Reincarnation

Other Books by Sylvia Cranston

REINCARNATION, AN EAST-WEST ANTHOLOGY
REINCARNATION IN WORLD THOUGHT
REINCARNATION: THE PHOENIX FIRE MYSTERY
(with Joseph Head)

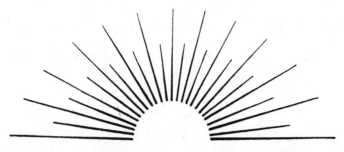

Reincarnation

A NEW HORIZON IN SCIENCE, RELIGION, AND SOCIETY

•

SYLVIA CRANSTON AND CAREY WILLIAMS

Julian Press

Published by Julian Press, a division of Crown Publishers, Inc., One Park Avenue, New York, New York 10016, and simultaneously in Canada by General Publishing Company Limited

Manufactured in the United States of America

Library of Congress Cataloging in Publication Data

Main entry under title:

Reincarnation: A new horizon in science, religion, and society.

1. Reincarnation—Addresses, essays, lectures.
I. Cranston, Sylvia. II. Williams, Carey.
BL515.R427   1984   133.9′01′3   84-3796
ISBN 0-517-55496-8

10 9 8 7 6 5 4 3 2 1

First Edition

Contents

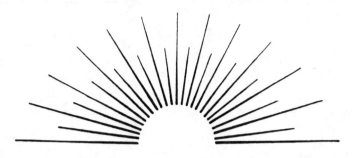

It would be curious if we should find science and philosophy taking up again the old theory of reincarnation, remodeling it to suit our present modes of religious and scientific thought, and launching it again on the wide ocean of human belief. But stranger things have happened in the history of human opinion.

JAMES FREEMAN CLARKE

The eye seems to demand a horizon. We are never tired (or unhappy) so long as we can see far enough.

RALPH WALDO EMERSON

Preface

Of all living creatures, human beings alone know they will someday die. They do not know, however, when that dread moment will occur, whether the next instant, the next day, the next year, or decades hence. Furthermore, they do not know what, if anything, happens beyond the door of death. Nobody knows the answers to these mysteries, many people say, so it is a waste of time to engage in foolish conjectures. Ignorance gives rise to fear, and when the unknown is deemed unknowable, fear stalks the human mind.

Even when people are convinced they will survive death, they are nevertheless afraid, owing to doubts and uncertainties as to where they will go after death. Will they be in a blissful place called heaven? Or a horrible place called hell? Furthermore, the pictures they have conjured up in their minds about heaven are not particularly inviting. Thus few "true believers" long to go there. And so, when old age approaches, they tenaciously cling to life on earth, despite its miseries and sorrows.

British Prime Minister David Lloyd George, of World War I fame, once confided:

> When I was a boy, the thought of heaven used to frighten me more than the thought of hell. I pictured heaven as a place where there would be perpetual Sundays with perpetual services, from which there would be no escape, as the Almighty, assisted by cohorts of angels, would always be on the lookout for those who did not attend. It was a horrible nightmare. The conventional heaven with its angels perpetually singing, nearly drove me mad in my youth, and made me an atheist for ten years. My opinion is that we shall be reincarnated.[1]

Is reincarnation, then, just another opinion, a pleasant idea evoked by wishful, magical thinking to offset the fear of dying and cushion the shock of our inevitable demise?

It may interest those who have always dismissed theories of immortality as comforting illusions that reincarnation is often rejected precisely because it is *not* the "easy way out." For instance, consider the fundamentalists and born-again Christians. They prefer an everlasting stay in heaven to the painstaking work of returning to earth to struggle more diligently for their redemption.

Consider also the scientists and psychologists of materialistic persuasions. They may instinctively reject rebirth because, if it were true, a lifetime of research based on the theory that matter and energy are the *only* realities could go for naught. Then there are the people who are weary and bitterly disillusioned with life. They may say, "What, one more round? Never. I do not want to come back."

This last view often rests on a misconception that being reborn means *immediate* rebirth. Most reincarnational philosophies teach that a long period of celestial rest usually intervenes between incarnations—a time for assimilating the harvest of life's experiences. Then, refreshed and invigorated, the individual returns, not in sadness and despair but, as childhood attests, in eager joyousness to undertake a new adventure in learning and growing.

To searchers for truth, however, neither likes nor dislikes are a legitimate basis for accepting or rejecting reincarnation. "What are the facts?" they will say. Is there any hard-core evidence supporting the many-lives theory? Yes, there is—not final proofs, but evidence, volumes of it. This will be considered in chapters 4 and 5, which focus mainly on the work of the leading scientist in reincarnation research, Dr. Ian Stevenson, Carlson Professor of Psychiatry at the University of Virginia Medical School and former chairman of that department. In an ongoing series, he has to date five large volumes of case histories of children around the world who provide evidence, often in incredible detail, that they lived before. Their claims have usually been found 90 percent accurate.[2]

In reviewing the first volume in Stevenson's series Cases of the Reincarnation Type, the *Journal of the American Medical Association* spoke of his "meticulous and extended investigations," saying he has "painstakingly and unemotionally collected a detailed series of cases in which the evidence for reincarnation is difficult to understand on any other grounds. . . . He has placed on record a large amount of data that cannot be ignored" (December 1, 1975).

Another indication of medical interest in reincarnation was evident at a symposium, The Child and Death, held at Columbia University's College of Physicians and Surgeons in January 1979. The meetings, lasting several days, were attended by doctors, nurses, and educators from many parts of the United States. Four speakers were invited to present the reincarnational viewpoint. Their talks appear in Part IV of this book.

At the Columbia symposium, the Nathan Lefkowitz Memorial Lecture was delivered by Dr. Paul Patterson, a renowned specialist in cystic fibrosis— the dread disease that often attacks children. Upon being introduced to Sylvia Cranston, an editor of *Reincarnation: The Phoenix Fire Mystery** who spoke at the conference, Dr. Patterson told of donating the volume to the library at the Albany Medical College of Union University, where he teaches. The librarian later informed him that the book was so avidly sought by the young doctors, she was obliged to limit borrowing to one week only.

In addition to cases of the reincarnation type involving children, the present volume offers a select number concerning adults with possible past-life recall. One of these is so remarkable it attracted the attention of Queen Elizabeth's husband Prince Philip, and his uncle, the late Lord Mountbatten, a great grandson of Queen Victoria. They were instrumental in having the case researched by high-ranking British naval personnel (chapter 7).

*

Many people who disbelieve in survival after death take comfort in the thought that, although death ends everything for them, their lives can acquire a kind of immortality through their influence on posterity. Such hope, however, is of only short-term significance when time is viewed on a cosmic scale, as this story makes clear.

A professor at Princeton spoke to Einstein about his son, a brilliant college student who was so dejected and depressed he refused to continue his studies or do anything else. What was the trouble? Worry about his own death? No. *He was concerned about the death of the solar system!* Someday, he said, it will all go to pieces, and then? Everything accomplished on planet Earth would go for naught. It would be as if nothing really happened here at all! So why bother to do anything now?

As Bertrand Russell remarked years ago in a BBC debate: "All the

---

**Reincarnation: The Phoenix Fire Mystery. An East-West Dialogue on Death and Rebirth from the Worlds of Religion, Science, Psychology, Philosophy, Art, and Literature, and from Great Thinkers of the Past and Present,* compiled and edited by Joseph Head and S. L. Cranston. New York: Crown, 1977 (cloth); Warner, 1979 (paperback).

labors of the ages, all the devotion, all the inspiration, all the noonday brightness of human genius, are destined to extinction in the vast death of the solar system, and the whole temple of Man's achievements must inevitably be buried beneath the debris of a universe in ruins."[3]

Darwin was concerned with the same problem. In a letter to his son, he spoke of the inevitable destruction of our solar system, when "the sun with all the planets will grow too cold for life."

> Believing as I do that man in the distant future will be a far more perfect creature than he now is, it is an intolerable thought that he and all other sentient things are doomed to complete annihilation after such long-continued progress. To those who fully admit the immortality of the human soul, the destruction of our world will not appear so dreadful.[4]

Darwin was not speaking of the ordinary view of immortality—that of permanent escape into a heavenly state after one brief sojourn here. Rather he intimated that evolution, as a process, might continue from world to world, if souls are in fact imperishable, which in this case would mean being reborn. The possibility that worlds reincarnate—even the galactic universes as a whole—is a subject currently engaging the serious attention of astronomers and physicists. It is discussed in our concluding chapter, "Horizons Far and Horizons Near."

*

It may come as a surprise to learn that the reincarnational outlook is not, as commonly supposed, a product of Eastern religions. It has had numerous adherents in the West, as the chapters on Christianity and Judaism demonstrate. It was also pervasively taught among our early European, African, and American Indian ancestors (see chapter 11). And as to the past and present centuries, Professor Geddes MacGregor observes that "preoccupation with the reincarnational theme has been so widespread among notable writers, it might be easier to make an inventory of authors who show no interest in it than to make a list of those who do." "Moreover," he adds, "the writers who do show deep interest in the notion are as diverse in temperament as they are varied in background."[5]

Among their number are leading Christian and Jewish religious scholars who write books and papers supporting the reincarnational outlook. Selections from their writings appear in chapter 12 on Judaism and chapter 13 on Christianity. Also featured is the unearthing of long-lost Christian Gnostic manuscripts. These have so astounded the academic world that the story of the origins of Christianity and what Jesus taught is being rewritten. Few people are aware that, among the Christian Gnostics, reincarnation was a widespread teaching.

Turning from present-day scholarly interest in reincarnation to that of the general public, this has now accelerated to such proportions that the 1981 Gallup poll on religion reveals that 38 million Americans—almost one-quarter of the adult population—now admit to being reincarnationists. The exact percentage is 23 percent. For Protestants it ranges between 21 and 26 percent; for Catholics, 25 percent (see chapter 2). Numbers do not prove or disprove anything, but when so many people have abandoned the one-life philosophy of their immediate forebears, we are faced with a phenomenon that invites investigation.

In response to this growing interest, numerous books on reincarnation are appearing. The current *Subject Guide to Books in Print* lists over one hundred as available. As yet, most of this literature treats only the surface aspects of the subject and rarely considers the possible transformative power inherent in this philosophy of life—how, for example, it could contribute to the solution of world problems or aid the individual in day-to-day stressful living. In Part IV, "Transformation of Life and Society," we examine these possibilities.

Western minds would appear especially fitted to apply reincarnation practically, precisely because they have not been born into this philosophy. Because it is not part of their cultural milieu, they are better able to objectively analyze its relevance in today's world. Some of our foremost thinkers, as we shall see, have commenced this challenging task. Significantly, they view the many-lives perspective as a new horizon to be explored, rather than as a lost horizon—a nostalgic return to something past and gone.

Unfortunately, in the Orient, where rebirth has been taught for ages, it has become a belief system put upon the child like a garment when it is born. Like other religious teachings, it has suffered from distorting interpretations, far removed from the elevated views of humanity's sages and prophets. As a result, progress has often been hindered not fostered. In India, for instance, priestly hierarchies have enforced separative caste practices by warning that the penalty for violation could be an ensuing birth as an animal or insect! Enlightened reincarnationists teach: "Once a human being, always a human being."[6]

We, too, in the West have inherited belief systems—religious and scientistic—that have colored much of our lives and thinking. They have not always nourished our minds or our souls. The time has arrived when, on every side, their constricting limitations are being recognized, and alternative philosophies are being eagerly investigated.

*

A concluding word on the presentation of material in this volume. As it seems presumptuous to claim expertise in the many areas through which a topic like reincarnation ranges, we prefer to allow the authorities in their respective fields to speak for themselves. Thus we quote directly from their writings, wherever possible. As to the final authority, that always rests with each individual. The open-minded inquirer examines, on its merits alone, every idea that may point the way to self-knowledge and wider horizons of thought.

I
THE HORIZON TODAY

How can we live turning a deaf ear to the last dramatic questions? Where does the world come from and whither is it going? Which is the supreme power of the cosmos, what the essential meaning of life?

Scientific truth is characterized by its exactness and the certainty of its predictions. But these admirable qualities are contrived by science at the cost of remaining on a plane of secondary problems, leaving unanswered the ultimate and decisive questions.

We cannot breathe confined to a realm of secondary and intermediate themes. We need a comprehensive perspective, foreground and background, not a maimed scenery, not a horizon stripped of infinite distances.

We are given no escape from last questions. In one fashion or another they are in us, whether we like it or not.
                    Ortega y Gasset, *Toward a Philosophy of History*

When there is no vision, the people perish.
                    Solomon, Book of Proverbs 29:18

1

The Cry for Meaning

In recalling childhood experiences, Henry Pickering, a nineteenth-century poet, told of an occasion that brought his first deep sorrow. He was observing, as usual, his baby brother asleep in his cradle, but this time something was strangely different. The cradle was "decked with sweet smelling flowers!"

> This sight so strange filled my young breast with wonder, and I gazed upon the babe more. I thought it slept—and yet its little bosom did not move! I bent me down to look into its eyes, but they were closed; then softly clasped its hand, but mine it would not clasp. What should I do? "Wake, brother, wake!" I then impatient cried; "open thine eyes, and look on me again!" He would not hear my voice.
>
> All pale beside my weeping mother sat, and gazed and looked unutterable things. "Will he not awake?" I eager asked. She clasped me in her arms, and in anguish faintly said, "My dearest boy, thy brother does not sleep; alas! He's dead; he never will awake."
>
> He's dead; I knew not what it meant, but more to know I sought not. For the words so sad, "*He never will awake*," sunk in my soul; I felt a pang unknown before; and in tears, that angels might have shed, my heart dissolved.[1]

On the grave of a little girl in Wrexham, Wales, appeared this inscription.

> I wonder what I was begun for
> Seeing I am so soon done for.[2]

But what about the rest of us? Do we know "what we were begun for"? Surely, soon enough, we too will be done for! How can human beings exist or have any direction in their lives without knowing the answer to such a simple, elementary question?

There was a time when the hope for a nation's future resided in its youth with its optimism and ideals, its dreams for a better world. But today? The president of Bard College, Leon Botstein, writing in *Harper's*, tells about today's students arriving at colleges and universities. "There happens," he says, "to be a real crisis out there. . . . The crisis is demonstrated by the growing illiteracy and ignorance in English, in the humanities, in science, in general knowledge and ability to think and to express oneself. It reflects a profound alienation among young people" (September 1979). And the reason for it is a devastating absence of inner motivation. Students find no satisfactory reason for living, and from their experience thus far in education, they have little hope that the colleges can supply one.

Much publicity has been given to the large numbers of students suffering from depression, melancholia, and schizophrenia. But most alarming is the increased suicidal rate. The *New York Times* carried the report that "suicides among teenagers and young adults have tripled in the last 20 years. . . . The yearly suicidal rate for people between 15 and 24 years old was now almost 5,000" (February 11, 1979). Since then the rate has risen higher.* Young adults appear to be pleading in overt ways, to attract attention to the basic problem of their lives—finding an enduring purpose for existence.

The psychiatrist Viktor Frankl says in his recent book, *The Unheard Cry for Meaning,* that "at an American University, 60 students who had attempted suicide were screened afterward, and 85 percent said the reason had been that life seemed meaningless." Most important, however, 93 percent of these students suffering from the apparent meaninglessness of life "were actively engaged socially, were performing well academically, and were on good terms with their family groups."

"This happens," Frankl says, "in the midst of affluent societies and in the midst of welfare states! For too long we have been dreaming a dream from which we are now waking up; the dream that if we just improve the socioeconomic situation of people, everything will be okay, people will become happy. The truth is that as the struggle for survival has subsided, the question has emerged: survival for what? Ever more people today have the means to live, but no meaning to live for."[3]

The Fear of Nothingness, the Horror of Emptiness.   The cry for meaning is not confined to young people. The problems discussed thus far are evidently symptomatic of our entire culture. Dr. Frankl says that the sense of meaninglessness now affects humankind on an almost epidemic scale. The majority of a psychiatrist's clientele, writes Erich Fromm, are "sick" because they know that life runs out of their hands like sand, and that they

---

*See chapter 22, "The Aching Problem of Suicide, and a Remedy That Works."

will die without having lived. "At the beginning of this century," he observed, "the people who came to the psychiatrist were mainly people who suffered from *symptoms*. They had a paralyzed arm or an obsessional symptom like a washing compulsion, or they suffered from obsessional thoughts." This sickness prevented them from functioning socially as normal people. They are the minority today. The many new "patients" function socially. They are not sick in the conventional sense. "They complain of being depressed, having insomnia, being unhappy in their marriages, not enjoying their work, and any number of similar problems." What they really suffer from, says Dr. Fromm, "is an inner deadness. They live in the midst of plenty and are joyless."[4]

At a recent gathering of psychiatrists, analysts, and other workers in psychotherapy held in New York, the group agreed that the underlying cause behind all psychiatric disorders is "the fear of nothingness, the horror of emptiness" (*New York Times,* April 21, 1978). As Ernest Becker, Pulitzer prize author, explains, "At the bottom of all phobias and neuroses is the fear of death."[5]

"Nothing really matters personally to me," said anthropologist Bronislaw Malinowski, "except the answer to the burning question, am I going to live, or shall I vanish as a bubble?" Commenting on this in his Gifford Lectures, Macneile Dixon observed, "If we have not here among men who reflect, however unwilling they are to acknowledge it, *the pivot of the human situation,* I know not where to look for it."[6]

Maybe we *will* vanish as a bubble. Maybe it is just wishful thinking to believe otherwise. Edmund Wilson, called the dean of American writers, thought so and described the effect upon himself of this philosophy: "The knowledge that death is not so far away, that my mind and emotions and vitality will soon disappear like a puff of smoke, has the effect of making earthly affairs seem unimportant and human beings more and more ignoble. It is harder to take human life seriously, including one's own efforts and achievements."[7]

Tolstoy's Experience.   No author of recent centuries put his finger on this problem with greater urgency and dramatic effect than Leo Tolstoy. During the 1978 celebration of the 150th anniversary of his birth, the United Nations determined that he is the most widely read author in the world. In *The Saturday Review* Norman Cousins wrote, "Through the magic of his words he brought sensitivities to life that helped shape the contours of human thought in millions of people everywhere. His words were sublime in a way that gave a vision of what human beings might achieve or become" (October 28, 1978).

In *My Confessions,* Tolstoy told why he decided to take his life at the height of his literary fame and prosperity.

> When I thought of the education of my children, I said to myself: "Why?" . . . Or, thinking of the fame which my works would get me, I said to myself: "All right, you will be more famous than Gogol, Pushkin, Shakespeare, Moliere, and all the writers in the world—what of it?" And I was absolutely unable to make a reply. . . .
>
> The mental state in which I then was seemed to me summed up in the following: my life was a foolish and wicked joke played upon me by I knew not whom. Illness and death would come, if not today, then tomorrow, to those whom I loved, to myself, and nothing would remain but stench and worms. All my acts, whatever I did, would sooner or later be forgotten, and I myself be nowhere. Why, then busy one's self with anything? How could men see this, and live? . . . I felt a horror of what awaited me. . . . I could not patiently await the end . . . and I longed to free myself . . . by rope or a pistol ball. . . .
>
> I now see that if I did not kill myself it was due to some dim consciousness of the invalidity of my thoughts.[8]

What was wrong? Not his logic, says Macneile Dixon, but his unstated premises, the assumption that all the facts are in with which we can form a true and final judgment as to the value of life.[9]

A solution to Tolstoy's dilemma came when he eventually asked and answered this question: "What am I?" "A part of the infinite. In these few words lies the whole problem." Here, he said, "was preserved the profoundest wisdom of humanity." As "part of the infinite," he was an enduring entity that the hand of death could never touch.[10] Later, his belief in immortality was extended to reincarnation as well.

In a letter to a correspondent, he affirmed this by saying that the experiences "of our present life are the environment in which we work out the impressions, thoughts, feelings of a former life," and that "our present life is only one of many thousands of such lives. . . . I wish you would understand me; I am not playing, not inventing this: I believe in it, I see it without a doubt."[11]

As to suicide, he wrote in his diary, "How interesting it would be to write the story of the experiences in this life of a man who killed himself in his previous life; how he now stumbles against the very demands which had offered themselves before, until he arrives at the realization that he must fulfill those demands. Remembering the lesson, this man will be wiser than others''[12] (February 13, 1896).

Tolstoy appears to have believed that, if we remembered our past lives, we would be wiser. This raises a problem many people ask respecting reincarnation, which we now consider.

Without Past-Life Memory, What Value Rebirth?   Corliss Lamont asks the above question in his once widely commended book, *The Illusion of Immortality,* and concludes that, if a person does not remember previous lives, he may just as well have never lived them! What meaning could they possibly have for him?[13] Lamont quotes Leibniz: ''Of what use would it be to you, sir, to become king of China, on condition that you forgot what you have been? Would it not be the same as if God, at the same time he destroyed you, created a king in China?''[14]

First let us ask, supposing we did recall all our past lives, would this be helpful to us now? Professor Geddes MacGregor responds to this question in his book *Reincarnation in Christianity.*

> If I were to remember hundreds of incarnations back to my life as a farmer in Babylonia and including my life as a court jester at the court of Philip the Fair, to say nothing of a brief life in the workhouse in Dickens' England and a tragic life as a Russian princess, you could hardly expect me to bear the burden of it all and still profit from yet another life on earth. . . . Deprivation of memory would be essential to new development and new growth, since it is precisely the burden of memory, with all the sense of guilt, all the remorse, all the heartaches from the past, that impede our genuine growth in our later years. . . . One of the greatest mercies is our capacity to forget. But for that merciful ability, we could not endure even one life let alone a succession of them, and eventually we could not but stop making any moral progress at all.

The professor further observes: ''No sensible person really expects an octogenarian, however vigorous his body and resilient his mind, to be open to radically new ideas that have been alien to him all his life. For that he would need an entirely fresh start. When we have led a full life, our minds are cluttered with memories; we need a clean slate to make that fresh start.''[15]

Gandhi writes similarly in a letter to his close disciple Madeleine Slade, daughter of the British Admiral Sir Edward Slade.

What you say about rebirth is sound. It is nature's kindness that we do not remember past births. Where is the good either of knowing in detail the numberless births, we have gone through? Life would be a burden if we carried such a tremendous load of memories. A wise man deliberately forgets many things, even as a lawyer forgets the cases and their details as soon as they are disposed of. Yes, "death is but a sleep and a forgetting."[16]

While all the foregoing seems obvious, the thoughts expressed do not actually answer our original question: What value has rebirth if past experiences are forgotten and consequently inaccessible? Perhaps their harvest *is* accessible, but in another form than detailed remembrance. Call it summation memory, if you will. Our characters, dispositions, innate talents—expressed or now asleep—can then be seen as essential memory. And right now, consciously or subconsciously, we are the sum total of all our past.

To use an analogy: a long column of figures contains a list of many numbers, each of which could represent the value of a particular incarnation; but the total is the sum of them all. Our monthly bank statement lists many individual transactions, but what counts is the final figure, the bottom line. A honey bee offers another example. Let each flower visited by the bee be analogous to a past life. Now what is important? That the flower was a clover, a columbine, or a snapdragon, or that it was growing in this field or that? No. Only one thing is important—how much nectar was gathered to be stored as honey for future use.

Professor John McTaggart, a distinguished Cambridge philosopher, about whom we will be hearing more in the talk at Harvard, suggests how summation memory, as related to reincarnation, works out practically in our lives. His first example concerns wisdom. Can we be wiser by reason of something the waking mind has forgotten?

Unquestionably we can. Wisdom is not merely, or chiefly, amassed facts, or even recorded judgments. It depends primarily on a mind qualified to deal with facts, and to form judgments. Now the acquisition of knowledge and experience, if wisely conducted, may strengthen the mind. Of that we have sufficient evidence in this life. And so a man who dies after acquiring knowledge—and all men acquire some—might enter his new life, deprived indeed of his knowledge, but not deprived of the increased strength and delicacy of mind which he had gained in acquiring the knowledge. And, if so, he will be wiser in the second life because of what has happened in the first. Of course he loses something in losing the actual knowledge. . . . And is not even this loss really a gain? For the mere accumulation of knowledge, if memory never ceased, would soon become overwhelming, and worse than useless.

Then McTaggart considers love.

> The problem here is more important, if, as I believe, it is in love, and in nothing else, that we find not only the supreme value of life, but also the supreme reality of life, and, indeed, of the universe. Much has been forgotten in any friendship which has lasted for several years within the limits of a single life—many confidences, many services, many hours of happiness and sorrow. But they have not passed away without leaving their mark on the present. They contribute, though they are forgotten, to the present love which is not forgotten. In the same way, if the whole memory of the love of a life is swept away at death, its value is not lost if the same love is stronger in a new life because of what passed before.

He points out, however, that such love can only be sustained if the lovers and friends meet again in another life, for "if the conditions which determine the circumstances of our birth, and through them our juxtapositions throughout life, were themselves determined by chance, the probability of meeting our friends in another life would be too small to be regarded." But, "if immortality is to give us an assurance or a hope of progressive improvement, it can only be if we have reason to believe that the interests of spirit are so predominant a force in the universe that they will find, in the long run, satisfaction in the universe. And, in this case, the constitution of the universe would be such that, whether with or without memory, love would have its way."[17]

In a letter to a woman in New Zealand, McTaggart wrote, "I can't help thinking it probable that people who meet once will meet often on the way up. That they should meet at all seems to show that they must be connected with the same part of the pattern of things, and if so they would probably often be working together. Very fanciful, no doubt, but more probable than thinking that it goes by chance, like sand grains in a heap, which is what one thinks in these scientific days, unless one thinks for oneself."[18]

In the Harvard talk that follows in chapter 3, it becomes evident that such thoughts were consonant with the philosophy of the great American transcendentalists Emerson, Thoreau, and Bronson Alcott. It is therefore not surprising that Alcott's famous daughter, Louisa May—who all her life lived in this atmosphere—wrote in a letter to a friend:

I think immortality is the passing of a soul through many lives or experiences, and such as are truly lived, used, and learned, help on to the next, each growing richer, happier and higher, carrying with it only the real memories of what has gone before. . . . I seem to remember former states and feel that in them I have learned some of the lessons that have never since been mine here and in my next step I hope to leave behind many of the trials I have struggled to bear here and begin to find lightened as I go on. This accounts for the genius and great virtue some show here. They have done well in many phases of this great school and bring into our class the virtue or the gifts that make them great or good. We don't remember the lesser things. They slip away as childish trifles, and we carry on only the real experiences.[19]

2

Current Western Belief in Many Lives

Truth is not decided by a show of hands.

A modern maxim

The truth of an idea does not stand or fall by numbers of adherents, yet when numerous people in all walks of life abandon the viewpoints implanted in them as children, replacing them with a new approach to life and death, such a phenomenon becomes worthy of investigation. In the Harvard talk, we speak of the awakening interest in rebirth that burgeoned in occidental lands beginning in the last century. However, it was not until the middle of the present century that statisticians began to take special note of the trend. The earliest survey of which we are aware is that taken by Mass-Observation, a British fact-finding organization. In the 1940s, it conducted "a study in popular attitudes to religion, ethics, progress and politics in a London borough." The results of the survey were disclosed in a book, *Puzzled People,* from which we quote.

> The conception of life after death was explored at various levels—by long informal conversations and through the written comments of Mass-Observation's National Panel. Perhaps the least expected, and in some ways the most significant fact which came to light was the extent of belief in reincarnation. Among the interview sample about one person in twenty-five spontaneously went into enough detail to show that they held some such belief. That amounts to about one in ten of those who have any definite belief in an afterlife at all, and is almost certainly an underestimate, since no attempt was made by direct questioning to go into the details of people's conception.[1]

A decade later, British anthropologist Geoffrey Gorer wrote in *Exploring English Character*, a volume based on a survey of 5,000 people living in a London borough, "A quarter of all those who believe in an afterlife do not appear to believe that this afterlife will be eternal. Eleven percent believe in future lives just like their present life, two percent believe in life on another planet, and eleven percent believe in reincarnation, either implicitly or explicitly on this earth." In other words, 24 percent of those believing in an afterlife accepted some form of reincarnation.

"The relative prevalence of the belief in reincarnation," Gorer continues, "is perhaps the most surprising single piece of information to be derived from this research." Commenting further, he adds,

> Reincarnation is a belief of the major Asiatic religions, but it is contrary to the creeds of all the established religions of Europe and the Near East. The Theosophists imported it into Europe at the end of the last century, but they comprise a minute portion of my sample; and, apart from the Presbyterians, some members of every denomination subscribe to this belief, though many of its holders must be "undenominational." . . . By and large the believers in reincarnation are very evenly distributed throughout the population.[2]

TWELVE-NATION 1969 GALLUP POLL

In February 1969, Gallup Opinion Index, based at Princeton, issued a "Special Report on Religion," covering the religious beliefs and practices of Protestants and Catholics in twelve widely scattered Western nations. One of the questions asked was, "Do you believe in reincarnation?"

As the percentages of those who answered yes were quite startling—considering that neither Protestantism nor Catholicism presently teaches reincarnation—one might imagine the report to be biased. Hardly. One editor was George Gallup, Jr., whom the report indicates to be "an active member of the Episcopal Church"! The other editor was John O. Davies III, "active in the Roman Catholic Diocese of Trenton, New Jersey."

Here are the percentages of belief in rebirth: Austria, 20 percent; Canada, 26 percent; France, 23 percent; Great Britain, 18 percent; Greece, 22 percent; the Netherlands, 10 percent; Norway, 14 percent; Sweden, 12 percent; United States, 20 percent; West Germany, 25 percent. When one of the present writers reported the figures covering the United States and Canada on Tom Snyder's television program "The Tomorrow Show" (April 13, 1978), Snyder exclaimed, "Why, that is almost one-quarter of the population!"

However, it would be a mistake to believe that, while 25 percent of the people in the census declared a belief in rebirth, 75 percent *did not*; for the survey also included "no opinion" figures. For example, in the Netherlands, where the believers were only 10 percent, 35 percent had no opinion; in the United States, those with no opinion numbered 16 percent; in Norway, 29 percent; and in Great Britain, 10 percent.

As to Great Britain, a new Gallup poll covering that country alone revealed that acceptance of reincarnation had risen from 18 percent in 1969 to 28 percent in 1979. The London *Daily Telegraph*, reporting these figures, added that "23 percent of the men and 33 percent of the women professed such a belief, the greatest percentage being in the 25–34 age group" (April 15, 1979).

GALLUP POLL (UNITED STATES) 1981

This poll was the subject of a book by George Gallup, Jr., *Adventures in Immortality*. The Gallup Organization describes the census as the most comprehensive survey on beliefs about the afterlife that has ever been undertaken. It was addressed to adults eighteen years old and over. The question asked on reincarnation was quite explicit: "Do you believe in reincarnation—that is, the rebirth of the soul in a new body after death— or not?"[3]

The query was addressed not just to religious people, as the 1969 poll was, but to the general United States adult population. George Gallup, Jr., reports: "Of those adults we polled, 23 percent, or nearly one-quarter, said they believe in reincarnation." There were 67 percent nonbelievers, and 10 percent had no opinion. Among women, there were 25 percent believers; among men, 21 percent. As to Protestants, 21 percent of the Baptists believed in rebirth, as did 22 percent of the Lutherans and 26 percent of the Methodists. Among Catholics the figure was 25 percent.[4] As to the 23 percent of the adult population who believe in reincarnation, using as a base the 1981 population figures of 166 million who are 18 years old and over, that would mean over 38 million reincarnationists in the United States.[5]

College Students. The foregoing poll did not take special note of this category, but psychologist Dr. Harold Leif mentions in a psychiatric journal that "a recent survey reported in the popular press showed that a substantial number of American college students hold this belief."[6] The figures, as we remember, were 31 percent.

Dramatic evidence of this interest was indicated when a national controversy erupted in 1978 over a course called Your Former Lives conducted by Professor David Weltha at Iowa State University. Several teachers at the university were adamantly opposed, and the conflict was brought to the attention of the state legislators, some of whom questioned the use of public funds to teach "a pagan religion" in the schools. *Time* magazine allotted an entire page in its science section to the dispute and was critical of Dr. Weltha's work. College newspapers around the country entered the fray, and thousands of students rallied to the professor's defense. He was invited to present his case on "The Tomorrow Show," and one of the authors of this book was asked to share the program with him.

YOUNG ADULTS IN HIGH SCHOOL AND GRADE SCHOOLS

The London *Daily Telegraph* reported that "there is a strong preoccupation among senior school children with some form of reincarnation, judged from informal talks among them on religious education in secondary modern schools" (August 6, 1960). This study, a survey of the relationship between contemporary Christianity and the youth of Great Britain, was subsequently published as a paperback titled *Teenage Religion*. The research was organized by Harold Loukes, Reader in Education at Oxford University, and was published under the auspices of the Study and Research Committee of the Institute of Christian Education. The method chosen was simply to report, via tape recordings, the actual replies of students to questions concerning religious belief. Mr. Loukes, himself a Christian, noted the frequent emergence in teenage thought of "the curious streak of reincarnation, respectable in the east, odd, yet morally attractive in the west." Students made such observations as:

> I'm not struck on saying there is a heaven. I think you come back to life again.

> I think when I die I will come back as someone else and carry on like that. I don't believe in heaven and hell because millions of people are dying every day, and there wouldn't be enough room for us all, we would be meeting stone age men and so on.

> I think that you kind of come back into the world again, to live and lead a better life, and you go on coming back until you're perfect, and then, well, there isn't a place, but I think you go to God when you're perfect.[7]

A piano teacher recently told of an experience with an eighth-grade pupil. Amazed at the girl's phenomenal ability in handling chords, the teacher inquired, "How is it that you know so much about chords?" The girl replied, "I must have learned about them in another life." Aware that the girl had a Catholic background and went to parochial school, the astonished teacher asked, "Where do you hear about such things?" "At school," the girl answered. "My friends and I talk about reincarnation all the time."

We learned of this after one of the authors appeared as the guest on a two-hour radio program, "Amplify," directed by Catholic priest Ronald Lengwin. It is broadcast on Sunday evenings over Pittsburgh's famous KDKA, a fifty-kilowatt station that reaches states as far as Florida. The topic that evening (February 8, 1981) was reincarnation.

The remark of the music student—"my friends and I talk about reincarnation all the time"—was also made to the authors by Valerie Gilbert, then a brilliant student at the fashionable Dalton School in New York, and who now attends Harvard. These young people will be the future parents in our society. What will they be teaching their children? (The Gallup poll, 1981, reported that the belief in reincarnation in the age group under thirty was 29 percent, as opposed to 21 percent of those over thirty.)

*

The many-lives theme appears frequently in novels, motion pictures, cartoons, and on television. Even greeting cards carry the message. The following words appear on a birthday card in the popular Ziggy series.

> Enjoy yourself on your birthday. Remember, you only live once.

> But just in case you believe in reincarnation, MANY HAPPY RETURNS!

Religious teachers find they no longer can ignore the reincarnation boom. Reverend Michael Paternoster, an Anglican priest, mentions this in a Christian periodical:

> I have before me as I write three books by Christian ministers [treating of reincarnation]: *Death and Eternal Life* by John Hick, *Christianity and Reincarnation* by Rudolf Frieling, and *Reincarnation in Christianity* by Geddes MacGregor. Of the three books I find MacGregor's approach the most congenial, though I am unconvinced by it. . . . Nevertheless, it must be admitted that these three books together—and the climate of opinion in which they could be written and published—indicate forcibly that the question of reincarnation is no longer one that Christians can simply assume to be closed for them.[8]

3

Lecture at Harvard University

With "Reincarnation and the Book of Life" as the title of her lecture, Sylvia Cranston spoke at Harvard on October 17, 1979. It is reprinted here in shortened form, but collateral and updated material has been added. The talk falls naturally into three divisions: Reincarnation and the Book of Life; Only Two Options—or a Third Alternative?; and Psychologists Discover Rebirth.

Time did not permit giving the lecture in its entirety at Harvard, but the complete text has been acquired by many college and university teachers for use in their classes in religion, philosophy, and death education. The original fifty-page typewritten talk is now in Yale University's Beinecke Rare Book and Manuscript Library.

REINCARNATION AND THE BOOK OF LIFE

The title for our discussion this evening, "Reincarnation and the Book of Life," came about in an unexpected way. I had been paging through the book *Reincarnation in Christianity* by Professor Geddes MacGregor, who is distinguished professor of philosophy emeritus at the University of Southern California. He is also an Anglican priest of forty years standing and, among recent honors, was special preacher at St. Paul's Cathedral in London in 1969 and at Westminster Abbey in 1970. MacGregor not only writes on reincarnation but, as visiting professor, has given courses thereon at some of our leading universities.

Now, among the books listed in the extensive bibliography in *Reincarnation in Christianity* was a volume on rebirth that evoked considerable amusement:

16

Death on the Installment Plan by a noted French author. Why not call it "Birth on the Installment Plan"? I thought. That would be closer to the Latin derivative meaning of reincarnation: "coming again into bodies of flesh"—human flesh, of course, not the distorted version common in the Orient of regression into animals and insects.

Death on the Installment Plan! Birth on the Installment Plan! In our money-oriented culture, this sounds like something we have to pay for, a debt incurred, strung out in neatly packaged payments. Why not think of it, I mused, as serialized installments of the chapter in a book—the Book of Life! (Our numerous incarnations—if we had them—could also be likened to a play, with many scenes and acts, unfolding the drama of the soul.)

If we were to read a story in a magazine and begin with installment ten, completely unaware that anything preceded, what possible meaning could the story have for us? The characters would make no sense; the plot would be nonsense.

Apply this analogy to our own lives and presume for a few moments that reincarnation is true, but we are ignorant of this "fact." What meaning could be discovered for our present existence?

We are born an infant and inherit a body that could be healthy or diseased, handsome or ugly, well-developed or maimed. Why? What did we do to deserve this good or evil fortune? Simultaneously, we inherit parents (rich or poor, loving or indifferent), a nation, a time and geographical environment, a culture, and so on—all of which powerfully affect us. Now we are stuck with it and call it the accident of birth. Why were we not born in the Middle Ages? Or in the jungles of South America, or among the war-ravaged, starving peoples of Vietnam and Cambodia?

Without a sensible answer to these questions, what reasons can be offered for living? Surely, Macbeth must have been right when, on the eve of his destruction and learning of the death of Lady Macbeth, he said, with scornful indifference, "All our yesterdays have lighted fools the way to dusty death. Out, out, brief candle! Life's but a walking shadow, a poor player that struts and frets his hour upon the stage and then is heard no more; it is a tale told by an idiot, full of sound and fury, signifying nothing" (Act V, Scene 5).

When I read MacGregor's *Reincarnation in Christianity,* it seemed quite coincidental that in his opening chapter, "The Universal Appeal of Reincarnation," he also uses the analogy of a book.

Reincarnation takes care of the problem of moral injustice. To the age-old question of Job (Why do the wicked prosper and the righteous suffer?) the reincarnationist has a ready answer: we are seeing, in this life, only a fragment of a long story. If you come in at the chapter in which the villain beats the hero to pulp, of course you will ask the old question. You may even put down the book at that point and join forces with those who call life absurd, seeing no justice in the universe. That is because you are too impatient to go on to hear the rest of the story, which will unfold a much richer pattern in which the punishment of the wicked and the vindication of the righteous will be brought to light. Death is but the end of a chapter; it is not, as the nihilists suppose, the end of the story.[1]

JUNG'S STORY WITHOUT A BEGINNING

In endeavoring to understand his own life history, Jung likewise felt obliged to invoke the ideas of preexistence and rebirth. "My life as I lived it," he said in *Dreams, Memories, Reflections,*

> had often seemed to me like a story that has no beginning and no end. I had the feeling that I was an historical fragment, an excerpt for which the preceding and succeeding text was missing . . . I could well imagine that I might have lived in former centuries and there encountered questions I was not yet able to answer; that I had to be born again because I had not fulfilled the task that was given to me. When I die, my deeds will follow along with me—that is how I imagine it. I will bring with me what I have done. In the meantime it is important to insure that I do not stand at the end with empty hands.
>
> In my case it must have been primarily a passionate urge toward understanding which brought about my birth. For that is the strongest element in my nature. This insatiable drive toward understanding has, as it were, created a consciousness in order to know what is and what happens, and in order to give a more complete answer. It might happen that I would not be reborn again so long as the world needed no such answer, and that I would be entitled to several hundred years peace until someone was once more needed who took an interest in these matters and could profitably tackle the task anew. I imagine that for a while a period of rest could ensue, until the stint I had done in my lifetime needed to be taken up again.[2]

BEN FRANKLIN'S "NEW EDITION"

Like Jung, this founding father envisioned another incarnation to go on with *his* work. And he also used the theme of a story or book. This appears in his epitaph, recorded when he was a printer at the age of twenty-two. (What a strange thing for a young man to write!) Carl Van Doren calls it "the most famous of American epitaphs."[3] It appears, slightly modified, in almost a dozen versions, which is not surprising, as

Franklin often made copies for friends at their request and did not always recall the original wording.[4] Here is how it usually appears.

> The Body of B. Franklin,
> Printer,
> Like the Cover of an Old Book,
> Its Contents Torn Out
> And
> Stripped of its Lettering and Gilding,
> Lies Here
> Food for Worms,
> But the Work shall not be Lost,
> For it Will as He Believed
> Appear Once More
> In a New and more Elegant Edition
> Revised and Corrected
> by the Author.

This epitaph was not used on Franklin's tombstone. It therefore seems likely to have been the idle dream of a young man's fancy. However, a letter he wrote when he was seventy-nine suggests otherwise. In fact, his original idea of returning only once more, now appears in larger perspective.

> When I see nothing annihilated and not a drop of water wasted, I cannot suspect the annihilation of souls, or believe that [God] will suffer the daily waste of millions of minds ready made that now exist, and put himself to the continual trouble of making new ones. Thus, finding myself to exist in the world, I believe I shall, in some shape or other, always exist; and, with all the inconveniences human life is liable to, I shall not object to a new edition of mine, hoping, however that the *errata* of the last may be corrected.[5]

Emerson in his *Journals* quotes the eighty-year-old Franklin: "I feel as if I was intruding among posterity when I ought to be abed and asleep. I look upon death to be as necessary to the constitution as sleep. We shall rise refreshed in the morning."[6]

JOHN McTAGGART OF CAMBRIDGE UNIVERSITY

This noted reincarnationist—who taught at Cambridge for a quarter of a century—also used the analogy of sleeping and waking. "We may die old but we shall be born young. And death requires a deeper and more gracious significance when we regard it as part of the continually recurring rhythm of progress—as inevitable, as natural, and as benevolent as sleep.''[7]

C. D. Broad, who succeeded McTaggart at Cambridge, said that his predecessor's system, in which reincarnation is one of the directive themes, was the work of genius that places its author ''in the front rank of the great historical philosophers,'' and one that ''may quite fairly be compared with the *Enneads* of Plotinus, the *Ethics* of Spinoza, and the *Encyclopaedia of Hegel.*''[8]

Incidentally, McTaggart was no wishful thinker. He had no rosy dreams of an immediate bright future for himself or for humanity. His biographer G. Lowes Dickinson relates:

> He believed that the world of appearance was moving, on the whole, towards the world of Reality, and that all souls would in the end arrive there. It was a very long, and might be a very terrible journey . . . and McTaggart himself anticipated very bad times for himself. He would say, as he observed the inhabitants of a slum, that he himself might be thus in some other life; and at times he would console himself for the fact that while he was so happy [and] his friends were not, by the reflection that his turn for a bad time might come later. . . .
>
> As he never lost touch with his old friends, so he never ceased to make new ones. Neither class, nor age, nor occupation could keep him apart from congenial souls. He went through life knitting up relations which he believed to have originated in former existences.

The test of his convictions, Dickinson remarks, came in 1925 when death by a heart attack overtook him unexpectedly at fifty-eight. ''I am grieved that we must part,'' he said to his wife, ''but you know I am not afraid of death.'' The doctor in attendance asked, ''What is this man? A philosopher? I never knew a philosopher was so serene.''[9]

IS THE BOOK OF LIFE A BOOK OF FATE?

Or to rephrase the question: When a person is born, does he turn the pages of an already written chapter in which each event is recorded without the possibility of escape? Was Omar Khayyam right when he said:

> The Moving Finger writes, and, having writ,
> Moves on: nor all thy Piety nor Wit
> Shall lure it back to cancel half a Line,
> Nor all thy Tears wash out a Word of it.[10]

For answer, we turn to Professor Huston Smith's classic study *The*

Religions of Man. (This teacher of philosophy taught for many years right here in Cambridge at M.I.T.) In writing of karma, as related to rebirth, he noted:

"Science has alerted the Western world to the importance of causal relationships in the physical world. Every physical event has its cause, and every cause will have its determinate effects. India extends this concept of universal causation to include man's moral and spiritual life as well. To some extent the West has also. 'As a man sows, so shall he reap'; or again, 'Sow a thought and reap an act, sow an act and reap a habit, sow a habit and reap a character, sow a character and reap a destiny'—these are ways the West has put the point. The difference is that India tightens up and extends its concept of moral law to see it as absolutely binding and brooking no exceptions. The present condition of each individual's interior life—how happy he is, how confused or serene, how much he can see—is an exact product of what he has wanted and got in the past; and equally, his present thoughts and decisions are determining his future states. Each act he directs upon the world has its equal and opposite reaction on himself. Each thought and deed delivers an unseen chisel blow toward the sculpturing of his destiny.

"This idea of karma, and the completely moral universe it implies, commits the Hindu who understands it to complete personal responsibility. Most persons are unwilling to admit this. They prefer, as the psychologists would say, to project—to locate the source of their difficulties outside themselves. This, say the Hindus, is simply immature.

"Because karma implies a lawful world, it has often been interpreted as fatalism. Karma decrees that every decision must have its determinate consequences, but the decisions themselves are, in the last analysis, freely arrived at. Or, to approach the matter from the other direction, the consequences of a person's past decisions condition his present lot, as a card player finds himself dealt a particular hand, but is left free to play that hand in a number of ways. This means that the career of a soul as it threads its course through innumerable human bodies is guided by its choices." [11]

This last thought correlates well with an old aphorism on karma: "No person but a sage or true seer can judge another's karma. Hence while each receives his deserts, appearances may deceive, and birth into poverty or heavy trial may not be punishment for bad karma, for souls continually incarnate into poor surroundings where they experience difficulties and trials which are for the discipline of the individual and result in strength, fortitude, and sympathy." [12]

KARMA, A FOOLPROOF LAW?

What assurance is there that the right person reaps what he or she actually sowed, not what somebody else sowed? How is karma carried from life to life, so one can be assured there are no mistakes?

Applied within the span of one life, William James offers a suggestive answer in his *Talks to Teachers on Psychology*. Every moment, he says, we are spinning our own fates for good or evil.

> Every smallest stroke of virtue or of vice leaves its never-so-little scar. The drunken Rip Van Winkle, in Jefferson's play, excuses himself for every fresh dereliction by saying, "I won't count this time!" Well, he may not count it, and a kind Heaven may not count it; but it is being counted none the less. Down among his nerve cells and fibers the molecules are counting it, registering and storing it up to be used against him when the next temptation comes. Nothing we ever do is, in strict scientific literalness, wiped out.[13]

Furthermore, as is now well known, the record is also stored in the subconscious mind. And, according to reincarnational theory, the deeper levels of that mind endure from life to life. Hence, the record of what we do could well survive death.

Incidentally, Professor John Hick used the just-quoted words of James in explaining the Buddhist teaching of rebirth and karma, and commented: "This is the reflexive operation of the moral law of karma, seen by James as physical as well as mental; and if the agent lives a second or third or any number of lives, so long as he is the same person he must take with him the character which he has been forming and reforming in all his past volitions."[14] Such character, like a magnet, draws to itself, as a learning and compensating experience, peoples and events appropriate to its nature.

EMERSON AND THOREAU

As Harvard is so close to Concord, it would be particularly fitting this evening, if time permitted, to survey the views of Emerson, Thoreau, Alcott, and the other transcendentalists on our subject. Here only a few thoughts of two of them will be shared.

In Emerson's essay "Experience," he uses the simile of a stairway rather than a book, but in effect tells the same story.

> Where do we find ourselves? In a series of which we do not know the extremes, and believe that it has none. [When born] we wake and find ourselves on a stair; there are other stairs below us which we seem to have

ascended: there are stairs above us, many a one, which go upward and out of sight.

But the Genius which according to the old belief stands at the door by which we enter, and gives us the lethe to drink, that we may tell no tales, mixed the cup too strongly, and we cannot shake off the lethargy now at noonday. Sleep lingers all our lifetime about our eyes.[15]

In his essay "Compensation," Emerson employs another analogy, that of a house: "Every soul is by intrinsic necessity quitting its whole system of things, as the shell-fish crawls out of its beautiful and stony case, because it no longer admits of its growth, and slowly forms a new house." Yet we resist making this transition. "We cannot part with our friends," says Emerson. "We cannot let our angels go. We do not see that they only go out that archangels may come in. We do not believe in the riches of the soul, in its proper eternity and omnipresence. We linger in the ruins of the old tent where once we had bread and shelter and organs, nor believe that the spirit can feed, cover and nerve us again. But we sit and weep in vain. The voice of the Almighty saith, 'UP AND ONWARD FOREVERMORE!' "[16]

One more selection is from Emerson's "Nominalist and Realist."

It is the secret of the world that all things subsist and do not die, but only retire a little from sight and afterwards return again. Nothing is dead; people feign themselves dead, and endure mock funerals and mournful obituaries, and there they stand looking out of the window, sound and well, in some new strange disguise. Jesus is not dead; he is very well alive; nor John, nor Paul, nor Mahomet, nor Aristotle; at times we believe we have seen them all, and could easily tell the names under which they go.[17]

Whether Emerson remembered his previous lives is not known, but that Thoreau and he discussed past-life memories is evident from a sentence that appears abruptly, without antecedent explanation, in a letter from Thoreau to Emerson dated July 8, 1843: "And Hawthorne, too, I remember as one with whom I sauntered in old heroic times along the banks of the Scamander amid the ruins of chariots and heroes."[18]

Writing to Harrison Blake, Thoreau observed, "I lived in Judea eighteen hundred years ago, but I never knew that there was such a one as Christ among my contemporaries" (April 3, 1850). In another letter to Blake, he wrote, "As the stars looked to me when I was a shepherd in Assyria, they look to me now as a New Englander" (February 22, 1853).[19]

THE HERO IN OUR BOOK OF LIFE

We have yet to consider more in depth who or what in the human constitution is supposed to incarnate from life to life. But is it not first necessary to discover something within us that can survive all transformations in *this* life? Our bodies, feelings, and ideas change, but is there anything more permanent than those? Some might say, "Yes, there is the I-am-I consciousness and my enduring sense of identity." However, in attempting to identify the "I" in "I am," philosopher David Hume found only a conglomeration of thoughts, sensations, and wishes. But Immanuel Kant, pondering on Hume's answer, asked, Who is it that carries on the scrutiny of his own performance? Whose memory is at work permitting self-identity? Are there not two selves in man?

In *Walden,* Thoreau replies affirmatively and observes: "I am conscious of the presence and criticism of a part of me, which, as it were, is not a part of me, but spectator, sharing no experience, but taking note of it. . . . When the play, it may be the tragedy, of life is over, the spectator goes his way. It was a kind of fiction, a work of the imagination only, so far as he was concerned."[20]

The scoffing skeptic may comment: "Who ever saw the inner Self? Let's stick to observable facts." But does the scientist himself limit himself to observable facts? The limits of our perceptions are so restricted that, if the researcher did not permit himself to go beyond them, his efforts would long since have been unproductive. What physicist—even with his newest electron microscope that magnifies 15 million times—has seen or experienced an electron or a neutron, or a quark, or the host of other elements believed to exist within the atom? Yet he speaks of these things as realities. As one professor, J. Paul Williams, wryly remarks, "Let no one think that he has reached perfection in his habits of thought if he accepts inferential logic in physics but rejects it in theology."[21] It appears of considerable significance that today some scientists—in fact, very prestigious ones—are using inferential logic, supported by evidence, to investigate whether an immortal entity exists within the human frame.

This is reported in an essay by John Gliedman in *Science Digest* (July 1982) titled "Scientists in Search of the Soul." "From Berkeley to Paris and from London to Princeton, prominent scientists from fields as diverse as neurophysiology and quantum physics are coming out of the closet and admitting they believe in the possibility, at least, of such unscientific entities as the immortal human spirit."

Among those mentioned is Sir Karl Popper, "the most famous philosopher of science of our age and who singlehandedly created the orthodox theory of scientific explanation held by most working scientists.'' He postulated ''the existence of a nonmaterial conscious mind that influences ponderable matter.'' The famed physiologist Sir Charles Sherrington believed similarly.

As to physicists, some of the foremost today have come to the same conclusion based on the work in the 1930s in quantum mechanics of John von Neumann, ''whose intellect was so great he may have been the smartest man that ever lived. . . . It was not until the early 1960s that one of the greatest physicists of the century, Eugene Wigner, winner of the 1963 Nobel Prize in physics, boldly spelled out in public what von Neumann's followers had been whispering in their laboratories . . . man may have a nonmaterial consciousness capable of influencing matter.''[22]

A Modern Breakthrough.   The interminably unresolved speculations of philosophers and psychologists as to whether there is or is not within us an independent self appears to have been dramatically bypassed in the mounting evidence of out-of-body experiences. Such happenings have become so numerous that the initials OBE have been resorted to in referring to them. Many of these involve individuals pronounced clinically dead. [See chapter 8.] Others concern people who, at the time of near fatal accidents or during surgical operations, find themselves outside their bodies and accurately observing events transpiring while their bodies are unconscious.

Former Air Marshal Sir Victor Goddard, president of England's College of Aeronautics, in an article titled ''The Night My Number Came Up,'' told of such an experience that had happened to a friend. Sir Victor recalled the incident while his own plane, *Sister Ann*, was about to be involved in a possible fatal crash landing.

> I recalled how, in the first World War, at East Fortune, my friend Jenkins had crashed in a Sopwith Pup and broken his skull. He remained unconscious for three weeks. When he came around he told me how, immediately after the crash, he had found himself outside the wreckage, observing himself, inert and apparently dead, in the pilot's seat; saw spectators arrive, running and breathless; saw how they anxiously wrestled with the wreckage to get at his own body, and how their expressions of regret and anxiety distressed him. He saw the ambulance arrive and the stretcher men. He felt regard but not concern for his own body.
>
> I wondered how I myself, my real self, would ''see'' all that was to be enacted on that forlorn beach when physical nature had its way with *Sister Ann* and her human cargo.[23]

Another such experience occurred to Peter Sellers when he had his first heart attack. The doctors pronounced him dead. He recalled leaving his body and looking down and seeing his open chest cavity and the surgeon holding his heart in his hands (*New York Times*, October 31, 1980).

Ernest Hemingway also had a startling OBE when he was seriously wounded while serving as an ambulance corpsman during World War I. The strange experience affected him so profoundly that he talked about it and wrote about it at various times throughout his life. One description occurs in *A Farewell to Arms:* "There was a flash, as when a blast-furnace door is swung open. . . . I tried to breathe but my breath would not come and I felt myself rush bodily out of myself. . . . I went out swiftly, all of myself, and I knew I was dead, and that it had all been a mistake to think you just died."[24] Another vivid account by Hemingway appears in Malcolm Cowley's *A Second Flowering: Works and Days of the Lost Generation.* Hemingway told a friend: "I died then, I felt my soul or something coming right out of my body like you'd pull a silk handkerchief out of a pocket by one corner. It flew all around and then came back and I wasn't dead anymore."[25]

Raymond Moody, in his classic book on this subject, *Life After Life,* has a chapter on parallel experiences recorded in ancient literature. He reports that The Tibetan Book of the Dead—compiled by Oxford anthropologist W. Evans-Wentz—contains a lengthy description of the various stages through which the soul goes after physical death. Dr. Moody comments: "The correspondences between the early stages of death which it relates and those which have been recounted to me by those who have come near to death is nothing short of fantastic."[26]

Speaking of Tibetan Buddhism, how interesting that this very evening Harvard is honored by the presence of His Holiness, the Dalai Lama who, in the course of his historic seven-week visit to the United States, is presenting a talk on the Buddhist idea of the Self to a select audience at Sanders Theatre [in Harvard's Memorial Hall]. The subject was not publicized, and I learned of it by chance from Dr. L. A. Wickremeratne of Harvard who visited me this morning in Boston. This doctor is engaged in special research (under a grant received from the Harvard Center for the Study of World Religions) that borders on my own researches into reincarnation. [An excerpt from the Dalai Lama's talk is given in chapter 15 and reveals he is convinced that there is an immortal, reincarnating mind in human beings.]

The Personality and the Individuality. In answering more definitely the question "who is the hero of our Book of Life?" Western reincarnationists usually employ the terminology first used by the theosophists of the last century. They called the perishable Self the personality, and the enduring Self the individuality. The choice of terms seems warranted from their derivative origins, as we shall see, but first an example from theosophical writings of how these terms were originally used. The selection is from Helena Blavatsky's chief work, *The Secret Doctrine: the Synthesis of Science, Religion and Philosophy.* (According to a niece of Albert Einstein, *The Secret Doctrine* was always on his desk.[27]) Madame Blavatsky wrote:

> Intimately, or rather indissolubly, connected with Karma is the law of rebirth, or of the reincarnation of the same spiritual individuality in a long, almost interminable, series of personalities. The latter are like the various costumes and characters played by the same actor, with each of which that actor identifies himself and is identified by the public, for the space of a few hours.

"The Inner, or real man, who personates those characters," she continues, "knows the whole time that he is Hamlet for the brief space of a few acts, which represent, however, on the plane of human illusion the whole life of Hamlet. And he knows that he was, the night before, King Lear, the transformation in his turn of the Othello of a still earlier preceding night; but the outer, visible character is supposed to be ignorant of the fact."

> In actual life that ignorance is, unfortunately, but too real. Nevertheless, the permanent individuality is fully aware of the fact, though through the atrophy of the "spiritual" eye in the physical body, that knowledge is unable to impress itself on the consciousness of the false [or illusionary] personality. . . .
> "That which is part of our souls is eternal," says Thackeray, and though "the book and volume" of the *physical* brain may forget events within the scope of one terrestrial life, the bulk of collective recollections can never desert the divine soul within us. Its whispers may be too soft, the sound of its words too far off the plane perceived by our physical senses; yet the shadow of events that were is within its perceptive powers, and is ever present before its mind's eye.[28]

As to the derivation of "individuality," it comes from the Latin *individuus,* meaning indivisible, which suggests permanence and continuity. As to "our word 'personality,' " observes Professor Huston Smith, it "comes from the Latin *persona* which originally meant the mask an actor donned as he stepped on to the stage to play his role. The mask carried the make-up of the role, while the actor behind it remained hidden and anonymous.'' The professor continues:

> This mask is precisely what our personalities are—the roles into which we have been cast for the moment in this greatest drama of all, life itself. The disturbing fact, however, is that we have lost sight of the distinction between our true self and the veil of personality that is its present costume, but which will be laid aside when the play is over. We have come completely under the fascination of our present lines, unable to remember previous roles or to anticipate future ones.
>
> The task is to correct this false identification. Turning his awareness inward a human being must pierce and dissolve the innumerable layers of the manifest personality until, all strata of the mask at length cut through, he arrives finally at the anonymous actor who stands beneath.[29]

A great transformation will take place in human relationships when people cease identifying themselves and others with the mask selves rather than with the transcendent Self within. Eugene O'Neill seems to suggest this in his play *The Great God Brown.* On stage, the players wear masks when their ordinary selves speak, but when the inner being shines through, the masks are removed. The performance closes with these lines: "It's only our lives that grow old. We *are* where centuries only count as seconds, and after a thousand lives our eyes begin to open."[30]

From all the foregoing, then, the reincarnating actor is a *Hero with a Thousand Faces,* to use the title of Joseph Campbell's renowned work on mythology.[31] Our usual Western concept of the hero, he says, "is of the actual, particular individual, who indeed is mortal and so doomed. Whereas in the Orient the true hero of all mythology is not the vainly striving, empirical personality, but that reincarnating one and only transmigrant, which—to quote a celebrated verse from the *Bhagavad-Gita*—'is never born; nor does it die. . . . Unborn, eternal, and of great age, it is not slain when the body is slain.' "[32]

Why Are We Not Further Advanced?   If all of us have lived many lives and our Book of Life up to now is a long, long saga, then why is humanity not further advanced?

While it is natural to equate reincarnation with progress, this is not necessarily correct. Rebirth only provides the *opportunity* for progress. Consider the daily "reincarnation" cycle: if mere repetitions of days and nights made one automatically wise, then all octogenarians would be sages!

In terms of the cosmic time scale, humanity may still be in its infancy, or at most its adolescence—probably the latter, in view of the turbulent international and domestic scene and the present inability of the human family to live in peace.

Buddha well appreciated that the vast majority advance very slowly. He likened our pilgrimage to climbing a mountain. His words on this that follow are taken from Sir Edwin Arnold's *The Light of Asia,* a volume on the life and teachings of Buddha that deeply impressed the New England transcendentalists and prompted a twenty-six-page review by Oliver Wendell Holmes. (How interesting that, exactly ninety years ago this month [October 1889], Charles Eliot, president of Harvard, invited Arnold to lecture here at Sanders Theatre where the Dalai Lama is speaking tonight.) Here are the lines:

> Manifold tracks lead to yon sister-peaks
> Around whose snows the gilded clouds are curled;
> By steep or gentle slopes the climber comes
> Where breaks that other world.
>
> Strong limbs may dare the rugged road,
> The weak must wind from slower ledge to ledge
> With many a place of rest.
> The firm soul hastes, the feeble tarries. All
> Will reach the sunlit snows.[33]

ONLY TWO OPTIONS— OR A THIRD ALTERNATIVE?

THE IMPASSE OF MODERN SCIENCE

"The only solid piece of scientific truth about which I feel totally confident," writes a physician and biologist of distinction, Dr. Lewis Thomas, "is that we are profoundly ignorant about nature. Indeed, I regard this as the major discovery of the past hundred years of biology."[34]

He is not alone in his observation. In 1977, *The Encyclopaedia of Ignorance* was published at Oxford,[35] in which the world's eminent scientists surveyed the unsolved problems in their fields. A similar work, involving astronomical research, was recently published: *Mysterious Universe: A*

Handbook of Astronomical Anomalies, by William R. Corliss. The reviewer in the *New York Times* remarks that the volume is composed "almost entirely of articles published by professional scientific journals," and is "a remarkably full compilation of scientific head-scratching regarding the heavens surrounding our planet"[36] (October 2, 1979). (Corliss is a specialist in anomalous science and is presently compiling a twenty-five-volume *Catalog of Anomalies.*)

It is not only the unsolved problems regarding the universe presently perceived that create difficulties for scientists in arriving at logical theories to explain life, but what they realize must exist in the unseen universe beyond the reach of their finest instruments. If this unseen physical universe could be perceived how would it alter their theories?

Gregory Bateson spoke of this in *Mind and Nature.* This British scientist was visiting professor of anthropology at Harvard in 1947 and, moving on to other fields, markedly influenced an entire generation of social scientists. He wrote:

> The invention of the microscope or the telescope or of means of measuring time to the fraction of a nanosecond, or weighing quantities of matter to millionths of a gram—all such improved devices of perception will disclose what was utterly unpredictable from the levels of perception that we could achieve before that discovery. . . . It follows that what we, as scientists, can perceive is always limited by threshold. That is, what is subliminal will not be grist for our mill. *Science probes; it does not prove.*[37]

The truth of this statement has recently been dramatically demonstrated with the exploration of the world within the cell. An electron microscope that magnifies 140,000 times was used, along with a new technique of freezing tissue specimens so quickly—in one-thousandth of a second—that there is no time for the delicate structures within cells to disintegrate. Structures in the cell never seen before have been revealed. Their chemical makeup and functions are still unknown and remain subjects of intense debate.[38]

Why Mystery?   If we live in a mechanistic universe, composed of nothing but matter and energy, why should there be so many mysteries, and why should nature exhibit an apparently never-ending series of invisible "layers"? Have we ever thought of that? A mechanism, however complicated, has no mysteries for a master mechanic. He can take it apart and reassemble it. This is not so with living forms.

Until recently the problem of man and the cosmos has been rigidly regarded in terms of two options, two alternatives. Biologist Jacques Monod, the famed author of *Chance and Necessity*, made this plain in an interview. He was asked, "You write that man was the product of pure chance. How do you come to that conclusion?" He replied, "Well, it's relatively simple in principle, unless we accept the pure creationist view of the origins of the universe. Unless we do that, we have to find some natural interpretation."[39]

The creationist view poses insuperable difficulties for most scientists. How, they ask, can an extracosmic, or even an intracosmic god, create and manage a universe so vast that it includes in our Milky Way galaxy—according to the latest figures—150 billion suns (*Astronomy*, August 1980)? In addition, astronomers tell us there are billions of companion galaxies spaced at about one million light-years apart. One light-year is approximately 6 trillion miles! A quasar has recently been discovered to be 18 billion light-years away (*New York Post*, March 31, 1982)!

Monod admits that the "naturalistic" concept of blind matter as the only reality has its problems too. The core problem of biology, he says, is how to account for a biosphere full of systems that behave as if they had a project and a purpose, existing in a world devoid of a project and a purpose. In a key passage in *Chance and Necessity*, he also admits:

> When one ponders on the tremendous journey of evolution over the past 3 billion years or so, the prodigious wealth of structures it has engendered, and the extraordinarily effective performance of living beings from bacteria to man, one may well find oneself beginning to doubt again whether all this could conceivably be the product of an enormous lottery presided over by natural selection.[40]

Nevertheless, he feels he has no alternative but to opt for lottery and chance, acknowledging that his answer and that of the school he represents is a "pure postulate, because you can't prove that this is right."[41]

Simply put, the theory regards the origin of life as an "improbable chemical accident," which perpetuated itself in more and more complex organisms through a series of additional accidents. Viewing all this objectively, Joseph Wood Krutch once asked, "But is not the assumption of an 'improbable chemical accident' which results ultimately in something capable of discussing the nature of 'improbable chemical accidents' a staggering one? Is it not indeed preposterous?"[42]

By "chance" and "accident," scientists do not mean either uncaused or haphazard action, but simply *unplanned* action, involving no design or free choice. Though unplanned, such action is predetermined by previous actions, and hence the theory has been called determinism. Henri Bergson, the noted French philosopher, disclosed its obvious implications in a rather startling way, as reported by Will Durant: "If the present moment contains no living and creative choice, and is totally and mechanically the product of the matter and motion of the moment before, then so was that moment the mechanical effect of the moment that preceded it, and that again of the one before, and so on, until we arrive at the primeval nebula as the total cause of every event, of every line of Shakespeare's plays—all written far off in the distant skies by the structure and content of that legendary cloud"—or in modern speculation "the Big Bang."

"What a draft upon credulity!" Bergson exclaims. "What an exercise of faith such a theory must demand in this unbelieving generation! What mystery or miracle, of old Testament or New, could be half so incredible as this monstrous fatalistic myth, this nebula composing tragedies?"[43]

The mental and moral confusion resulting from such deterministic theories is underscored in this open letter by an undergraduate to the president of Yale:

> A logical inference from every psychology lecture we have ever attended would be that man's least thought and act . . . every choice is dictated by a million strings of deterministic factors leading back to the dawn of time. . . . If man is a slave of determinism, incapable of free choice, what is the value of the ballot, trial by jury, and civil liberties in general? . . . Isn't it palpably obvious to you that at the root of the trouble lies an apparent contradiction between the implications of our studies and the ideals we are expected to revere?"[44]

The Typewriting-Monkeys-Myth Demolished. Science writers who are convinced that intelligence can arise through natural selection acting on random mutations of genes, are fond of declaring that "if enough monkeys pecked away at typewriters long enough, they could eventually write the complete works of Shakespeare." This old cliché has now been effectively overthrown by a professor of physics at Yale University, Dr. William R. Bennett, a specialist in designing computer programs. As reported in the *New York Times,* Dr. Bennett has discovered that "if a trillion monkeys were to type ten randomly chosen characters a second, it would take, on the average, more than a trillion times as long as the universe has been in existence just to compose the sentence: 'To be or not to be, that is the question' " (March 6, 1979).

When one contemplates the whole biosphere, observes Dr. Lewis Thomas, how could it have turned out to possess such stability and coherence, resembling as it does a sort of enormous developing embryo, with nothing but chance events to determine its emergence?[45]

If, then, after generations of reductionist labors to prove that the universe and all living forms are the product of blind, mechanical laws, without plan or purpose, and the effort has failed, has not the time come to consider other explanations?

A THIRD ALTERNATIVE

A proposed third alternative is ancient wisdom, grounded in the reincarnational outlook and the universal pervasiveness of God, but adapted to modern scientific, philosophic, and religious thought.

The first individual to attempt such a monumental task was the Russian theosophist, Helena Petrovna Blavatsky (1831–1891), founder of the Theosophical Society, which is known more generally as the theosophical movement. It originated in New York City in 1875 and soon became worldwide. It had, and has, three declared objects, quite acceptable today, but in the Victorian age daring and innovative: 1. To form the nucleus of a Universal Brotherhood of Humanity, without distinction of race, creed, sex, caste, or color. 2. The comparative study of ancient and modern religions, philosophies, and sciences. 3. The investigation of the unexplained laws of nature and the psychical and spiritual powers of human beings.

Professor Carl Jackson, in his article on theosophy in the current *Encyclopedia Britannica*, writes,

> Theosophy is a religious philosophy with definite mystical concerns that can be traced to the ancient world but is of catalytic significance in religious thought in the 19th and 20th centuries. . . . The movement has been a catalytic force in the 20th century revival of Buddhism and Hinduism, and a pioneering agency in the promotion of greater Western acquaintance with Eastern thought. In the United States it has influenced a whole series of religious movements. . . . In the estimation of some scholars, no other single organization has done more to popularize Asian religions and philosophical ideas in the West.[46]

Jung writes in *Psychology and Religion: West and East* that, in the last century, Eastern wisdom was at first "the preserve of Sanskrit scholars and philosophers, but it was not so very long before the theosophical movement inaugurated by Madame Blavatsky possessed itself of the Eastern traditions and promulgated them among the general public."[47]

Blavatsky's major work is *The Secret Doctrine: The Synthesis of Science,*

Religion, and Philosophy. The social historian Theodore Roszak, author of *Where the Wasteland Ends*, has a section on this book in his *The Unfinished Animal.*[48] First, he mentions that Helena Blavatsky "has had a bad press ever since she appeared in 1875 as organizer of the Theosophical Society. One of the great liberated ladies of her day—she could not help but draw withering, critical fire by her every act and word, especially when she presumed to challenge the most intellectual orthodoxies of the age." "Still today," he adds, "people who have never read a line she wrote remain adamantly convinced she was a fraud and a crank." At issue, he says, is "the quality of her thinking," and "in this she is surely among the most original and perceptive minds of her time. . . . Above all, she is among the modern world's trail-blazing psychologists of the visionary mind."

It seems clear, from Roszak's selections from her writings and his comments thereon, that he regards Blavatsky as exercising a fundamentally emancipating influence on the Western mind through the conception of evolution as moral, mental, and spiritual, as well as physical. Her books reveal, he says, "the first philosophy of psychic and spiritual evolution to appear in the modern West."

> Her effort, unlike that of the Christian fundamentalists, was not to reject Darwin's work, but to insist that it had, by its focus on the purely physical, wholly omitted the mental, creative, and visionary life of the human race; in short, it omitted *consciousness,* whose development followed a very different evolutionary path. Darwin simply did not go far enough; his was not a big enough theory to contain human nature in the round.

Blavatsky, says Roszak, traces from the universal deific source to the incarnate human spirit one uninterrupted series of entities. This immersion of spirit is for the purpose of vastly enriching our consciousness. "By our collective evolutionary course, and by innumerable personal incarnations, we make our way through all the realms of being: mineral, plant, animal, human, divine. And it is by virtue of this hard-won 'harvest of experience' that each human being becomes a microcosm of the universe." It was this teaching of evolution through rebirth, pervasively promulgated by the theosophical movement that was chiefly responsible for the beginning of the reincarnation renaissance of modern times. [See chapter 7 in *Reincarnation, the Phoenix Fire Mystery.*]

Alfred Russel Wallace, coauthor with Darwin of the theory of evolution, was an admirer of Blavatsky's writings. He saw the limitations of natural selection. It could not explain, he said, how art, music, and other aesthetic powers of the mind arose, inasmuch as they gave no competitive advantage in the struggle for survival. Roszak notes that Wallace "agreed natural selection explains adaptation; but in his eyes adaptation was essentially conservative and unenterprising. It moves in a purely horizontal direction. . . . If evolution was merely a matter of survival by adaptation, we might still be a planet of hearty bacteria. . . . Overlaying it Wallace saw a more daring vertical movement which boosts evolution toward higher levels of complexity and consciousness."[49] And this vertical movement had its impulse from a spiritual source, Wallace thought.

Wallace once wrote to Helena Blavatsky regarding her two-volume work, *Isis Unveiled,* "I am amazed at the vast amount of erudition displayed in these handsome volumes and the great interest of the topics on which they treat. Opens a whole world of new ideas and cannot fail to be of the greatest value."[50]

Not a Revelation. In the preface to *The Secret Doctrine,* the author makes clear that these ideas

> are in no sense put forward as a revelation; nor does the author claim the position of a revealer of mystic lore, now made public for the first time in the world's history. What is now attempted is to gather the oldest tenets together and to make of them one harmonious and unbroken whole. The sole advantage which the writer has over her predecessors, is that she need not resort to personal speculations and theories. For this work is a partial statement of what she herself has been taught by more advanced students, supplemented, in a few details only, by the results of her own study and observation.[51]

Her teachers, she said, were some of the wise men of the East.

Eastern and Western Science Contrasted. It was Blavatsky's opinion that the perpetual mysteries and missing links confronting scientists in every field will continue to plague them until the hidden side of nature, the "occult" cosmos is deemed a worthy subject of research. In *The Secret Doctrine,* she assures, however, that

> there can be no possible conflict between the teachings of occult and so-called exact science where the conclusions of the latter are grounded on a substratum of unassailable fact. It is only when its more ardent exponents, overstepping the limits of observed phenomena in order to penetrate into the arcana of Being, attempt to wrench the formation of Kosmos and its *living* Forces from Spirit, and attribute all to blind matter, that the Occultists claim the right to dispute and call in question their theories.

Science cannot, owing to the very nature of things, unveil the mystery of the universe around us. Science can, it is true, collect, classify, and generalize upon phenomena; but the occultists, arguing from admitted metaphysical data, declare that the daring explorer, who would probe the inmost secrets of Nature, must transcend the narrow limitations of sense, and transfer his consciousness into the region of noumena and the sphere of primal causes. To effect this he must develop faculties which are absolutely dormant—save in a few rare exceptional cases—in the constitution of our Race.[52]

On this latter point, an interesting contrast between Western and Eastern science is made by Dr. Walt Anderson: "We are, in the West, so in awe of our machines that we believe they alone are capable of discovering the truth. It does not seem to have occurred to many physicists that the reality unfolded in their research and theory might be experienced." In the West, he says, "the cosmos is explored by cyclotrons and lasers and telescopes," while Eastern science "has been largely non-technical, relying on the apparatus of the disciplined human body and mind," as in practices of deep meditation.[53]

In an ancient Hindu treatise, *Patanjali's Yoga Aphorisms*, there is this instruction: "By concentrating his mind upon minute, concealed or distant objects, in every department of nature, the ascetic acquires thorough knowledge concerning them." The commentator states that "the term 'knowledge' as used here has a greater meaning than we are accustomed to giving it. It implies full identification of the mind, for any length of time, with whatever object or subject it is directed to."[54]

Science Digest reports that "no world-famous physicist takes the claims of Eastern mystical philosophy more seriously than Cambridge University's Brian Josephson, winner of the 1978 Nobel prize in physics." Josephson "has staked his enormous scientific reputation on the possibility that he can gain insights into objective reality by practicing traditional Eastern meditational techniques" (July 1982).

The mathematical wizard and electrical engineer Charles Steinmetz told the world of science sixty years ago that, when it finally turned toward spiritual discoveries, it would make more progress in fifty years than in all its past history.[55]

Physicist Sir James Jeans, in his book *The Mysterious Universe,* foresaw that "the stream of knowledge is heading toward a non-mechanical reality; the universe begins to look more like a great thought than a great machine. Mind no longer appears as an accidental intruder into the realm of matter; we are beginning to suspect that we ought to hail it as the creator and governor of the realm of matter."[56]

*

The one thing that would be fatal for materialism, says Chapman Cohen in *Materialism Restated,* would be the necessity for assuming a controlling and directing intelligence at any part of the cosmic process.[57] Having in mind the unwelcome concept (to an atheist) of an anthropomorphic creator, as immaturely presented in some orthodox religions, he was sure there is no such necessity. Bertrand Russell in his introduction to Lange's *History of Materialism* observed regarding science: "As a rule, the materialistic dogma has not been set up by men who loved dogma, but by men who felt that nothing less definite would enable them to fight the dogmas they disliked."[58]

These able thinkers took for granted there could be only two alternative answers to the mysteries of life and death. There is, as shown, *a third alternative*, which possibly provides a more rational theory to account for the astonishing development of life on earth and the wondrous drama of human evolution. But like all theories it will stand or fall as facts do or do not support its suppositions.

Providing an overview of how this alternate theory relates to the reincarnational outlook, we briefly turn to some provocative thoughts of two noted nineteenth-century thinkers.

Evolution Through Reincarnation. A founder of the transcendentalist movement in America, the Boston clergyman James Freeman Clarke devoted a chapter of his book *Ten Great Religions* (1887) to "The Soul and Its Transmigration in All Religions." Quoting therefrom:

> That man has come up to his present state of development by passing through lower forms is the popular doctrine of science today. What is called evolution teaches that we have reached our present state by a very long and gradual ascent from the lowest animal organizations. It is true that Darwinian theory takes no notice of the evolution of the soul, but only of the body. But it appears to me that a combination of the two views would remove many difficulties which still attach to the theory of natural selection and the survival of the fittest.

> The modern doctrine of evolution of bodily organisms is not complete, unless we unite with it the idea of a corresponding evolution of the spiritual monad, from which every organic form derives its unity. Evolution has a satisfactory meaning only when we admit that the soul is developed and educated by passing through many bodies. If we are to believe in evolution, let us have the assistance of the soul itself in this development of new species.[59]

The leading nineteenth-century Darwinist, Thomas Huxley, also related reincarnational ideas to evolution. He wrote, in *Evolution and Ethics,* "In the doctrine of transmigration, whatever its origin, Brahmanical and Buddhist speculation found, ready to hand, the means of constructing a plausible vindication of the ways of the Cosmos to man. . . . Yet this plea of justification is not less plausible than others; and none but very hasty thinkers will reject it on the ground of inherent absurdity. Like the doctrine of evolution itself, that of transmigration has its roots in the world of reality; and it may claim such support as the great argument from analogy is capable of supplying."[60]

However, in this century, using the methods of empirical research, there are additional ways to demonstrate the possibility of more lives than one. [At this point of the lecture the reincarnation research of Dr. Ian Stevenson was considered. See chapter 4.]

Advanced Intelligences Beyond Our Humanity?   Thomas Huxley even went so far as to theorize that, if consciousness survives death, there is no end to the possibilities of its development in future lives. He suggests that intelligences advanced far beyond our present humanity could then play an indispensable though not compelling role, as guiding factors in cosmic and human evolution. Here is what Huxley—an arch skeptic and materialist most of his life—wrote.

"Looking at the matter from the most rigidly scientific point of view, the assumption that, amidst the myriads of worlds scattered through endless space, there can be no intelligence, as much greater than man's as his is greater than a blackbeetle's, no being endowed with powers of influencing the course of nature as much greater than his, as his is greater than a snail's, seems to me not merely baseless, but impertinent. Without stepping beyond the analogy of that which is known, it is easy to people the cosmos with entities, in ascending scale until we reach something practically indistinguishable from omnipotence, omnipresence, and omniscience. . . .

"I understand the main tenet of Materialism to be that there is nothing in the universe but matter and force. . . . *Kraft und Stoff*—force and matter—are paraded as the Alpha and Omega of existence. . . . Whosoever does not hold it is condemned by the more zealous of the persuasion to the Inferno appointed for fools or hypocrites. But all this I heartily disbelieve. . . . There is a third thing in the universe, to wit, consciousness, which I can not see to be matter or force, or any conceivable modification of either. . . .

"The student of nature, who starts from the axiom of the universality of the law of causation, can not refuse to admit an eternal existence; if he admits the conservation of energy, he can not deny the possibility of an eternal energy; if he admits the existence of immaterial phenomena in the form of consciousness, he must admit the possibility, at any rate, of *an eternal series of such phenomena*"[61] [italics added].

PSYCHOLOGISTS DISCOVER REBIRTH

WILLIAM JAMES

At Harvard in 1893, William James delivered his famous Ingersoll Lecture, "Human Immortality." As most of you know, he received his medical degree here and subsequently taught at Harvard for over a third of a century. Tonight, on the way to this lecture, I saw the magnificent building the university has erected in honor of this most renowned of American psychologists and philosophers.

In James's early life, he was under the influence of deterministic philosophies that apparently deeply depressed him. Horace Meyer Kallen, author of *William James and Henri Bergson,* writes that, from adolescence, James seemed to have been a delicate boy, always ailing. During his stay in Germany (1867–1868), he suffered a breakdown, with thoughts of suicide.

When he returned home, in Nov. 1868, after 18 months in Germany, he was still ill. Though he took the degree of M.D. at the Harvard Medical School in June 1869, he was unable to begin practice. Between that date and 1872 he lived in a state of semi-invalidism in his father's house, doing nothing but reading, and writing a very occasional review. Early in this period he experienced a sort of phobic panic which persisted until the end of April 1870.

"It was relieved, according to his own statement, by the reading of Renouvier on freewill and the decision that 'my first act of freewill shall be to believe in freewill.' . . . The decision carried with it," says Kallen,

the abandonment of all determinisms—both the scientific kind which his training had established for him, and which seems to have had some relation to his neurosis, and the theological, metaphysical kind. . . . His revolutionary discoveries in psychology and philosophy, his views concerning the methods of science, the qualities of men and the nature of reality, seem all to have received a definite propulsion from this resolution of his poignant personal problem. . . . The old neurasthenia practically disappeared. He went at his tasks with a zest and an energy his earlier record had given no hint of. It was as if some deeper level of his being had been tapped; his life as an originative thinker began in earnest.[62]

James on Immortality and Reincarnation. In his Ingersoll Lecture on immortality, the views expressed in support of a future life were so strikingly original, they became the focus of much dialogue and debate. James denied that the findings of physiological psychology had rendered the idea of immortality without scientific justification. These findings, he said, rested on the view that the brain functions only in a productive capacity in relation to thought. The brain, he said, could as easily transmit ideas having an origin elsewhere.

He argued that "when a brain stops acting altogether, or decays, that special stream of consciousness which it subserved will vanish entirely from this natural world. But the sphere of being that supplied the consciousness would still be intact and in the more real world with which, even while here, it was continuous, the consciousness might, in ways unknown to us, continue still."[63]

Elaborating on James's views, Professor J. Paul Williams wrote in an essay in *The Yale Review*,

> William James pointed out that we can take two positions concerning the relation between the body and life; one is that the body *produces* life; the other that the body *reflects* life. Light is produced by a candle; if the candle is put out its light disappears. Light is reflected by a mirror; if the mirror is taken away the light still continues. . . . Now is it not at least as easy to suppose that the body reflects the soul as it is to suppose that it produces the soul? It may be that this human carcass, full of aches and diseases, produces things like *Hamlet*, the theory of evolution, psychoanalysis, and the fortieth chapter of Isaiah, but it is a great deal easier to believe that these things are the work of living souls who used bodies as instruments [Spring 1945].

In the preface to the second edition of *Human Immortality*, James enlarged upon his theory and spoke of reincarnation.

> So many critics have made one and the same objection to the doorway to immortality which my lecture claims to be left open by the "transmission theory" of cerebral action, that I feel tempted, as the book is again going to press, to add a word of explanation.
>
> If our finite personality here below, the objectors say, be due to the transmission through the brain of portions of *a pre-existing larger con sciousness*, all that can remain after the brain expires is the larger con-

sciousness. . . . But, this, the critics continue, is the pantheistic idea of immortality, survival, namely, in the soul of the world, not the Christian idea of immortality, which means survival in strictly personal form. . . .

The plain truth is that one may conceive the mental world behind the veil in as individualistic a form as one pleases, without any detriment to the general scheme by which the brain is represented as a transmissive organ. If the extreme individualistic view were taken, one's finite mundane consciousness would be an extract from one's larger, truer personality, the latter having even now some sort of reality behind the scenes.

It is true that all this would seem to have affinities rather with pre-existence and with possible reincarnations than with the Christian notion of immortality. But my concern in the lecture was not to discuss immortality in general. It was confined to showing it to be not incompatible with the brain-function theory of our present mundane consciousness. I hold that it is so compatible, and compatible moreover in fully individualized form.[64]

The Buddhist Idea of Karma.   William James was especially honored in Europe when he was invited to give the Gifford Lectures in 1901 and 1902, which became his famous book *The Varieties of Religious Experience*. In the preface, he calls attention to the postscript at the end of the volume, which, he says, indicates his own philosophic conclusions. Therein he speaks of the Buddhist idea of karma, which is, of course, intimately associated with reincarnation in Buddha's philosophy.

> I am ignorant of Buddhism and speak under correction, and merely in order the better to describe my general point of view; but as I apprehend the Buddhist doctrine of Karma, I agree in principle with that. All supernaturalists admit that facts are under the judgment of higher law. . . . I state the matter thus bluntly, because the current of thought in academic circles runs against me, and I feel like a man who must set his back against an open door quickly if he does not wish to see it closed and locked.
>
> In spite of its being so shocking to the reigning intellectual tastes, I believe that a candid consideration of piecemeal supernaturalism and a complete discussion of all its metaphysical bearings will show it to be the hypothesis by which the largest number of legitimate requirements are met. That of course would be a program for other books than this; what I now say sufficiently indicates to the philosophic reader the place where I belong.[65]

Occult Interests.   James refers to the foregoing admission as being shocking to the colleagues of his day. Another of his interests was occultism, which was so embarrassing to Harvard that it was hushed up for many years, as I learned from Eugene Taylor here in Cambridge who is doing research in this field. By "occult interests," something more is meant than

James's rather well known investigation of paranormal phenomena and his becoming president of the American Society for Psychical Research in 1894. What was shocking was that he became interested in theosophy and joined the Theosophical Society on July 25, 1891.[66] In theosophy, of course, reincarnation is a foundational teaching.

A Closed Door. The door that William James said he tried to keep open in psychology was tightly sealed after his death, and concepts such as the existence of soul and immortality became anathema in orthodox circles for over half of a century. As Erich Fromm wrote in *Psychoanalysis and Religion*,

> Academic psychology, trying to imitate the natural sciences and laboratory methods of weighing and counting, dealt with everything except the soul. It tried to understand those aspects of man which can be examined in the laboratory. . . . It was more often concerned with insignificant problems which fitted an alleged scientific method than with devising new methods to study the significant problems of man. Psychology thus became a science lacking its main subject matter, the soul. [In Greece, the word *psyche*, from which psychology comes, was a name for the soul.][67]

SIGMUND FREUD

One would hardly expect Freud to be guilty of evincing any interest in soul and spirit, yet on occasion he made some unusual admissions thereon. In a conversation reported in Ludwig Binswanger's *Being-in-the-World*, Freud startled his friend and colleague by admitting that *"mankind has always known that it possesses spirit. I had to show it that there are also instincts."* And when Binswanger delivered an address commemorating Freud's eightieth birthday, the latter wrote him regarding religion and art: "If I had another lifetime of work before me, I have no doubt that I would find room for these noble guests."[68]

At one period, Freud even thought he had missed his true vocation. In a letter to the American psychologist Hereward Carrington, Freud wrote in 1921: "If I had my life to live over again I should devote myself to psychical research rather than psychoanalysis." This letter is quoted in Ernest Jones's three-volume *Sigmund Freud: Life and Work*, in the chapter titled "Occultism." It was a subject that, as the biographer says, "truly wracked" Freud and "perplexed him to distraction."[69]

Freud frequently used the word "soul" in his writings, as Dr. Bruno Bettelheim recently revealed in his book *Freud and Man's Soul*. He used such expressions as "a dream is the result of the activity of our soul," "the structure of the soul," and "the life of the soul." However, James Strachey, in the American edition of Freud's complete psychological works, invariably translated "soul" as "mind" or "mental activity"! The *New York Times* reviewer of Bettelheim's book comments that, by purposely mistranslating this word and others, Freudian theory has been transformed in America from "'an introspective psychology, into a *behavioral* one, 'which observes from the outside' and by doing so trivializes Freud's thought" (January 6, 1983). The overall effect, says Bettelheim, is to make it appear as "abstract, depersonalized, mechanized, 'scientific' statements about the strange and very complex workings of our mind." Freud was not only disturbed by the strong influence of behaviorism in America, but "was disgusted by a civilization that could explicitly deny the phenomenon of consciousness."[70]

*

Is there any evidence that Freud's philosophy could include a reincarnational outlook? Professor Herbert Fingarette concluded it could, when more fully worked out. This Fingarette does in *The Self in Transformation*, where there is a seventy-page chapter on reincarnation and karma.[71] Fingarette emphasizes: "I am not psychologizing reincarnation. I want to present it as a reality, not a metaphor."

In the foreword to the Harper Torchbook edition of *The Self in Transformation,* Benjamin Nelson remarks, "Fingarette escapes the logical and spiritual blunders which have regrettably dogged orthodox Freudianism from the time the earthshaking insights of psychoanalysis were prematurely encased in rigid molds."[72] Reviewing the book in *The Library Journal*, psychiatrist Louis De Rosis calls it a major contribution to psychoanalytic thought and adds,

> This volume is a high-powered microscope used by a brilliant philosopher to bring profound illumination into psychoanalysis—not only to its basic theoretical underpinnings but to its relationships in the whole scheme of man's being. This is truly required reading for all psychiatrists, psychoanalysts, and clinical psychologists of any school or persuasion. It should also have more than passing meaning for the informed layman [April 15, 1963].

CARL JUNG

Jung agreed with Freud that "mankind has always known that it possesses spirit," but Jung concerned himself with the therapeutic value of this conviction. In a commentary on an old Chinese text, *The Secret of the Golden Flower,* he wrote,

Death is psychologically just as important as birth, and an integral part of life. It is not the psychologist who must be questioned as to what happens finally to the detached consciousness. Whatever theoretical position he assumed, he would hopelessly overstep the boundaries of his scientific competence. He can only point out that the views of our text with respect to the timelessness of the detached consciousness, are in harmony with the religious thought of all times and with that of the overwhelming majority of mankind. He can say, further, that anyone who does not think this way would stand outside the human order, and would, therefore be suffering from a disturbance in his psychic equipment.

As physician, I make the greatest effort to fortify, so far as I have the power, a belief in immortality, especially in my older patients to whom such questions come menacingly near.[73]

As to reincarnation, Jung, as we have said, had a persistent feeling that he had lived in previous centuries, that he had to be reborn because of his "insatiable drive toward understanding," and that, after several hundred years of rest, he imagined he would be returning to continue with this world-task. In *Memories, Dreams, Reflections,* he also revealed that it was only in later years he obtained direct evidence for reincarnation. This was in a series of dreams that seemed to illustrate the processes of reincarnation in a deceased person of his acquaintance.[74]

Desiring more information on this, I wrote to Dr. Aniela Jaffé, who was the recorder and editor of the just-named work. Accompanying my letter was a copy of the anthology *Reincarnation, the Phoenix Fire Mystery,* as it contained a number of selections from Jung's writings on preexistence and reincarnation. Replying from Zurich on August 22, 1980, she wrote, "I am not informed about the dream series which you mention. Jung never told it to me, maybe because some other personalities were involved. But the quotations in your book are already most revealing as to what Jung believed concerning rebirth." Incidentally, I had obtained Dr. Jaffé's address through a good friend of hers, a Jungian analyst Armin Wanner, now living in New York. He informed me that, among Jung's intimate associates, it was well known that Jung believed in reincarnation.

Eric Erikson, one of the patriarchs of psychoanalysis, apparently has similar leanings. In his volume *Gandhi's Truth,* which received the 1970 National Book Award, he said,

And let us face it: "deep down" nobody in his right mind can visualize his own existence without assuming that he has always lived and will live hereafter; and the religious world-views of old only endowed this psychological instinct with images and ideas which could be shared, transmitted, and ritualized.[75]

A QUANTUM LEAP IN HUMAN EVOLUTION

Another patriarch in psychology, Carl Rogers, also admits to sympathy for the many-lives perspective, and that "the more we know, the nearer our thinking is to that of the ancient sages." In Rogers's chapter, "Some New Directions: A Personal View," in Thomas Hanna's *Explorers of Humankind,* he adds how paranormal experiences of close friends have enlarged his own outlook. As a result, he says, "I have been forced to consider the possibility of reincarnation, which in the past I had thought a ridiculous belief." Speaking generally of these transcendental experiences, he writes,

> Perhaps our more primitive capability, our largely unused right brain, is beginning to function again as it so often does in less "civilized" societies. Perhaps this "metaphoric mind" can come to know a universe which is nonlinear, in which the terms time and space have very different meanings. I do not know how this world of the paranormal may change us. But I believe we are perhaps opening up vast new fields of knowledge and power—a quantum leap. And every time new forces or energies have been discovered in our universe, they have changed our perception of reality and have opened new doors and new opportunities for the human being. . . . Contrary to the belief of many, this expanding discovery of the psychic world is in no way antiscientific.
>
> Perhaps we are entering a transitional stage of evolution similar to that of the first sea creatures who laboriously dragged themselves out of the swampy bogs to begin the difficult and complex task of coping with the problems of living on land. . . . Are we entering new worlds of psychic space, as well as the world of outer space? What is the future of the human spirit? To me these are tantalizing, but definitely hopeful questions.[76]

The Book of Life, then, may have strange developments in store for humanity in the centuries ahead, and it may be that each of us will be there to turn the pages!

II
SCIENTISTS INVESTIGATE REINCARNATION

First and above all, an explanation must do justice to the thing to be explained, must not devaluate it, interpret it away, belittle it, or garble it, in order to make it easier to understand. The question is not "At what view of the phenomenon must we arrive in order to explain it in accordance with one or another philosophy?" but precisely the reverse: "What philosophy is requisite if we are to live up to the subject, be on a level with it?" The question is not how the phenomenon must be turned, twisted, narrowed, crippled so as to be explicable, at all costs, upon principles that we have once and for all resolved not to go beyond. The question is: "To what point must we enlarge our thought so that it shall be in proportion to the phenomenon."

FRIEDRICH VON SCHELLING

It is enough for me to contemplate the mystery of conscious life, perpetuating itself through all eternity; to reflect upon the marvelous structure of the universe; and to try humbly to comprehend even an infinitesimal part of the intelligence manifested in nature.

ALBERT EINSTEIN

4
The Research of Ian Stevenson, M.D.

In September 1977, the 165th volume of a distinguished psychiatric periodical, the *Journal of Nervous and Mental Disease (JNMD)*, marked an unusual occurrence in medical publishing. Almost the entire issue was devoted to the research of Dr. Ian Stevenson into survival after death—and more particularly into reincarnation as a means for such survival. This event had been preceded in May of that year by the publication of Dr. Stevenson's lengthy paper "The Explanatory Value of the Idea of Reincarnation" in the same journal.

What was the reaction of readers? Dr. Eugene Brody, editor of the journal and a psychiatrist at the University of Maryland Medical School, said when interviewed, "I must have had three or four hundred requests for reprints from scientists in every discipline. It's pretty clear that there's a lot of interest in this topic."[1]

Ian Stevenson is Carlson Professor of Psychiatry at the University of Virginia Medical School and was formerly chairman of that department. He specializes in cases in which children, both in the West and East, have spontaneous detailed memories of what they claim are former lives. Five volumes of his case histories have thus far been published by the University of Virginia Press, while the number of reincarnation cases now in his files totals over 2,000.

In an editorial titled "Research in Reincarnation and Editorial Responsibility," Dr. Brody explained the decision of the *JNMD* to publish articles by Dr. Stevenson.

> The world of science and the journals essential to it seem at times to erect boundaries which can have an imprisoning rather than a facilitating effect on the search for new information and ways of organizing it.
>
> Many reputable journals almost automatically tend to reject work on certain topics as inappropriate to current scientific belief. Extrasensory perception,

reincarnation, and the paranormal in particular, carry an aura of abandonment of ordinary standards of logic and reality testing. For some they suggest
rejection of the total body of knowledge accumulated by systematic observation and experiment. Publication of papers on these topics may imply editorial endorsement of nonscientific philosophies and conclusions. We do not
imply such endorsement through this issue's focus on reincarnation and the
paranormal.

Our decision to publish this material recognizes the scientific and personal
credibility of the authors, the legitimacy of their research methods, and the
conformity of their reasoning to the usual canons of rational thought. . . .
This number of the *Journal* featuring Ian Stevenson's work on reincarnation reaffirms our commitment to the freedom of scientific and medical
information. This is the freedom of the professional community and of
concerned citizens to participate in generating new ideas and data, to dissemi-
nate them, or to have access to them [September 1977].

The *JNMD* is not the only psychiatric journal to take note of Dr.
Stevenson's work. The *American Journal of Psychiatry* (December 1979)
published an article, coauthored by him, concerning the case of a woman
who claims to recall a life lived 150 years ago in Bengal and is able to
speak fluently a language not learned in this life. This ability is called
xenoglossy, and a number of such cases will be reported in chapter 6.

Stevenson persistently avoids spectacular publicity and, in his published
writings, emphasizes that he has uncovered possible evidences for
reincarnation, not final proofs. Although he finds the past-life recall of the
children he investigates usually to be 90 percent accurate—some remembering over fifty verified items, including names of people, places, and
incidents—he downplays rather than exaggerates his cases, carefully weigh-
ing alternate theories that may apply. (See "Alternate Theories to Explain
the Cases," page 57.)

REACTIONS OF DR. STEVENSON'S PEERS

An article on Stevenson, "Is There Another Life After Death?" (*Look*,
October 20, 1970), relates how some of his colleagues in psychology and
psychiatry regard him.

Dr. Albert J. Stunkard.   A professor and chairman of the department of
psychiatry at the University of Pennsylvania in Philadelphia, Dr. Stunkard
says, "Stevenson's present work seems queer to many conventional scientists.
It is certainly controversial. But he is the most critical man I know of
working in that sphere, and perhaps the most thoughtful, with a knack for
building into his research appropriate investigative controls."

Dr. Herbert S. Ripley. This professor of psychiatry and chairman of the department at the University of Washington in Seattle says, "I think very highly of Stevenson. I regard him as thorough and honest. We are lucky, I feel, to have someone of his ability and high integrity investigating this controversial area."

Dr. Gertrude Schmeidler. A professor of psychology at the City College of the City University of New York, Dr. Schmeidler says, "Stevenson is a most careful and conscientious person of great intellectual ability and high professional standards. He has a most painstaking approach to collection and analysis of raw data."

Speaking of Stevenson's articles in the *Journal of Nervous and Mental Disease*, a staff writer for the *New York Times,* Tom Buckley, comments in *Quest/78* (September/October) that to get his research "published in so establishmentarian a journal was a triumph for Stevenson, a tribute to the scrupulousness of his methods, and a sign that his psychiatric colleagues were accepting him back out of the wilderness." As to his other colleagues at the university, Stevenson told Buckley, "I seem to have been pretty well rehabilitated. If I'm seeking information on anthropology, genetics, biology, and so on, I can consult with them and be reasonably sure of a friendly reception."

"Either he is making a colossal mistake in his changed career," said Dr. Harold Lief in the *JNMD* of September 1977, "or he will be known as the 'Galileo of the 20th century.' . . . I can think of no one better to continue man's endless quest for some sense that his presence on earth is more than fleeting and relatively unimportant."

BACKGROUND HISTORY

Ian Stevenson, one of four children, was born in Montreal, October 31, 1918. His father was chief Canadian correspondent of the *Times* of London. Stevenson studied medicine and psychiatry at McGill University in Montreal, graduating in 1943. As to how he came to the United States, *Quest/78* (September/October) reports that "Stevenson was subject to respiratory infections, which eventually became so severe that after his graduation from McGill he was obliged to cut short his residency at the Royal Victoria Hospital there and transfer to St. Joseph's Hospital in warm and dry Phoenix, Arizona. . . . Indeed, his need for warmth led him to associate himself with the Louisiana State University School of Medicine in New

Orleans from 1949 through 1957, when he went to the University of Virginia at Charlottesville as head of the psychiatry department and chief psychiatrist of the university hospital.''

He has written scores of papers on psychiatry in the professional journals and two standard books on psychiatric interviewing and diagnosis. In addition, he saw private patients and taught at the university. "He is a fully qualified psychoanalyst," the magazine continues. "Beyond all that, he has been, ever since completing his own training, a member of the medical elite—a holder of fellowships at the New York Hospital and the Ochsner Clinic in New Orleans. . . . In other words, Stevenson was at the top of his profession when at the age of 48 he abandoned psychiatry to devote himself full time to his reincarnation research."

In another interview, Eugene Kinkaid, a writer for *The New Yorker,* asked Stevenson, "What caused you to abandon a traditional medical and academic career for one so unorthodox?" Stevenson replied, "I became dissatisfied with the methods for helping people that had been developed in psychiatry. Orthodox theory in psychiatry and psychology conceives human personality to be the product of a person's genetic material (inherited from his ancestors through his parents), and the modifying influences of his prenatal and postnatal environment. But I found that there are cases that we cannot satisfactorily explain by genetics, environmental influences or a combination of these" (*Family Circle,* June 14, 1978).

Investigating the Cases. *   Stevenson explains that "in studying cases of reincarnation I have to use the methods of the historian, lawyer, and psychiatrist. I gather testimony from as many witnesses as possible. It is not uncommon for me to interview 25 people in regard to one case of reincarnation. And I have frequently gone back to interview the same people several years later."[2] A tape recording is made of interviews.

As a routine part of investigation, Stevenson checks written materials

---

*It should be noted that, throughout this chapter, as well as others where Dr. Stevenson is quoted, for reasons of space, it has not been feasible to include his references to either his own published cases, or to medical books and other records that are cited to support statements made. However, this material is readily accessible to anyone interested, for, wherever he is quoted, we provide in the text or the notes the name of the published paper or books from which the selections are taken.

such as diaries, letters, certificates of birth and deaths, autopsy records, hospital charts, and newspaper reports. Autopsy and medical records are particularly important in birthmark cases in which the child claims to have been murdered and points to scars on his body where, he says, he had previously been shot or knifed. In such cases, when medical records could be located, the child's memories proved accurate. (See pages 66–68 on birthmarks.)

In investigating cases where the parties involved speak foreign languages, Stevenson needs no interpreters for French and German, as he speaks both fluently. He also knows some Spanish and Portuguese. For Asian and Middle Eastern languages, he usually uses two or three interpreters.

Stevenson travels to many parts of the globe. During the eleven years between 1966 and 1977, he "traveled an average of 55,000 miles annually, or a total of over 600,000 miles."[3] Since that time his schedule has not appreciably diminished.

He keeps in touch with other scientists engaged in reincarnation research and has built up an international network of agents who inform him on cases in their localities. This is important so that he can arrive on the scene as soon as possible after cases begin to develop.

In the United States, puzzled parents contact him to help them understand the past-life memories of their children. To alert families of his research, Stevenson accepted an invitation to be interviewed in the June 14, 1978 issue of *Family Circle,* a magazine that has a circulation of 8½ million readers in the United States. The interview appeared in the "Ideas for Living" column, under the headline "Have You Lived Before?" The subhead read, "The World's Leading Scientific Authority on the Subject of Reincarnation Discusses His Unique Research."

Why Children and Not Adults. In another interview, Stevenson explained why he "is mostly interested in cases involving young children who claim to have had a previous life, especially when the child spontaneously offers evidence of this previous personality in his conversation. 'I'm suspect of cases in which the subject is an adult,' he says, 'because you can't really control the subconscious influences derived from information to which the adult has been exposed.' "[4]

"One of the problems with adults in the West who talk of the possibility of reincarnation," Stevenson told another interviewer,

> is the tendency to interpret too quickly, to have a glimpse of some past life and rush to the encyclopedias and the history books and try to fit it together

and make their own interpretations. Often the person will come up with the name of someone famous and decide, that fits me.

That's really very foolish. They're building a kind of inverted cone of imagination on a small base of *primary* experience. That is another reason why I prefer the cases of children, because they do not usually interpret their cases; they just say: "This is it; my name is so and so." To them, it is very clear, very vivid.[5]

Furthermore, as most of the children start speaking of their former life between the ages of two and four, they have limited access to information upon which they could consciously or subconsciously build a case of reincarnation. In addition, the children in many of Stevenson's published cases go into incredible detail concerning their former lives, correctly naming relatives and towns or villages where they lived. They accurately describe houses in which they dwelt, where money, jewelry, or weapons have been secretly hidden. Thus their stories are not the product of childish imagination. "One thing you look for in a good case," says Stevenson, "is richness of obscure detail."[6]

Another strong feature of these cases is that they lend themselves to accurate verification because most of the previous lives terminated only a few months or years prior to the present incarnations. Consequently, former parents and relatives are still alive to attest to, or contradict, what the children say.

Consulting the Psychics. As might be expected, Dr. Stevenson is critical of the practice prevalent today of consulting psychics and yogis to ascertain who we were in other lives. Here is what he wrote in "Reincarnation: Field Studies and Theoretical Issues," which appeared in *Handbook of Parapsychology,* edited by Benjamin B. Wolman and published in 1977 by Van Nostrand, specialists in scientific textbooks.

> Of the several different types of evidence adduced in support of a belief in reincarnation the weakest by far consists of statements made by one person, usually a sensitive, or medium, or yogi, concerning the supposed previous life or lives of another person. In no department of parapsychology, if it may be called such, is the volume of utterance so disproportionately large in comparison with the weakness of presented evidence. In nearly all instances of this type the statements of the person claiming to "read" another person's previous lives consist of completely unverifiable assertions about the previous life allegedly perceived.
>
> Some persons have exploited claims to "read" other persons' past lives in

sordid commercialism with regard to which one does not know whether to deplore more the cupidity of the profiteers or the gullibility of the deceived. The simple and not too expensive device of having several such "sensitives" make statements about the same person seems rarely to be adopted, although it would quickly unmask the pretensions of most of the practitioners in this field.

Number and Range of Cases.   A census of Stevenson's cases according to geographic areas was taken in July 1974, by Professor J. Gaither Pratt, who worked for many years with J. B. Rhine, the renowned parapsychologist. For several years prior to Dr. Pratt's death in 1979, he was on Stevenson's staff at the university and also taught there. The results of the census were reported in a chapter by Pratt in *The Psychic Realm: What Can You Believe?*, which he coauthored with Naomi Hintze. While it is commonly supposed that cases are chiefly found in Eastern countries where reincarnation is generally accepted, Dr. Pratt stated that, of the 1,339 cases then on file, "the United States has the most, with 324 cases (not counting American Indian and Eskimo), and the next five countries in descending order are Burma (139 cases), India (135), Turkey (114), and Great Britain (111)."[7] This totals 823 cases, and the remaining 516 come from other parts of the world.

The professor adds: "These figures should not be taken, however, as giving the relative density of cases in the various countries, since the conditions that influence whether or not existing cases will be reported to the investigator vary widely from one part of the world to another." In the West, where reincarnation is not generally accepted, there is a tendency to ignore, suppress, or indulgently smile at statements of children who wish to talk about a previous life. "Such statements usually are not taken very seriously," says Naomi Hintze. "A friend says she has been told that when she was about three she frequently made such comments as, 'When I was old—when I was eighty, before I was born. . . .' She had no recollection of this, and since her mildly puzzled parents never pressed their little girl for an explanation, whatever memories she may have had were never explored."[8]

Commenting on the Western cases Stevenson remarks that there is evidence such cases are not reported more frequently, either by the subject himself or by his parents, because of "fear of ridicule or ostracism." "Since the subjects (and their parents) of some American cases have expressed such fears to me, and often have only revealed the cases known to them with much trepidation, one may suppose that many other cases are completely hidden by the subject, or, if he is rash enough to tell his parents, suppressed by them."[9]

Strangely enough, reincarnation cases are suppressed not only in the West but, to some extent, in the East also. One reason derives from a prevalent superstitious fear that children remembering previous lives will die young. Consequently various devices are used to prevent memories from further surfacing—such as whirling the child on a potter's wheel counterclockwise or filling his mouth with filth or soap.

Too Many Cases to Investigate.   "Although the belief in reincarnation is an ancient one throughout large parts of Asia, Africa, and North America," observes Stevenson, "it was not known until recently that many persons claim to remember previous lives."[10] He reports that the number of cases that seem worth considering far exceeds his staff's ability to investigate them. "I should have no difficulty whatever in indicating places in several countries where an investigator can easily find more cases of this type than he could possibly study."[11]

Stevenson's cases have proliferated to such a degree that analysis by his staff is too time consuming and impractical, and therefore an elaborate computer program has been set up in his laboratory at the university. A computer specialist is on his staff.

Richness and Quantity of Remembrances.   "The subjects of these cases," notes Stevenson,

> vary greatly both in the quantity of their utterances and in the richness of the memories of the previous lives talked about. Some children make only three or four different statements about a previous life, but others may be credited with 60 or 70 separate items pertaining to different details in the life remembered.
>
> It is conjecturable that in all cases the subject remembers more than he tells because his telling depends very much both on his own related emotions that lead him to confide in others about his memories, or to conceal them, and on the willingness of other persons to listen to him. (Even in Asia, busy parents often do not make suitable audiences for the talk of small children.)[12]

Also, it seems likely that the child's limited vocabulary presents an obstacle to revealing all he remembers.

ALTERNATE THEORIES TO EXPLAIN THE CASES
The quoted selections are from Dr. Stevenson's writings.

Fraud—Conscious or Otherwise. To begin with, financial rewards for Dr. Stevenson's cases are nonexistent. It is his policy to make no payment for testimony. Publicity also is usually undesired, whether in the East or West. Furthermore, "it would be difficult to simulate a case with a child as the subject. Small children are not easy to coach for the assumption of roles that do not seem natural to them."[13]

A consideration of the large number of witnesses for many of Stevenson's cases also makes the hypothesis of fraud unlikely. To accomplish a hoax would require the collusion of many confederates in both the present family and the previous family, who usually live in another city or village. "To these difficulties," writes Stevenson regarding his Asian cases, "we must add those of directing and staging some of the highly emotional scenes I myself have witnessed in the villages. I cannot believe that simple villagers would have the time or inclination to rehearse such dramas as occurred in Chhatta when the family of Prakash thought—or said they thought—I favored his returning to the former family. The complexity of the behavioral features of these cases alone seem to make fraud virtually out of the question. . . ."[14] Incidentally, witnesses are usually subjected to hours of exhausting cross-examination by Stevenson, which does not make him an enjoyable visitor.

As to unconscious deceit, Stevenson, a psychiatrist and a psychoanalyst who has specialized in analyzing the testimony of patients, would appear to be well equipped to detect psychological and other influences that could impeach the testimony of witnesses in the reincarnation cases he investigates. (He is the author of *The Psychiatric Examination*, published in Boston by Little, Brown, 1969, and *The Diagnostic Interview*, Harper & Row, 1970.)

Fantasizing and Personation. Daydreaming and fantasizing are natural aspects of childhood. So cannot these reincarnation cases be dismissed on such grounds? The main difficulty here is that the "fantasies" turn out to be woven around a nucleus of facts and can be verified where the child has given sufficient information.

"Psychoses of any kind are extremely rare in children; delusional false identification with another person seems even rarer. I have discussed this question with two child psychiatrists, one specially expert in childhood schizophrenia. Neither had ever heard of a case in which a child claimed to be someone else. Children do occasionally identify briefly in play with other people or animals, and some psychotic children have identified themselves with machines. But I have not discovered a case in the literature of psychiatry of prolonged claims to another identity on the part of children outside the cases here under discussion."[15]

Cryptomnesia.   "Cryptomnesia," writes Stevenson, "involves an illusion of memories."

> A person afflicted by it thinks that what he is saying or writing is original with him. He has, however, learned normally the content of his communication earlier, either from a person or from some other (usually printed) source. Either he has not been aware that he was absorbing this information at the time he acquired it, or he has later forgotten that he obtained it normally. . . . My main objections to cryptomnesia as applied to cases of the reincarnation type derive . . . from consideration of the young age at which most of the subjects first begin to talk about the previous lives they claim to remember. . . . Some subjects refer to their memories when less than two years old.[16]

Paramnesia.   This refers to the possibility that after the two families concerned have met, the adults attribute to the child many more correct statements about his previous personality than he actually made before the families met. Dr. Stevenson's exhaustive cross-examination of witnesses is aimed at uncovering such weak cases. Paramnesia cannot apply, says Stevenson, to those cases in which someone made a written record of what the subject said about the previous life before the two families met.[17] Nor would it apply where the investigator has come on the scene and received an advanced report before the families met. These cases naturally have top priority on Stevenson's agenda because of their verifiability, and several of them are recorded in our next chapter.

It would be a mistake to imagine that both families in such a situation find being united an occasion of cordial fraternization and mutually joyful exchange of memories. When a child claims to have formerly lived in a wealthy family or one of higher caste, it does not reflect credit on such a family that their child has been "demoted" in his new incarnation. Nor is such a family likely to welcome the child or his new parents with open arms, any more than families in this life welcome poor relations into the bosom of their home life. The same conflict occurs, but in a reverse sense, when the child is reborn into a "superior" state. The new family does not relish hobnobbing with a poor or low-caste previous family, nor does it enjoy thinking that its child had such an ancestry.

But in either case, or in cases where both families are of equal status, the present parents may understandably be fearful that the previous father and mother may claim the child, or that the child himself will prefer the prior parents and insist on living with them. There also may be anxiety, on the part of the former relatives, that the child may reveal old family secrets. In one case, a former relative "fainted dead away" when the reborn child disclosed such private information. (See "An Embarrassing Domestic Secret Revealed," pages 88–89.)

Inherited Memory and/or the Collective Unconscious. In volume 3 of *Cases of the Reincarnation Type,* Dr. Stevenson indicates that this alternate theory "merits some discussion in a footnote, if only because correspondents so persistently bring it to my attention, for the most part, not having thought through what they are saying." Their view is "that the apparent memories of previous lives experienced by the subjects of these cases might be adequately accounted for by concepts such as those of the 'collective unconscious' or 'inherited memory.' (I think that these two concepts are substantially similar, although not exactly so.)" "Inherited memory" implies that, instead of an individual remembering his own past life, he is actually remembering the life of some ancestor whose memories have been genetically transmitted to him. In analyzing both theories, Stevenson says,

> There exist a few cases in which the subject *might* be a lineal descendent of the related personality. According to my knowledge, however, no one has claimed that imaged memories as detailed as those we find in many of these cases could be transmitted by "inherited memory" or through the "collective unconscious." These concepts have been used not implausibly to explain the occurrence of similar legends, such as of a great flood, in widely separated parts of the world; and they may also help us to understand the occurrence of similar symbols in many different cultures. But the suggestion that numerous detailed imaged memories might be inherited extends the concept of "inherited memory" far beyond what even its most ardent advocates have hitherto claimed for it.
>
> Even more serious objections permit us to exclude "inherited memory" as an interpretation for the majority of cases of the reincarnation type. First, in most cases—certainly in most Asian ones—subject A is born a few years or less after the death of person B, whose life A subsequently claims to remember. B, however, lived in a family and village completely different from that of A and his parents. Therefore, A could not possibly be a descendent of B. Second, a parent could only transmit genetically to his or

her offspring memories of events that had happened to the parent *before* that child's conception. *It follows, therefore, that the memory of a person's mode of death could never be inherited* [italics added].[18]

As will be seen on page 63, the events children remember most vividly are connected with the death of the previous personality and the events leading thereto.

Clairvoyance and Telepathy.   When the evidence in the cases is overwhelmingly in favor of their authenticity—as Stevenson's cases usually are—and it appears that some paranormal explanation must be involved, critics frequently wish to bypass reincarnation as an explanation by attributing a child's knowledge not to remembrance of its own "nonexistent" past life but to clairvoyant or telepathic powers. Thus, they say, the child obtains its information by tuning into the minds of living persons who know all about the deceased individual that the child claims to have been himself. Such a hypothesis, one investigator points out, appears to be more involved and extravagant than the simple explanation of rebirth; nevertheless, it should be seriously explored as to its merits.

1. The first difficulty to be overcome is explaining how and why these children, who with rare exceptions do not exhibit extrasensory powers in connection with other matters in this life, should manifest their ability only with one particular stranger, thus manifesting what in parapsychology is called a one-target manifestation. Furthermore, in tapping the minds of living relatives and acquaintances to obtain that information, they are able to exclude all other items of memory and knowledge these people have.

2. Considering the enormous number of facts the children remember in the more elaborate cases, we would have to credit them with *super* extrasensory perception, far beyond any presently known cases of ESP where sensitives and psychics are concerned.

3. The child would have to tap the memories of not just one living person who is a relative of the deceased individual, but a number of other relatives and acquaintances as well. For, as Stevenson writes regarding some of his cases, *"all the information known to the child did not reside in a single living mind,"* and consequently "the information had to be gathered from two or more minds, each of which possessed a portion only of the available information. In short, multiple agents would be required for the explanation of such cases of extrasensory perception."[19]

4. As Stevenson points out, no amount of extrasensory perception will account for the behavioral features and the elements of personation that occur in most of them. "The subject attributes this information to a personality with which he identifies himself. I think it is difficult for persons not acquainted with these cases at first hand to imagine the magnitude of these features of behavior and personation."[20]

5. Another important difficulty in applying the ESP theory is that children often display a knowledge of how things *were* in their past life and are unaware of changes that subsequently occurred and presently exist. Such changes are well known to the people whose minds they are supposed to be reading. To illustrate, Stevenson cites the famous case of Shanti Devi. Among her numerous accurate past-life remembrances was that she had buried 150 rupees in the corner of a room in the house of her former husband's parents. When the spot was dug up under her direction and the money was missing, the husband admitted shamefacedly that he had removed it after her death. Her being totally ignorant of its removal, says Stevenson, "requires a particularly complex explanation," if one excludes reincarnation as the answer.[21]

6. The birthmark evidence, shortly to be discussed, is clearly beyond the scope of ESP.

Mediumistic Possession. "Possession" refers to the mind of an individual being taken over by a deceased person, whose memories become those of the living person. Could this not apply to children with past-life recall?

Mediumship, Stevenson reports, rarely arises in children two or three years old. In the reincarnation cases, the vast majority of the children make their declarations during ordinary consciousness and under ordinary circumstances of life, not in a trance or in other abnormal states of withdrawal. "They talk about the past lives sporadically here and there without interrupting their habitual play or work. Something which reminds them of some event in the previous life stimulates a brief flow of talk about the life and then it ceases. . . . This general normality of behavior contrasts obviously enough with that of most mediums who, on entering a trance, show a more or less complete change of personality and do not usually answer to the call of their regular names, much less go about their ordinary business in an intelligently responsive way."[22]

Another argument against this theory is that the evidence of birthmarks is difficult to explain on the basis of possession. Are we to suppose that the possessing spirit went to the trouble of transferring the mark to the child in the womb?

"The theory of possession," says Stevenson, "also cannot explain the knowledge shown by a number of the children of how buildings were arranged or people looked during the life of the previous personality," while being totally ignorant of changes that have taken place since their death. For example, a child will be amazed at a relative now being old and wrinkled and having no teeth. If a disincarnate personality is so close to earth-life that it can take possession of children, why does it not keep up with changes in people and buildings in its former environment? Why does knowledge of these things cease with the date of death?[23]

FREQUENTLY RECURRING CHARACTERISTICS IN CASES OF THE REINCARNATION TYPE

Stevenson's cases have now accumulated sufficiently that recurrent features can be discerned. In his opinion, this provides evidence of their authenticity. Inasmuch as they recur in cases all over the world, they cannot be regarded as mimicked in a particular culture that believes in reincarnation. "If anyone suggests that the similarities in the cases . . . derive from normal communications between the informants, he has to assume an international plot of great magnitude and effectiveness."[24]

Following are eleven characteristics commonly appearing in the cases. These do not include the birthmark manifestations, which are yet to be discussed. The quoted selections are from Dr. Stevenson's writings.

Age When Memories Appear.   The typical case "starts when a child between the ages of two and four, but occasionally older, begins to narrate details of a previous life. The child often begins talking about this previous life as soon as he gains any ability to speak. Sometimes he begins before his capacity for verbal expression is equal to his need to communicate, so he mispronounces words that are later better understood, or uses gestures to supplement what he cannot yet say clearly with words."[25]

At a lecture given by Stevenson at the United Engineering Center in New York (April 2, 1980), he mentioned that often the first words children say are names of people they knew previously or places they lived. Such references completely mystify their parents until the child is able to speak in detail about his former life.

Ages When Memories Fade.   "One of the universal features of cases of the reincarnation type is the almost invariable tendency for the subject to forget the memories of a previous life between the ages of five and eight.

This coincides with the age at which the child leaves his narrow home circle and begins a wider participation in life outside the home at school and elsewhere. I have suggested that these new experiences become deposited among the child's memories in a layer above those of the previous life which then gradually became inaccessible."[26]

Characteristics of Behavior. "Unexpected behavior of various kinds nearly always accompanies the statements the child makes about the previous life he claims to remember, or occurs contemporaneously with them. This behavior is unusual for a child of the subject's family, but concordant with what he says concerning the previous life, and in most instances it is found to correspond with what other informants say concerning the behavior of the deceased person about whom the subject has been talking, if such a person is traced. . . . The child often also shows 'adult' attitudes and behaves with gravity, wisdom, and sometimes patronizing condescension toward other children. The latter conduct apparently derives, in instances with unusually vivid memories, from the conviction on the part of a subject that he is still an adult, not a child."[27]

Strangeness of New Body. The subjects "frequently have commented on the strangeness of the physical bodies in which they found themselves as young children. . . . They often remark—and sometimes grumble—about the small bodies in which they feel confined."[28] When a long period has elapsed between incarnations, as might occur when the person that dies has lived to a ripe old age, the transition to a new body may not appear so puzzling. The long period of rest perhaps tends to erase past-life memories.

The Most Vivid Events Remembered. The events that children remember most vividly are connected with the death of the previous personality and the events leading thereto.[29] The next chapter will deal with several examples of this.

Incidence of Violent Deaths. "In a large percentage of the cases from all countries so far studied, the deceased person whose life the child claims to remember died in some violent manner—through accidents, murder, suicide or war. . . . This incidence of violent death far exceeds that of the general population in the areas where the cases occur."[30] This does not mean that only people who have died violently reincarnate. It may suggest that the shock of such a death was so intense its memories more easily penetrate the brain consciousness of the new personality. If a previous life occurred in which the individual died a normal death, the likelihood of remembering may be diminished.

Phobia for Objects or Circumstances Causing Death. Another common feature of the cases of violent death is that the child usually, but not always, has a strong phobia for the object or circumstances that caused the death. One child remembered that her death occurred as a result of moving aside on a bridge to let a bus pass. She fell in the water and drowned, and in her next birth had a phobia for buses, bridges, and water. It took four people to hold her down to give her a bath.[31]

In another case, a child who previously died of knife wounds had an intense phobia for knives. When Stevenson later interviewed him as a grown man, he insisted that he no longer had an aversion for knives. However, his wife informed Stevenson privately that her husband never used a knife in eating. If anything on his plate required cutting, he severed it with the edge of his fork. Stevenson observed this too. But the man himself was unaware of deliberately avoiding a knife![32]

Changes in People and Surroundings Detected by Children. It frequently occurs that, when a child arrives at the scene of its former home, it indicates changes—either in the surroundings or people—that have taken place since its death. Children will make such comments as these to former relatives: "Your hair is now white." "You have lost your teeth." "You now wear glasses." One young boy led the way to where he said he formerly lived. He was surprised to find only an empty lot! His former house had been torn down.

Announcing Dreams. This refers to the phenomenon in which someone has a dream, prior to the rebirth of a child, foretelling that an individual who lived before is returning to incarnate in a particular family. Such instances, says Dr. Stevenson, are reported among the cases of every culture so far studied.

He writes in the *International Journal of Comparative Sociology* that "occasionally two or more members of the family will have such a dream" (March 1970). But, whether one or more persons have such dreams, they nearly all "occur towards the end of the pregnancy and most often just before delivery, but a few have occurred after delivery."

Abnormal Appetites During Pregnancy. "During pregnancy many women experience strange longings for unusual foods or for those that are out of season. These are called *pica* in clinical medicine. Husbands sometimes relate tales of submissively going out in a blizzard to find a store that could provide a pregnant wife with fresh strawberries in January. We do not usually examine deeply accounts of this kind. It seems sufficient to attribute them to a caprice on the part of the pregnant woman taking advantage of the special devotion that most husbands feel toward their wives when they are pregnant. But here again, there may be something else to inquire about.

"In a number of cases of the reincarnation type known to me, the subject has shown a craving (or perhaps an aversion) for a particular food. His mother has reported that during her pregnancy with him she experienced an unusual appetite (or aversion) for the same food, and the food in question has been found to be one for which the related previous personality had a similar craving or dislike. If such cases are interpreted as instances of reincarnation, they suggest that the previous personality in its nascent state had influenced the pregnant woman to its tastes."[33]

Possessing a Skill Not Taught or Learned.   Among Stevenson's cases are children who have "shown skills in early childhood that, according to informants for their cases, they could not have learned through instruction or imitation of older persons. . . . In each case, the skill in question was one which the related previous personality was known to have had."[34]

Stevenson also includes the unusual behavior of children who are remembering a past life as possible incidences of a skill unlearned in this life. "We do not usually think of the totality of a person's behavior as a *skill*; and yet his behavior is a learned way of responding to social events just as much as his style of hitting a tennis ball is a learned response to a physical event."[35]

As an example of a skill unlearned in this life, there is the case reported by Stevenson of a Belgian boy named Robert, who lived in the town of Knocke. Robert vehemently insisted that a portrait of his Uncle Albert was a portrait of himself. The uncle had been killed in World War I in 1915. He was one of two sons and the marked favorite of his mother—Robert's grandmother. Robert had an overwhelming affection for her, "in contrast to her other grandchildren who largely ignored her." He was happy and healthy with her, sullen and disobedient with his own parents. In fact, she was "the light of his life." The grandmother reported that Robert called her by "pet names Albert had used and told her of likes and dislikes which Albert and she had privately shared."

When the lad was three and a half, he saw a swimming pool for the first time. He ran to the diving board and plunged in, leaving only the barest ripples. His uncle Albert had been a magnificent diver. When children first dive—either under instruction or in imitation of others—they invariably make a resounding, awkward splash. The bodily coordination involved in a perfect dive, especially from the height of a diving board, is an art that comes with much practice.

Another incident occurred when a visitor to Robert's home took a picture of him, using an old-style motion picture camera. When the handle was turned with a clicking noise, the boy screamed, "Don't! Don't! They killed me that way the last time!" Albert had been killed by machine gun fire while trying to destroy a German emplacement.[36]

The most arresting cases of unlearned skills occur when a person speaks a foreign language to which he has never been exposed in this life (see chapter 6).

BIRTHMARKS AND DEFORMITIES

In his paper "The Explanatory Value of the Idea of Reincarnation," Dr. Stevenson has a section on this subject, from which we quote:

> The subjects of cases of the reincarnation type often point to marks on their bodies (which their parents say are birthmarks) and assert that it was at these locations that bullets or bladed weapons fatally wounded them in the previous lives which they seem to remember. I have (as of 1977) examined at least 200 such birthmarks. . . . Many such birthmarks cannot be distinguished, at least by me, from scars of acquired wounds with which they would be confused except for the strong affirmations of parents that the marks in question existed at birth, or were noticed soon after birth.[37]

Other subjects have major deformities in which arms or legs are grossly malformed, or fingers, toes, or hands are missing. When these subjects begin to talk about a prior existence they recall having been killed and that the assailant cut off the deformed or missing organs "before delivering the *coup de grace* that terminated the existence."

Dr. Stevenson considers both types of cases of sufficient import to warrant publication as a collection in separate volumes yet to be published. In a number of cases he has obtained hospital and/or autopsy reports concerning the claimed past personality, and the records reveal that such injuries not only occurred but the bodily areas *where* they occurred exactly correspond to the location of the present birthmark or deformity. The children, furthermore, often recall considerable other detailed information about the prior deceased person that could not have been learned in this life through ordinary channels.

Two Examples of Birthmark Cases. The first is that of Ravi Shankar. He recalled being brutally decapitated as a child by two persons, one a relative hopeful of inheriting the wealth of the boy's father. The reborn boy was found to have a linear mark, closely resembling the scar from a knife wound, encircling his neck! This case is reported in *Twenty Cases Suggestive of Reincarnation*, now in paperback.[38]

The second case (as yet unpublished) is quite dramatic, and was described by Stevenson in his talk at the United Engineering Center in New York at which one of the present authors attended. A child in Turkey recalled being a bandit in his former life. He had committed suicide when about to be captured by the French police, who then had jurisdiction in that country. They surrounded the house where the outlaw took refuge, but before the police gained entrance, he wedged the muzzle of his long rifle under the right side of his chin, resting the handle on the ground, and then pulled the trigger. In his new life, the boy was born with a huge gash mark under his chin. While Stevenson was investigating the case, an old man turned up who had remembered the bandit's death and seen the condition of his dead body.

The highlight of the case came when Stevenson asked the reborn robber whether he had any other birthmarks, for the doctor privately reasoned that, if the bullet had gone through the brain in the manner described, there must be another scar where the bullet exited. The answer was "yes," and the Turk pointed to a spot a little left of the crown of his head. There, buried under the bushy hair, Stevenson found the scar mark. A slide picture of this was shown to the audience and also of the gash under the jaw. On another slide was traced the line of trajectory the bullet should have taken in its passage through the brain, and this was in perfect alignment with the scar mark on the top of the head. Here we have important evidence supporting the man's claim that the self-inflicted injury occurred in his prior life. If it had happened in this one, he would not be alive to tell the tale. His brain would have been destroyed.

Stevenson writes that "birthmarks occur so regularly in subjects claiming to remember previous lives in which they were shot or stabbed that a subject of this group without one arouses my curiosity. I wish to reserve a full discussion of this topic for another volume and will therefore mention here only that the length of the interval between the death of the previous personality and the birth of the subject seems to influence the occurrence (or absence) of birthmarks in these cases."[39]

What Is the Carrier of Scar Marks and Other Attributes from Body to Body? In a paper titled "Questions Related to Cases of the Reincarnation Type," Dr. Stevenson considers the problem of how the memories and attributes (including birthmarks) of a particular individual are carried over into a succeeding incarnation.

"I find myself thinking increasingly of some intermediate 'non-physical body' which acts as the carrier of these attributes between one life and another. . . . It seems to me that the imprint of wounds on the previous personality must be carried between lives on some kind of an extended body which in turn acts as a template for the production on a new physical body (to be occupied by the presumably reincarnating personality) of birthmarks and deformities that correspond to the wounds on the body of the previous personality." This nonphysical body, he theorizes, must exist in a state of which we know almost nothing, "although some subjects of reincarnation cases have claimed to remember experiences after death and before (presumed) rebirth when they were apparently housed in such a body."[40] Stevenson plans to publish accounts of such experiences in a forthcoming work.

Many readers, no doubt, are familiar with the reports of people pronounced clinically dead in which the patients when revived tell of functioning in a body having different powers than the physical, which can go through walls as if they did not exist. While in such a body, the individual as spectator can objectively observe his "dead" body and its surroundings (see chapter 8).

*

In the chapter that follows, "Cases of the Reincarnation Type from Around the World," six of the eleven presented are from Dr. Stevenson's large accumulation of cases personally investigated by him.

He is frequently asked whether all this research has led him to believe in reincarnation. Such questions he invariably refuses to answer. As he explained to one interviewer, "I think my personal belief is unimportant to anyone but myself. For people to believe something because I—or any scientist—says he believes is to return to authoritarian decisions about beliefs. . . . So I believe that everyone should examine the evidence for reincarnation for himself and make up his own mind."[41]

On another occasion, Stevenson remarked, "What I do believe is that, of the cases that we now know, reincarnation—at least for some—is the best explanation that we have been able to come up with. There is an impressive body of evidence, and it is getting stronger all the time. I think a rational person, if he wants, can believe in reincarnation on the basis of evidence."[42]

5

Cases of the Reincarnation Type from Around the World

It needs only one case to be "real" for many accepted ideas about life to be turned upside down (or right side up!).

JEFFREY IVERSON, *More Lives Than One?*

Our journey in this chapter begins in the Americas, proceeds eastward to Europe, then to the Middle East, and ends in the Orient with an international case linking both East and West. The opening case dates back to the early part of this century before scientists took an interest in such matters.

"I WAS A SOLDIER AND I TOOK THE GATES"

The account that follows received first prize in a national contest titled "The Most Extraordinary Coincidence I Know Of." It was conducted by *The American Magazine,* and the winning story appeared in the July 1915 issue. Whether it was merely a coincidence or something more, the reader can judge. The contributor, a woman in Minneapolis, provided this introduction.

Perhaps the best internal evidence of the truth of this little story is its simplicity. Another matter worth noting is that the diary in which the record was made many years ago and the documentary history in which the note was

found are still in existence, and the characters are still living to bear witness—if
their word be believed.

And this is the way one of the most absolutely truthful women I ever
knew or can hope to know told the story:

"Anne, my little half-sister, younger by fifteen years, was a queer little
mite from the beginning. She did not even look like any member of the
family we ever heard of, for she was dark almost to swarthiness, while the
rest of us all were fair, showing our Scotch-Irish ancestry unmistakably.

"As soon as she could talk in connected sentences, she would tell
herself fairy stories, and just for the fun of the thing I would take down her
murmurings with my pencil in my old diary. She was my especial
charge—my mother being a very busy woman—and I was very proud of
her. These weavings of fancy were never of the usual type that children's
fairy tales take; for, in addition to the childish imagination, there were bits
of knowledge in them that a baby could not possibly have absorbed in any
sort of way.

"Another remarkable thing about her was that everything she did she
seemed to do through habit, and, in fact, such was her insistence, although
she was never able to explain what she meant by it. If you could have seen
the roystering air with which she would lift her mug of milk when she was
only three and gulp it down at one quaffing, you would have shaken with
laughter. This particularly embarrassed my mother and she reproved Anne
repeatedly. The baby was a good little soul, and would seem to try to
obey, and then in an absent-minded moment would bring on another occasion for mortification. 'I can't help it, Mother,' she would say over and
over again, tears in her baby voice, 'I've always done it that way!'

"So many were the small incidents of her 'habits' of speech and thought
and her tricks of manner and memory that finally we ceased to think
anything about them, and she herself was quite unconscious that she was
in any way different from other children.

"One day when she was four years old she became very indignant with
Father about some matter and, as she sat curled up on the floor in front of
us, announced her intention of going away forever.

" 'Back to heaven where you came from?' inquired Father with mock
seriousness. She shook her head.

" 'I didn't come from heaven to you,' she asserted with that calm
conviction to which we were quite accustomed now. 'I went to the moon
first, but— You know about the moon, don't you? It used to have people
on it, but it got so hard that we had to go.'

"This planned to be a fairy tale, so I got my pencil and diary.

" 'So,' my father led her on, 'you came from the moon to us, did you?'

" 'Oh, no,' she told him in casual fashion. 'I have been here [since then] lots of times—sometimes I was a man and sometimes I was a woman!'

"She was so serene in her announcement that my father laughed heartily, which enraged the child, for she particularly disliked being ridiculed in any way.

" 'I was! I was!' she maintained indignantly. 'Once I went to Canada when I was a man! I 'member my name, even.'

" 'Oh, pooh-pooh,' he scoffed, 'little United States girls can't be men in Canada! What was your name that you 'member so well?'

"She considered a minute. 'It was Lishus Faber,' she ventured, then repeated it with greater assurance, 'that was it—Lishus Faber.' She ran the sounds together so that this was all I could make out of it—and the name so stands in my diary today. 'Lishus Faber.'

" 'And what did you do for a living, Lishus Faber, in those early days?' My father then treated her with the mock solemnity befitting her assurance and quieting her nervous little body.

" 'I was a soldier'—she granted the information triumphantly—'and I took the gates!'

"That was all that is recorded there. Over and over again, I remember, we tried to get her to explain what she meant by the odd phrase, but she only repeated her words and grew indignant with us for not understanding. Her imagination stopped at explanations. We were living in a cultured community, but although I repeated the story to inquire about the phrase—as one does tell stories of beloved children—no one could do more than conjecture its meaning.

"Someone encouraged my really going further with the matter, and for a year I studied all the histories of Canada I could lay my hands on for a battle in which somebody 'took the gates.' All to no purpose. Finally I was directed by a librarian to a 'documentary' history, I suppose it is—a funny old volume with the s's all like f's. This was over a year afterward, when I had quite lost hope of running my phrase to earth. It was a quaint old book, interestingly picturesque in many of its tales, but I found one bit that put all the others out of my mind. It was a brief account of the taking of a little walled city by a small company of soldiers, a distinguished feat of some sort, yet of no general importance. A young lieutenant with his small band—the phrase leaped to my eyes—'*took the gates'* and the name of the young lieutenant was 'Aloysius Le Fèbre.' ''

The part where the child states that humanity once lived on the moon may sound fantastic, but theosophists might find it corroborative of their views that the moon was once a living planet and our former home.[1] Interesting that it is now known that the moon rocks brought back by the astronauts are older than any found today on earth.

A CASE OF DISAPPOINTED LOVE

This is one of Dr. Stevenson's cases.[2] It was published with several other American cases in his *Twenty Cases Suggestive of Reincarnation*. His volumes devoted entirely to American and European cases have yet to be published in his series *Cases of the Reincarnation Type*. However, his paper, "American Children Who Claim to Remember Previous Lives," appeared in 1983 in the *Journal of Nervous and Mental Disease* (vol. 171, no. 12).

*

In Rio Grande do Sul, the southernmost state of Brazil, a baby was born to a prosperous rancher, Señor C. J. de Oliveiro. The child was named Maria, but everyone called her Sinhá, or more affectionately Sinházinha. As the girl grew up, she loved the rural life of her father's land but, requiring companionship, often visited the closest village, Dom Feliciano, twelve miles away. There she made friends with Ida Lorenz, wife of the district's schoolteacher.

She subsequently fell in love twice, but each time her father, a stern, stubborn man, disapproved, and one of the young men took his life in desperation. Sinhá became inconsolably despondent, and her father, now worried, arranged a trip to the coastal city of Pelotes during the carnival season, but the girl's spirits did not improve. She purposely neglected herself by inviting exposure to cold, damp weather and engaging in exhausting activities. Her voice became hoarse, a throat infection spread to the lungs, and tuberculosis set in. In a few months she was gone.

Before she died, Sinhá confessed to her dear friend Ida that the illness had been self-caused. She then made two solemn predictions: first, she would be reborn as Ida's daughter; and second, "when reborn and at an age when I can speak on the mystery of rebirth in the body of the little girl who will be your daughter, I shall relate many things of my present life, and thus you will recognize the truth.'' Ida shared this confidence with her schoolteacher husband, but they agreed simply to await developments and say nothing to their family or to others.

Months after Sinhá died, a daughter was born to the Lorenz family and given the name Marta. Save for character similarities, the earliest indication that she could have been Sinhá reborn occurred when Marta was less than a year old and Sinhá's father visited the Lorenz family. Another family acquaintance, a Mr. Valentin, happened to drop in at the same time. The latter evinced great friendliness to the child, but Marta immediately went to Sinhá's father, and despite his forbidding, unwelcome attitude toward children, she caressed his beard and said, ''Hello, papa.'' This had no significance for him; not until eleven years later was he informed of Sinhá's supposed rebirth as Marta.

What happened next is taken from the recorded words of Mr. Lorenz, Marta's present father. The translation is that of Dr. Stevenson, who thoroughly investigated the case. The Lola mentioned in the excerpts that follow is Marta's older sister.

> One day, when Marta was two-and-a-half years old, as she was returning from the stream near our house with Lola, after they had been washing clothes, she asked her sister: ''Lola, carry me on your back.'' Her sister who (like all our children and neighbors) knew nothing of the deceased girl's promise [to return], replied: ''You can walk well enough. I don't need to carry you.''
>
> To this Marta replied: ''When I was big and you were small, I used to carry you often.'' ''When you were big?'' asked Lola, laughing. Then the little girl answered: ''At that time I did not live here; I lived far from here where there are many cows, oxen, and oranges and where also there were animals like goats, but they were not goats.'' (Here she referred to sheep, which the child had never seen.) These words described the farm of the dead Sinhá's parents in the country.
>
> Thus conversing, Lola and Marta walked on and reached the house. Then Lola told us about the strange ideas of her little sister, and I said to the latter: ''My little daughter, I have never lived there where you say you have lived.'' To this she replied: ''Yes, but in those days I had other parents.''
>
> Another one of Marta's sisters then jokingly said: ''And did you then have a little Negro servant girl such as we now have?'' (She was referring to a little Negro orphan girl whom my wife and I had sheltered.) The girl was not embarrassed and replied: ''No. Our Negro servant there was already big and so was the cook; but we did have a small Negro boy and one day he forgot to fetch water and my father beat him.''
>
> On hearing this, I said: ''I have never beaten any Negro boy, my little

girl." She replied: "But it was my *other* father who beat him. And the Negro boy cried out to me, 'Sinházinha, help me!' and I asked my father not to beat him and the little Negro boy ran off to fetch water."

"Who was this Sinhá or Sinházinha?" I asked. "That was myself," she replied, "but I then [also] had another name. My name was Maria, and I had one other name which I cannot remember now."

Her full name had been Maria Januaria de Oliveiro.

Ida also took part in the cross examination of the child. One question was: "In what manner did you as Sinhá greet me when I used to visit you on your father's ranch?" Marta replied that she would prepare coffee and wait in front of the house, playing a phonograph she placed on a stone. Upon interviewing Sinhá's younger sister, Dr. Stevenson learned that this, in fact, was the way Sinhá in advance prepared for the cherished visits of her beloved friend and present mother.

Ida inquired from the child how Sinhá had spoken to her the last time she visited before the girl died. Marta dramatized what occurred: she whispered in her present mother's ear and pointed to her own throat, saying that she could not speak because her voice was gone. This final scene was known only to Ida.

During the next few years, Marta made 120 separate declarations either about the life of Sinhá or of recognitions of persons known to Sinhá. Her present father kept detailed records of these statements. Some of these concerned matters entirely unknown to him, to his wife, or to the other children of the family, but they subsequently proved correct.

Now, Marta often spoke about Sinhá's home and her desire to be taken there. The wish was not granted until she was twelve, but by then she rarely talked about her prior life. On arrival she immediately recognized a clock on the wall, saying it belonged to her and that her name would be found on the back engraved in gold letters. The former father was at first loathe to take it down, apparently fearing Marta would claim it. On the back was written "Maria Januaria de Oliveiro." It developed that Sinhá herself had bought the clock and personally attended to its winding. This was the only object Marta recognized at the ranch.

After Marta's visit, a relative of the Oliveiro family heard about the supposed rebirth of Sinhá. Without warning, she descended upon the Lorenz household and challenged Marta: "If you were really Sinhá, tell me what our relationship was?" The girl replied correctly: "You were my cousin and my godmother." The lady was a complete stranger in Dom Feliciano where Marta and her family lived.

Another unexpected confirmation occurred when Marta was nineteen and employed on a ranch to teach children. The family there were strict Roman Catholics, and she dared not breathe a word about such unorthodox subjects as reincarnation. An elderly black woman employee was especially drawn to Marta and exclaimed to others: *"This girl looks like Sinhá!"* The woman turned out to be one of the former black servants who had worked at the Oliveiro ranch and whom Marta mentioned when she was a child of two and a half.

Sinhá's unfortunate act of suicide through self-neglect—causing her death from tuberculosis of the lungs and larynx—apparently had two karmic repercussions on the present life. First was her extreme susceptibility to colds and bronchial troubles. None of the other Lorenz children were thus afflicted. When these troubles arose, she felt she was about to die and also felt her body to be large as if she were an adult. Dr. Stevenson comments: "The laryngeal pain and hoarseness evidently led through association to the full reproduction of the last scenes in the life of Sinhá. . . . I believe that we may reasonably consider Marta's vulnerability to bronchitis and laryngitis a kind of 'internal birthmark' related to the previous life and death of Sinhá."

The second consequence was a tendency, when life became difficult, to wish to destroy herself. She admitted to Dr. Stevenson that, although she never attempted suicide, she might have done so if a gun had been available.

On the positive and encouraging side, however, she brought through a beautiful side of her former self. In that incarnation she had been especially remembered by many people because of her loving, compassionate nature, and this was preserved in her present makeup. As to her rebirth experience, she sought to use it effectively to relieve others of pain and sorrow. Stevenson reports:

> On one occasion a lady who was visiting the Lorenz family complained of the recent death of her father and said: "Oh, dear, the dead never return." At this Marta said: "Don't say that. I died also and look, I am living again."

> On another occasion, during a rainstorm, when one of her sisters expressed concern that the deceased sister Emilia of the family would get wet in her grave, Marta said: "Don't say that, Emilia is not in the cemetery. She is in a safer and better place than this one where we are, the soul never can be wet."

DID THIS AMERICAN PSYCHIATRIST LIVE IN SEVENTEENTH-CENTURY EUROPE?

It is not usual for a psychiatrist to write a novel, much less a story on reincarnation. And when such a story has at its core—if not in its plot—the author's own experience regarding a possible previous life, it would appear to have taken considerable courage to write the book. The psychiatrist in question is Frederic F. Flach, M.D. He is Associate Clinical Professor of Psychiatry at Cornell University Medical College in New York. He is also attending psychiatrist at the Payne Whitney Clinic in New York Hospital and conducts a private practice as well. Dr. Flach's novel is called *Fridericus* and was published in 1980.

Dr. Flach first became interested in reincarnation while researching his psychiatric work *The Secret Strength of Depression*. In amazement he came upon—through a colleague's discovery—a 1620 treatise in Latin on the same subject by a Swiss doctor *with his own name:* Friederich F. Flacht. (Latinized, the name reads M. Fridericus Flacht.) Although his immediate conclusion was that this must be a bizarre coincidence, he could not help wondering whether that physician was himself in another life.

After the publication of *Fridericus,* Dr. Flach told an interviewer that he really believes he was Dr. Fridericus. This Swiss doctor in Basel "was a medical practitioner interested in depression, as I am, which was quite a rarity in his day. And there is even a curious similarity between what he wrote and what I study."

"Another parallel," the doctor said, "is the part of Europe Fridericus came from. The cities he went to during his lifetime were in the same area my family lived in. Part of my family originated near Zurich. There is a town called Flach. Some came from just north of the border which is the very southern part of what is now Germany. Others came from Strasbourg. And if you draw a circle around that area, it is the same area he came from. He was the physician for the city of Worms, which is just north of Strasbourg, and he was in Basel, Heidelberg, and Mulhouse. What's more, he was married twice. I have been married twice. He had three children. I have three children."

In 1977, Dr. Flach went to Europe to search out more about Fridericus. "My main goal was to go back and retrace Fridericus's steps. I went to Basel, Worms, Heidelberg, Strasbourg, and Mulhouse. I wanted to get a feeling of the area. In Basel I had a sense of familiarity. It was a sense of warmth and a sense of being home."[3]

As to the novel *Fridericus*, it is written from the viewpoint of a clinically trained and experienced psychiatrist. It is truly fascinating to follow the arguments on the solutions to the problems of the main character, as presented by four different and differing professionals. Much of this dialogue revolves around the validity (or not) of reincarnation.

The case of Dr. Flach, meager in details, is not a strong case, but an interesting sign of the times. Surely, fifty years ago, no psychiatrist would dare reveal his involvement with such a subject.

A VICTIM OF THE INQUISITION IN THIRTEENTH-CENTURY FRANCE

This remarkable case was investigated by a British psychiatrist, Dr. Arthur Guirdham. In fact, the woman in the case was his own patient. He first met Mrs. Smith in 1961 when he was chief psychiatrist at Bath Hospital in England. (Before his retirement in the 1970s, he was also medical superintendent of Bailbrook House and consultant psychiatrist to the Bath Child Guidance Clinic.) Mrs. Smith's problem was that she had persistent nightmares, accompanied by shrieks so loud that she and her husband feared they would wake the whole neighborhood. In an interview, Dr. Guirdham told of his patient's background:

> She had been suffering for years from dreadful dreams of murder and massacre. . . . I examined the woman for neuroses. She had none, but as the dreams had occurred with such regularity since the age of 12, she was worried about them. She was a perfectly sane, ordinary housewife. There was certainly nothing wrong with her mental faculties.
> After a few months, she told me that when she was a girl . . . she had written [the dreams] down. She had also written things that came into her mind, things she couldn't understand about people and names she had never heard of. She gave me the papers and I started to examine them.[4]

What first amazed him was the verses of songs she had written as a schoolgirl. They were in medieval French and in langue doc, the language spoken in southern France in the twelfth and thirteenth centuries. The doctor ascertained that she had never studied such obscure subjects in school.

"I sent a report of her story to Professor Père Nellie of Toulouse University and asked his opinion. He wrote back immediately that this was

an accurate account of the Cathars in Toulouse in the thirteenth century.
"She also told me of the massacre of the Cathars. She told in horrid
detail of being burned at the stake. . . . I was astounded, I had never
thought of reincarnation, never believed in it or disbelieved. . . . She also
said that in her previous life she was kept prisoner in a certain church
crypt. Experts said it had never been used for this purpose. Then further
research showed that so many religious prisoners were taken on one occasion that there was no room for all of them in regular prisons. Some had
been kept in that very crypt. . . .

"In 1967 I decided to visit the south of France and investigate. I read
the manuscripts of the thirteenth century. Those old manuscripts—available
only to scholars who have special permission—showed she was accurate.
She gave me names and descriptions of people, places, and events, all of
which turned out to be accurate to the last detail. There was no way she
could have known about them. Even of the songs she wrote as a child, we
found four in the archives. They were correct word for word. . . .

"I started this as a clinical exercise and I have proved that what a
twentieth-century person told me about a thirteenth-century religion—without
any knowledge of it—was correct in every detail."[5]

In Dr. Guirdham's book on the case, *The Cathars and Reincarnation,*
he accumulates much evidence of the subject's knowledge of life in the
thirteenth century, although she claimed never to have read books on the
subject. She made correct drawings of old French coins, jewelry worn, and
the layout of buildings. She was able to name and place accurately in their
family and social relationships people who do not appear in the textbooks,
but were ultimately traced by going back to the dog-Latin records of the
Inquisition. These minor characters "are still traceable owing to the ant-
like industry of the Inquisitors and their clerks." She remembered members of the Fanjeaux and Mazerolles' families, in particular, giving their
first names and the roles they played. She recalled treating her friend
Roger de Grisolles with sugar loaf as a tonic. However, the existence of
sugar at this time in Europe was doubted. Investigation disclosed that
sugar in loaf form was derived from Arab medicine and existed at that
period in France.

As to her burning, the patient transcribed for Dr. Guirdham this description of a dream written in shorthand many years previously—a "firsthand"
report of how it feels to be consumed by fire! Hundreds of thousands of
"heretics" have thus died, but who could suspect what the experience was
really like.

The pain was maddening. You should pray to God when you're dying, if you can pray when you're in agony. In my dream I didn't pray to God. . . . I didn't know when you were burnt to death you'd bleed. I thought the blood would all dry up in the terrible heat. But I was bleeding heavily. The blood was dripping and hissing in the flames. I wished I had enough blood to put the flames out.

The worst part was my eyes. I hate the thought of going blind.

In this dream I was going blind. I tried to close my eyelids but I couldn't. They must have been burnt off, and now those flames were going to pluck my eyes out with their evil fingers. . . .

The flames weren't so cruel after all. They began to feel cold. Icy cold. It occurred to me that I wasn't burning to death. I was numb with the cold and suddenly I started to laugh. I had fooled those people who thought they could burn me. I am a witch. I had magicked the fire and turned it into ice.[6]

In his lecture "Reincarnation and the Practice of Medicine," Dr. Guirdham adds further details in the case.

Twenty-five years ago, as a student, a school girl at the age of 13, she was insisting that Cathar priests did not always wear black. You'll find the statement that they did in any book on the subject written in any language until 1965. . . . [Yet] she said that her friend in the thirteenth century wore *dark blue*. It now transpires that at one sitting of the Inquisition (the Inquisition of Jacques Fournier, who was bishop at Palmiers), it came out ten times in one session that Cathar priests sometimes wore dark blue or dark green. But that fact had been lying in the archives in Latin for long enough, and was only accessible to the public in 1965 when Duvernoy edited the record of the said Inquisitors that was published at Toulouse in 1966. But this woman knew this in 1944 as a school girl.

Again she could describe rituals in a house, a kind of convent. . . . Professor Nellie, the greatest living authority on the Troubadours—who definitely are spiritually connected with the Cathars—wrote to me and said, This is almost exactly Cathar ritual, making allowance for local deviations. He also added later that he could tell me where the place was, the convent of Montréal. By way of future advice he added that, in case of doubt, one should "go by the patient." Professor Nellie is a most meticulous and skeptical assessor of evidence.

When I first wrote to another specialist, Professor Duvernoy at Toulouse, he said, "Get in touch with me about anything you want, I am astonished at your detailed knowledge of Catharism." I couldn't say, "I've got this by copying down the dreams of a woman of thirty-six or seven which she had when she was a Grammar School girl of thirteen." He's found out since, but he's all the more keen to supply me with the evidence. . . .

If the professors at Toulouse are amazed at the accuracy with which an English girl can produce details of Catharism known to few, that is good enough for me. . . . All I have done in this matter was to listen to the story, act as an amateur historian, and to verify from many sources the details she had noted. I believe this to be a unique and entirely valid experience.[7]

AN UNUSUAL CASE OF DÉJÀ VU

This French expression means "already seen" and is the name given to the fairly frequent experience of recognizing as strangely familiar a scene, a house, a street, never seen before in this life—or so it appears.

"The true explanation," observes Professor C. J. Ducasse, "is usually that the new situation is similar in prominent respects to some situation the person has experienced before in his *present* life but which he does not at the moment recall."[8]

The following case, however, is clearly of another order. It was written up in—of all places—the *New York Times*. We say "of all places," because it is rare to find items on reincarnation therein. In a four-column spread, the *Times* of April 17, 1979, featured a special dispatch from Christopher Wren in Egypt, headed "Briton with a Sense of Déjà Vu Calls Ruins 'Home.' " A better title might have been: "Were Discoveries of a Noted Woman Egyptologist Based on Past-Life Recall?"

It all began when Dorothy Eady, at the age of three, fell down a flight of stairs in her home in Plymouth, England. She was pronounced dead by the local doctor. "When he came back with the death certificate, the body was sitting on the bed playing," she recalled. Then she began to cry. "They asked why I was crying, and I said, 'I want to go home.' They assured me I was home."

Wren writes: "From then on she was convinced that she belonged in another, dimly remembered time. She played hooky from school and hung around the Egyptology Room of the British Museum in London. When she first saw a magazine photograph of the magnificent temple at Abydos, she told her parents: 'Here is my home, but why is it in ruins and where are the gardens?' "

However, it was not until 1933, when she was in her late twenties that she was able to go to Egypt. "I never left; I never wanted to." She took a job with the Egyptian Antiquities Service and acquired experience in field excavations, but it was some years before she had time to travel to Abydos.

"As soon as I saw the mountain, I knew where I was. The train stopped, and I got off. . . . There was no other place for me to be."

"In 1956," the *Times* continues, "she managed to get transferred to help with the excavation and restoration of Abydos, which has some of the finest bas-reliefs of pharanonic art. Her colleagues were surprised by her immediate familiarity with the temple. 'In the pitch dark I went to each place they told me to.' " She would then describe the scene. "Every time I was right."

As to the gardens she spoke of as a child, no archaeologist had yet discovered where they were, but on her arrival she revealed their location. The tree roots and vines were still there and the water canals too. As the *Times* adds:

> She also correctly estimated the height of damaged columns where the temple roof was missing and she translated some of the more enigmatic hieroglyphics.
>
> In a previous incarnation, she believes, she was the orphaned daughter of a common soldier and a vegetable seller and was adopted by the temple, where the spring resurrection rituals to the god Osiris were conducted. "I can't remember any ordinary life, so I think I must have been stuck in the temple. I have a vague memory of the processions. I can remember an awful old killjoy of a high priest."

This was a period 3,200 years ago in the nineteenth dynasty under Seti I and his successor Ramses II. Seti was the name Dorothy Eady gave her son when she married an Egyptian. The marriage lasted only two years, her husband preferring a woman who could cook and disliked monuments. For many years, both among her colleagues and in the village where she lives, she has been known as Om Seti, which means mother of Seti—such usage being traditional among Egyptian peasants.

She concedes that "her odyssey from the middle-class gentility of Plymouth to the rural poverty of a remote Egyptian village (where she is now retired on a modest pension) sounds bizarre." Some people say that when "I fell downstairs it knocked a screw loose."* But there is no screw

---

*There are other cases where a bodily shakeup has triggered supposed past-life memories. One such was reported in a German newspaper. It concerned a small girl in Ihansi, India, who fell out of a third-story window. She did not suffer any bodily harm, but suddenly started to talk in several languages, which scholars discovered to be old Indian dialects not used for centuries. *Rheinischer Merkur* (May 31, 1947), published in Koblenz.

loose in her knowledge as an archeologist. "Her grasp of ancient Egypt is formidable," writes Wren. "Egyptologists still visit her sparsely furnished house in Abydos to benefit from her knowledge and her lively self-deprecating wit. James P. Allen of the American Research Center in Cairo has described her as a patron saint of the profession. 'I don't know of an American archaeologist in Egypt who doesn't respect her.' "

A DREAM OF THE TOWER OF LONDON

A British physicist, Dr. Raynor Johnson, has taken time from his scientific experiments to investigate the inner side of nature as well as the outer. In one of his books, *A Religious Outlook for Modern Man*, he records this dream experience of a young girl, using her own words.

"The dream was of being a prisoner in a place that I knew to be the Tower of London. I had not seen it in real life, but I had no doubt where I was. It was very cold weather (in waking life, a hot summer). I was aware that I had been condemned to death. This, I used to dream over and over again, and after being in the dream a vigorous man, to wake up and be a little girl felt rather strange.

"At last the dream changed, and I was standing on a scaffold which must have been newly erected as it smelt of sawdust. Everything was decorous and decent. The executioner knelt and apologised for what he was about to do. I took the axe from his hand and felt it, and handed it back, bidding him do his duty. When I woke up I made a drawing of the axe, which was of a peculiar shape.

"Sometime after this I asked to be taken to the Tower of London, and I explained to a friendly gunsmith that I wanted to write history but could not understand the battles perfectly until I understood the weapons. 'You are right, Missy,' he said, and demonstrated to me the various uses of pike, lance, crossbow, etc. I then asked had he an axe that beheaded people? He said, 'Yes, this certainly beheaded the Jacobite Lords, but it is supposed to be very much older.' Somehow, I was not surprised that it proved to be the exact shape of the axe in my dream."[9]

Dr. Stevenson reports that he has "collected and is analyzing many dreams suggestive of a previous life. . . . A few," he says, "contain verifiable and verified information; most do not. . . . Certain features of these dreams recur in many of them and justify a careful study of the patterns they show." One feature is that the individuals experiencing them "often relive the past as if it were now happening."

Characteristically, in these dreams the subject experiences himself with a different identity living a scene in some past time and different place. For the duration of the dream, and sometimes for a little longer, he experiences himself as a different personality. Subjects experiencing these "previous life" dreams sometimes examine themselves in a mirror upon awakening to make certain that they do or do not have a beard, for example.[10]

AN AMAZING CASE IN LEBANON[11]

While Dr. Stevenson was in Brazil in 1962 investigating a case, he met an émigré from Lebanon who said that in his native village, Kornayel, there were many cases of rebirth. The man provided Stevenson with a card of introduction to his brother there, but it was not until two years later that the doctor could visit the place. So, one day in early March of 1964, without advance warning, he suddenly appeared, only to learn that the brother had escaped the cold winter of this mountainous area and was spending the winter in Beirut.

When the villagers learned of Stevenson's mission, they told him of a five-year-old boy, Imad Elawar, who had been incessantly talking about his former life since the age of one. This was not a matter of astonishment to the natives; they were familiar with such revelations. In fact, Stevenson relates that, among these people—who are not Muslims but members of the Druse religion, the incidence of reincarnation cases is among the highest in the world. The 200,000 existing Druses live mainly in Lebanon, Syria, northern Israel, and Jordan. Quite a few have now emigrated to the United States and Brazil.

Stevenson located the father of Imad and found he was the cousin of his friend in Brazil. The case turned out to be one of his strongest and is especially valuable because he was able to investigate it *before* the two families involved—past and present—knew of each other's existence. Dropping in "out of the blue," he was able to freshly examine the behavior of the boy at home and also when he first met his supposed former relatives. Consequently, before any attempt was made to locate these people, Stevenson recorded over fifty items the child said he remembered. Now, for the story itself.

Imad was born December 21, 1958, and when he began to speak, the first words he said were the names Jamileh and Mahmoud. As he became more fluent, he soon revealed many facts about his prior life, the names of people he formerly knew, the property he owned, and some of the events of his life. He recalled being a member of a Bouhamzy family that lived in Khriby—a village separated from Kornayel by a twenty-five-mile winding mountainous road. Among his present family, only his father had ever visited Khriby, and this was on the occasion of a prominent Druse's funeral.

Imad would talk to himself about the people whose names he mentioned, and ask aloud how these people were getting along. He also spoke of these things in his sleep. There were fourteen names of individuals he mentioned, but the one he spoke about most was Jamileh, whose beauty he raved about, comparing it with that of his more unattractive mother. Jamileh, he said, wore red clothes that he had bought for her; she wore high heels— unusual even today among women in her village. Imad's mother reported that, when he was about three years old, his longing for Jamileh reached its height, and one day, lying on a bed with his mother, he suddenly asked her to behave as Jamileh would under such circumstances.

Among his other memories was his fondness for hunting. He had a rifle in that previous life and also a doubled-barreled shotgun, he said. To describe the latter he held two fingers together. Among other property, he owned a house, which he described, a small yellow car, a bus, and a truck that hauled rocks.

Among events in his former life, he remembered beating a dog. But the one thing that bothered him most was a serious accident in which a truck ran over a man, broke his legs, and crushed his trunk. The man, said Imad, was taken to the "doctor's place" and had an operation. To Imad's mother and grandmother, this revelation seemed particularly significant, because when the child first learned to walk he constantly exclaimed how wonderful it was to be able to walk again!

His father discounted all these stories and called the child a liar. Thereafter the son spoke of such matters only among the female members of his family.

However, everyone took notice one day when two-year-old Imad, stopping a complete stranger on the street, joyously threw his arms around him. The startled man exclaimed: "Do you know me?" "Yes, you were my neighbor." The man was Salim el Aschkar, a native of Khriby. He once lived close to Imad's former house, a fact that was only discovered later, for at this point no one knew which Bouhamzy family the boy really belonged to. However, this did not prevent his present family from coming to rather definite conclusions—*but quite incorrect conclusions, as we shall see*. Thus, in the beginning, Stevenson was given some very misleading clues.

Here is the story the parents had pieced together: as the first words the child had spoken as a baby were Mahmoud and Jamileh, they must have been the names of himself and his wife. Mahmoud must have been killed by a truck. This seemed to be confirmed not only by Imad's recall of the accident, but because as a child he had a notable phobia for large trucks and buses. Even as a toddler, he would run and hide from them.

With little more to go on, Stevenson, accompanied by Imad and his father, went to Khriby the next day. The child was in ecstasy, as he had been nagging his parents for years to take him there. En route the boy made a number of additional statements to Stevenson regarding his memories. But the visit turned up nothing consequential in solving the mystery of Imad's claimed pre-life history. Yes, they discovered a Mahmoud Bouhamzy did exist; *in fact, he was very much alive*. His wife was not called Jamileh, and the description of his house did not conform to Imad's description.

So Stevenson decided to leave the father and son behind the following day and make some preliminary investigations of his own in Khriby. He located a Bouhamzy by the name of Haffez whose father had been run over by a truck that broke his legs and crushed his trunk. And, despite two operations performed that very day, he had lost his life. However, the dead man's wife was not called Jamileh, and his house did not match Imad's description. So Stevenson's research again dissolved into nothing.

Then suddenly light dawned! Haffez revealed that there was a cousin who was greatly attached to his father and who was deeply upset by the truck tragedy. His name was Ibrahim Bouhamzy. Ibrahim had an *uncle* named Mahmoud—and also had a mistress called Jamileh. In fact, this relationship scandalized the whole village. In a land where women are renowned for their beauty, Jamileh was exquisitely beautiful and dressed in the fashion previously described by Imad. Furthermore, Ibrahim's house also matched Imad's description. What was especially significant was that Ibrahim died in his late twenties of tuberculosis and had been bedridden for almost a year before his death. No wonder Imad had been so happy about walking around again! After Ibrahim's death, Jamileh married and moved to another village.

Commenting about his first failures in the case, Stevenson said, "As it turned out, the errors of inference made by Imad's family add considerably to the evidence of their honesty and also to the improbability that they themselves could have provided a source or a channel for the information given by Imad.'' Furthermore, ''among the Muslims and Christians who surround them, the Druses have an extraordinary reputation for honesty.''

When Stevenson got back to Imad's home and told his parents about the results of the investigation, they were not happy about who their son was in his former life. The story of his relationship with Jamileh brought to his present mother's face an expression of shocked consternation—but Stevenson also noted a tinge of amusement.

After this successful visit to Khriby, Stevenson was now in a position to bring Imad and his father there the following day, to see what identifications the boy could make at Ibrahim's house, which had been boarded up since his death in 1949. Among the declarations the boy had made before the first trip was that there were *two wells* at the house, *one full and one empty*. Dr. Stevenson now saw these for himself. They had been closed up since Ibrahim's death. They were not spring wells, but concrete cavities or vats used for grape juice. A rather intricate mechanical device, which Stevenson describes, allowed them to be alternately used, so that one would be empty while the other was full.

At this point, three ladies unexpectedly arrived on the scene and escorted Imad around the house. They were the mother and sister of Ibrahim accompanied by a neighbor. In this situation, Imad made thirteen correct recognitions or statements relating to his former life and relatives. However, he did not recognize his mother, although he said he liked her very much. She was now an elderly woman, and her appearance had altered greatly. His sister asked him, ''Do you know who I am?'' He rightly replied, ''Huda.'' He identified a large oil painting on the wall as his brother Fuad. A rather large photograph of Ibrahim was shown him. ''Which was it,'' they asked, ''your brother or your uncle?'' Neither, he said. ''It was me.''

His former sister probed further: ''You said something just before you died. What was it?'' Imad answered: ''Huda, call Fuad.'' This was correct. His brother Fuad had left shortly before, and Ibrahim wanted to see him again, but died immediately. Fuad was especially loved by Ibrahim, and when a small photograph of him was given Imad as a keepsake, he clung to it and kissed it affectionately.

At they toured the house, Huda said she heard him say that his mother once crushed her finger in the door leading to the courtyard. This injury actually occurred, and Stevenson later noted that the mother's finger still had a flattened end.

The boy was asked, "How was the bed arranged when you slept in it?" He indicated it used to be in a position crosswise from its present position. Then a pertinent question followed: "In what manner did your friends talk to you during your last illness?" He replied, "Through a window." Why? They dared not enter his room owing to his infectious disease, and so the bed had been arranged in the aforementioned manner.

Another challenging question: "Where do you keep your rifle?" Imad pointed to the back of a closet fitted into a partition wall. Ibrahim's mother confirmed that this was the place and added that he and she alone knew where the gun was kept, this being a closely guarded secret. (It was unlawful to possess such weapons at the time.)

*

The case has two interesting sequels. They were revealed by Imad's uncle Mahmoud on one of the several occasions when Dr. Stevenson returned to Lebanon to interview the witnesses again.

It will be recalled that Mahmoud was one of the two persons whose names Imad first spoke as an infant. When Imad had gone to Khriby, he did not meet this relative, but in the summer of 1970, when the lad was twelve, the uncle made a surprise visit to Imad's house. The boy did not recognize him. When the latter displayed an old photograph taken when he wore a moustache and inquired who the person was, the boy answered, "It is my uncle Mahmoud." The uncle then invited Imad to spend a few days with him in Khriby. (The boy had not been there since Stevenson accompanied him in 1964.)

The second incident that particularly impressed the uncle occurred while Imad and he were walking in Khriby. Imad appeared to recognize a man on the street and asked permission to speak to him. The uncle asked, "What do you want to talk to that man for? He is a former soldier." The boy replied that this was just the reason why he wanted to talk with him. Imad then had a long talk with the ex-soldier, explaining to him that he was Ibrahim reborn and reminding him of experiences the two of them had shared in that other life. The man confirmed to the uncle that Ibrahim and he had entered the French army on the same day and had been close companions during their army service.

In summation, Dr. Stevenson reports that, of the fifty-seven direct and verifiable claims about his past life Imad had made *before* he met his previous relatives, he was correct in fifty-one. These included the yellow car, bus, and truck referred to previously, which Imad said he owned in his former birth.

AN EMBARRASSING DOMESTIC SECRET REVEALED[12]

A child of two-and-a-half hands a family guest a glass of water. When later asked to remove the empty glass, he makes the startling announcement: "I won't pick it up. I am the son of a Sharma"—a high caste in India. Then, in a fit of anger, he breaks several glasses.

Who is this boy, and where does he live? His name is Gopal Gupta, and he lives in Delhi with his parents, who have little education and know no English. When asked to explain his rude conduct, he said he formerly lived in Mathura, where he had many servants to carry away dishes. Why should anyone ask him to remove glasses?

He also spoke of his previous father and two brothers, one of whom shot him in the chest. He told of quarreling with his former wife, and mentioned that he had owned a large company named Sukh Shancharah, which dispensed medicine. Gopal gave out most of this information on the evening of his temper tantrum.

These statements, and many others later revealed, were subsequently verified. Of the forty-six items and recognitions listed in Dr. Stevenson's investigation of the case, only one was partially incorrect, and three could not be verified.

When the previous family—wealthy and well educated—heard rumors of this boy in Delhi talking about having once lived with them, a few members came to see Gopal—first, his former wife, a sister, and her son, and later, his oldest brother. Gopal identified them all. Another sister also came, but he recognized her with difficulty. She invited him to the marriage of her son in another town, and there the child came face to face with the brother who killed him. The brother had been sentenced to life imprisonment, but owing to illness had been released. He was instantly named by Gopal.

Why did that younger brother shoot him? Gopal had previously disclosed that the brother drank a good deal and had married a woman from Assam who apparently wanted lots of money. Prior to the shooting the brother was heavily in debt and demanded money from his older brother, but at the time the latter was short of funds. Because of this and various imagined grievances, the shooting occurred.

It was not until Gopal was nine years old that he himself visited Mathura and his old home. He also visited the home of his former wife. When the boy had first seen her in Delhi, his father noted that Gopal was very cool to her. What the quarrel had been about was not clear, but now it was to become public knowledge. To her great embarrassment, and before all those assembled, the boy revealed that, when the younger brother had demanded money, Gopal sought to appease him by obtaining 5,000 rupees from this former wife, but she refused the request. As a result, the quarrel between the brothers intensified and became a contributing factor in the shooting.

At this disclosure the lady fainted dead away! Dr. Stevenson explains that a blend of astonishment at Gopal's remarks and embarrassment at the disclosure of a domestic secret probably altered the flow of blood to her head, and so she collapsed. On regaining consciousness, as might be expected, she denied Gopal's story. Later, however, she had the courage to confess to its truth. In fact, when Stevenson later wrote her asking permission to publish this information, she willingly consented. And so this rather remarkable piece of evidence was rescued from oblivion.

AN OUTSTANDING CASE OF DEMOTION[13]

Bishen Chand, the subject of this case of Dr. Stevenson, was born in poverty in Bareilly, a large city in northern India. His father was a poor railway clerk. When only ten months old, the child uttered the words *pilvit* or *pilivit*. A large town some thirty miles away from Bareilly is called Pilibhit, and as the child began to speak connectedly, he revealed numerous details of a previous life there. The case is important because much of what he said about the prior life was recorded in writing before verifications were attempted.

His name, he said, had been Laxmi Narain, and his father was a wealthy landowner. He also spoke of an "uncle," Har Narain. The parents had never heard of such people and fearfully sought to discourage such strange revelations, owing to the widespread superstition that children who utter them die soon. However, the child could not be silenced and, every day during his early years, spoke of that other life and contrasted his present life with it in a contemptuous way. "Bishen Chand reproached his father for his poverty," writes Stevenson, "demanded money, and cried when he did not receive it. He said: 'Even my servant would not take the food cooked here.' He blamed his father for not building a house. He tore cotton clothes off and demanded silk ones." Like the members of his prior family, he ate meat and drank alcohol—secretly obtaining these things as a young child. His present parents did not drink and were the strictest vegetarians.

When he was four years old, Bishen Chand accompanied his father to a wedding party to a town beyond Pilibhit. When they were returning, the train conductor announced the stop of Pilibhit and the lad insisted on getting off, because he "used to live here." When he was refused, he cried all the way back to Bareilly.

A lawyer, K.K.N. Sahay, somehow learned of the boy's past-life revelations. He visited the family, recorded the boy's statements, and then undertook to take him and his father to Pilibhit to see what he would recognize. The lawyer published a full report, and later Dr. Stevenson made a complete investigation.

Among the particulars the child revealed before he was taken to Pilibhit was that his former self, Laxmi, died unmarried. In that life, he could speak Urdi, Hindi, and English. He had a neighbor, Sunder Lal, who had a green gate, a sword, and a gun, and that nautch-dancing parties were held in the latter's courtyard. He described his own house, including the existence of a shrine room, and separate apartments for ladies and men. In referring to such apartments, he used the Urdi word *masurate,* instead of the Hindi word *zenana* familiar in his family, and later, when speaking of a lock on a door of his home, he used the upper-class Urdi word *kofal,* instead of the Hindi word *tala.*

As to schooling, he claimed to have reached Class VI in the government school near the river. Class VI was a low grade of attainment, so the child could not have been bragging, for it indicated he was a lazy student.

He also made the alarming disclosure that, in his former life, he had a mistress and, when he saw a man coming out of her room, he killed him—pridefully adding that, due to family influence, he escaped punishment.

His father reports that the child said to him on one occasion, "Papa, why don't you keep a mistress? You will have great pleasure from her." Although shocked and astounded, the father quietly replied: "What pleasures, my boy?" "You will enjoy the fragrance of her hair," Bishen answered, "and feel much enjoyment from her company."

Now when the boy was finally taken to Pilibhit, the first place the party visited was the government high school. However, the boy could not recognize it as his school. They then learned that the present building was new and recently erected. The headmaster agreed to take the party to various places in Pilibhit. In the course of their tour, Bishen Chand recognized the old government high school, which was by a river—just as he had said. He also identified the room where Class VI met and correctly recognized and named a former classmate from an old photograph.

When they passed one house, Bishen Chand said it was that of his neighbor Sunder Lal. He pointed to the green gate and to the courtyard where nautch parties were held—a fact corroborated by nearby shopkeepers.

Later the boy recognized his own house. He shouted that this was the house of Har Narain. The latter turned out to be Laxmi's father not his uncle, as the boy had previously said. This mistake, if mistake it was, can be explained by the fact that, in the city of Bareilly, there was a famous person known as Uncle Har Narain. The boy, in loving fashion, may have attached that name to his own father who bore the same name. However, Bishen was wrong in saying that the house was in the Mohalla Ganj area; it was in Mohalla Sarai Khan, some distance away. The home was in a state of deterioration, and it was considered amazing that the lad, when asked, could correctly point out among the ruins where a former stairway to the upper floor once existed. He bitterly complained that his family had allowed his house to be kept in such disrepair after his death.

An old, faint photograph was shown him by a surviving member of the family who lived nearby. The child said, "Here is Har Narain and here I," pointing to a boy seated on a chair. This established his identity as Laxmi Narain. The uncle of Laxmi acknowledged in a written report that some of the incidents the boy related had long been forgotten by the family.

The boy was given a pair of tablas (drums), which he played with ease. His father in this life reports that the boy had never previously seen this kind of drum. Dr. Stevenson comments: "When I first heard about the playing of tablas, I conceived it as a very primitive skill amounting to a mere tapping on a drum. I revised this opinion after watching Dr. Jamuna Prasad play the tablas with great dexterity during a musical performance at his house in 1969. I then realized that playing well on the tablas requires discipline and practice."

A crowd of neighbors had now gathered around the lad, and they kept baiting him to name the prostitute with whom Laxmi consorted, and thus prove he really was that man. Bishen embarrassedly resisted answering, but finally said "Padma"—which was correct.

Upon inquiry, it developed that Laxmi Narain was the only son of his father, who spoiled him and encouraged his taste for luxury and extravagance. After the father died, his son was left a large inheritance, and he freely indulged his fondness for good food, fine clothes, beautiful women, and alcohol. Yet, strangely enough, he was also deeply religious in a ceremonial way. He would seclude himself in the shrine room in his house for ten to fifteen days and even have his meals there. After this, he devoted the rest of the month with equal zeal to debauchery. It was while drunk that he killed the man who emerged from Padma's apartment. He seized a gun carried by a servant and shot the man dead.

However, he was also noted for his great generosity and was known to give his own food to beggars. He once presented 500 rupees (an enormous sum then) to a Moslem watch dealer to help him start in business. How significant, then, that in his new life, when his father indicated one day his intention of buying a watch, the child said "Papa, don't buy. When I go to Pilibhit, I shall get you three watches from a Moslem watch dealer whom I established there." Then in Pilibhit, as the touring party passed through the business district, the child stopped the tonga, got down, and went to a particular shop. He looked at it intently and said it was the shop of his friend Ismail, where he had his watch repaired. No sign on the shop revealed Ismail's name. In fact, he had died by that time, and the shop had changed hands some years earlier.

While at Pilibhit, Bishen Chand was taken to see his former mother. She posed several test questions, and his answers assured her that the boy was indeed her late lamented son. One question may sound like a leading one, but the answer could hardly have been invented. She asked, "Did you throw away my pickle?" He replied, "I did throw away the pickle, but how is it possible to eat worms? You wanted me to eat worms, hence I threw the pickle away." The mother explained that one time her pickles became rotten and had worms in the jar. She threw the worms out and kept the pickles in the sun. Laxmi threw them away to her great annoyance.

"Who was your servant?" she challenged. "My servant was Maikua, a black, short Kahar" (a low caste group who work as domestics). "He was my favorite cook." This was correct.

Another question led to an astounding discovery. The mother asked for the location of the family treasure. (After the death of her husband and Laxmi, it was thought money had been concealed in the house, but no one knew where.) Bishen led the way back to his former home and showed the room where it was hidden, but without revealing the exact location. After he left, a new search was made, and the family was rewarded to find a hoard of gold coins!

Bishen expressed deep affection for his former mother and, when he returned home, tried to persuade his father to let her live with them:

"Papa, she would not cost you much. She wears a plain sari and a petticoat and spends the greater part of the day in prayers and worship." When the mother later visited the boy and his family, they found he had described her perfectly.

As to Padma, his former mistress, Bishen confided to Stevenson an incident that took place in *this* life when he was twenty-three. He had not seen her since he was six, when she had visited his family after hearing the stories of Laxmi's rebirth. The incident occurred when Bishen was working in a town north of Pilibhit. Unexpectedly Padma and several other women came into the office where he was employed. She was now in her fifties. Bishen recognized her and said, "Are you Padma?" She said, "Yes." He put his arms around her and was so emotionally excited he fainted.

Padma was then living in the hills three miles away. That same evening, wanting to renew their former relationship, he went to see her and brought with him a bottle of wine. He had not drunk alcohol since he secretly imbibed it as a child. When Padma saw him, she reproached him, "I am an old woman like your mother. Please go away. You lost everything in your previous life. Now you want to lose everything again." She broke the bottle of wine and sent him away. Two years later Bishen married and, according to himself and the report of others, lived an exemplary conjugal life.

Even before the incident with Padma, Bishen's character had undergone a remarkable change. As he approached manhood, his poverty and ceaseless struggle to earn a meager livelihood brought him to reflect that his problems were the consequence of his arrogant, dissolute life as Laxmi, particularly the murder of Laxmi's rival lover. Significantly, this tragic event was still vividly recalled by Bishen. All the other memories had faded away. Stevenson remarks that, when he last interviewed Bishen, he felt himself "in the presence of a person who had learned that material goods and carnal pleasures do not bring happiness." As to the case as a whole, Stevenson concludes, "It seems unusually strong with regard to authenticity."

A CASE OF GENDER DYSPHORIA[14]

If you were in a doctor's office leafing through a psychiatric journal and came upon a serious discussion as to whether a certain girl in Burma could have been a man in her previous life, would you not be rather startled that such an enquiry should appear in a medical periodical? Well, one such case was published in the *Journal of Nervous and Mental Disease* of September 1977, under the title "A Case of Gender Dysphoria." It was reported by Dr. Stevenson.

"Gender dysphoria" is a psychiatric term for an individual who feels trapped in his or her present sex and is convinced he or she belongs in the opposite one. In the West, this is usually considered a psychological abnormality derived from parents desiring their child to be the sex opposite to its present one. Without denying this may happen, Dr. Stevenson presents an alternate possibility that could apply in some cases.

The present case developed in this way: A four-year-old Burmese girl by the name of Ma Tin Aung Myo—whom we will call Myo—was walking with her father one day in Na-Thul, the village where they lived, when an airplane flew overhead. The child was frightened and began to cry. After this, every time an airplane flew over she cried. "What are you afraid of?" her father asked. "I'm afraid they will shoot me," she answered.

Soon thereafter she became very depressed and often wept. "I am pining for Japan," she said, adding that her real home was in northern Japan, where, as a man, she was married and had several children, and longed to be with them. In her last life, she continued, she had been a cook in the Japanese army, stationed in Burma during World War II and had been strafed by a war plane and killed. She recalled being close to a pile of firewood and had begun to cook a meal when the plane that killed her flew over.

She also recalled that, at the time, she (he) was wearing short pants and a big belt, but had taken off her shirt. Myo's mother told Dr. Stevenson that, when she was pregnant several months with Myo, she had a recurring dream of a husky Japanese soldier, wearing short pants and no shirt, who followed her. He said he would come to stay with her, but fearing the man, she ordered him away.

Stevenson ascertained that the village where Myo was born was occupied in 1942 by the Japanese Army, soon after they invaded Burma. The allied bombers struck the area twice daily for a time, and fighter planes descended, machine-gunning any person they saw on the ground. To avoid this, the Burmese residents left the village during the day and returned only at night, but the Japanese soldiers were obliged to remain, and many of them were killed.

It was not possible to investigate this case in Japan, as Myo did not remember her former name nor the exact part of northern Japan where she had lived.

As to her tastes, she did not like the hot climate of Burma, nor did she enjoy its spicy food, preferring sweet foods. When she was young, she loved half-raw fish, a popular Japanese dish. As just mentioned, she claimed to have been a cook in the occupying army. In her present life, she longed to prepare meals for her family, but they refused to let her because she omitted all the spices and chillies!

At an early age, she insisted on wearing boys' clothes and absolutely refused to wear girls'—they gave her a headache, she said. When the school authorities insisted she dress as a girl, she refused and dropped out of school. She wore her hair short like a man's. As a child, she played at being a soldier and asked her parents to buy toy guns. She played football and cane ball just like a boy.

To those skeptical of the reincarnation interpretation of the case, Dr. Stevenson asks: "If Myo wanted for needs of her own to identify herself with a deceased person, why did she select a Japanese soldier?" As a result of the Japanese occupation, they "were unpopular and detested in Burma, and the personation by a Burmese girl of a Japanese soldier certainly gained her no credit in her family or village." "The simplest explanation sometimes *is* the best one," he adds, "and I believe that Western psychiatrists and psychologists should seriously consider and investigate further the basis for the Southeast Asian interpretation of cases of gender dysphoria"—that in the previous incarnation the individual was a member of the opposite sex and still clings tenaciously to that role.

WAS A BRITISH PILOT REBORN IN SRI LANKA?[15]

In this, our final case, the scene opens in a Sinhalese household in the city of Kotte in Ceylon—or Sri Lanka as it is now called. It is the home of Mr. and Mrs. de Silva, the parents of seven children. The year is 1944, and their latest child, a boy named Ranjith, is now two years old. Mr. de Silva, although a kindly man and a Buddhist, has an intense dislike for the British, who until recently had occupied his country for almost 200 years. What then should be more unwelcome than to discover his own boy exhibiting many of the qualities of the hated British.

Dr. Stevenson, who investigated the case with his late associate Francis Story, a noted Buddhist scholar, reports that these Anglo-Saxon traits,

or a certain attitude which underlay them, made the boy an outsider in the family. He regarded them with coolness and showed less affection for his parents than the other children. The parents on their side regarded him as a "freak" who had somehow strayed into their midst. This did not prevent a flow of affection from them to the boy, however, although the strong independence and refractoriness to parental guidance which Ranjith showed perplexed and often sorely troubled them.

In eating habits, too, the lad was more British than Sinhalese. He cared little for rice, the staple dish in the Orient. He ate bread liberally spread with butter and held it in his fingers as the English do. When only two, his father noticed that, if the child's stomach was upset, he used the English method of putting fingers down his throat to induce vomiting, a practice foreign to Sinhalese. When the family ate in a hotel, he skillfully manipulated his knife and fork while the other children clumsily handled theirs. The hot chillies and spices were repugnant to him.

When Ranjith was almost four, his father heard him announce to his mother, brothers, and sisters: "You are not my mother, brothers, and sisters. My mother, father, and others are in England." The father said nothing, but, as the boy continued in his aloofness, he eventually asked him questions about his other family.

Ranjith could not recall his name or his parents' names, but he did remember two brothers, Tom and Jim, and a sister Margaret. His father, he said, worked on big steamers and sometimes brought home pineapples. The boy brought him lunch at noontime. He said his home was isolated from other houses, being on a hill. In the mornings, it was at times so cold in the house he wore both a jersey and an overcoat and moved closer to the fireplace. At such times, there was ice in the garden and on the roads. Wagons came to remove the ice on the roads. "Were they motor wagons?" the father asked. "No," was the reply, "they were horse wagons." (Natural ice never occurs in the tropical lowlands of Ceylon where Ranjith lived, nor had he ever seen a horsedrawn wagon.)

The lad volunteered that he was a Christian not a Buddhist in that other life and that he took his brothers and sisters to church every Sunday on the pillion of his motorcycle. He also spontaneously mentioned that he and his mother were very fair, much fairer than the Burgher lady who lived next door. (Holland controlled Ceylon from 1640 to 1796, and these Dutch descendants are lighter in complexion than the Sinhalese.) In reply to the question of what his mother wore, he said, "a skirt and jacket." This contrasts strongly with the saris worn by women in Sri Lanka.

On the day of Ranjith's fourth birthday, his father arranged with the local British radio station to announce the birthday on the air. The boy's older sisters, to please the lad, told him that at 5:00 P.M. his "mother" would speak to him from England! At the scheduled time, the family gathered around their radio, and Ranjith waited spellbound for the message. A voice with English accent came over the wire announcing the birthday. Ranjith cupped his hands around his mouth and spoke into the radio: "Mother, I am staying in a Sinhalese family's house. Take me there"— that is, to England. "Happy Birthday," in a rendition that includes the word "darling," was then heard. After the song Ranjith said, "That is my mother. My mother calls me 'darling' and sometimes she calls me 'sweetheart.' " The boy was asked how he recognized his mother's voice. He answered, "My mother speaks softly like that."

"This usage of the word 'softly,' " reports Stevenson, "was new to Ranjith's family for, although correctly used by Ranjith, it happens that in Sinhalese-English the word 'slowly' is used to refer to the quality meant by 'softly' " in occidental English. "Mr. de Silva said he first learned of this other meaning of the word 'softly' from his son."

If the family had thought that this birthday message would bring happiness to little Ranjith, they were mistaken. The child became very sad, and the father instructed his other children to try to help the child forget his memories. For the next fourteen years, it appeared as if he had, although when he was in his early teens he made a strange request. Instead of completing his education as most serious students in Sri Lanka do, he asked to leave school and work in a garage—even to wash cars if that was all that was available. His father was amazed and upset, but granted permission. The boy learned with such astonishing rapidity how to repair and drive cars and motorcycles that, when he was eighteen, his father mentioned that sometime he should go to England to perfect himself in this field. That was all Ranjith needed to hear. Without consulting his father, he immediately booked passage on a ship to that country. At a farewell party, he told friends he still believed he had lived there before.

Ranjith remained in England for two years and considered them the happiest period of his life. He not only got along wonderfully well with the British, but they loved him—this young man with the heavily pigmented skin common in Sri Lanka. His sister, who lived in London, reported that he found his way around with ease. (When the present writers were there in 1978, they found the streets so complicated and unexpectedly tangential they would not venture more than a few blocks without a guide.)

Ranjith anticipated that additional memories of his previous life would surface while in Europe and he would be able to identify his former house and town, but this did not occur. Nevertheless, his passion for automobiles and his precocious knowledge of their workings continued. He entered an automobile race in Scotland and was first among twenty-two contestants, none but himself being Asiatic.

When Stevenson interviewed him in Sri Lanka, Ranjith said he would live permanently in England if it were not that his present parents were now elderly and he felt they needed his help. He confided that all his life, even as a small child, he had a strong urge to kill animals, and he still liked to hunt and kill animals in the jungles of Ceylon. Aware that this violated the precepts of Buddhism, he struggled against it, but sometimes struggled in vain. "This may have been a residue," says Stevenson, "of a previous life as a Christian (whose religion would not have condemned the killing of animals) and as an Englishman, many of whose countrymen are well known for hunting and killing animals with enthusiasm."

Inasmuch as Ranjith spoke of being a Christian in his last incarnation, Stevenson inquired why he thought he was born a Buddhist this time. He answered he believed that during World War II he had been a British air pilot who crashed near Kotte, in Ceylon, where the Royal Air Force had a base. In his present life, he had a deep yearning to fly but could not afford going to aviation school. Stevenson comments that Ranjith's disclosure came as a surprise to him, but he recalled similar statements made by some of his Burmese subjects. "These are children who remember previous lives as British or American pilots (or other airmen) shot down over Burma during World War II." Interesting that, unlike Ranjith, these Burmese subjects had fair complexions and hair.

The foregoing study appeared in Stevenson's *Twenty Cases Suggestive of Reincarnation,* with this introductory comment. "Unlike many of the others in this entire group of twenty cases, it does not provide any direct evidence for reincarnation, although it does *suggest* it. But it seems worth presenting at this time because it provides an excellent example of a type of case which occurs even more commonly than do the cases with rich detail susceptible of verification." Elsewhere, Stevenson remarks that, in international cases where the subjects are supposedly reborn in other cultures, they usually recall very few verifiable facts concerning previous lives. As to this, "A generalization slowly emerges: *the greater the 'cultural distance' between the subject and the life he seems to remember, the less likely he is to recall specific verifiable facts"* [italics added].[16]

Space limitations have permitted only a sampling of Dr. Stevenson's cases. However, even such a meager presentation makes understandable this review of the first volume of Stevenson's series Cases of the Reincarnation Type that appeared in the ultraconservative *Journal of the American Medical Association,* and which we noted in our Preface: "In regard to reincarnation Stevenson has painstakingly and unemotionally collected a detailed series of cases in which the evidence is difficult to explain on any other grounds. . . . He has placed on record a large amount of data that cannot be ignored" (December 1, 1975).

6

Did They Speak a Past-Life Language?

Out of the mouth of babes . . .

Psalms 8:2

Cases where children or adults speak a foreign tongue not consciously learned in this life are rare, but they do occur often enough to warrant scientific classification. "Xenoglossy" is the word for them, a term coined by Dr. Charles Richet, the noted French physiologist, Nobel prize recipient, and parapsychologist. Derived from the Greek, *xeno* (pronounced zeno) means "strange" or "foreign," while *gloss* means "language." Dr. Ian Stevenson, the leading researcher in this field, has two volumes of such cases, one titled *Xenoglossy* and the other, *Unlearned Language: New Studies in Xenoglossy.*

Two forms of xenoglossy are known: recitative and responsive. In the first, the subject repeats, without necessarily understanding, fragments of a strange language. Usually, he exhibits only rote memory. Such memories often derive from earlier subconscious or unremembered exposure to the language in this life and are subsequently triggered by an incident or association—or perhaps during hypnotic regression, as in this example given by Stevenson.

> A young man while hypnotized began to talk in a strange language eventually recognized as Oscan, a dialect of Italy in the third century B.C. The subject wrote out what he was saying, which proved to be an Oscan curse. Further investigation showed that the subject had sometime before daydreamed in a library while his eyes rested on a grammer of Oscan which happened to be lying open on the table before him. Quite unconsciously he had absorbed the phrases of Oscan which he had read. Then subsequently in the hypnotic trance these phrases reached expression.[1]

However, in responsive xenoglossy, the subject is able to converse in the foreign language. Thus, if it develops that the subject never learned or was exposed to the language in this life, some paranormal explanation may be in order. Stevenson remarks that "authentic cases of responsive xenoglossy provide for me important evidence of the survival of human personality after death."[2] Either the individual learned the language in a prior life or was subject in this life to the influence of a deceased personality who learned it.

The earliest known case of responsive xenoglossy, he says, is one in the last century: in 1862, Prince Galitzen was conducting a hypnotic experiment upon a poor, unlearned German woman in Hesse, Germany. To his amazement and that of other people present, the woman told in excellent French of a prior life in the eighteenth century, when she lived in Brittany. There, as a woman of high position, she found a new lover and got rid of her husband by throwing him off a cliff. Under hypnosis, she spontaneously admitted that her present life of impoverishment was a result of this murder. Prince Galitzen subsequently went to Brittany and verified the woman's story of her claimed previous life. He also investigated whether, in her present life, she had ever learned French. He discovered that she was uneducated and knew only the German dialect she spoke.

The foregoing case appears in Dr. Stevenson's *Xenoglossy*,[3] his first volume on the subject. The main case in the book concerns the hypnotic regression of a Jewish-American woman conducted by her husband, a medical doctor. During the regression she spoke the Swedish language of 200 years ago. That she could converse in that language was demonstrated in one session attended by Swedish experts who gave written attestations to this remarkable fact. Prior to publishing his book, Dr. Stevenson spent sixteen years investigating this case, and his report on it is over 200 pages. It cannot be adequately summarized or analyzed in this chapter, which is concerned not with regression cases but with the spontaneous manifestations of xenoglossy among children.

EXAMPLES OF XENOGLOSSY AMONG CHILDREN

1. Lynn is a housewife who lives with her husband and daughter in Evanston, Illinois. Her husband Roger works for a large bank in Chicago. One night she and her husband were awakened from sleep by a strange voice coming from their daughter's room. The mother writes,

> We got out of bed and went into her room but found her sleeping quietly.
> We were puzzled and were about to return to our own room when she began

to talk in her sleep. She spoke rapidly in French in an unfamiliar voice. My daughter is only six and has never been outside this country and has never been exposed to anyone who speaks French.

She spoke in French for several nights in a row. Neither I nor my husband has ever had more than an elementary course in French in college, so we had trouble following what she was saying. My husband borrowed a portable tape recorder from his office, and we made a recording of one of her conversations. We brought the recording to the French teacher at our local high school. She listened to it and told us that the little girl on the tape was looking for her mother, whom she had been separated from when her village was attacked by the Germans. She said the little girl seemed to be lost and, judging from her tone of voice, was very distressed.

The mother had not previously accepted reincarnation, but she ended her story saying: "It is my feeling that our daughter lived before in a village in France and probably died in one of the world wars."[4]

2. The following case was told to the writers by friends of a prominent New York physician, Dr. Marshall W. McDuffie, now deceased. To the mystification of Dr. McDuffie and his wife Wilhelmina, their twin baby boys were found to be conversing together in some unknown vernacular. There are other known cases where children speak thus, but it usually develops they have invented a private, primitive language for conversational purposes. However, in this case, the speech seemed more sophisticated. So the puzzled parents eventually brought the boys to the foreign language department of Columbia University, hoping to identify their speech—but without success. By chance, a professor of ancient languages passed by and was amazed to find the children speaking ancient Aramaic! Here we have tiny tots of Scottish descent speaking a Semitic language current at the time of Christ! This disclosure prompted the McDuffies to investigate reincarnation, and they became interested in theosophy.[5]

3. This is a Stevenson case concerning Wijanama, a Sinhalese boy living in Sri Lanka. In the small village where he lived, about fifteen miles north of Kandy, all the inhabitants are Buddhists. When he was four years old, he talked of a previous life in which conditions were very different from those in his village. The former family, he said, ate meat; there was electricity in the house (not available in the village); water came in a pipe, not a well or stream; streets were paved with asphalt. The previous family worshiped in a place that had no idols nor any statues as found in Buddhist temples.

Now, idols are forbidden in Muslim mosques, and many of this child's habits of eating and dress were characteristic of Muslims, not Buddhists. Yet, in the village and surrounding area, there were no Muslims who could have influenced him.

The most remarkable feature of the case was that a year before he began to speak of his former life, he would rouse himself from sleep at some time during the night, sit cross-legged on his bed, and for five minutes chant words in a strange language. Then he would go back to sleep. He continued this practice until he was at least eleven years old when Stevenson last saw him.

The psychiatrist was able to obtain a tape recording of Wijanama's nocturnal mutterings, and this was given to Muslim scholar T. S. Miskin for study. Among the words he identified were *umma* and *vappa*—corrupted Tamil words used by Muslims in Kandy for "mother" and "father." The child could also be heard saying *Allaha*—not *Allah,* the usual way of pronouncing the Arabic word for God. Mr. Miskin was particularly impressed by Wijanama's pronunciation of these words, which he said only a Muslim child could have spoken so well. The child's prayer appeared to be a call to God and to the boy's former parents.

The lad also used Tamil words in daily life, words totally unknown to his family. One was *podung,* when the boy was asked if he had enough to eat, rather than *hari*—the corresponding expression in Sinhalese, the language of Sri Lanka.[6]

4. The well-known actor Melvyn Douglas reported this case at a gathering in Hollywood some years ago.

"Robin Hull was a little fellow, just five years old. He talked well for his age, for the most part. But often his mother noticed him uttering strange sounds. They were, she decided, an unintelligible abracadabra left over from his infancy. However, as time went on and Robin came to speak more and more fluently, she really thought it odd that he should continue uttering these same strange sounds. 'I really don't understand it,' she told her dinner guests one evening. 'Robin really says these sounds as if they had definite meaning to him. Moreover, he repeats many of them so frequently that I have come to recognize them.'

"One of the Hull guests was a woman interested in reincarnation. 'Would you let me come and sit with you in the nursery one afternoon just on the chance Robin might talk this way?' she asked. 'I'd be glad to,' Mrs. Hull told her. So the next afternoon found the two women in the nursery with

Master Hull. He was extremely obliging. He said dozens of strange sounding words. His mother's guest was fascinated. 'I'm sure he is saying real words,' she said, 'words which would mean something to someone . . . if we could only find the right someone. Please let me bring a professor I know. He is familiar with a number of the Asiatic languages.'

"Mrs. Hull agreed to have the professor come, although now she admits that she wished she hadn't mentioned anything about Robin's curious jargon. She didn't relish a lot of people with strange beliefs trooping into his nursery and proceeding to read their own meaning into everything he said.

"A week later her friend came with the professor. Robin talked as usual. He very evidently wasn't at all self-conscious about these strange sounds he made. Finally after more than an hour had passed, they left the nursery. The professor turned to Mrs. Hull. 'The words Robin keeps saying are from a language and dialect used in northern Tibet,' he told her. 'There's no doubt about many of them. Others I do not recognize at all. Was he, by any remote chance, there as a baby? Have you or your husband, or any of your family, or any of your husband's family ever been there?' To all these questions Alice Hull shook her head.

"Then the professor called Robin. 'Where did you learn the words you say?' 'In school,' Robin told him. 'But, Robin dear,' interrupted his mother, 'you've never been to school.' 'When I went to school—before,' said Robin, his little brow furrowed. 'Do you remember what the school looked like?' the professor asked. For a long minute Robin was thoughtful. Then he said, 'Yes, I remember. It was in the mountains. But they weren't the kind of mountains we went to in the summer, mamma.'

" 'Was this school you went to made of wood or of stone?' 'It was stone,' said Robin. 'And tell me, what were the teachers like? Were they ladies or men?' 'They were men.' Robin showed no hesitancy on this score. 'But they didn't dress like you and my daddy. They had skirts, with a sash around their waist that looked like a rope.' And Robin gave a detailed description of the school."

The professor was so impressed with everything the boy said he undertook the long journey—long in those days—to northern Tibet in search of the school. Fortunately, the latter area is close to China and not so difficult of access then as eastern Tibet. Eventually, the Hulls received this letter from him. "I have found the school about which Robin told us. It is in the Kuen-lun mountains, rocky and arid, and, of course, not at all like the mountains where Robin now spends his summers. And it tallies with

Robin's description in every detail. So do the lamas (priests) who teach there."[7]

Readers interested in exploring more elaborate cases of past-language recall may wish to consult Dr. Stevenson's volume *Unlearned Language: New Cases in Xenoglossy*, just published by the University Press of Virginia. One of the cases, that of Sharada, is of sufficient medical interest to have appeared as a clinical and research report by Stevenson in the *American Journal of Psychiatry* (December 1979).

Hypnotic Regression Experiments

No rule is so general, which admits not some exception.

ROBERT BURTON, *Democritus to the Reader*

The following by Dr. Ian Stevenson, appeared in the October 1976, newsletter of the American Society for Psychical Research:

Here is a short statement in reply to the many letters I receive from people who apply to me for hypnotic regression to previous lives; who ask me to recommend a hypnotist; or who request me to investigate some material that has emerged from such experience.

Many persons who attach no importance whatever to their dreams—realizing that most are merely images of the dreamer's subconscious mind without correspondence to any other reality—nevertheless believe that whatever emerges during hypnosis can invariably be taken at face value. In fact, the state of a hypnotized person resembles in many ways—though not in all—that of a person dreaming. The subconscious parts of the mind are released from ordinary inhibitions, and they may then present in dramatic form a new "personality."

If the person has been instructed by the hypnotist—explicitly or implicitly—to "go back to another place and time" or given some similar guidance, the new "personality" may be extremely plausible both to the person having the experience and to others watching him or her.

In fact, however, nearly all such hypnotically evoked "previous personalities" are entirely imaginary, just as are the contents of most dreams. They may include some accurate historical details, but these are usually derived from information the person has acquired normally through reading, radio and television programs, or other sources. He may not remember where he obtained the information, but sometimes this can be brought out in other hypnotic sessions designed to search for the sources of the information used in making up the "previous personality."

However, something of value may emerge, even though very rarely, during experiments with hypnotic regression to previous lives—for example, when the subject proves able to speak a foreign language not normally learned. Instances of this responsive xenoglossy are included in the very small group of reports that I myself might perhaps be interested in investigating.

There are some hazards in this procedure of regression to "previous lives." In a few instances the previous personality has not gone away when instructed to do so, and the subject in such cases has been left in an altered state of personality for several days or longer before restoration of his normal personality.

Among the few cases of hypnotic regression that have interested Dr. Stevenson is the Swedish-speaking case referred to in the last chapter. Another is Bridey Murphy. These, he says, are "exceptional examples."* In both cases the subjects were capable of going into deep hypnosis. "In my opinion," the doctor adds, "it is only in deep hypnosis that subjects can get back to mental contents that may derive from real previous lives. At the more superficial levels of hypnosis the material elicited resembles that of ordinary dreams. . . . Subjects at these levels are likely to talk about imaginary 'previous lives.' "[1]

THE FAMOUS BLOXHAM TAPES

These tapes contain the past-life regressions conducted by a Welshman, Arnell Bloxham, president of the British Society of Hypnotherapists. Several of them were dramatized on a BBC television documentary in 1976 and created a national sensation. Two of these will now be presented, the first being so extraordinary that, prior to its being seen on the BBC, it

---

*To appreciate Dr. Stevenson's conclusion that the Bridey Murphy case is an "exceptional example," one should read the latest edition of The Search for Bridey Murphy by Morey Bernstein, to see how that famous case stands today (New York: Pocket Books, 1978). Bernstein advises the present authors that a new up-to-date edition will be published in 1985 by Doubleday. In the 1950s, the public eventually turned against the case and regarded it as a hoax, owing to the persistent unfair attacks from the Hearst newspapers and the backlash from the religious community.

attracted the attention of Queen Elizabeth's husband, Prince Philip, and his uncle, the late Lord Mountbatten, a great grandson of Queen Victoria. They were instrumental in having the case studied by top naval historians. Lord Mountbatten had been First Lord of the British Navy.

The television producer in the documentary was Jeffrey Iverson, who himself had researched the Bloxham tapes. His book thereon, *More Lives Than One?*[2] appeared simultaneously with the BBC production. It reports eleven of Bloxham's regressions. The foreword, by a noted television historian, Magnus Magnusson, who collaborated in the investigation, explains that they "visited places where these 'regressions' were set. We checked and cross-checked against known or presumed historical facts. We spoke to historians, archaeologists, archivists, psychologists. We dug and we delved, we questioned and we argued."

Over a period of many years, Bloxham recorded in all 400 regressions, and Iverson's first task was to discard those tapes that could not be researched or proven. He wrote:

> To listen to the full collection would take something like a thousand hours—to research them all would take years. But I needn't have worried. The vast majority were of ordinary humdrum lives, stories from the past but incapable of any sort of objective proof. It was interesting that if what the psychiatrists said was true, that the people were fantasizing about themselves, then most were pitching their fantasies modestly and surprisingly low.
>
> Most of the so-called previous lives were in fact so ordinary the hypnotist himself became bored with them long before his twenty years of research was completed. Latterly Bloxham would hypnotise and regress only people in whom he sensed the possibility of an interesting or unusual regression. . . . Some certainly could be fantasies—the mind and imagination deal in both fiction and fact. But it needs only one regression to be "real" for many accepted ideas about life to be turned upside down.[3]

THE GUNNER'S MATE ABOARD THE HMS AGGIE[4]

As to evidence of xenoglossy in the Bloxham tapes, Iverson reports that "perhaps the closest anyone came, in the regressions I have heard, to using a strange tongue was Graham Huxtable as the gunner's mate. Some of his naval slang and archaic phrases he could not understand himself, when he came out of trance, and they made no sense to me—in fact some were wrongly transcribed, until naval historians at Greenwich heard the tape and explained their meaning."

> Bloxham told me that Lord Mountbatten, former First Lord of the Admiralty, had a copy of this tape "on permanent loan." Researchers and the opinions

of some of Britain's finest naval historians dropped into my lap as a result of Earl Mountbatten's interest.

He had been so fascinated by the tape that he had his nephew, Prince Philip, and some other top naval men try to trace the ship in which the "gunner's mate" was serving.

Introducing the story, Iverson writes that "in the HMS *Aggie* regression, an impressed sailor aboard a British frigate two centuries ago tells of a fight with a French ship off Calais." It "is as powerful and bloodcurdling as any dramatic work I have ever heard." The swearing of this "illiterate gunner's mate, with his hacking cough and earthy chuckle, is as far removed as it is possible to imagine from the man under hypnosis, Graham Huxtable, a charming and soft-spoken Swansea man. The voices of the two are not recognizable as that of the same person—the mate has a much deeper tone and a strong South-of-England country accent."

Huxtable had never been to sea nor served in the navy, nor had any interest in such matters. During World War II, he served in the army and was involved in tanks, not naval vessels. As to his regression, he did not visit Bloxham to be hypnotized, but merely to accompany a patient, and then was induced "to go under."

Iverson reports that "several ships' captains and ships have been suggested as possibly matching the captain of the *Aggie* and his vessel but no one can specifically identify the action off the French coast. This is hardly surprising, for in a century of blockades of French ports, chancing upon this one minor incident is truly expecting to find the needle in the naval haystack." However, the naval historian Oliver Warner was convinced of the authenticity of the mate's story "simply by the reality of the conditions described, the man's general attitude and as much by his overall ignorance as by any facts of history he appears to be familiar with."

The regression opens with Huxtable visualizing himself aboard a ship that is "always rolling." The men call the ship *Aggie,* but it has a fancy name he can't recall. The captain's name is Pearce. "What sort of man is he?" asks Bloxham. "He's fond of the cat! Aye, too fond!" Iverson explains that "the cat-o'-nine-tails, a whip with nine lashes, was the standard method of discipline in the British navy."

"So they used to flog the men?" inquires Bloxham. "What do you mean '*used* to flog 'em, they flog 'em now!' " To avoid punishment, he tells his men, "Keep your eyes down boy! Keep your eyes down! Keep 'em in the boat! I learned. . . . Cold, cold." (He appears to be shivering and Bloxham puts a blanket over his body.)

Asked whether Captain Pearce had ever beaten him, the reply was, "No, not me, no, I can lay a gun. Aye, I can lay the sixteen of 'em, aye." In describing the *Aggie,* he said it has thirty-two guns, "sixteen a side. Aye, good guns." Iverson adds, "G. J. Marcus says of the eighteenth century in his naval history—'there was a numerous class of thirty-two-gun frigates.' "

"Have you been in any battles?" asks Bloxham. "Where do you think I got these marks?" came the belligerent reply. "Who did you fight?" "Bloody Frogs! Aye, Frenchies. Bastards!" The mate tells of an occasion when they sank a French boat "with all hands." "Did any of your men get hurt?" "Hurt, aye, hurt—splinters . . . it's when the shot comes in—aye—splinters fly." (Iverson: "Splinters were a main hazard in actions between the wooden warships of the time.")

"What port was that?" "Any port—we done it—we done it before. . . . Up and down, we've done for months—patrol, patrol, patrol—got to keep 'em in, that's what the bosun says." "Which is your favorite port?" "Ports are all the same—taverns and bumboats and stinks." "Does your ship stink?" "Aye, to the wood she stinks. Come up windward of her and you're all right. But she stinks to the wood."

Endeavoring to probe the mate's personal history, Bloxham asks, "Have you got a wife?" "Wife? Wife? Sailors? No, sailors don't 'ave wives—women! When we can get 'em . . . when they lets 'em on, high jinks then, when they do, catch one. Hah, hah." "Catch one, do you?" "Some, some. They're all right for what they are, they'll do. A man's too long afloat and they don't let us off. . . . Not them that's been pressed." Iverson comments,

> The "press" gangs were notorious in the eighteenth century and by law they could "impress" any able-bodied man with experience of the sea between the ages of eighteen and fifty-five. In practice, *they took anyone,* sometimes penetrating miles inland if the need to crew a ship was great enough. In 1770 only one-fifth of Britain's sailors were "volunteers." . . . Even the founder of the Methodist Church, John Wesley, was once a victim of a press gang in that century! And once aboard ship, there was no getting off when the ship was in port. Women were taken in "bumboats" to naval ships in harbor and were allowed aboard for the benefit of the ordinary seamen.

The gunner's mate was proud that he no longer was an impressed seaman, but when asked how he originally was caught, he replied: "They chased me." "What were you doing at the time?" "Was with old Moll."

Bloxham amusingly *mis*understands. "Oh, with a moll were you?" The mate impatiently responds: "Old Moll, old Moll . . . *a mare*! Old Moll, aye, you couldn't keep 'er in the furrow. [Chuckles] Old Moll, she used to pull off all the time." "Were you ploughing?" asked Bloxham. "Ploughin' —saw 'em coming—they were at the other end as well—they got me. . . . That's how I got this burning cold." (Huxtable's dialogue is often halted with a bout of deep coughing.)

"What is your name?" inquired Bloxham. "Don't have names on ships." "What was your name before you came aboard?" "When I were a boy— Ben." "What are you to look at, dark or fair?" "Dirty." "Are you short, short and fat?" "Not fat! Not fat on this ship! Don't get fat on weevils . . . worms and weevils and worms. Worms in the water tank too." (Iverson: "The provisioning of ships was usually appalling during the eighteenth century. Worms were commonplace in food and water.")

"Who is the monarch, who is king?" "King, king! Him! [rolling words contemptuously] German George." (Iverson: "For over a century, from 1714 until 1820, all the kings of England were called George and might have been referred to mockingly and for various reasons as 'German George,' as they were either born in Germany or of German descent.")

"What is the most exciting battle you've been in?" "Excitin'? hmm— lads ask questions like that." "What do you usually tell them?" "It's not excitin', lad, you'll be frightened. . . . They'll be frightened—like I were. They'll learn, they'll learn."

The *Aggie* tape now approaches its climax. Iverson writes:

> As if excited, perhaps by the proximity of battle, Huxtable's voice be-
> comes louder and more confident. Sometimes, he describes [to Bloxham]
> what is happening; at other times, he calls out his order to the gun crews,
> and sometimes he mimics orders he hears. . . .
>
> The matches he refers to were lengths of rope soaked in tar and lit to
> provide the sparks by which the guns were fired. It has been thought likely
> that sailors *blew on the spark* to keep it alight, but the method described
> here of *swinging the match* seems more sensible and likely. A watchful
> gunner's mate could quickly see who was neglecting that vital spark, by
> watching the swing of an arm.

"Do you know what port you're waiting outside?" asks Bloxham. "It is [pause] Calais, Calais, Calais." "Have you come out of Dover?" "Out of the Sound we came this time, out of the Sound." "Plymouth Sound?" "Aye, we've been out a month, a month or more." He breaks off with

Bloxham, to shout back an answer to some command he has heard. "Aye aye, sir! Aye aye, ready sir! [softly] You bastard!"

"Who gave you the order? The captain?" "The gunner, the lieutenant." "Do you know his name?" "Guns—Jolly Guns. [chuckles grimly] He's a jolly man I don't think!" Ignoring Bloxham, the mate shouts a command: "Swing that match, boy, swing it—keep it alight!"

"Is your ship yawing a bit?" "Ah, she's just holding, just holding, holding up against the wind . . . in close—can hear the breakers now." "Can you?" comments Bloxham, "That's a bit too close." "Ah, we're close in. Ah, Pearce does this, he does this. He lays in close and waits. . . . They say he can smell the sand. [pause] Ah God, wish they'd come."

Bloxham instructs his subject: "Now this is a bit later, is the enemy leaving his anchorage?" Answer: "He's still not coming—not much mist now! Not much mist now. We'll be clear—in five minutes we'll be clear." The ship appears, and the mate is busy giving orders, getting the men ready behind their cannons.

"Have you fired your cannon?" "Waiting, waiting! Waiting for the order—steady, lads, steady—now hold it, hold it, hold it, wait for the order, wait for it—swing those matches, aye, siree—stand clear from behind."

Then the order comes, and the mate yells: "NOW you fool. *Now up,* fool, now. NOW! [screams in exultation as the shot is fired] Well done, lads—run 'em up, run 'em up, get 'em up, get 'em up—get 'em up the front—[shrieks] pull that man out, pull 'im out—send him in the cockpit . . . get up there—get on the chocks there—run them up again."

Another series of shots is fired. "Again, lads—you had him then—hurry, men—by God you bastard—got him that aim—that's the way to lay a gun."

And then their ship is hit by the French. "My Christ, they've got old Pearce, they've got Pearce. [sudden terrible screaming] MY BLOODY LEG [screaming and moaning uncontrollably] MY LEG—MY LEG!"

Iverson tells us, "With some difficulty, Bloxham who appears to be slapping Huxtable's face, manages to bring him out of the trance and reassures him that his leg is still in one piece. Both men are clearly shaken by the experience."

This portion of the Huxtable tape was heard by the present writers when they were in England at the Wrekin Trust Conference on Reincarnation. The tape was played by Iverson who was one of the speakers. For the audience it was a shattering experience to hear Huxtable's prolonged pitiful screaming when he felt his leg was shot off.

"The *Aggie* is certainly the most dramatic tape in Bloxham's collection," Iverson reports in his book. "The gunner's mate, with every word he utters, his coughing and cursing, reeks of the sea and his own time. He has a credible personality, displayed in chuckling affection for his lost youth as a ploughboy with 'old Moll,' to his sour acceptance of life at sea. His pride in being able to 'lay a gun' is well founded, as naval experts who have heard the tape have verified."

MASSACRE IN TWELFTH-CENTURY BRITAIN[5]

A Welsh housewife, Jane Evans, visited Arnell Bloxham for health reasons—a chronic rheumatic condition. When he inquired about her interests, she spoke of a fascination for Greece and Tibet. This prompted him to regress her, but during six sessions not a word emerged about Greece or Tibet! It was her regression as a twelfth-century Jewess in York, a place she had never visited, that was repeated on the BBC television program.

Her name in that life was Rebecca. As the story unfolds, she speaks of the uprisings against the Jews in Chester, Lincoln, and London, and how worried they are in York of the uprisings soon spreading there. The date is the year 1189. She tells of a representative of the pope, a man named Massotti, being in York to obtain recruits to join the crusades in the Holy Land and fight the infidels. "And when he said 'take up your arms against the infidels,' the people in the crowd said 'what about the infidels in York, all Jews are infidels.' And we are frightened, we are frightened. My husband has sent money out of York to our uncle in Lincoln in case something terrible happens. King Henry is good to us, but King Henry is getting old—where would we be if it were anyone but Henry?" Rebecca also refers to him as King Henry Plantagenet. "He helps us when we have to take our cases to the courts for the money that is owed us. In return we give him ten parts of the money that we gather back."

(Iverson: "This seems to present a quite accurate picture of King Henry of the House of Plantagenet and his relations with the Jews. They were certainly given protection in his courts and it is known that the king exacted a payment for this. But Rebecca is speaking of the year of Henry's death and already forces are built up within this medieval society that will soon have a tragic consequence for the Jews of York.")

The reference to "sending money to our uncle in Lincoln" appears authentic, according to Professor Barrie Dobson of York University, an authority on Jewish history of this period. There were close ties between the Jewish communities of York and Lincoln.

King Henry dies, and Richard the Lion-Hearted ascends the throne but immediately goes off to the crusades. Rebecca bemoans: "Now that good King Henry has died, King Richard is away, who is going to help us now? I hear whispers about what has happened to some Jews. An old Jew called Isaac in Coney Street, he was murdered—he was murdered. Before they murdered him they made him eat pork and they poured holy water on his head and then they murdered him. And we are frightened of what they will do to us and our children. We will have to leave." (Iverson: "It is known, too, there was a murder of a Jew living in Coney Street, but there is no detail," as Rebecca gives it.)

Rebecca speaks of one man that especially hates them. His name is Mabelise. (Iverson: "Here Rebecca appears to be talking about a man labelled by chroniclers at the time of the York Massacre as 'the arch-conspirator against the Jews'—one Richard Malebisse, a name almost identical with Rebecca's 'Mabelise' . . . a hated nobleman, referred to by the medieval chronicler, William of Newburgh, as 'Richard rightly called Mala Bestia' or 'evil beast.' ")

Bloxham progresses Jane to the time of the massacre and inquires, "Did you have to leave?" "Yes. Yes we all had to go. [The mobs] came to the house of Benjamin next to us and we could hear the screams and smell the smoke. My husband and our son are carrying money on their backs in sacks—we had to go—we fled. [pause] We wanted to go [for shelter] to the castle but they were pursuing us so my husband slit a sack of silver and let it pour into the road so the people pursuing us would stop pursuing us and pick up the silver so that we could get a bit ahead of them. . . . But when we got to the castle, they wouldn't let us in." (Many Jews had managed to get into the castle, but Rebecca and her family were too late.) "We took shelter in a Christian Church, just a small church, outside the gates of York," but close to the castle. Bloxham asks whether this is the Cathedral of York, and she answers, "No, no—just a small church outside the gates of York, outside the big copper gate, the big copper gate of York.

"We are hiding. We are cold. We are hungry . . . and we're hoping that they won't think we're there. . . . They hate us because we do not believe in their beliefs." (Voice full of stress, and in a desperate situation she casts around for a crumb of comfort and debates aloud the possibilities.) "But we are in their church and God's house is still God's house—but if they find us here they will surely kill us."

Her voice resumes in increasing agitation and hysteria. Her daughter,

"Rachel is crying—my husband has gone to see if he can find food for us—he's gone to see if he can get food and my son has gone with him. . . . We can hear the screaming and the shouting and the crying—'burn the Jews, burn the Jews, burn the Jews.' [pause] Where is Joseph? Why doesn't he come back, why doesn't he come back? [pause then almost screams] Oh God—they're coming—they—they are coming—Rachel's crying—don't cry—don't cry—don't cry. Aah, they've entered the church—we can hear them—they've entered the church . . . they're coming—they're coming . . . they're coming down."

(Her voice is almost incoherent with terror.) "Oh not—not not not Rachel! No don't take her—don't, stop—they're going to kill her—they—don't—not Rachel, no, no, no, no—not Rachel—oh, don't take Rachel—no, don't take Rachel—no, no, no, no, no, don't take Rachel—no. [grief-stricken voice] They've taken Rachel—they've taken Rachel."

"Are you all right?" Bloxham asks. "They have left you alone, have they?" "Dark . . . dark," are her last words. The subject is then awakened.

*

What proved significant about the Rebecca regression was that it did not revolve around the best known historical facts about the massacre—the unfolding drama in the castle, where the Jews were temporarily sheltered from the howling mobs. As Iverson points out,

> Rebecca knew nothing of the actions taken by the Sheriff and the Constable of the Castle, nor of the [false] promises of safe conduct and the final scenes of murder. This ignorance is perhaps quite natural if Rebecca is viewed as a genuine eye-witness with an inevitably limited knowledge of *overall* events during the riots. If we view her regression as a fantasy based on a reading of history books, it is perhaps strange she should have omitted to fantasize about the best known features of most textbook versions of the massacre. If Rebecca had claimed to have been murdered with the others in the castle, her story would have been historically almost irrefutable.

Yet, he adds—and this is the most impressive part of the whole regression—"her version was ultimately all the more impressive for being made plausible only by a curious workman's accidental discovery in an ancient church." It will be recalled that she said her family had taken refuge in the crypt of a small church. The snag here is that none of the old churches in York—and there were forty at that time—had underground crypts save the big Cathedral of York, and Rebecca specifically said they were not hiding there. Professor Dobson was certain that the small church outside the "copper gates" of York could only have been St. Mary's, Castlegate. Yet when Professor Dobson and Iverson visited it, there definitely was no crypt. However, six months later the professor informed Iverson of a new development. The church was now being converted into a museum. He wrote,

> In September, during the renovation of the church, a workman certainly found something that seems to have been a crypt—very rare in York except for the Minster—under the chancel of that church. It was blocked up immediately and before the York archaeologists could investigate it properly. But the workman who looked inside said he had seen round stone arches and vaults. . . .
>
> So, if one wanted to carry this argument to a conclusion, this crypt could be the place where, if you believe her story, Rebecca met her doom. More certainly still, the further discovery of re-used Roman and Anglo-Saxon columns and masonry this summer below the present floor level in St. Mary's, makes it absolutely clear there was a church on the site in Rebecca's time.

Hazards of Past-Life Hypnotic Regressions.   Both the regressions discussed in this chapter had undesirable repercussions upon the subjects involved. The cannon shot that destroyed the seaman's leg shook Graham Huxtable up to such a degree, he never returned for another hypnotic session. Then there was the experience of Jane Evans as Rebecca while another of her lives—the most recent in time—was painful and unpleasant. There she saw herself as an American nun, Sister Grace, in a remote convent in Des Moines, Iowa. (Jane was never in the United States.) She lived a sad, misfit, religious life, ignorant of events in the outside world, full of doubts and imaginary sins, eating too much, and singing tunelessly— the other nuns said. The regression ends with a scene at the close of the nun's life. Bloxham asks, "How old are you now?"

"Sixty—sixties—very crippled—terrible pain—terrible pain in my stomach. It seems to be eating me away—I try and smile and laugh but it's a terrible pain—terrible pain." She was in so much discomfort that the hypnotist ended the session.

After Jane's experience as Rebecca, she walked out of Bloxham's consulting room and fainted. For days she felt sick, confessed to being frightened by it all, and refused to do any more. Five years later, she reluctantly consented to repeat two of the regressions on television, on the conditions that a pseudonym (Jane Evans) would be used and no camera shot of her face would be shown.

American television shows also feature hypnotic regressions. One repeated many times was seen on David Susskind's program in 1977 wherein two strangers from the audience volunteered as subjects. One, a man, was taken back to a Roman life where he was a weak king who murdered his wife's mother. He relived being pursued by an angry mob who stoned him to death. As he related this in gasping voice, his face and body writhed in excruciating torture. In the other case, that of a woman, two lives were relived, one of a prostitute in a wild and woolly western town, another in a similar setting where, as a young girl, she was trapped in a slowly rising flood that inexorably swept on to drown her. Her pitiful screams for her mother presented a nerve-wracking experience for the viewers.

One does not have to be a psychiatrist to understand that hypnotically inducing someone to reenact these dreadful tragedies could be an irresponsible tampering with the subject's psyche. Granting the possibility of reincarnation, it appears to be nature's great kindness that, before birth, she draws the curtain between the past and present. Or, as the Greeks said, the soul passes through the river of forgetfulness. Dr. Stevenson reports that a marked and therapeutic modification of psychological disorders, "even a dramatic improvement," can sometimes arise from these regressions, but they can also cause "a worsening of a symptom."[6] Thus no hypnotherapist can guarantee that a subject will not have "a bad trip," despite the posthypnotic suggestion given that no detrimental effects will ensue when the person wakes.

8
Near-Death and Beyond-Death Encounters

There are some odd things about human dying, anyway, that don't fit at all with the notion of agony at the end. People who almost die but don't, and then recover to describe the experience, never mention anguish or pain, or even despair; to the contrary they recall a strange feeling of tranquility and peace. We might be learning more about this. Something is probably going on that we don't yet know about.

LEWIS THOMAS, *New England Journal of Medicine*, June 1977

The above observations are reminiscent of some passages in Dr. Thomas's classic work, *The Lives of a Cell*. The dying, he learned from experience with patients, accept death serenely, without fear. Most of his patients "appeared to be preparing themselves with equanimity for death, as though intuitively familiar with the business." He then expresses surprise at his own feeling that "dying is an all right thing to do." Death, he concluded, is not evil but natural. And now, for him, there comes a logical question.

But even so, if the transformation is a coordinated, integrated physiologic process in its initial, local stages, there is still that permanent vanishing of consciousness to be accounted for. Are we to be stuck forever with this problem? Where on earth does it go? Is it simply stopped dead in its tracks, lost in humus, wasted? Considering the tendency in nature to find uses for complex and intricate mechanisms, this seems to me unnatural. I prefer to think of it as somehow separated off at the filaments of its attachment, and then drawn like an easy breath back into the membrane of its origin, a fresh memory for a biospherical nervous system, but I have no data on the matter.[1]

The foregoing was written in the early 1970s. Since then, has there been any data on the matter? The general public is likely to answer yes, for they have read numerous testimonials of people pronounced clinically dead (heart stopped, breathing stopped, all vital signs gone) who experienced life beyond death. Owing to modern resuscitation techniques, they lived to tell the tale.

Most doctors, however, were dubious about the conclusions being drawn from these experiences. Among them was cardiologist Michael Sabom. When, in 1976, he read the internationally famous *Life After Life* by Raymond Moody, M.D., the kindest thing he could say about it was, "I don't believe it." His philosophy had been: "With death you are dead, and that is the end of it."

> I identified these experiences as part of "some new mind trip" designed to titillate the imagination of the public and the media. And titillate it did: personal testimonials of others claiming similar "afterlife voyages" became commonplace in newspapers and magazines; headlines on popular tabloids regularly announced that "proof" of life after death had finally arrived. . . . Dozens of books were published to cash in on the lucrative sensationalism of the subject.

At this time, it happened that a church group approached Dr. Sabom to participate as a medical consultant in a program on Dr. Moody's book. Reluctantly agreeing, he prepared for the program by making a brief survey of patients in his hospital who had a near-death crisis following a cardiac arrest. Thus he could document his negative views of this phenomenon—if he found such patients. The third patient he interviewed was a middle-aged housewife from Tampa.

> As soon as she was convinced that I was not an underground psychiatrist posing as a cardiologist, she began describing the first near-death experience I had heard in my medical career. To my utter amazement, the details matched the descriptions in *Life After Life* (although she never heard of the book). I was even more impressed by her sincerity and the deep personal significance her experience had had for her. At the conclusion of the interview, I had the distinct feeling that what this woman had shared with me that night was a deeply personal glimpse into an aspect of medicine of which I knew nothing.

Dr. Sabom then embarked upon a rigorous scientific investigation of these experiences, probing every alternate explanation that could reveal the answer lay not in the religious interpretation but in physiological, pharmacologic, and psychological facts.* He was in an excellent position to do this, having daily access to hospital patients and the complete records of their cases. He had participated himself in the revival of numerous cardiac arrests.

Five years later, the results of his investigations appeared in his book, *Recollections of Death, a Medical Investigation,* published by Harper & Row. The front jacket read: "Striking new clinical evidence, having crucial implications for our understanding of the near-death experience, presented by a noted cardiologist and professor of medicine." He has since spoken before many medical groups and appeared on numerous television programs. All the quotes from Dr. Sabom in this chapter are from his book.

His book largely supports the findings of Dr. Moody. *Time* magazine, in a full page review of Sabom's book, quotes him as saying that, after reading Moody's works, "5 years and 116 interviews later, I am convinced that my original suspicions were wrong" (February 8, 1982).

Thus he was able to write, in the *Journal of the American Medical Association,* in answer to an article by Dr. Richard Blacher, who argued that the near-death experiences were mere fantasy: "Dr. Blacher points out that 'the physician must be especially wary of accepting religious belief as scientific data.' I might add that equal caution should be exercised in accepting scientific belief as scientific data" (June 4, 1980).

*

Before presenting case histories—several of which involve reincarnation—we will review the scientific investigations in this field. Then, alternate theories for explaining the phenomena—now widely known by the initials NDE (near-death experiences)—will be offered. Later, the possible relationship between NDEs and being reborn in another body will be discussed, for, if it is a fact that near-death survivors provide accurate out-of-body experiences, then there is evidence that the real individual is not his or her body. In theory, at least, if such persons can return to their old body, they may have the power to incarnate in other bodies as well.

---

*Dr. Sabom writes: "If there was any bias on my part during the first year or so of the study, it was weighted toward a disbelief in the validity of these near-death reports. (I was recently reminded of this fact by a patient I interviewed early in the study. She spontaneously remarked during a conversation we had four years later, 'You seemed to be out to mainly disprove the experience as much as anything when I talked with you the first time.')"

At the outset, it should be emphasized that doctors Sabom and Moody have not been alone in their investigations of the NDEs. Dr. Sabom reports in his book:

> Dr. Kenneth Ring, a professor of psychology at the University of Connecticut, is currently investigating the NDE and has recently published many of his findings in a book *Life at Death: A Scientific Investigation of the Near Death Experience*. Another study is being conducted by John Audette and several physicians in East Peoria, Illinois. The NDE is also being investigated at the University of Michigan, University of Iowa, the University of Virginia, Western New Mexico University, the University of California at Berkeley, Seattle Pacific University, and in Denver, Colorado, by Fred Schoonmaker, M.D.

The latter doctor is director of Cardiovascular Services at Denver's St. Luke's Hospital. Over the past twenty years, Dr. Schoonmaker has amassed medical records and case histories of over 2,300 patients who came close to death. Of these, more than 1,400 reported having near-death encounters.[2] An International Association for Near-Death Studies, based at the University of Connecticut, has now been formed. Recently it sponsored a symposium at Yale Medical School (May 1982).*

An esteemed cardiologist, Dr. George E. Burch, past president of the American College of Cardiology and editor of the *American Heart Journal*, writes, "If one considers death as a continuum or as a process, then certainly these patients who have been resuscitated after several minutes of absent heart action have experienced and retrieved psychic information from as deep within this continuum as is possible."[3]

*

Just what are these experiences? And are they only psychic, or objective as well?

In his chapter, "The Experience of Dying," in *Life After Life,* Dr. Moody writes,

> Despite the wide variation in the circumstances surrounding close calls with death and in the types of persons undergoing them, it remains true that

---

*Earlier studies were made by Dr. Karlis Osis. In 1959 he sent 5,000 physicians and 5,000 nurses questionnaires regarding deathbed visions of their patients. The replies were followed by interviews with the respondents. The results were reported by Dr. Osis and an associate in *At the Hour of Death* (New York: Avon Books, 1977), based on research of over 1,000 afterlife experiences. They support the later findings of Dr. Moody.

there is a striking similarity among the accounts of the experiences themselves. In fact, the similarities among various reports are so great that one can easily pick out about fifteen separate elements which recur again and again in the mass of narratives that I have collected. On the basis of these points of likeness, let me now construct a brief, theoretically "ideal" or "complete" experience which embodies all of the common elements, in order in which it is typical for them to occur. [The italics are Dr. Moody's.]

A man is dying and, as he reaches the point of greatest physical distress, he hears himself pronounced dead by his doctor. He begins to hear an uncomfortable noise, a loud ringing or buzzing, and at the same time feels himself moving very rapidly through a long dark tunnel. After this, he suddenly finds himself outside of his own physical body, but still in the immediate physical environment, and he sees his own body from a distance, as though he is a spectator. He watches the resuscitation attempt from this unusual vantage point and is in a state of emotional upheaval.

After a while, he collects himself and becomes more accustomed to his odd condition. He notices that he still has a "body," but one of a very different nature and with very different powers from the physical body he has left behind. Soon other things begin to happen. Others come to meet and to help him. He glimpses the spirits of relatives and friends who have already died, and a loving, warm spirit of a kind he has never encountered before—a being of light—appears before him. This being asks him a question, nonverbally, to make him evaluate his life and helps him along by showing him a panoramic, instantaneous playback of the major events of his life. At some point he finds himself approaching some sort of barrier or border, apparently representing the limit between earthly life and the next life. Yet, he finds that he must go back to the earth, that the time for his death has not yet come. At this point he resists, for by now he is taken up with his experiences in the afterlife and does not want to return. He is overwhelmed by intense feelings of joy, love, and peace. Despite his attitude, though, he somehow reunites with his physical body and lives.

Later he tries to tell others, but he has trouble doing so. In the first place, he can find no human words adequate to describe these unearthly episodes. He also finds that others scoff, so he stops telling other people. Still, the experience affects his life profoundly, especially his views about death and its relationship to life.*[4]

---

*Based on the 1981 Gallup poll on religion in the U.S., George Gallup, Jr., reports in his book *Adventures in Immortality* that 2 million Americans described an out-of-body experience in connection with a near death; 1.2 million adults perceived the bright-light phenomenon mentioned above; and 2.7 million experienced a highly compressed reexamination of their lives, or "death" review.

Of all these elements composing the near-death experience, Dr. Moody discovered that the one that had "the most profound effect upon the individual" was the encounter with the "Being of Light." "The love and warmth which emanate from this being to the dying person are utterly beyond words, and the person feels completely surrounded by it and taken up in it, completely at ease and accepted in the presence of this being."

AUTOSCOPIC OR OUT-OF-BODY EXPERIENCES

All the foregoing elements in the NDEs were investigated by Dr. Sabom, but his chief focus was the autoscopic visions of patients and ascertaining how accurate these reports were, by checking them against hospital records. Where records were available, he found that "the details of these perceptions were found to be accurate in all instances." In the book, detailed comparisons are given between hospital reports and the NDEs in individual cases. Elaborating on the experiences as a whole, the doctor reports:

> All persons in this study who related an NDE described it as if it had taken place outside their physical body. They felt the "essential" part of themselves had separated from the physical, and that this part was able to perceive objects and events visually. During the NDE, the "separated self" became the sole "conscious" identity of the person, with the physical body remaining behind as an "empty shell." . . .
> During the autoscopic experience, the "self" which had "separated" from the unconscious physical body was perceived to be situated above the level of the physical body—a point specifically identified as "ceiling height" in all but three cases.

In these three cases, the height was described as 60 feet by one man, 150 feet by another, and by an army colonel, as if he were "flying high over Womack so that I was looking down into the intensive care unit where they had taken my body."

Beyond the autoscopic episodes, forty-one of Sabom's cases experienced what he calls the "transcendental NDE" because they transcend or surpass our earthly limits into realms no present-day scientific investigation can penetrate.

The reaction of the patients who had out-of-body experiences was enormous. In most cases, they no longer wondered whether they could survive death. They said they *know* they can survive, because they have experienced their consciousness existing outside of their physical body.

Sabom found that of those having NDEs in his study, 15 percent had been agnostics with no belief whatever in a hereafter, but they now accepted it as a reality. Also he discovered that many of his subjects had previously snickered and laughed at stories they heard of people having NDEs. Thus, with these people, it was only "seeing is believing" that could *convince* them. Hence it is understandable that skeptical doctors and scientists who have no personal experience of such events themselves, or have not investigated the phenomena, have been busy at work finding alternate explanations for the NDEs.

ALTERNATE EXPLANATIONS

Dreams and Fancies.   Dreams, as well known, are infinitely varied in nature. If the NDE is merely a dream, investigators ask, why is its basic pattern of unfoldment so consistently uniform. The details are unique to each subject, but the core experience is fundamentally the same. Furthermore, the subjects insist again and again that, during their out-of-body experience, they are acutely alert and fully awake. To quote two of Dr. Sabom's subjects: (a) "I've had a lot of dreams and it wasn't like any dream that I had had. It was real. It was so real. And that peace, the peace made the difference from a dream, and I dream a lot." (b) My NDE was "realer than here, really. After that the world seemed like a mockery to real life—make-believe. Like people playing games. Like we're getting prepared for something but we don't know what."

When the subjects are faced with a choice whether to return to earth-life, they claim their thinking is clear and sharp, governed by rational not emotional considerations. They longed for a final release, but knew they had obligations to fulfill here, children to care for, etc. Another point is that most dreams are ephemeral, and their effect is soon dissipated, rarely making a deep impression. But the NDE experience is so overwhelming that it affects the individual's whole life, changing his or her behavior and modes of living. And those who have experienced NDEs lose all fear of death. Many consider it the peak experience of their life.

Drug-Induced Delusions or Hallucinations.   Dr. Kenneth Ring, in his aforementioned book, reports that one of his subjects was "a psychiatrist . . . who, accordingly, should know something about both dreams and hallucinations. She told me without qualification that, in her opinion, her own experience was neither the one nor the other."[5] Dr. Sabom writes: "Medical studies of the content and structure of drug-induced hallucinations have found these experiences to be highly variable and idiosyncratic. The administration of narcotics for either medicinal or illicit purposes can be associated with a 'high' of euphoria and bliss or a 'bad trip' of terrify-

ing distorted perceptions. . . . The NDE, on the other hand, is characterized by a clarity of thought and 'visual' perception."

Educated Guesses. Was it possible that some chronic cardiac patients
who had NDEs were simply familiar enough with cardiopulmonary resusci-
tations from viewing television to fantasize accurately about what took
place? Sabom conducted a control experiment on this. He asked twenty-
five longtime heart patients who never had an NDE to describe such
procedures. Twenty made major errors, such as saying mouth-to-mouth
resuscitation was used—which is never necessary in hospitals with their
sophisticated equipment. Two could not remember at all, and three made
correct but very superficial descriptions lacking details. However, those
claiming out-of-body visualizations were surprisingly correct in their
observations, and "these autoscopic details" says Sabom, are "fairly specific for the actual resuscitation being described and are not interchange-
able with the clinical circumstances of other near-death crisis events."

Subjects Relive Their Birth Experience. The tunnel and the Being-of-
Light experience is explained by some critics in this way. The dying
person, fearing death, regresses to the time of birth, the tunnel being the
passing through the mother's genital passage. And the light? Nothing more
than the high intensity floodlights in the delivery room! Yet, as the world-
renowned obstetrician Frederick Leboyer points out in his revolutionary
book *Birth Without Violence,* to the newborn child, opening its acutely
sensitive eyes to those lights is an occasion for tortuous pain. "The infant
howls. And why should this surprise us? Its eyes have just been burned. . . .
They say a newborn child is blind? No, it is blinded."[6] And this traumatic
experience is recalled by the dying person as a joyous, healing encounter
with a wondrous luminous Being?

Depersonalization. The theory here is well explained by Dr. Ring in his
book.

> The phenomena associated with the prospect of impending death, such as a
> sense of peace and well-being, feelings of bodily detachment, a panoramic
> life review, and mystical transcendence are all to be understood as ego-
> defensive maneuvers to insulate the individual from the harsh realities of
> imminent annihilation by providing a cocoon of compensatory fantasies and
> feelings. In other words, the perception of death results not in physical
> ejection from one's body, but in psychological detachment from one's
> (apparent) fate.

This would be an excellent theory except that no sense of psychological detachment can explain actual out-of-body experiences that accurately report what is going on when the subject is clinically dead.

Dr. Sabom points out further that, in a number of his cases, the person had an NDE when he was unaware that he was in danger and hence had no time to set up ego defenses.

Cerebral Hypoxia or Cerebral Hypercarbia. This theory gives the cause of NDE as either a low oxygen level in the brain or high levels of carbon dioxide. Obviously, if a subject has just "died," the blood stops feeding oxygen into the brain. Also the carbon dioxide already there cannot be released. Dr. Sabom reports on experiments where the level of oxygen was slowly withdrawn from volunteer subjects. "The person's mental and physical abilities became progressively impaired until convulsions occurred and respiration ceased. No experiences resembling an NDE were reported." Experiments with elevated levels of carbon dioxide have produced experiences strongly resembling the NDE, but at the same time very different. The subjects have frightening perceptions of shapeless and objectless horror. They have compulsions to solve mathematical puzzles and do other odd things. They demonstrate signs of extreme neurological dysfunction: "The pupils became rigid, the eyes roll upward." Tonic seizures ensue, "followed by stupor for one to two minutes" after the experiment.

In considering this alternate theory, it is important to bear in mind what Dr. Moody explained in the sequel to *Life After Life*. "I have emphasized from the beginning that I have dealt with some near-death experiences in which no apparent clinical death took place, and that these contain many of the same features as those in which there was such a 'death.' " Thus "all the phenomena alluded to—the noise, the panoramic memory, and the light—have been experienced in the course of near-death encounters in which this cut-off of blood flow to the brain never took place."[7]

Let us bear in mind all these alternate explanations as we turn to a few case histories:

NEAR-DEATH
AND OUT-OF-BODY
EXPERIENCES

THE EXTRAORDINARY CASE OF PRIVATE GEORGE RITCHIE

• The near-death experience of George Ritchie—now a physician and a psychiatrist—so amazed another doctor and subsequent psychiatrist, Raymond Moody, that the latter undertook a five-year investigation of such cases. So it was that Moody's *Life After Life,* with a readership now in the millions, first alerted the Western world that such strange things occur. Moody's book is dedicated to Dr. Ritchie. In the motion picture *Beyond and Back,* this case was the main feature.

At the age of twenty, Ritchie, a medical student, decided to forego temporarily his dream of becoming a doctor and enlist in the army. He had been a brilliant student and, except for a man named Hitler, would likely have been the youngest doctor to graduate from the Medical College of Virginia. After the war, he did complete his medical studies. He later became president of the Richmond Academy of General Practice and then went into psychiatry, eventually becoming chairman of the department of psychiatry at Towers Hospital in Charlottesville, which later became affiliated with the University of Virginia in that city. He now carries on a private practice in Richmond. He is also president-founder of the Universal Youth Corps.

Our report is based on Dr. Ritchie's book *Return from Tomorrow* and on one of his tape-recorded talks, which provides details not in the book.[8]

While in training as a private at Camp Barkeley in Texas, Ritchie soon became depressingly disabused of the value of foot soldiers in a modern mechanized war. He was consequently ecstatic when, owing to the army's need for doctors, he was ordered to the Medical College of Virginia to complete his studies. However, on the eve of his return he came down with double lobar pneumonia. The miracle drug penicillin was then not available. His condition worsened, and the ward boy making the hospital rounds found him dead. Confirming this, the medical officer ordered the attendant—when he finished his duties—to prepare the body for the morgue. And it was during this nine-minute interval that the major portion of this incredible experience occurred.

Dr. Donald G. Francy, chief medical officer at Camp Barkeley, called Ritchie's recovery "the most amazing medical case I have ever encountered." In a notarized statement he wrote: "Private George Ritchie's . . . virtual call from death and return to vigorous health has to be explained in terms of other than natural means."[9] It is one thing for a cardiac arrest case to be revived, but in a death from pneumonia the body is so toxic and deteriorating that a successful resuscitation is practically impossible. Furthermore, Ritchie was "dead" for nine minutes or more and there should have been irreparable brain damage.

Now, at an undetermined time *before* Ritchie was officially discovered to be dead, it appears he became mentally conscious in a separated intangible body and found himself in a tiny room where he had apparently been moved when his condition became grave. The time was around midnight. His first thought was that he must catch that early morning bus in order to return to the medical school in Richmond for the new session. Strange! Where were his clothes? He searched everywhere in that tiny room. Ah, maybe they are under the bed. "I turned around, then froze. Someone was lying in that bed. I took a step closer. He was quite a young man, with short brown hair, lying very still. But . . . the thing was impossible! I myself had just gotten out of that bed! For a moment I wrestled with the mystery of it. It was too strange to think about—and anyway I didn't have time."

Frantically searching for the ward boy to get his clothes, Ritchie saw a sergeant in the corridor and sought his help. But the man neither saw him, nor heard him speak, and would have walked right through his "body" if Ritchie had not quickly jumped aside.

Consumed by his overwhelming desire to return to school, Ritchie found himself outside the hospital, and then he took off with enormous speed flying northward to Richmond. As he traveled, he wondered if he was really going in the right direction.

> An extremely broad river was below me now. There was a long, high bridge, and on the far bank the largest city I had come to yet. I wished I could go down there and find someone who could give me directions.
>
> Almost immediately I noticed myself slowing down. Just below me now, where two streets came together, I caught a flickering blue glow. It came from a neon sign over the door of a red-roofed one-story building with a "Pabst Blue Ribbon Beer" sign propped in the front window. "Cafe," the jittering letters over the door read. . . .
>
> Down the sidewalk toward the all-night cafe a man came briskly walking . . . I fell into step beside him. "Can you tell me, please, what city this is?" He kept right on walking. . . . We reached the cafe and he turned, reaching for the door handle. Was the fellow deaf? I put out my left hand to tap his shoulder. There was nothing there. It had been like touching thin air. And yet I had distinctly seen him, even to the beginnings of a black stubble on his chin where he needed a shave.

Ritchie pondering his plight, leaned against the guy wire of a nearby telephone pole, and went right through it.

Before relating what happened next, we report that a year later Ritchie accidentally discovered the name of the city. He was returning to duty at

Camp Barkeley before leaving for Europe. Ritchie with other medical students traveled by car to the camp. On the third day, they reached Mississippi, a state he had never visited. Arriving at the outskirts of Vicksburg, he writes that "something about the layout of this town seemed strangely, impossibly, familiar: I knew exactly how the shoreline would look around the next curve. How the streets would intersect. There! Just as I'd known they would! And all at once I knew for sure that straight ahead on that very street we would come in a few blocks to a white frame building with a red roof and the word 'Cafe' in neon letters over the door." As the car approached, he saw the cafe and "the sidewalk where I walked beside a man who could not see me. There was the telephone pole where I had stood so long . . . how long? In what kind of time and what kind of body?"

In Ritchie's out-of-body dilemma, he now saw the futility of going on to Richmond—nobody would see him or hear him. "What if I got home and even my own family couldn't see me? A terrifying loneliness swept over me. Somehow, some way I had to get back that solidness that other people saw and responded to." And then he thought of that body he saw lying so very still in his hospital bed. So back to the hospital he sped.

On arrival, he frenziedly sought to find his body in one of the 200 hospital barrack rooms where 5,000 GI's were sleeping. (There were 250,000 men in training at Camp Barkeley.) In the dim light, he could barely see their faces. Hours seemed to transpire as he raced madly in and out of rooms. And then he remembered! He had a Phi Gamma Delta fraternity ring on his left hand. A new search disclosed a tiny room where a man's face was covered by a sheet, and on his left hand was Ritchie's ring.

> Slowly I crept forward, eyes riveted on that hand. There was something terrible about it. Even in the dim night-light I could see that it was too white, too smooth. Where had I seen a hand like that before? Then I remembered: Papa Dabney lying in the parlor at Moss Side.
>
> I backed toward the doorway. The man in that bed was dead! I felt the same reluctance I had the previous time at being in a room with a dead person. But . . . if that was my ring, then—then it was me, the separated part of me, lying under that sheet. Did that mean that I was . . . It was the first time in this entire experience that the word "death" occurred to me in connection with what was happening. But I wasn't dead! How could I be dead and still be awake? . . . Frantically I clawed at the sheet, trying to draw it back, trying to uncover the figure on the bed. All my efforts did not even stir a breeze in the silent little room.

At last in despair I sat down on the bed. Or did so mentally: actually my disembodied being made no contact with it. There, right there, was my own shape and substance, yet as distant from me as though we inhabited separate planets.

He wasn't sure just when the light in the room began to get brighter. He whirled to look at the 15-watt night-light. Surely it could not turn on that much light! "I stared in astonishment as the brightness increased, coming from nowhere, seeming to shine everywhere at once. All the light bulbs in the ward couldn't give off that much light. All the bulbs in the world couldn't! It was like a million welders' lamps all blazing at once."

Now he saw that it was not a light but a Man who had entered the room, or rather, *a Man made out of light*. "This Person was power itself, older than time and yet more modern than anyone I had ever met." Presently he was shown a panoramic view of his entire life. This Person "knew every unlovable thing about me," yet he "accepted and loved me just the same." He asked Ritchie, "What have you done with your life?" The question was repeated again and again, and each time Ritchie gave evasive answers. It finally dawned on him that he had not done very much with his life at all.

What now transpired is impossible to adequately portray in a few paragraphs. His celestial companion escorted Ritchie on what the latter describes as "an educational tour." He was shown the astral world that interpenetrates the earth, then a higher world, and still beyond that a higher one. In the astral world, as Ritchie called it, he saw dreadful sights of souls temporarily earthbound owing to strong sensuality. Former alcoholics were seen drawn to bars and cafes, and their "hell" was this: they could see others drinking and they would longingly reach out for a glass too, but could never pick it up. He saw others enslaved by sexual desires unable to consummate them. That was their "hell." He saw the desperate plight of suicides. He was also taken to a business office and watched a disembodied person shouting and shouting to an unhearing employee, telling him how to run the business. It was his deceased employer.

Owing to Ritchie's strict Southern Baptist upbringing, one experience truly startled him. He found himself in a place where there was a marvelous library. Here were housed all "the key books of the universe" ever written—and the Bible was only one of the world scriptures.

When they rose to the third plane or world, Ritchie was amazed to see many Beings of Light of the nature of his exalted companion, although he was certain the latter was the highest and grandest of all—the Christ. (A

Buddhist having this experience would probably identify him as Buddha; a Hindu, as Krishna; a Jew as someone of the nature of the Messiah. *Perhaps they all would be right.*)

Regretfully, the time came to return to the earthly plane of consciousness. "Walls closed around us. Walls so narrow and boxlike that it was several seconds before I recognized the little hospital room we had left what seemed a lifetime ago." Struggling to reenter the body on the bed, he finally managed to open its eyes, but was annoyed that something covered his face—the sheet! He could not remove it. To lift his arms was like lifting lead bars. He slowly brought his hands together, but that was all he could manage, except to turn the ring around several times.

Then his mind blurred. He lapsed into unconsciousness and apparently died once more, for it was *after this* that his body was resuscitated, although his mind did not regain consciousness until three days later. This time, when he opened his eyes, he saw a nurse smiling down at him. "It's good to have you back with us," she said. "For a while there we didn't think you were going to make it."

Later, Ritchie learned that, when the ward boy returned to prepare his body for the morgue, the arms seemed to have changed their position. Originally, when the doctor had covered Ritchie's face, he had straightened the arms and put the hands face down—that was why Ritchie was able to identify his ring. Noting the change, the boy galloped for the doctor, who carefully reexamined the body for vital signs, and again pronounced it dead.

However, the ward boy refused to accept the verdict of his superior officer. "Maybe," he suggested, "you could give him a shot of adrenalin directly into the heart muscle." Ritchie comments: "It was unthinkable, in the first place, for a private to argue with an officer, a licensed physician. In the second place, what the ward boy was suggesting was medically ridiculous. When the entire system was deteriorated from an illness like pneumonia, simply getting the heart muscle to contract a few more times achieves nothing. Indeed my condition, any medical man would have known, was totally irreversible. And yet this knowledgeable O.D., fully aware of the unreasonableness of what he was doing, accepted the suggestion of the uninformed enlisted man at his side." And the suggestion worked!

The period of recovery was enormously difficult, and when he returned to Richmond, he was literally "a bag of bones," in no condition to successfully complete a crash medical course. It took a year to recuperate.

He was sent back to Camp Barkeley and from there went abroad to serve as a medic with our army in Europe. At the end of the war, he continued his studies and became a doctor, later a psychiatrist. He writes:

> When I applied for my residency in psychiatry at the University of Virginia Hospital I was advised by a friend on the staff not to mention my [out of body] experience since he didn't know how the others might take this.
>
> The very first person to interview me turned out to be Dr. Wilfred Abse, Professor of Psychoanalysis and Analytical Psychotherapy in the Department of Psychiatry, and one of the top men in the Virginia Psychoanalytic Society. I had no sooner stepped into his office than Dr. Abse confronted me with, "Well, Dr. Ritchie, I understand that you feel that you have met the Christ." I saw my chances at the University of Virginia floating out the window. Dr. Abse was Jewish, a Freudian analyst, and he was asking me a direct question which demanded an answer. . . .
>
> I said, "I can no more deny the reality of what happened to me in Barkeley, Texas, than Saul of Tarsus could deny what happened to him on the road to Damascus" [when he saw Christ].

"And that was that, I thought, for my chances of becoming a psychiatrist. Imagine my surprise, a couple of weeks later, to receive a letter telling me that I had been accepted unanimously by the examining staff"—every one of whom had put him through the third degree. "Years later, when Dr. Abse and I had become good friends, he told me that that particular conversation had been critical indeed. 'All of us up here knew that you claimed to have had an out-of-the-body experience. If you'd pretended with me even for a moment that it hadn't happened, I'd have put you down as a deeply insecure person, and most probably an emotionally disturbed one who couldn't distinguish between fact and fancy.' " It was in this hospital that Dr. Ritchie rose to the position of chairman of the department of psychiatry.

*

One question, no doubt, must puzzle readers. As we will recall, Ritchie not only claimed to see *one* incredibly radiant Being of Light, but *many*. Who are these beings? Are they created as such by God? Or could they have once been human like ourselves who, through repeated experience in many lives, are now advanced far beyond us? Dr. Ritchie is inclined to believe that evolution through reincarnation is the answer. His belief in rebirth was made plain in his aforementioned taped talk on his near-death experience. It is titled "To Live Again and Again." In the question period, answering a query on many lives, he said, "As a physician, as a youth leader, as a psychiatrist, being at a place like the University of Virginia—where we have the privilege of having here what I think will twenty-five years from now be known as the Freud of this coming century, Dr. Ian Stevenson—I believe the evidence is so preponderantly in favor of reincarnation that you cannot doubt it if you have anything like an open mind.''

Dr. Raymond Moody also speaks of reincarnation in *Life After Life*. Asked whether the near-death experiences reveal evidence of more lives than one, he replied,

> It is important to bear in mind that not one of them rules out reincarnation. . . . If reincarnation does occur, it seems likely that an interlude in some other realm would occur between the time of separation from the old body and the entry into the new one. . . . It is also worth noting that the Tibetan Book of the Dead, which so accurately recounts the stages of near-death encounters, says that reincarnation does occur at some later point, after the events which have been related by my subjects.*[10]

Moody goes on to say that ''readers who wish to pursue this question further are referred to the excellent study, *Twenty Cases Suggestive of Reincarnation,* by Ian Stevenson, M.D.'' (see our chapter 4).

Incidentally, in some of Stevenson's cases of children remembering past lives—reported in *Twenty Cases* and elsewhere—the subjects speak of encountering holy men in the after world and that these beings directed them to incarnate in a certain body. This correlates well with the NDE experiences of Beings of Light.[11] In fact, in Dr. Stevenson's latest volume in the Cases of the Reincarnation Type series—which covers Thailand and Burma—he reports that 55 percent of Thai children who have past-life recall remember that in the disincarnate period between lives they encountered ''a 'man in white,' a sagelike person wearing white robes.'' (Buddhist holy men, with whom the children are familiar, wear ochre colored robes, never white.)

---

*In Jung's commentary on *The Tibetan Book of the Dead*—included in the current Oxford University Press edition of this work—he declares that this book, compiled and edited by Dr. W. Y. Evans-Wentz, contains a ''magnificent world of ideas. . . . For years, ever since it was published, it has been my constant companion, and to it I owe not only many stimulating ideas and discoveries, but also many fundamental insights.'' Describing its contents, Jung mentions that ''it falls into 3 parts,'' the first ''describes the psychic happenings at the moment of death,'' the second, ''the dream-state which supervenes immediately after death,'' and third, ''concerns the onset of the birth-instinct and of prenatal events. . . . I am sure that all who read this book with open eyes will reap a rich reward.''

Now these tiny tots indicate that the men in white welcomed them when they previously died and acted as their "guide and companion." Significantly, when the time arrives to be reborn, "these 'men in white' do not appear to influence the *choice* of the home for the next birth." They only lead the subjects to the place where they belong.

Stevenson further reports that just before rebirth the man in white or another holy person offers the incoming soul something to eat, usually fruit, which erases the past-life memories. This fruit has been called "the fruit of forgetfulness." "Subjects who remember previous lives sometimes claim that when offered this fruit, they managed not to eat it. . . . They may attribute the preservation of their memories to this successful disobedience." Stevenson comments that these case histories of Thai children resemble the old Greek tradition of drinking the water of lethe, or forgetfulness, before being reborn.[12]

As to Dr. Ritchie's extraordinary experience, he avers that Stevenson has told him he investigated a number of equally remarkable cases yet to be published.[13]

PETER SELLERS'S ENCOUNTER WITH DEATH

In Shirley MacLaine's best-selling book *Out on a Limb*,[14] she shares this conversation she had with the British actor. (We use the excellent condensed version, which appeared in the *Ladies' Home Journal*, June 1983.)

"Peter Sellers was one person who seemed certain that he had lived before. One day when we were on the set while making the movie *Being There*, he told me that he had often felt that he *knew* the characters he had acted because he '*was* each of those characters at one time or another.' At first I didn't understand what I was hearing, but as he continued, I realized he was talking about having lived those characters in some of his own past-life incarnations.

" 'Oh,' I said casually, 'you mean you feel you are drawing on experiences you had in previous lifetimes?' Peter's eyes lit up as though he had finally found somebody he could talk to, to share this belief of his.

"Abruptly he said, 'This sound stage gives me the creeps. . . . This is the sound stage where I died.' I tried not to overreact for I remembered reading in the papers what an awful brush with death he recently had.

" 'Dr. Rex Kennamer saved my life,' he said, 'and I saw him do it.'

"Like a person recounting a scene that had happened to somebody else, Peter told me:

" 'I felt myself leave my body. I just floated out of my physical form and I saw them cart my body away to the hospital. I went with it. I was curious. I wondered what was wrong with me. I wasn't frightened or anything like that because I was fine; and it was my body that was in trouble.

" 'Then, I saw Dr. Kennamer come. And he felt my pulse and saw that I was dead. He did everything but jump up and down on me to get my heart beating again. Then I saw Rex shout at somebody and say there was no time to prepare me for heart surgery. He commanded somebody to carve me open right there on the spot. Rex took my heart out of my body and tried to massage it back to life.

"At this point, 'I looked around myself and I saw an incredibly beautiful bright loving white light above me. I wanted to go to that white light more than anything. I knew there was love, real love, on the other side of the light that attracted me so much. Then I saw a hand reach through the light. I tried to touch it, to grab onto it, to clasp it so it could sweep me up and pull me through it. Then I heard Rex say below me, "It's beating again. I'm getting a heartbeat." At the same moment a voice attached to the hand I wanted to touch said, "It's not time. Go back and finish. It's not time." '

"Sellers ended his story with this remark: 'I know I have lived many times before, and that experience confirmed it for me, because in *this* lifetime I felt what it was for my soul to actually be *out* of my body.' "

"About a year and a half later," relates Shirley MacLaine, "I was sitting with some friends in my apartment in Malibu. I had been traveling and didn't know that Peter had had another heart attack. We were chatting amiably when suddenly I jumped up from my chair. 'Something has happened to Peter Sellers.' When I said it, I could feel his presence. It was as though he was right there in my living room watching me.

"Then the telephone rang. I disguised my voice and said hello. It was a newspaper reporter. 'I'd like to speak to Miss MacLaine,' he said. 'Actually I wanted to get her reaction.'

" 'To what?' I said. 'Oh,' he said. 'If you haven't heard, I'm sorry, but her friend Peter Sellers just died.' I wanted to say, 'Yes, you probably *think* he's dead, but he's really only left his latest body.' "

A TRAGIC LIFE THAT ALMOST REPEATED ITSELF

This case is of special interest because it dates back to the later part of the eighteenth century, before there was public awareness of after-life experiences and possible reincarnations. It is related by the noted Danish author Johan Ludwig Heiberg in his *The Newly Married,* which reveals events that transpired on his own honeymoon. (We are indebted to a Danish friend for the translation that follows.)

In the present episode the newlyweds, to escape a storm, have received shelter and lodging for a few days in the home of a poor widow and her adopted son Fredrick. As an orphaned child, he had found her in a strange way, filling an empty place in her heart, her own son being dead. Fredrick, now grown, falls passionately in love with Heiberg's bride and secretly plans to "accidentally" kill the husband the next day on a pre-arranged hunting trip. However, the couple alarmed by his erratic and erotic behavior, make preparations to leave as soon as possible. Meanwhile Fredrick's stepmother has a dreadful premonition of his intentions and speaks to him thus.

" 'I have never told you, my son . . . maybe the heart gets rest when I speak to you of my fate; maybe it becomes easier when we are two to carry the secret tortures. That son, which was given me in my marriage, oh—you don't know how he died!—he was decapitated and his blood covered the scaffold. Rejected by a young and beautiful maiden, who was deaf and blind to his love, he killed a more lucky lover while hunting.

"That morning, when he was to suffer his horrible doom—my son sank to my breast and exclaimed: 'Give me a word, a powerful word, which will comfort me on my last walk alive!' And I said . . . But Fredrick, you frighten me! You stare at me as white as a corpse.

" 'Oh mother! You said: "When before your savior you stand say: My God and my Brother! Forgive me for your martyr-wounds; for my anger and for my mother!" '

" 'How do you know that?' the mother exclaims in astonishment.

" 'It was I! I am your real son, and now he lives the life anew.'

" 'Fredrick, has insanity overtaken your mind?'

" 'No, mother, don't be afraid! But up to now, I walked as one blind, through all these long years. My consciousness awoke in this hour. Now I see my entire self, now I see the basis of my life and at the same time I hope and I tremble. Ah, I feel again my horrible fear, when my head I laid on the block. But still my thought held the comforting words you spoke.

" 'When the ax fell my consciousness left me. I woke up in strange places; and in my wanderings my eye rested on a man in white garments. . . . Maybe he was my Saviour, but ah! I did not know him, so my prayer to him I did not say, though his eyes were so mild looking . . . his hair was shining light. He said, "Turn around! Your place is not here. On earth you suffered death for your crime; here is no punishment, no penalty. So go back, down to earth to live over again your days.''

'' 'Then I turned back on fearful foot, wandering ever so long. I needed rest and slept a sleep so deep I knew nothing of what happened. But, when I woke up as a child I sensed I was another.

'' 'Oh mother, look at me; I need you to console me now. Not another time, that I can promise for certain, shall your son make sad your heart. She does not answer! What a deep sigh she draws. She is dead!' ''

The shock from such revelations, accompanied by amazement and joy, brought the poor woman's life to a close.

A NEAR-DEATH EXPERIENCE IN A SEVEN-YEAR-OLD CHILD

The American Medical Association published this case under the above title in its October 1983 issue of the *American Journal of Diseases of Children*. The author of the paper, Melvin Morse, M.D., was the chief doctor in the case. He is on the staff of The Children's Orthopedic Hospital and Medical Center in Seattle and is associated with the Department of Pediatrics, University of Washington School of Medicine. His investigation was supported in part by a grant from the Public Health Service. Here is the story.

A young seven-year-old girl—a responsible child, bright, cheerful, and in excellent health—experienced an unwitnessed near-drowning in a community swimming pool. A physician at the center found her comatose with fixed dilated pupils—a sign of death. After three days of heroic efforts at revival, she regained consciousness. Dr. Morse entered the case on the first day, when the child was taken to a nearby hospital.

Two weeks later, the doctor asked the girl what she remembered of the near-drowning. "She said that she remembered 'talking to the heavenly Father.' " Then she became embarrassed and would say nothing further until the next visit to the doctor. "It now feels good to talk about what happened." Dr. Morse reports:

> The patient indicated that the first memory she had of her near-drowning was "being in the water." She stated, "I was dead. Then I was in a tunnel. It was dark and I was scared. I couldn't walk." A woman named Elizabeth appeared, and the tunnel became bright. The woman was tall, with bright yellow hair. Together they walked to heaven. "Heaven was fun. It was bright and there were lots of flowers." She said that there was a border around heaven that she could not see beyond. She met many people, includ-

ing her dead grandparents, her dead maternal aunt, and Heather and Melissa, two adults waiting to be reborn. She then met the "heavenly Father and Jesus," who asked her if she wanted to return to earth. She replied, "No." Elizabeth then asked if she wanted to see her mother. She said yes and woke up in the hospital.

The nurses in the hospital reported that the child frequently asked for Heather and Melissa, apparently expecting they had already been reborn. As to religious background, the family of the child were active Mormons, and the girl attended church and Bible school once a week. Reincarnation is not one of their teachings.

Dr. Morse enumerated the usual alternate theories to explain the case, and comments that they do not "explain how so many persons, including children, can describe the identical core near-death experience despite wide differences in religious beliefs and cultural backgrounds." Summing up, he writes: "The patient in the present study had a near-death experience consistent with the typical case that has been reported among adults in the medical literature. Her experience contains many elements in common with the prototype near-death experience that differ from her religious training, including the dark tunnel, the border around heaven, and the choice to return to earth."

A CHOICE BETWEEN TWO KINDS OF REBIRTH
In 1935, William Martin of Liverpool reported this strange experience that happened to him in 1911 at the age of sixteen.

"I was staying about twelve miles away from my own home when a high wall was blown down by a sudden gust of wind as I was passing. A huge coping stone hit me on the top of the head. It then seemed as if I could see myself lying on the ground, huddled up, with one corner of the stone resting on my head and quite a number of people rushing toward me. I watched them move the stone and someone took off his coat and put it under my head, and I heard all their comments: 'Fetch a doctor.' 'His neck is broken. Skull smashed.'

"One of the bystanders asked if anyone knew where I lived, and on being told I was lodging just around the corner, he instructed them to carry me there. All this time it appeared as though I were disembodied from the form lying on the ground and suspended in midair in the center of the group, and I could hear everything that was being said.

"As they started to carry me, it was remarked that it would come as a blow to my people, and I was immediately conscious of a desire to be with my mother. Instantly I was at home and father and mother were just sitting down to their midday meal. On my entrance mother sat bolt upright in her chair and said, 'Bert, something has happened to our boy.'

"There followed a long argument, but my mother refused to be pacified and said that if she caught the 2:00 P.M. train she could be with me before 3:00 P.M. She had hardly left the room when there came a knock at the front door. It was a porter from the railway station with a telegram saying I was badly hurt.

"Then suddenly I was again transported—this time it seemed to be against my wish—to a bedroom, where a woman whom I recognized was in bed, and two other women were quietly bustling around, and a doctor was leaning over the bed. Then the doctor had a baby in his hands. At once I became aware of an almost irresistible impulse to press my face through the back of the baby's head so that my face would come out at the same place as the child's.

"The doctor said, 'It looks as though we have lost them both,' and again I felt the urge to take the baby's place to show him he was wrong, but the thought of my mother crying turned my thoughts in her direction, when straightaway I was in a railway carriage with her and my father.

"I was still with them when they arrived at my lodgings and were shown to the room where I had been put to bed. Mother sat beside the bed and I longed to comfort her, and the realization came that I ought to do the same thing I had felt impelled to do in the case of the baby and climb into the body on the bed. At last I succeeded, and the effort caused the real me to sit up in bed fully conscious. Mother made me lie down again, but I said I was all right, and remarked it was odd she knew something was wrong before the porter had brought the telegram.

"Both she and Dad were amazed at my knowledge. Their astonishment was further increased when I repeated almost word for word some of the conversation they had had at home and in the train. I said I had been close to birth as well as death, and told them that Mrs. Wilson, who lived close to us at home, had had a baby that day, but it was dead because I would not get into its body. We subsequently learned that Mrs. Wilson died on the same day at 2:05 P.M. after delivering a stillborn girl."[15]

A PHYSICIAN WITNESSES A REAL-DEATH OUT-OF-BODY EXPERIENCE

Between clinical death and what doctors call biologic death, a difference exists. In clinical death, all vital signs cease and the patient is pronounced dead. But in certain cases, particularly those of heart arrests, the person can sometimes be revived. Biological death occurs when the organs have so deteriorated that revival is impossible.

From an occult standpoint, however, there may be other criteria for determining real death, and this appears to be demonstrated in the case shortly to be considered. What are such criteria? Helena Blavatsky writes that "a resuscitation, after the soul and spirit have entirely separated from the body and the last electric thread is severed, is impossible."[16] In *The Secret Doctrine*, she adds that a person can still be revived "whose astral 'vital body' has not been irreparably separated from the physical body by the severance of the magnetic or odic cord."[17] Interesting that in the Old Testament it is averred that, when death occurs, "the silver cord is loosed" (Ecclesiastes 12:6).

There have been a number of reports of deathbed visions experienced by onlookers who claim to have actually seen this loosening or severing of the silver, magnetic cord. Dr. Kenneth Ring in his aforementioned *Recollections at Death* cites several and quotes the following remarkable description given by a physician, Dr. R. B. Hout, who witnessed the death of his aunt. During the experience he saw not only the silver cord but what Blavatsky called the severing of "the last electric thread."

First, in his vision, the doctor's attention "was called to something immediately above the physical body, suspended in the atmosphere about two feet above the bed. At first I could distinguish nothing more than a vague outline of a hazy, foglike substance. There seemed to be only a mist held there suspended, motionless. But, as I looked, very gradually there grew into my sight a denser, more solid, condensation of this inexplicable vapor. Then I was astonished to see definite outlines presenting themselves, and soon I saw this foglike substance was assuming a human form.

"Soon I knew that the body I was seeing resembled that of the physical body of my aunt; the astral body hung suspended horizontally a few feet above the physical counterpart. I continued to watch and the Spirit Body now seemed complete to my sight. I saw the features plainly. They were very similar to the physical face, except that a glow of peace and vigor was expressed instead of age and pain. The eyes were closed as though in tranquil sleep, and a luminosity seemed to radiate from the Spirit Body.

"As I watched the suspended Spirit Body, my attention was called to a silverlike substance that was streaming from the head of the physical body to the head of the spirit 'double.' Then I saw the connection-cord between the two bodies. As I watched, the thought, 'The silver cord!' kept running through my mind. I knew, for the first time, the meaning of it. This 'silver cord' was the connecting-link between the physical and the spirit bodies, even as the umbilical cord unites the child to its mother.

"The cord was attached at the occipital protuberance immediately at the base of the skull. Just where it met the physical body it spread out, fanlike, and numerous little strands separated, and were attached separately, to the skull base. But other than at the attachments, the cord was round, being perhaps an inch in diameter. The color was a translucent luminous silver radiance.

"The cord seemed alive with vibrant energy. I could see the pulsations of light stream along the course of it, from the direction of the physical body to the spirit 'double.' With each pulsation the spirit body became more alive and denser, whereas the physical body became quieter and more nearly lifeless. By this time the features were very distinct. The life was all in the astral body; the pulsations of the cord had stopped.

"I looked at the various strands of the cord as they spread out, fanlike, at the base of the skull. Each strand snapped, the final severance was at hand. A twin process of death and birth was about to ensue. The last connecting strand of the silver cord snapped and the spirit body was free."

Then came the dramatic moment when the luminous body rose up from its reclining position. "The closed eyes opened and a smile broke from the radiant features. She gave me a smile of farewell, then vanished from my sight."[18]

If it were suspected that such awesome events transpire when human beings die, how differently people would view the process and how differently they would react. They would soon realize emotional grief could disturb the departure of a beloved friend or relative.

The solemnity and transcendental nature of death is described in Isaac Bashevis Singer's novel *Shosha*. One of his characters relates a mystical experience of "universal oneness" that permeated his being years ago. "I had merged with eternity. At times I think it was like the state of passing over from life to what we call death. We may experience it in the final moments or perhaps immediately after. I say this because no matter how many dead people I have seen in my life, they have had the same expression on their faces: Aha, so that's what it is! If I had only known! What a shame I can't tell the others."[19]

*

In our next chapter we turn from the mysteries of death to the mysteries of birth, opening with a consideration of the puzzling problem of reincarnation in relation to the genetic inheritance of the newborn child.

Heredity: Problems
and Puzzles in Genetics

We have found a strange footprint on the shores of the unknown. We have devised profound theories, one after another, to account for its origin. At last we have succeeded in reconstructing the creature that made the footprint. And lo! It is our own!

SIR ARTHUR EDDINGTON, *Space, Time, and Gravitation*

Does Heredity Invalidate Reincarnation? A distinguished biologist, Sir Julian Huxley, once answered this question affirmatively. Speaking of the conception of a child, he wrote in *What Dare I Think?*,

> Egg and sperm carry the destiny of the generations. The egg realizes one chance combination out of an infinity of possibilities; and it is confronted with millions of pairs of sperms, each one actually different in the combination of cards which it holds. Then comes the final moment in the drama—the marriage of egg and sperm to produce the beginning of a large individual. . . . Here too, it seems to be entirely a matter of chance which particular union of all the millions of possible unions shall be consummated. One might have produced a genius, another a moron and so on. With a realization of all that this implies, we can banish from human thought a host of fears and superstitions. *No basis now remains for any doctrine of metempsychosis* [italics added].[1]

Why does Sir Julian so conclude? Because, under the scheme of rebirth, the incoming entity brings with him the fruitage of his own thoughts and actions in previous lives. He inherits from himself. Whereas, according to biologists, all his endowments and disabilities are the replication of ancestral traits. It is all in his genes.

Do not be misled, however, that the expression "he inherits from himself" means reincarnationists deny in the least the *facts* of heredity. An eminent theosophist, William Q. Judge, explains:

142

Some urge that heredity invalidates reincarnation. We urge it as proof. Heredity, in giving us a body in any family, provides the appropriate environment for the Ego. The Ego goes only into the family which either completely answers to its whole nature, or which gives an opportunity for the working out of its evolution, and which is also connected with it by reason of past incarnations or causes mutually set up. This points to bodily heredity as a natural rule governing the bodies we must inhabit. Transmission of trait and tendency by means of parent and body is exactly the mode selected by nature for providing the incarnating Ego with the proper tenement in which to carry on its work. Another mode would be impossible and subversive of order.

But when we look at the characters in human bodies, great inherent differences are seen. This is due to the soul inside, who is suffering or enjoying in the family, nation, and race his own thoughts and acts which past lives have made it inevitable he should incarnate with.[2]

In this, justice reigns, but in the scientistic scheme, chance and randomness rule. One person, as Huxley says, becomes a moron, another a genius, owing to the random combination of genetic material. So why honor great men? *It was all in their genes!* Why blame the criminal, and have courts of law? The criminal is not at fault; defective genes are the culprit. When Watson and Crick won the Nobel prize for deciphering the genetic code and diagramming it in the famous double helix, thus giving rise to the modern revolution in biology, why did they not turn down the coveted award and give credit to their genes? Would not a society based on the current interpretation of the science of genetics collapse? Individual responsibility and individual initiative would cease to exist.

As to the many-lives view that the incoming entity is drawn to the hereditary line most suitable to its karmic needs, Professor John McTaggart of Cambridge used this analogy. Likening the inherited body and tendencies to a hat and the wearer thereof to the reincarnating soul, he points out that "hats in general fit their wearers with far greater accuracy than they would if each man's hat were assigned to him by lot. The adaptation comes about by each man selecting, from hats made without any special reference to his particular head, the hat which will suit his particular head best." And McTaggart goes on to say: "This may help us to see that it would be possible to hold that a man whose nature had certain characteristics when he was about to be reborn, would be reborn in a body descended from ancestors of a similar character, which determined the fact that he was reborn in that body rather than another."[3]

An amusing comment comes from Professor C. J. Ducasse.

McTaggart's use of the analogy of the head and the hats if taken literally would mean, as a correspondent of mine suggests, that, like a man looking for a hat to wear, a temporarily bodiless soul would shop around, trying on one human foetus after another until it finds one which in some unexplained manner it discovers will develop into an appropriate body. McTaggart, however, has in mind nothing so far-fetched, but rather an entirely automatic process. He refers to the analogy of chemical affinities.[4]

Another noted Cambridge philosopher, James Ward, used the same analogy of chemical affinities in his Gifford Lectures, "The Realm of Ends." (Ward was professor of mental philosophy at Cambridge from 1897 to 1925. In addition to his philosophical pursuits, he was a psychologist and also deeply interested in science. He received doctorates in that field from Cambridge and Oxford.) If the series of rebirths, he says,

is to have any real continuity or meaning, if it is to be not merely a series but a progression, then at every return to life, either Providence must determine, or the . . . soul must itself select, its appropriate reincarnation. Otherwise, if disembodied souls are to be blown about by the winds of circumstance like other seeds, we should only have a repetition of that outrageous fortune which the doctrine of transmigration was supposed to redress. . . .

This difficulty in turn has been met by the further and bolder assumption, that disembodied souls do in fact steer their own way back to a suitable rebirth. An atom liberated from its molecular bonds is described as manifesting an unwonted activity, technically known as "the nascent state"; but still it does not recombine indifferently with the first free atom that it encounters, but only with one for which it has an "affinity." And "there seems to be nothing more strange or paradoxical in the suggestion that each person enters into connection with the body that is most fitted to be connected with him." . . . A liberated spirit ought to be credited with vastly more *savoir vivre* than a liberated atom.[5]

THE ELECTRICAL ARCHITECT (OR ASTRAL BODY)

Reincarnationists add another dimension to the foregoing process. In the East, where rebirth has been taught for ages, sages have naturally concerned themselves with the mysteries of birth and the life of the unborn child in the womb. They teach that the soul is appropriately clothed on higher planes of consciousness with bodies of the material existing on those planes.[6] The lowest of these inner bodies is called the *linga sarira,* or design body. According to this view, it is the model upon which the physical body is built and which the incarnating mind-soul projects as a link between its world and this. This design body is not separate from the physical body, as a blueprint is, but permeates and sustains the physical. Without the design body, the physical body could not function or cohere. The design body corresponds to "the electrical architect," discovered by the Yale scientists Harold Saxton Burr and F. C. Northrop to exist within all living forms. We will be discussing this discovery shortly. The theosophists call the *linga sarira* the astral body or astral double. In European cultures, the etheric counterpart has had various names: *doppelganger* in Germany; *perisprit* in France; *verdoger* in Scandinavia; *zelem* in Hebrew; in ancient Greece, *eidolon* and ancient Rome, *umbra*.

The major channels or plexi between the astral and physical bodies are known in Hinduism as *chakras* and in Buddhism as *padmas* (lotus centers). The acupuncture points and meridian lines, which Chinese physicians have used for many centuries in healing disease, are mediating channels between the two bodies.

As indicated in chapter 8, evidence for the astral body exists in the near-death, out-of-body experiences where individuals tell of functioning in a finer body that can go through walls as if they did not exist and travel hundreds of miles seemingly with the speed of thought.

There is also the birthmark evidence discussed by Dr. Stevenson in chapter 4. In considering the puzzling phenomena of children who claim to have lived before replicating former scars or injuries in their new body as birthmarks, the doctor remarked: "I find myself thinking increasingly of some intermediate 'non-physical body' which acts as the carrier of these attributes from one life to another," and which serves, he says, "as a template,"[7] or pattern.

According to Eastern philosophy, when a human fetus is conceived, the nucleic acids DNA and RNA—the memory centers in the nucleus of the germ cell—are activated and governed by these finer bodies, undetected by our most powerful electron microscopes. Yet it would appear that the astral body, as it merges with the physical, can be detected by humanly devised instruments. And this is where "the electrical architect" experiments of Burr and Northrop at Yale University enter. Their paper on this was presented before the National Academy of Science after four years' study of the organic development of salamanders and mice, as well as human beings. The professors described the electrical phenomena accompanying all growth, the patterns of which were recorded on electrocardiographs and electroencephalographs, revealing definite characteristics for each species. In a *New York Times* report, the science editor provided this nontechnical statement of the significance of the experiments:

There exists in the bodies of living things an electrical architect who molds and fashions the individual after a specific predetermined pattern, and remains within the body from the pre-embryonic stages until death. All else in the body undergoes constant change; the individual myriads of cells of which the body is made, excepting the brain cells, grow old and die, to be replaced by other cells, but the electrical architect remains the only constant throughout life, building the new cells and organizing them after the same pattern of the original cells, and thus, in a literal sense, constantly recreating the body. Death comes to the individual after the electrical architect within him ceases to function.

The electrical architect promises a new approach to the understanding of the nature of life and the living processes. It indicates that each living organism possesses an electrodynamic field, just as a magnet emanates all around it a magnetic field of force. Similarly, the experimental evidence shows, according to Dr. Burr, that each species of animals and very likely also the individuals within the species have their characteristic electric field, analogous to the lines of force of the magnet.

This electric field, then, having its own pattern, fashions all the protoplasmic clay of life that comes within its sphere of influence after its image, thus personifying itself in the living flesh as the sculptor personifies his idea in stone [April 25, 1939].

Thirty-three years later, Burr published his *Blueprint for Immortality: The Electric Patterns of Life*. He reported that "for nearly half a century the logical consequences of this theory have been subjected to rigorously controlled experimental conditions and met with no contradictions."[8]

From the foregoing experiments, it can be postulated that the etheric, electrical design body is not unique to human beings, it being a universal phenomenon in nature. In Kirlian photography the astral body of vegetation has been occasionally captured on film.[9]

Unfortunately, the geneticists and molecular biologists have largely ignored the experiments at Yale. They seek to reduce all the processes of nature to "miracle" chemicals, "miracle" protein molecules called RNA and DNA. A hundred years ago, Blavatsky wrote in *The Secret Doctrine*: "The whole issue of the quarrel between the profane and the esoteric sciences depends upon the belief in, and demonstration of, the existence of an astral body within the physical, the former independent of the latter."[10] She also speaks in this connection of the "inner soul of the physical cell—the 'spiritual plasm' that dominates the germinal plasm," as "the key that must open one day the gates of the *terra incognita* of the biologist now called the dark mysteries of embryology."[11]

CURRENT MYSTERIES IN GENETICS

With the deciphering of the genetic code by Watson and Crick in 1953, the scientific world hailed the discovery as solving all the major mysteries in cell biology. Today, however, biologists are keenly aware that the puzzles are more perplexing than ever.

First, the source of the genetic code is a total enigma. How did nature produce it? Scientists do not know. Sir Fred Hoyle points out that, within the genetic material in the nucleus of each cell, there are 200,000 chains of amino acids arranged in a very special, intricate pattern (diagrammed by Watson and Crick in their double helix model). The odds against arriving at this arrangement by a series of accidents via natural selection and random mutations, says Hoyle, is similar to the odds against throwing 5 million consecutive sixes on a single dice![12]

Second, the switching on and switching off mechanisms in the genes are unknown. It should be explained that every cell in our body carries in its nucleus a complete set of genes and contains all the information to reproduce a new human being. It is fortunate, however, that, at any one time, only a few of them are functional. In a skin cell, for instance, or a liver cell, a muscle cell, or the lens of an eye cell, only those genes are "turned on" that can produce that kind of cell. All the other genes are "turned off." If all the genes operated simultaneously, disorganized, undifferentiated growth would occur, and the name for this is cancer. So now the biologists talk about—but have not yet discovered—*operator* genes, whose functions are switched on by *activator* genes and then switched off by *regulator* genes. And so, appropriately enough, the following heading appeared in bold letters across the science page of the Sunday, May 29, 1983, issue of the *New York Times:* "GENE TRIGGER IS HOTLY SOUGHT CLUE TO PUZZLE OF LIFE." The article opens with an admission of ignorance.

> All animals, from frogs to rodents to elephants to humans, begin as a single fertilized egg. Then, during the species' allotted days or months of gestation, the single fertilized cell differentiates into a vast, close-knit community, a myriad of different specialized cells all functioning in harmony. How does this process of differentiation proceed? No one knows. It is one of the central puzzles of modern biology, hotly pursued in laboratories everywhere because answers would almost certainly give clearer understanding of the nature of life.

Commenting on all this, a group of British scientists observed that this theorized "hierarchy of intricate interlocking control systems does not resolve the ultimate mystery, but on the contrary deepens it,'' for ''the more complex the mechanisms, the more need there is to postulate intelligent programming.'' These scientists, members of the Theosophical Research Centre in England, have a reincarnational outlook in regard to evolution, and the quote is from their book, *Intelligence Comes First,* edited by Dr. E. Lester Smith, F.R.S.[13]

THE MYSTERY OF THE HUMAN BRAIN

To emphasize the dilemmas in cellular biology and genetics, Dr. Lewis Thomas draws attention to the problem concerning the birth of the human brain.

> The real amazement is this: you start out as a single cell; this divides into two, then four, then eight, and so on, and at a certain stage, as the cells differentiate, there emerges one cluster of cells which will have as its progeny the human brain.
>
> The mere existence of those special cells should be one of the great astonishments of the earth. One group of cells is switched on to become the whole trillion-cell massive apparatus for thinking and imagining. All the information needed for learning to read and write, playing the piano, or the marvelous act of putting out one hand and leaning against a tree, is contained in that first cell. All of grammar, all arithmetic, all music.
>
> It is not known how the switching-on occurs. . . . No one has the ghost of an idea how some of [the embryonic cells] suddenly assume the special quality of brainness.[14]

Furthermore, the brain itself is so astonishingly complex, notes *Fortune* science editor Tom Alexander, that ''a long-standing puzzle is how a structure so elaborate and highly organized gets wired together.'' ''Elementary calculations suggest,'' he says, ''that there simply cannot be enough information encoded in the DNA molecules that constitute the body's genetic blueprint to specify how two neurons—the most primitive of the brain's computers—are connected'' (January 24, 1983).

Perhaps with all these ''dark mysteries of embryology'' haunting the genetic scientists, the evidence thus far offered for the existence of an electromagnetic pattern body—call it the electrical architect, as Dr. Burr does, or the astral body, as many reincarnationists do—may prove worthy of serious attention.

Addressing those who think the reincarnational hypothesis sounds too complicated and mysterious, James Ward remarked in his Gifford Lectures, ''The Realm of Ends,'' that after all it should give the scornful objector pause, to think how many of the vital processes, about which we have definite knowledge, involve an elaborate adjustment of multifarious details that would be utterly incredible but for its familiarity. Is it then unreasonable to expect still more marvelous conjunctions in the wider dimensions of the world beyond the grave? And is it not also possible—just because of such wide dimensions—that what to us seems complicated or impossible is really as simple as say movement into a third dimension, which a being confined to two might fail to understand?[15]

It is interesting that biologist Julian Huxley, who was so adamantly convinced that reincarnation ranked as a superstition, changed his mind years later. In a contribution to a series of papers included in *Where are the Dead?*, he spoke of rebirth as a possibility:

> There is nothing against a permanently surviving spirit-individuality being in some way given off at death, as a definite wireless message is given off by a sending apparatus. But it must be remembered that the wireless message only becomes a message again when it comes in contact with a new, material structure—the receiver. . . . Our personalities are so based on body that it is really impossible to think of survival which would be in any true sense *personal* without a body of sorts. . . . I, therefore, can think of *something* being given off which would bear the same relation to men and women as a wireless message to the transmitting apparatus . . . until it came back to actuality of consciousness by making contact with something which could work as a receiving apparatus for mind.[16]

This receiving apparatus, of course, would be the brain. On another occasion, Huxley affirmed that the brain does not create thought; it is an instrument that thought finds useful.[17] Consequently, when the brain dies, the thinker and his thoughts could operate through future brains, yet to be born.

10
Unexplained Cases of Genius

The virtues we acquire, which develop slowly within us, are the invisible links that bind each of our previous existences to the others—existences which the spirit alone remembers, for matter has no memory for spiritual things. The endless legacy of the past to the present is the secret source of human genius.

BALZAC, *Seraphita*

"A genius is born, not made," is a common observation. To this, a reincarnationist would add that it is the flowering of many lives of effort. As evidence, the case of Mozart is often mentioned because his musical powers manifested at such an early age. However, Mozart, as well as Bach, Beethoven, and Brahms, all came from musical families; hence genetic factors could explain their powers. Not really explain, some might interject, because compared to others of similar backgrounds, they are as magnificent suns to candlelight. In this chapter, we will consider two cases where heredity does not appear to play a part, nor environment either.

A MATHEMATICAL MARVEL

The subject of this case is internationally renowned as a mathematical genius. Her name is Shakuntala Devi, and she was born in India. She travels everywhere, baffling experts with her incredible ability to figure problems faster than any known electrical device. When she toured the United States in 1977, there were accounts about her extraordinary talents in every major newspaper and in many magazines. She outdid one of the world's most advanced computers—the U.S. National Bureau of Standards' prized Univac 1108—by figuring out the twenty-third root of a 201-digit number in less than fifty seconds, thus winning a place in the *Guinness Book of World Records*. Not only was she quicker than the computer, she needed no programming. The computer, on the other hand, had to be fed some 13,466 instructions and 4,883 data locations. The odds against her figuring the result by chance were 598 million to one—as calculated by the same computer.*[1]

Mrs. Devi's talents were first discovered when she was three years old. Her parents, puzzled by her uncanny knack for numbers, took her to local academics for an explanation. After she convinced Bangalore University professors that she could work out logarithms, complicated roots, and sums in a matter of minutes, she was launched on the route to fame. She has had little formal education, but she says, "I've always loved numbers; they fascinate me. Everything in life—art, science and philosophy—is based on numbers." As a child, her powers appeared so natural to her, she believed everybody had the same talent for computations, and it was a real surprise to learn otherwise.[2]

Does she travel around the world exhibiting her powers to make money? No. In an interview reported in the *Ottawa Citizen* and titled "The World's Most Calculating Woman," she said: "I believe human achievements are most important and that it is necessary to demonstrate that humans are still superior to machines. The world doesn't yet understand the possibilities of the human mind. The mind has immense potential; this is why I demonstrate" (January 3, 1974).

Another interview conducted at this time was on the Ottawa television

---

*Before the age of computers, there were other mathematical prodigies with powers hardly explainable by heredity and environment. One was a black boy, William Marcy, who lived in Kentucky in the mid-nineteenth century. He could neither read nor write, but his feats in mental arithmetic were amazing. Quoting from the *New York Herald Tribune*: "He could multiply or divide millions by thousands in a few minutes from the time the figures were given to him—and always with the utmost exactness. Once, in the presence of several scholars, Marcy added a column of figures, eight in a line and 180 lines long, making the sum total of several millions, within *six minutes!* The feat so astounded his incredulous audience, that several of the men took off their coats and, dividing the sum among them, went to work. Two hours later they arrived at identically the same answer" (April 8, 1952).

program "This Day." To a question on how her ability could be explained, she answered that in India the explanation would be "by reincarnation," and she intimated recalling a past life in Egypt. It cannot be denied that there were once extraordinary mathematicians in that land of the pharaohs. The mathematical basis for the Great Pyramid of Cheops in its overall as well as detailed construction has so puzzled investigators that a century of theorizing has still not solved all the mysteries.

A BLACK, BLIND SLAVE BECOMES
A FAMOUS MUSICIAN

To be born blind and in slavery in Georgia in the year 1849 was hardly a propitious entry into this world. In a magazine article, "Blind Tom: Mystery of Music," Webb Garrison related that for business reasons, "most Georgia farmers of a century ago were very particular about their annual crop of slaves, and Perry H. Oliver, of Muscogee County, was no exception." So, when the baby of one of his slaves was born stone blind, he was keenly disappointed. "Later, Oliver sold the mother at a slave auction to General James Bethune of Columbus, Georgia. Then he pulled the blind youngster from hiding. 'Here,' he chuckled, 'I forgot to tell you she has a boy. I'm throwing him in free' " (*Coronet*, July 1952). And so the poor mother with her one-year-old child was torn from her home and friends, to live among strangers. General Bethune named the boy Thomas Greene Bethune, but the world was to know him as "Blind Tom." In her novel *My Antonia,* Willa Cather told a fictionalized version of his story, and called him Blind d'Arnault.

Among the many accounts of this astounding prodigy, the best researched is that of Ella May Thornton, honorary state librarian of Georgia. Her study, "The Mystery of Blind Tom," was published in the Winter 1961 issue of *The Georgia Review.* We quote here from that article.*

> While he was still an infant in arms, Tom's extraordinary susceptibility to any and every sound manifested itself—but to music in particular. . . . All

---

*We discovered the study in the Music Division of the Performing Arts Research Center at Lincoln Center in New York. An attached handwritten note from Miss Thornton reads: "Sent in appreciation of the valuable information obtained from your collections in the research which produced this article."

of the Bethunes, who were of high intelligence, cultivation, and benevolence, recognized the unusual qualities of the small Negro.

The first amazing demonstration of Tom's musical virtuosity was the occasion when he, unexpectedly [at the age of three], joined his voice with those of the Bethune girls as they were singing on the verandah steps one evening. It was not the melody that he carried, but the more difficult second part. . . . He, spontaneously and perfectly, carried on to the end of the song.

The next surprising exhibition was the following year when he was four, upon an evening when the young ladies had had several hours of music at the piano. After they had scattered to other parts of the house, all that had been played earlier was heard again. When the original performers hastened back to the parlor, there was the little black mite at the keyboard, giving back, in ecstasy, all that he had received.

"No one knew of his ever having touched a piano before," adds Miss Thornton, "and it seems probable that he never had," because "sounds attract attention, and a slave boy playing the piano in a busy household would soon be detected."

It is reported by the music magazine *Etude* (August 1940) that, right from the start, Blind Tom used both the black and white keys. Thus he was aware of the major and minor scales of Western music. As the black and white keys are not a natural arrangement, but an ingenious device invented by man, it is difficult to understand how a blind child could use them without some prior acquaintance with the piano and a period of training in its use. Miss Thornton emphasizes that, when he began to play the great classics, he approached them "differently from those who play 'by ear' and know nothing of the placing of the fingers." He "displayed an absolute accuracy of fingering which a highly professional reviewer in 1862 declared was 'of the schools.' "

Although Tom's mental faculties were quite limited, it would be a mistake to confine him to that class of rare retarded children who, having computerlike brains, can record and play back compositions heard only once. While Tom had this faculty to a remarkable degree—he could hear a new piece twenty pages long and repeat it perfectly—he had unusual creative talent, too, as we shall see.

"There were music teachers of the first class in Columbus at this time," relates Miss Thornton,

one of them being Carlo Patti, the brother of the noted Madame Adelina. General Bethune sought instruction for Tom, thinking perhaps that formal teaching might be beneficial. The Columbus teacher, who may have been Patti himself, for he instructed the Bethune girls, declined the request saying:

"No sir, I give up; the world has never seen such a thing as this little blind Negro and will never see such other. I can't teach him anything; he knows more of music than we know or can learn—all that great genius can reduce to rule and put in tangible form; he knows more than that; I don't even know what it is, but I see and feel it is something beyond my comprehension. All that can be done for him will be to let him hear fine playing; he will work it all out by himself.''

Tom's public concerts began when he was eight years old. When he was twelve, at "the very time of Georgia's secession, on January 19, 1861, Tom appeared in concert in New York City and, throughout the war, played in towns in both Confederate and Union territory, as well as behind the lines of both armies. Thousands of soldiers heard him, and many recounted these occasions, in wonder and amazement, in their diaries and journals, later numerously published. In 1866 and 1867 he performed widely in the British Isles and on the Continent and, for nearly twenty years thereafter, far and wide throughout America. He played at the White House by command performance.''

While Tom played Beethoven, Mendelssohn, Bach, Chopin, and many others, he was no mere repeater of the music of others.

Of his countless hours at the keyboard, a liberal portion of these was given over to improvising. And, once given form, these melodies were forever afterward a part of his repertoire, which was said to embrace seven thousand pieces. In more than one critique it was pointed out that those who undertook to set down his compositions were never able to lay hold of the mystery and beauty of his musical phrases. . . . His grasp and mastery of the sciences of counterpoint and harmony were complete. . . . Indeed, all the elements requisite to the formation of a total musical power seemed to have been fused into his being.

Miss Thornton ends her study with a problem: "A question is often raised as to whether there have been any findings by psychologists, physiologists, and other men of science, as well as musical authorities, in explanation of the astounding attainments of Blind Tom. The answer I make, after long study, is that there has been no explanation.'' Yet explanation there must be. If reincarnation proves to be true, then one could say that somewhere, sometime, this blind slave boy must have learned to become a superb musical artist.

It may be significant that the appearance of Blind Tom on the Western scene was especially timely. It was toward the close of the black night of human slavery in the United States when he demonstrated to millions of listeners that the poor, despised, seemingly degraded, uneducated black person was capable of accomplishments that white people with the best education could not duplicate.

How Talents Can Manifest Without Past-Life Recall.   Blind Tom had no known awareness of having lived before. And so it is with most people who display extraordinary talents. Sometimes their teachers, however, are so puzzled they find themselves turning to reincarnation as an explanation. One such is Sister Teresa, a Catholic nun who was an art instructor in a parochial school in Brooklyn. When one of the present writers, as guest speaker at Columbia University, discussed reincarnation at a meeting of the Thanatology Foundation, Sister Teresa was present. She later spoke of a young boy in her art class who displayed such professional skill in portraiture—having the intimate knowledge of the fine points and shadings that comes only with years of training and practice—she was convinced he must have learned this in another life.

Among Dr. Ian Stevenson's reincarnation cases involving children, there are numerous examples of talents and skills transmitted from claimed former lives. He discusses this in his paper "The Explanatory Value of the Idea of Reincarnation."[3] For those who do not remember their past lives, yet exhibit talents and behavioral characteristics from other lives, he uses an arresting analogy. He refers to posthypnotic instructions directing a subject in trance to perform a certain act on waking, with no recollection that the suggestion was given. The subject then appears to do what he was asked spontaneously, although the subconscious mind actually prompts him to so act. Similarly, Stevenson says, the habits and abilities of previous lives could be reproduced in the present even though the individual has no awareness as to when and where he originally developed them.

Stevenson points out that a comparable situation occurs with every one of us in our present life. "We know how to walk but few of us remember the days of infancy when we learned to walk." This, he says, "makes it possible to envisage that persons may have had previous lives of which they have no imaged memories, but from which nevertheless they may have derived important ingredients of their characters." This, in fact, occurs in Stevenson's reincarnation cases. Most of the children, from about eight onward, lose all imaged memories of their previous life but retain into adulthood the talents and character traits supposedly brought over from the past.

A moving case that bears out the foregoing was related by the late

Reverend Dr. Leslie Weatherhead, a former president of the Methodist Conference in Great Britain and for many years leading preacher at London's renowned City Temple. The account that follows appears in his lecture, "The Case for Reincarnation." Dr. Weatherhead met the parties involved in Melbourne, Australia. He was introduced to them by the British physicist Dr. Raynor Johnson, who investigated the case.

"Captain and Mrs. Battista, Italians, had a little daughter born in Rome, whom they called Blanche. To help look after this child they employed a French-speaking Swiss 'Nannie' called Marie. Marie taught her little charge to sing in French a lullaby. Blanche grew very fond of this song and it was sung to her repeatedly. Unfortunately Blanche died and Marie returned to Switzerland. Captain Battista writes, 'The cradle song which would have recalled to us only too painful memories of our deceased child, ceased absolutely to be heard in the house; all recollection of it completely escaped from our minds.'

"Three years after the death of Blanche, the mother, Signora Battista, became pregnant, and in the fourth month of pregnancy she had a strange waking-dream. She insists that she was wide awake when Blanche appeared to her and said, in her old familiar voice, 'Mother, I am coming back.' The vision then melted away. Captain Battista was skeptical, but when the new baby was born in February, 1906, he acquiesced in her being also given the name Blanche. The new Blanche resembled the old in every possible way.

"Nine years after the death of the first Blanche, when the second was about six years of age, an extraordinary thing happened. I will use Captain Battista's own words: 'While I was with my wife in my study which adjoins our bedroom, we heard, both of us, like a distant echo, the famous cradle song, and the voice came from the bedroom where we had left our little daughter Blanche fast asleep. We found the child sitting up on the bed and singing with an excellent French accent the cradle song which neither of us had certainly ever taught her. My wife asked her what it was she was singing, and the child, with the utmost promptitude, answered that she was singing a French song.'

" 'Who, pray, taught you this pretty song?' I asked her. *'Nobody, I know it out of my own head,'* answered the child"[4] [italics added].

*

How interesting that, when the child prior to birth announced to her mother she was coming back, she was aware of rebirth, but by the age of six she had forgotten. Yet she carried forward an ability previously acquired. So may it be with all of us.

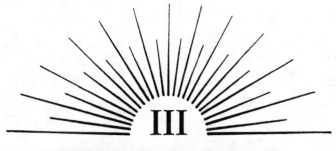

III
RELIGIOUS TEACHERS: THEIR MODERN MESSAGE

Humanity's sages have their bodies based on earth; but for their souls they have made them wings. Dwelling in cosmos as their city, they are the true world citizens. Such sages, though few in number, secretly keep alive the hidden spark of wisdom throughout the cities of the world in order that virtue may not be absolutely quenched and vanish from our human kind.
PHILO JUDAEUS, *De Septenario*

Humanity has every reason to place the proclaimers of high moral standards and values above the discoverers of objective truth. What humanity owes to personalities like Buddha, Moses, and Jesus ranks higher than all the achievements of the enquiring and constructive mind.
ALBERT EINSTEIN, *The Other Einstein*

When Jesus was sent to the human race, it was not as though he had just awakened from a long sleep. Jesus has at all times been doing good to the human race.
ORIGEN, *Contra Celsum*

11

Early Instructors of the Human Race

Jung speaks of reincarnation as "an affirmation that must be counted among the primordial affirmations of the human race,"[1] while seventeenth-century divine Thomas Burnet, startled by the universal prevalence of the belief in reincarnation, declared it "fatherless, motherless, and without genealogy."[2] The father of anthropology, Sir Edward Tylor, in his classic work *Primitive Culture,* traced the extensive belief in reincarnation through stage after stage of the world's civilizations and found it had immense antiquity.[3] If this is true, it seems logical to suppose that rebirth was taught by the primeval instructors of which so many legends speak, those wise beings who are said to have taught the early races not only religion but their arts, crafts, and social sciences.[4]

The critic might object that primitive man and his teachers could only think primitive, immature thoughts, the mental lispings of an infant humanity that merit little attention. This might be true, but such is not the consensus of modern scholars. In the present century, a remarkable change has taken place in the study of the myths, religions, and symbols of early peoples. Gone is the Victorian's simple faith in his own racial, moral, and cultural superiority, and in the so-called comparative method that was the application of these standards outside their legitimate context. Limited by this parochial outlook, the renowned author of *The Golden Bough,* Sir James Frazer, "in some 20,000 pages, had discovered how all the thoughts, imaginings and yearnings of archaic man, all his myths and rites, all his gods and religious experiences, are only a monstrous mass of beastliness, cruelty and superstition, happily abolished by scientific human progress." Thus speaks the distinguished contemporary scholar Mircea Eliade when contradicting the validity of Frazer's conclusion.[5]

Another eminent scholar, Lord Raglan, a past president of the Royal Anthropological Institute, observes that "the 'primitive man' of Frazer," was "always asking himself questions and giving himself the wrong answers." The word "primitive," this authority avers, "has led to more muddled thinking than all the other words in the dictionary put together," and it should be banished from our vocabulary.[6]

*

In Ernst Cassirer's celebrated *An Essay on Man,* he proposes an intriguing view of our earliest ancestors' belief in rebirth. He first mentions that "to mythical and religious feeling, nature becomes one great society, the society of life," for it is realized that "life possesses the same religious dignity in its humblest and its highest forms." In early thought, he then adds, "we find the same principle—that of the solidarity and unbroken unity of life—when we pass from space to time." Thus "the generations of humankind form a unique and uninterrupted chain, and this chain is preserved by reincarnation."

"The conception that man is *mortal,*" Cassirer further tells us, "seems to be entirely alien to mythical and 'primitive' religious thought."

> If we read Plato's *Phaedo,* we feel that the whole effort of philosophical thought is to give clear and irrefutable *proof* of the immortality of the human soul. In mythical thought the case is quite different. Here the burden of proof always lies on the opposite side. If anything is in need of proof it is not the fact of immortality but the fact of death. . . . By virtue of this conviction of the unbroken unity and continuity of life . . . "primitive" religion is perhaps the strongest and most energetic affirmation of life that we find in human culture.[7]

TANTALIZING FRAGMENTS OF LOST WHOLE

It appears probable that the mythical mode of thought mentioned by Cassirer was taught by the sages of old in order to awaken the intuitional faculties of humanity. Furthermore, ancient mythology was not mere pabulum for infants according to Giorgio de Santillana. In his much-quoted *Hamlet's Mill,* he says it was a "great world-wide archaic construction of thought," which is no longer understood. The original themes, notes this professor of the history and philosophy of science at the Massachusetts Institute of Technology, were preserved by the Pythagoreans and Plato "as tantalizing fragments of a lost whole." Plato, he says, understood "the language of archaic myth" and gave to the West the foundation of all modern philosophy. Most Platonic myths "act like a floodlight that throws bright beams upon the whole of high mythology."[8] As already indicated, the reincarnational outlook pervades Plato's philosophy.

The theme of life, death, and rebirth into new bodies is unfolded in numerous myths. It is perhaps of some significance that the same basic stories, with appropriate variations, are found in many cultures often remotely situated around the globe, suggesting that the teachers among our early ancestors had access to a common fount of learning. The more important of the myths on rebirth may be found in Chapter 2 of *Reincarnation: the Phoenix Fire Mystery*.

In this chapter, we will focus on specific many-lives beliefs as they occur in living representatives of early peoples. But where such cultures have died out or become submerged, as in Europe, the records of history will be used.

The chapter will conclude with "Rebirth of Humanity's Great Souls." Here will be found the remarkably concordant conviction—both in the West and the East—that these beings incarnate again and again to assist the human race in its growth toward mental and spiritual enlightenment. From the reincarnational outlook, these sages and saviors are the product of evolutionary experience in prior worlds. For, as a family cannot start without parents or a school without teachers, so it may be that the human family, when it commenced life on this earth, owed its beginning to humanity's Great Teachers.

REINCARNATION AMONG EARLY CULTURES

OUR EUROPEAN ANCESTORS

In early Europe, long before its conversion to Christianity, the belief in reincarnation was widespread.[9] Starting in the far north, the peoples that embraced it were the natives of Finland, Iceland, and Lapland. Then there were the Norwegians, Swedish, Danish, and Germans. Forming another group were the Letts, Old Prussians, and Lithuanians. Going south, there were the Celts of Ireland, Scotland, England, Wales, and Brittany in France. The Celtic culture also included the ancient Gauls, who occupied a vast area, including France, northern Italy, Belgium, parts of the Netherlands, western Switzerland, and Germany west of the Rhine. Farthest south, of course, were the Greek and Roman civilizations. Selections from the reincarnational writings of Greek and Roman philosophers are found in chapter 5 of *Reincarnation: the Phoenix Fire Mystery*.

Nordic and Germanic Peoples. "We shall come again," said the old

people in Norway when death called them from their ancestral home. Axel
Olrik tells of this in *Viking Civilization*. He also reports that "a special
form of family relationship was that in which one newly deceased was
reborn in his descendants, and the latter were accordingly given the name
of the deceased. This belief appears as late as the period of the Migration,
first among the East Goths, from whom it spread far and wide. . . . It
continued to exist as a current folk belief for many centuries." (Among the
Lapps, anthropologists find comparable beliefs, one being that the spirit of
a deceased ancestor who is about to be incarnated instructs the pregnant
mother in a dream how her child is to be named."[10])

"It is clear that the doctrine of metempsychosis was held by the early
Teutonic peoples," writes Bruce Dickins, author of *Runic and Heroic
Poems of the Old Teutonic Peoples*.[11] The Teutons included the Scandinavians,
the Dutch, and a large percentage of the Germans. Belonging to the northern Caucasian stock, they were all tall in stature with blond hair and blue
eyes. The Anglo-Saxons of Britain were of this origin, having come from
the North Sea area of Germany.

Dickins says that mention of reincarnation is to be found chiefly in
Teutonic prose. The only reference he found in early poetry is when Hogin
refuses to hold back Brunhilde from self-immolation in the fiery funeral
pyre that consumed the hero Siegfried. Hogin says: "Let no man stay her
from the long journey, and may she never be born again." Richard Wagner
preserved this thought in the final lines of his opera *The Götterdämmerung*,
where Brunhilde silently sings:

> The home of desire I leave behind
> Illusions forever avoid.
> The open door of return and being
> I close forever.
> Yearning for regions of peace,
> The holy land of choice,
> Released from the path of return,
> So wanders the Wise one forth.

Wagner specifically directed that these lines be unsung because "the
musician cannot help seeing for himself that the verses have to be omitted
in the live production inasmuch as their meaning is emphatically expressed
in the orchestral music itself"[12]—those glorious closing passages that end
the four operas comprising the Ring Cycle. However, contrary to Wagner's
intention, the stanza is omitted in current librettos.

These operas revolve around the Scandinavian and Germanic myth of the twilight and death of the gods. Again the idea of rebirth enters in, for, as Carlyle observes in *Heroes and Hero Worship,* "It is not a final death. There is to be a new Heaven and a new Earth"—not in some distant sphere but here in our world, after a purifying conflagration. "Curious," Carlyle adds, that "this law of mutation which also is a law written in man's inmost thought, had been deciphered by these old earnest Thinkers in their rude style; and how, though all dies, and even gods die, yet all death is but a phoenix fire-death, and new-birth into the Greater and the Better! It is the fundamental Law of Being for a creature made of Time, living in this Place of Hope. All earnest people have seen into it; may still see into it."[13]

IRISH, SCOTTISH, AND WELSH

Julius Caesar wrote of the Celtic peoples: "They wish to inculcate this as one of their leading tenets, that souls do not become extinct, but pass after death from one body to another, and they think that men by this tenet are in a great degree stimulated to valor, the fear of death being disregarded."[14]

A past president of Ireland, Douglas Hyde, confirms the foregoing in his *Literary History of Ireland*: "The idea of rebirth, which forms part of a half-a-dozen existing Irish sagas, was perfectly familiar to the Irish Gael." Another authority, Alfred Nutt, adds that the conception of reincarnation was a "dominant factor" in the Celtics' religious system.[15]

M. F. Cusack in *A History of the Irish Nation* speaks of a high civilization in Innis Fail (the old name for Ireland) long before the Christian missionaries came in the fifth century. In Druidic times, the scholars entrusted with the ancient records were called Ollamhs. Cusack says their diplomas were obtained after a collegiate course that might deter many a modern aspirant to professional chairs. As prescribed by the Brehon Laws, the course lasted twelve years. The studies included philosophy, law, and knowing and practicing the druidical secrets. On the arrival of the missionaries, many of the ancient records were burned.[16]

As indicated earlier, the Celtic culture included not only Ireland, but Scotland, Wales, the Bretons of France, and the vast area known as ancient Gaul. The Scottish poet Fiona Macleod tells in *Winged Destiny* that "students of Gaelic will remember that Tuan gave out the same ancient wisdom as Pythagoras gave" and, like the Greek sage, "remembered his many transformations." "I think the soul knows," adds Macleod. "I think the soul remembers. I think that intuition is divine and unshakeable. We have travelled a long way, and forgotten much. The secret road of the soul is a long road."

As to the Welsh and the Bretons of France, Bryher writes in the foreword to her book *Ruan* that they believed "the spirit rested after death until the moment came for another return to earth. This continued until, after many lives, some attained the state of spiritual perfection that admitted them to Gwenved, the "white" heaven where they became fully conscious of God. They chose, however, to return as teachers to mankind from time to time until that ultimate and future moment should come when all humanity would attain their state."[17]

OUR AFRICAN ANCESTORS

"Africans and their descendants may well be proud of their past," observes a writer in *The New Yorker* (August 6, 1963). "The great empires of Ghana, Mali, and Songhai and the powerful kingdoms of Ashanti, Ife, and Benin all flourished centuries before the Europeans arrived in Africa. Timbuktu, in Mali, formerly the Sudan, was a seat of advanced learning in the fifteenth century; the records of the old university are still there."

Janheinz Jahn in *Munti—The New African Culture* says that "the Africans' zeal for learning, which so delights the educators, is not the zeal of an illiterate people to whom writing comes as a revelation. It is the zeal for learning of a civilized people whose own script has been destroyed and who therefore need a new medium for communicating and preserving information."[18]

Dr. E. G. Parrinder, author of *African Traditional Religion, West African Psychology,* and similar volumes, wrote in the 1950s that,

in tropical Africa, belief in rebirth is deeply enrooted. The studies made by anthropologists and other serious writers in many different parts of Africa, especially in the last forty years, have revealed deep-seated beliefs in reincarnation held by many different African peoples. Reincarnation, to most Africans, is a good thing. There is little idea of an end to the number of incarnations, or a search for that as desirable. . . . On the contrary, it is bad not to be reborn, and childlessness is a great curse because it blocks the channel of rebirth. . . . It is a common practice for the diviner to be called in at the birth of a child to declare which ancestor is reincarnated, and family resemblances are explained as due to use of the same soul-stuff. . . . Various phrases are used to describe reincarnation. One West African people calls it "the shooting forth of a branch," and another "a recurring cycle." In the latter case the same word is used to describe a vine which twines round a post, reappearing continually higher up.[19]

Thus cycles of rebirth are not merely repetitive cycles but spirals!
As to the Yorubas and the Edo-speaking peoples of West Africa, a native
of Ghana, K. Brakatu Ateko, outlines four of their important beliefs:

> I. *God.* A maxim says *"Obi Nkyere abofra Nyame,"* and literally means:
> No one teaches a child God. Over and above the tutelary, tribal and family
> gods and goddesses is the Supreme Being to whom no sacrifices are made. . . .
> It is crystal clear that the African conception of the High God is not of recent
> growth. . . .
>
> II. *Karma.* There are proverbs which illustrate this law: (1) When Mr.
> Lizard eats pepper, it is he who perspires and not Mrs. Lizard. (2) When
> Akosua commits evil, Akua is not punished.
>
> III. *Reincarnation.* The Yoruba and the Edo-speaking tribes, among
> whom I sojourned as a teacher half a century ago, have a strong belief in
> reincarnation. At that period the white man's influence had not affected the
> beliefs and the ways of life of the hinterlands of Nigeria. The Yorubas, for
> instance, name a boy Babatunde, meaning "Father has returned," and the
> girl, Yetunde (Iyantude) signifying "Mother has returned." In Ghana, the
> name Ababio "he has come again," carries the same meaning.
>
> IV. *Death.* Our traditional philosophy of death was grander than that
> acquired in the wake of Christianity. Death was not looked upon as an
> enemy to be feared and propitiated. If one died, he was believed to have
> been born on the other side of the veil and vice versa in the case of birth in
> our world.[20]

In a volume of her experiences among the Ibibios of southern Nigeria,
Mrs. D. Amaury Talbot provides individual case histories, reported by the
natives, of how incidents and actions in previous lives had repercussions
on the present. As to the culture of these people, she says, "fragments of
legend and half-forgotten ritual still survive to tell of times shrouded in the
mists of antiquity, when the despised Ibibio of today was a different being,
dwelling not amid the fog and swamp of fetishism, but upon the sunlit
heights of a religious culture hardly less highly evolved perhaps than that of
Ancient Egypt."[21]

A Society of Wise Men in Africa. A most remarkable report on the
existence of such a society is told by Captain Patrick Bowen, who lived in
Africa during his youth. His father was a physician, and Patrick as a boy
followed his father's wagon through the wild Bushlands of the Northern
Transvaal. He gained the friendship of several Isanusi (wise men) of the
Zulus. When he was older, one of these, Mankanyezi (the Starry One),
told him of a society to which he belonged, "whose members are the
guardians of the *Wisdom-which-comes-from old*; they are of many ranks,

from learner to Master, and Higher Ones whose names may not be spoken; and there is one member at least in every tribe and nation throughout this great land of Africa.''

> The Brotherhood is called, in the ancient Bantu speech, Bonabakulu Abase-Khemu, i.e., The Brotherhood of the Higher Ones of Egypt. It was founded by a Priest of Isis in the reign of the Pharaoh Cheops, to spread the Wisdom which comes from of Old, among all races and tribes of Africa. . . . The grades of the Brotherhood are: (1) the Pupil, (2) the Disciple, (3) the Brother, (4) the Elder, (5) the Master, (6) Those who Know (Isangoma), (7) Abakulu-bantu, i.e., Perfect Men, for whom rebirth has ceased, who dwell on earth in physical form by their own will, and can retain or relinquish that form as they choose.

Mankanyezi also told Captain Bowen of the stages undergone by the soul after death and between incarnations: ''Within the body is a soul; within the soul is a spark of the Itongo, the Universal Spirit. After the death of the body, Idhlozi (the soul) hovers for awhile near the body, and then departs to Esilweni, the Place of Beasts.'' This, the wise man said, is very different from entering the body of a beast. ''In Esilweni, the soul assumes [temporarily] a shape, part beast and part human'' before it rises higher.

This strange teaching correlates with what is taught in Eastern religions concerning the *bardo* state after death, akin to the purgatory of the Christians. Here the passionate animal nature is thrown off, releasing the purified soul to ascend to a heavenly condition. It is interesting that Emanuel Swedenborg and other seers have claimed seeing some newly departed humans wearing for a time the garment of animals that corresponded to their earthly nature. It is easy to see how a misunderstanding of this teaching could have conveyed the idea that after death the soul incarnates into animals!

To continue with Mankanyesi's words: ''After a period, long or short, according to the strength of the animal nature, the soul throws aside its beast-like shape, and moves onward to a place of rest. There it sleeps, till a time comes when it dreams that something to do and learn awaits it on earth; then it awakes, and returns to the earth, and is born again as a child. Again and again does the soul travel thus, till at last the man becomes the true Man, and his soul, when the body dies, becomes one with the *Itongo*, whence it came.''[22]

THE NATIVES ''DOWN UNDER''
''In every tribe without exception,'' writes Baldwin Spencer and F. J.

Gillen in *Northern Tribes of Central Australia,* "there exists a firm belief in the reincarnation of ancestors. Emphasis must be laid on the fact that this belief is not confined to tribes such as the Arunta, Warramunga, Binbinga, Anula, and others amongst whom descent is counted on the male line, but is found just as strongly developed in the Urabunna tribe, in which descent, both of class and totem, is strictly maternal."[23]

Sir James Frazer commends the researches of Spencer and Gillen and remarks, "We naturally ask whether the belief in reincarnation of the dead, which prevails universally among the Central tribes, reappears among the tribes in other parts of the continent. It certainly does so, and although the evidence on this subject is very imperfect it suffices to raise a presumption that a similar belief in the rebirth or reincarnation of the dead was formerly universal among the Australian aborigines."[24] Later research supports the presumption raised by Frazer.[25]

Now all this is particularly interesting, because scientists have suggested that the Australian native—coexisting as he does with an archaic fauna and flora to be found practically nowhere else on the globe—probably dates back to an enormous antiquity. Commenting on the religion and mythology of the tribes, Edward O. Schmidt writes, "The statement that the Australian civilization indicates a [previous] higher grade, is nowhere more clearly proved than here, where everything resounds like the expiring voices of a previous and richer age."[26]

It may be that the Australian natives themselves are aware that the old culture is dying, for one researcher, James Bonwick, discovered that "they certainly entertain the idea that after death they will again exist," but "in the form of white men." This "is not without consolation for when one was being executed in Melbourne, he exclaimed, 'Very good—me jump up Whitefellow.' "[27] Here is perhaps an intuitional feeling that races, like bodies, grow old and die out, but the being within incarnates in ever newer races offering better opportunities for growth and development.

THE BEAUTIFUL BALINESE

Margaret Mead wrote of reincarnation in one of her books to illustrate the possible practical and psychological effect such ideas can have on the culture of various peoples. She found that, among the Balinese and the Eskimos—both of whom she says accept rebirth—"infants are treated as having prophetic powers at birth, and in both of them children learn complex skills early." "I may add a question here," she continues. "Is the relationship between learning and a theory of birth and immortality perhaps a key point?'' She then compares ''the Balinese position—in which the individual is reincarnated over and over''—with

> the Manus position, where human beings are originally built from fathers' and mothers' bodies, reach their full powers at maturity, survive a little as strong ghosts immediately after death and then dribble off into lower and lower levels of sea-slugs and slime. . . .
>
> The Balinese believe you can learn at any age—the very young and the old learn with great relative effortlessness, beauty lasts into old age—while among the Manus, people are finished at forty. Perhaps we may suggest that there is a relationship here which it would be worth while to explore further.
>
> From there I may go on to consider whether I know any instances of a group who believe in reincarnation but also have a sharply marked decline in vigor during the life-span—thus looking for negative instances to disprove my developing hypothesis.

She mentions that, with topics in mind like ''belief in reincarnation'' and ''life-cycle,'' ''it would be possible to go up to Yale University and pull out a card catalog in which material on a great many societies has been arranged in such categories, so that it is possible to see how the two things fit together.''[28]

In respect to the Balinese, a further example of how the two ideas of reincarnation and life-cycle fit together in their culture can be gleaned from a travel page in the *New York Times* concerning their practices at the time of death:

> ''If you are lucky you may observe a cremation. . . .'' That's what a guidebook on Bali may say. Westerners may shudder at the thought. But the Balinese believe in reincarnation and regard death as passing from this life to a far better one. ''It is a most joyous time,'' an islander said. ''After the body is consumed by flames, the ashes are taken in a long procession to the sea, to be scattered on the waters.'' (October 28, 1973)

HAWAIIANS, OKINAWANS, AND OTHER PACIFIC ISLANDERS

In the vast area of the Pacific Ocean, many peoples believe in some form of reincarnation. In the South Pacific, they include the New Zealand Maoris, the Tasmanians, Tahitians, Fijians, Trobriands, Solomon Islanders, Marquesans, the tribes of New Caledonia, and the Melanesians.

In the North Pacific, where there are few islands, reincarnation is indigenous to the Okinawans and to the Ainu in northern Japan. It was once prevalent in Hawaii, and to that story we turn first.

Hawaiians. Anthropologists believe the islands of Hawaii were first colonized by the Polynesians and later by the Tahitians. From ancient times there existed, first in Polynesia and then in Hawaii, native priests known as the Kahunas. By the year 1900, only remnants of the order remained. Among these were unworthy representatives of their noble predecessors, and they were feared as sorcerers.

The word *Kahuna* means "keeper of the secrets." Investigation of their ancient lore began in 1880 by Dr. William Tufts Brigham, longtime curator of the Bishop Museum in Honolulu, and was continued by Max Freedom Long, whom he trained. According to the Kahunas—whose religious philosophy is known as Huna—there are three departments of the human being, a low, a middle, and a higher self. The first is concerned with the physical body and the emotions; the second is a reasoning entity, while the third is the High Self, the source of spiritual wisdom and power. It is by opening up to this High Self that genuine healing of the total individual can be achieved.

In Long's *Introduction to Huna,* he writes that, "in Huna the matter of evolution through a series of incarnations was part of the general system," but "the involutionary idea of a man being forced back to become an animal in some incarnation because of 'sin' has no part in Huna, so far as has been ascertained." Each of these three selves had its appropriate ethereal body. "The Huna system presents a theory of evolution in which units of consciousness evolve upward step by step from the group units of rocks and waters, through the vegetable kingdom, to insects, birds and animals,"[29] and finally become human.

Okinawans. During World War II, an American soldier interviewed the former chief librarian of the Okinawan Prefecture concerning the religious views of his people. The librarian, Shimabuku Zenpastu informed him that, "according to the Okinawan God-idea, deity is without shape and sexless. The majority of Okinawans believe in reincarnation." The original Okinawan belief, the soldier reports, is this.

> After a man's death, the spirit stays in his home for 49 days; on the 49th day, when the memorial services are complete, the spirit enters Gusho— "after this present world." The period in the after-death state varies, but the Okinawans believe that the spirit will return within seven generations, producing an individual who strongly resembles its former embodiment. Not all spirits reincarnate. Some remain in Gusho indefinitely, and will greet new arrivals in that state. It should be understood that the Okinawan conception

of Gusho is a spiritual state, where only the spirit of man exists. . . . Not mind, but spirit, reincarnates . . . mind being received by the individual through ancestral descent.[30]

Time reported that a United States Navy psychiatrist discovered the psychic health of the Okinawans to be superior to that of other people. Of five hundred natives subjected to terrible bombardment—"a nerve-shattering ordeal that drove many a Jap to suicide and many a G.I. into the mental ward"—only one became mentally unstable. The early training of the Okinawan child, the psychiatrist said, is such that, by the time he is five, "he has such a sense of security that his mental foundation is sturdy enough to survive catastrophe" (February 4, 1946). The indication seems to be that a person's belief in reincarnation can contribute to his mental stability.

THE FIRST AMERICANS

Anthropologists are greatly puzzled as to when, and from where, the earliest Americans arrived in the New World. Did they travel across the Bering Straits from Asia? Or across the Pacific in sailing vessels, as Thor Heyerdahl tried to demonstrate in the *Kon-Tiki*? Did they come from Africa, or Europe, or even from fabled Atlantis, when it supposedly sank? Or, what is more likely, did they come from various parts of the world, just as immigrants do today?

Whatever their origin, whatever diverse cultures they brought with them—for the Indians of north, south, and central America are not a homogeneous race—there are numerous evidences of their belief in reincarnation. This was doubted at one time, as these first Americans did not readily reveal their religious convictions to the white man. However, Professor Daniel Brinton, who wrote at the turn of the century, discovered that "this seemingly extraordinary doctrine which some have asserted was entirely unknown and impossible to the American Indians, was in fact one of their most deeply-rooted and widespread convictions, especially among the tribes of the eastern United States. It is indissolubly connected with their highest theories of a future life, their burial ceremonies, and their modes of expression."[31]

In *The Soul of the Indian*, Charles Eastman, himself an Indian whose tribal name was Ohiyesa, relates that "many of the Indians believed that one may be born more than once; and there were some who claimed to have full knowledge of a former incarnation." According to the Lenape of Delaware and New Jersey, it was the pure in heart who could recall their former lives.[32]

In a conversation with Marcia Keegan, who lived among the Hopis and Pueblos and writes books on their traditions, she told us that reincarnation is still very much alive with these artistic and peace-loving peoples, particularly among their chiefs. They, too, she said, are not prone to publicly share with the outside world their sacred beliefs.

Among the customs of the Pueblos and other tribes, writes Ernest Thompson Seton in his beautiful book *The Gospel of the Redman*, is their strange indifference to the body after death. "They consider it a mere husk, an empty case to be disposed of with view only to the comfort of the survivors. The soul that emerged will go on to the next life, and construct for itself a new and better body."[33]

The Eskimos. Margaret Mead reported some years ago that the Eskimo culture is based on the reincarnational outlook.[34] Explorer Vilhjalmur Stefansson discovered among his Eskimo friends in northern Canada "beliefs that resembled in a way, the reincarnation theories that we associate with India." Stefansson lived among the Coronation Gulf Eskimos for ten years. His article on their beliefs and customs is titled "Primitive People Are Far From Simple." The following excerpt suggests that many so-called primitives may be descendants of once highly civilized races; hence their reincarnational beliefs also may stem from that source.

> I know from experience that two men who speak English and Eskimo well are not going to converse in English unless what they are talking about is some particularly English subject, like the dramas of Shakespeare or the cotton-spinning of Lancashire. . . . You can say as much in one hour of Eskimo-speaking as you can in two hours with English, and you will say it more precisely as well as more concisely.
>
> In Eskimo a single noun, like "man" or "house," can have more than a thousand forms, each different in meaning from any other, and the difference is so precise that no misunderstanding is possible. . . . If you were to study in succession Latin, Greek, Hebrew and Russian, each till you could think in it and speak in it fluently and correctly, you would find those four languages combined easier to learn than Eskimo alone. . . . The most brilliant conversation I ever listened to has been among Stone Age Eskimos.[35]

REBIRTH OF HUMANITY'S GREAT SOULS

This theme, the reincarnation of mankind's saviors and teachers, is a universal one, expressed again and again in the world's religions. In the present chapter, we have seen how this inspiring idea has manifested in African, Germanic, and Celtic traditions. Now let us briefly touch upon what other traditions, both Western and Eastern, teach on the belief.

HIAWATHA AND OTHER INDIAN TEACHERS

In the magnificent lines that close Longfellow's *Song of Hiawatha*, this illustrious Indian chief announces his departure to the kingdom of death, the Islands of the Blessed. He promises, however, to return again. This promise was no poetic flourish of Longfellow, for Henry Schoolcraft—upon whom Longfellow drew for some of his story—reports the Indian conviction that Hiawatha "is again to appear and to exercise an important power in the final disposition of the human race."[36] Here are the verses from Hiawatha:

> I am going, O my people,
> On a long and distant journey;
> Many moons and many winters
> Will have come, and will have vanished,
> Ere I come again to see you . . .

> On the shore stood Hiawatha,
> Turned and waved his hand at parting;
> On the clear and luminous water
> Launched his birch canoe for sailing. . . .
> Westward, westward Hiawatha
> Sailed into the fiery sunset
> Sailed into the purple vapors,
> Sailed into the dusk of evening. . . .
> To the kingdom of Ponemah,
> To the land of the Hereafter!

Indian nations ruefully discovered that it is difficult to identify such great heroes when they are reborn, and unfortunate mistakes can be made. In fact, a disastrous error was made, one that changed the course of empire on the American continents and radically altered the lives of its rightful heirs. Professor Daniel Brinton wrote of this in *Myths of the New World:*

> The Maryland Indians said the whites were an ancient generation who had come to life again, and had returned to seize their former land. . . . [That such legends existed] is almost proved by the fact that in Mexico, Bogota, and Peru, the whites were at once called by the proper names of heroes of the dawn, Suas, Viracochas, and Quetzalcoatls. . . .

The dawn heroes were conceived of as of fair complexion, mighty in war, and though absent for a season, destined to return and claim their ancient power. . . . Historians have marveled at the instantaneous collapse of the empires of Mexico, Peru, the Mayas, and the Natches, before a handful of Spanish filibusters. The fact was, wherever the whites appeared they were connected with these ancient predictions of the spirit of the dawn returning to claim his own.

When the Central Americans "first beheld the fair complexioned Spaniards," Brinton adds, "they rushed into the water to embrace the prows of their vessels, and despatched messengers throughout the land to proclaim the return of Quetzalcoatl."[37] As to the great teacher of the Peruvians, Viracocha, he was pictured not only as white but bearded. Thus, when the bearded Spaniards came, riding on horses—unknown animals—the conquerors were mistaken for returning gods. In an article on Viracocha titled "Inca's Sun God," H. J. Maidenberg observes that, despite centuries of Christianizing, "today many Christian Indians still look to their holy lake [Titicaca] for the return of the Sun God and the restoration of the highly advanced civilization that was destroyed by Francisco Pizarro's expedition from Spain more than 400 years ago."[38]

D. H. Lawrence's haunting novel of Mexico, *The Plumed Serpent*, centers around the prophecy that Quetzalcoatl (symbolized as "the Feathered Serpent") will return and bring about a renaissance of the ancient culture. Professor William Tindall, who provides the introduction to the paperback edition, notes that in the novel "the theme of rebirth is supported by symbols so central and impressive that it would be accurate to say that theme and narrative serve them. . . . Lawrence makes his feathered snake not only a sign of unity but of those dying and reviving gods he learned about from Frazer. Quetzalcoatl like Attis, Osiris, and Adonis, has died in order to live."[39]

One of the main characters in the story, Don Ramón, is deeply convinced of the reality of the return of Quetzalcoatl. When his little Christian-raised son tells him that "there never was any Quetzalcoatl, except idols," his father replies, "Is there any Jesus, except images?" "Yes, papa." "Where?" "In heaven." "Then," said the father, "in heaven there is also Quetzalcoatl. And what is in heaven is capable of coming back to earth."

As to Quetzalcoatl's title, "the feathered snake," serpents and dragons frequently appear as symbols for wise beings in Eastern religions. In the New Testament, Jesus said, "Be ye wise as serpents, and harmless as doves!'' In *The Plumed Serpent,* Don Ramón exclaims, ''The universe is a nest of dragons, with a perfectly unfathomable mystery at the center of it.''[40]

EGYPTIAN TEACHINGS

A distinguished Egyptologist, Dr. Margaret Murray, writes in *The Splendour That Was Egypt* that one theory of the hereafter held by the Egyptians,

> which has received little attention from Egyptologists, is the theory of reincarnation. . . . The ka-names of the first two kings of the xx-th dynasty [a remote period in Egyptian history] show this belief clearly: Amonemhat I's name was ''He who repeats births,'' and Sensusert I's name was ''He whose births live.'' In the xix-th dynasty the ka-name of Setekhy I was ''Repeater of births,'' and it was by this epithet that he was addressed by the god Amon at Karnak. . . . Pythagoras is usually credited with having invented the theory of reincarnation, but it was already hoary with age before the Greeks had emerged from barbarism.[41]

In *The Book of the Dead,* the great teacher of the Egyptians, Osiris, asks of the god Thoth: ''How long have I to live?'' ''It is decreed that thou shalt live for millions of millions of years,'' replies the god. ''May it be granted,'' Osiris responds, ''that I pass on unto the holy princes, for indeed, I am doing away with all the wrong which I did, from the time when this earth came into being.''[42]

In commenting, noted British author J. B. Priestley remarks, ''I agree that it could be argued . . . that what the god Thoth was offering his questioner was not the false eternity of popular Christianity but the innumerable incarnations . . . accepted by the Buddhists. This Egyptian, it could be said, would live for millions of years because he would return again and again and again to Time, in one shape and personality after another, until finally purged of all desire for any further existence on this earth.''[43]

Other instructions of a most remarkable character received by Osiris have been preserved by the Christian church father Synesius in his *Treatise on Providence,* and have been singled out for translation by the distinguished Platonist Thomas Taylor.[44] Here, Osiris is informed of the periodical incarnation among humankind of saviors and heroes. Such beings ''descend according to orderly periods of time, for the purpose of imparting a beneficent impulse in the republics of mankind. . . . For this providence is divine and most ample, which frequently through one man pays attention to countless multitudes of men.'' Also, ''in this terrestrial abode'' Osiris learns, there is ''the sacred tribe of heroes who pay attention to mankind, and who are able to give them assistance even in the smallest concerns. . . . This heroic tribe is, as it were, a colony [from the gods] established here in order that this terrene abode may not be left destitute of a better nature.''

However, at certain critical cycles, the instruction continues, the return of saviors of the highest order becomes imperative. Why? Because at such time ''the whole order of mundane things, greatest and least, is corrupted,'' and therefore Great Souls must ''descend for the purpose of imparting another orderly distribution of things.'' In other words, ''a new order of ages'' must be commenced—something that many contemporary observers believe our sick, exhausted, war-torn world, with its dying political, economic, and social systems, desperately needs today.

RELIGIOUS SCHOOLS OF ISLAM

The Koran, the bible of Islam, is believed to have been revealed to Muhammed by Allah. It is largely ethical in nature. Honor is paid to Issa Ben Yussuf, or Jesus, son of Joseph, as also to the Hebrew prophets such as Moses. Muhammed affirmed that the Koran has an esoteric foundation. It was ''sent in seven dialects; and in every one of its sentences there is an external and an internal meaning. . . . I received from the messenger of God two kinds of knowledge: One of these I taught [but] if I had taught them the other it would have broken their throats.''[45]

''Typical passages in the Koran which are cited in support of the belief in reincarnation, are the following,'' notes Dr. Ian Stevenson in the *International Journal of Comparative Sociology* of March 1970.

> How disbelieve ye in Allah when ye were dead and He gave life to you. Then He will give you death, then life again, and then unto Him ye will return (*Surah*, 2, Verse 28).

> Allah hath caused you to grow from the earth, and afterwards He maketh you return thereto, and He will bring you forth again (*Surah*, 71, Verses 17–18).

In a series of articles titled ''Reincarnation—Islamic Conceptions,'' Dr. M. H. Abdi, a Moslem scholar, expresses some illuminating thoughts on how rebirth gradually lost popularity in Islam.

> The position adopted by the successive luminaries who followed [Muhammed] was to affirm the belief in reincarnation but not to propagate it as a

teaching for the masses. . . . Another factor to remember is that the defensive wars, which have been described as Jehad or holy wars, which the Muslims fought in the early days and the wars of conquests (therefore not holy) which the Muslims fought in later days . . . gave a different shift to Islamic teachings.

Philosophical, mystical and ethical teachings received an impetus in the first phase but they had subdued existence in the later phase. During this phase the republican character of the State was changed into monarchy and the supremacy no more belonged to the saints and philosophers. A subject like reincarnation demands a subtle mental attitude. It entails understanding of the higher planes of consciousness, the laws of cause and effect and the working of the laws of evolution. The monarchs had no interest in such subjects.

[However,] there is no danger for a Muslim being called a heretic if he believes and expresses himself in favor of reincarnation.[46]

In the centuries following the Prophet's death, a number of esoteric schools arose in Islam. E. G. Brown describes their doctrines in his three-volume *Literary History of Persia*. These schools, he says, accepted three forms of reincarnation:

Hulul.   The periodical incarnation of the Perfect Man or Deity.
Rij'at.   The return of the Imam or spiritual leader after death.
Tanasukh.   Reincarnation of the souls of ordinary men.[47]

In his book *Reincarnation in Islam,* N. K. Misra informs that one of the esoteric schools, the Ismailis, held that the Hindu Krishna incarnated as Buddha and then as Muhammed; while one of the Rafziah sects believes "that at no time is the world left without a Teacher as a guide; that in some person or another . . . this great soul, is manifesting all the time."[48]

The Sufis.   Although Islam became divided into two religious branches, with many subsects, Dr. Abdi tells us that there has always existed a "cementing class" that has brought all the sects together. They are the Sufis. "The soul of Islam always yearned after them. . . . Even now Rumi, Hafiz, Jami, Ibne Sina and a host of other Sufis command universal respect."[49]

Rumi exercised an enormous influence that reached even to Western lands.[50] In his great work *Mathnawi*—called the Koran in Persian—he wrote:

There have been thousands of changes in form. . . . Look always to the form in the present; for, if you think of the forms in the past, you will separate yourself from your true Self. These are all only states of the permanent which you have seen by dying.

Why then do you turn your face from death? As the second stage has always been better than the first, then die happily and look forward to taking up a new and better form. Remember, and haste not. . . . Like the sun, only when you set in the West can you rise again with brilliance in the East.[51]

In that seventeenth-century treasure source, *The Dabistan*, the Sufis are shown distinguishing between *tanasukh*, the rebirth of ordinary people, and *buruz*, the reincarnation of a perfect soul "for the sake of perfecting mankind."[52]

ORIENTAL SAGES AND AVATARS

In Eastern teachings, an avatar is the incarnation of a god or some exalted being who has progressed beyond the necessity of rebirths for his or her own individual progress. There are greater and lesser avatars. One of the greatest, Sri Krishna, says in *The Bhagavad-Gita:* "I produce myself among creatures whenever there is a decline of virtue and an insurrection of vice and injustice in the world; and thus I incarnate from age to age, for the preservation of the just, the destruction of wickedness, and the establishment of righteousness."[53]

As to the Chinese sage, Lao-tzu, Taoist traditions relate that he practiced Tao in previous incarnations: as Kwang Chang Tze in the era of Hwang-Ti (the Yellow Emperor) and also as Po-Chang in the time of Yao. The stone tablets of Hsieh Tao-Hang add that "from the time of Fu-Hsi down to that of the Chou dynasty, in uninterrupted succession, his person appeared, but with changed names."[54]

However, it is in Mahayana Buddhism, which is the Buddhism of China, Japan, Tibet, and North Korea, that the rebirth of perfected souls is prominently featured. These beings have renounced Nirvana in order to effectively help the human race, either by incarnation at critical cycles or as powerful, invisible presences.

According to the Dalai Lama, spiritual head of the Tibetans, there are various levels of higher development: Arahats, Bodhisattvas, and Buddhas. "They are reincarnated," he says, "in order to help other beings to rise toward Nirvana, and by doing so the Bodhisattvas are themselves helped to rise to Buddhahood, and the Arahats also reach Buddhahood finally. Buddhas are reincarnated solely to help others, since they themselves have already achieved the highest of all levels" attainable on this earth.[55]

CHRISTIANITY AND JUDAISM

According to the familiar Christian tradition, Christ is to return among humankind. In Matthew 24:7–8, as translated in the New English Bible jointly published by Oxford and Cambridge universities, he tells of the signs that will precede such coming: "The time is coming when . . . nation will make war upon nation, kingdom upon kingdom; there will be famines and earthquakes in many places. With all these things the birth-pangs of the new age begin." Note that he says "the new age," not the end of the world as some readers of the King James Bible understood these passages to mean. Whether Christ will descend bodily from heaven, as fundamentalists and other literalists insist, or through another birth—virgin or otherwise—is fundamentally not important. What is important is that he will come again. The world will be blessed by his presence, and life on earth will be transformed. In the Gospel of John (14:3), he promised, "I will come again, and receive you unto myself, that where I am, there ye may be also."

*

As to Judaism, from time to time in Jewish history, there has been an insistent belief that their prophets are reborn. The Samaritans held that Adam returned as Seth, then as Noah, Abraham, and Moses.[56] Among the Hebrew population at the time of Jesus, there were many speculations as to whether he was Elijah, Jeremiah, or one of the other prophets (Matthew 16:13–14).

Some centuries later, the Jewish Cabalists—whose teachings prevailed as the dominant thought in the Judaic world for three hundred years—taught that, when an individual no longer needs to be reborn for his own progress, he "can out of compassion for the world repeatedly return to help it."[57] These words are those of Professor Gershom Scholem, the leading scholar of Jewish mysticism in our time. Not only is it believed that advanced souls can do this, he reports that many Cabalists said they do so incarnate. "The righteous transmigrate endlessly for the benefit of the universe, not for their own benefit."[58]

*

In the ensuing four chapters, four of the six major religions will be the focus of attention: Judaism and Christianity from the West; Hinduism and Buddhism, from the East. As to the fifth, Islam, its teachings on rebirth have just been examined. Confucianism, the sixth major faith, has nothing to say on the subject. Confucius neither taught nor denied immortality and reincarnation, his mission being clearly that of a teacher of ethics and an elaborator of moral codes. He avoided metaphysical inquiry.

However, for centuries in China before the present Communist regime, many Confucianists embraced Buddhism and Taoism as well, thereby becoming intimately acquainted with reincarnation. As one writer metaphorically observed, these people "wore a Confucian cap, a Taoist robe, and Buddhist sandals"—a practice that could rewardingly be emulated everywhere. For religious wars and intolerance would cease if people included in their sacred beliefs the best in each of the world's religions. Then all of humanity's Great Teachers would become the teachers of us all.

12

Judaic Teachers and Prophets

Yea, though I walk through the valley of the shadow of death, I will fear no evil.

Book of Psalms 23:4

In 1978, when Isaac Bashevis Singer returned from Stockholm, where he was awarded the Nobel Prize for Literature, he was publicly interviewed in New York regarding his religious convictions. This took place at the temple B'Nai Jeshuran in a dialogue series conducted by his friend Rabbi William Berkowitz and was reported in the *Jewish-American Examiner* (December 24, 1978). Among the questions was "Mr. Singer, if I'm correct, you believe in *Gilgul,* in reincarnation. Hence: Has Isaac Bashevis Singer ever been here before on earth? And if so, when were you here, who were you and what were you? Do *you* know?"

Singer answered by using the analogy of the seasons of the year and how they repeat again and again. After the death of winter, there is always spring again. "I think this is also true of the human body and the human spirit," he said. "The Almighty did not create us just for one season and then send us to die. We are coming back."

As to the question when was I here, I can tell you only one thing, Rabbi. If I was here—you were here too and I'm sure that I once appeared in a Dialogue in your Synagogue. As a matter of fact, I have a feeling that I remember some of your questions from that old time!

In Singer's stories and plays, his characters frequently entertain thoughts concerning past lives. However, his belief in rebirth is not unique in Judaism. For more than three hundred years, from the sixteenth century onward, it was, as we shall see, a dominant teaching in the Jewish religion. Today, many rabbis still hold to this view. *Newsweek* accorded an entire page to one of them, Israel's Rabbi Adin Steinsaltz, from which we quote.

Jewish lore is filled with tales of formidable rabbis. Probably none living today can compare in genius and influence to Adin Steinsaltz. . . . When he is not writing, Steinsaltz is talking. Last year, he spoke at the Aspen Institute for Humanistic Studies and at Yale University. . . . "He is a genius of the highest order," marvels Dan Segre, a professor of International Relations at Haifa University. "Steinsaltz has the sort of mind that comes around only every couple of thousand years."

Steinsaltz believes in reincarnation. So few souls achieve spiritual perfection in one lifetime, he says, that they must be born in another body. "Almost every person bears the legacy of previous existences" [May 26, 1980].

Rabbi Steinsaltz is an authority on the Cabala, which is no doubt the source of his interest in reincarnation. We will investigate cabalistic teachings shortly, but first a few words as to Rabbi Steinsaltz's general outlook on this tradition, as indicated in the *Newsweek* article. He considers the Cabala, as well as the Torah, "as the authentic theology of the Jewish people."

According to kabbalistic doctrine, the Torah contains not only manifest but also hidden truths: the same transcendent God whom the Bible celebrates as supreme king and lawgiver is, from the mystical viewpoint, also an infinity of divine light that exists as the foundation of every human soul. For Steinsaltz, every soul is an emanation or spark of the divine, and its ultimate purpose is to rejoin the God it came from. . . . Steinsaltz hopes to demonstrate that the secrets of the kabbalah—which rationalistic rabbis of the nineteenth century dismissed as dangerous magic—are fully consonant with traditional rabbinic Judaism.

This view is also held by that large body of strictly orthodox Jews known as the Hasidim. Among them, reincarnation is universally taught. Martin Buber devoted much of his life to spreading their doctrines and way of living. One of his precious Hasidic tales will be told later when we discuss this colorful Jewish community in the United States and Israel.

REINCARNATION IN THE OLD TESTAMENT

While the doctrine of reincarnation pervades Cabalistic literature, the same cannot be said of the Old Testament. In fact, the soul, its life, and immortality are rarely mentioned therein. Why not? Isidore Epstein, an esteemed authority, who has edited the twenty-volume English edition of the Talmud, writes, "Scripture found it necessary to cast a veil over the whole question of survival beyond the grave, in order to wean people away from the idolatrous cult of the dead with which this belief was at that time associated."[1] Professor Gershom Scholem adds that "apart from basic ideas concerning reward and punishment, life after death, the Messiah, redemption, and resurrection, there is hardly a commonly held belief among the Jews regarding *eschatological details*."[2] And as to reincarnation, he says, there has never been an official pronouncement disclaiming it to be false and a heresy.[3] Nowhere in the Old Testament is reincarnation denied. In the Book of Job (14:14), Job plaintively asks "If a man dies will he live again?" but receives no answer.

How Old Is Reincarnation Teaching in Judaism?   This question is considered by Rabbi Moses Gaster in his article "Transmigration in Judaism," in *Hastings's Encyclopedia of Religions and Ethics*. Although not a reincarnationist himself, he makes some surprising admissions.

> There cannot be any doubt that these views are extremely old [in Judaism]. Simon Magus raises the claim of former existences, his soul passing through many bodies before it reaches that known as Simon. The Samaritan doctrine of the taheb teaches the same doctrine of a pre-existing soul which was given to Adam, but which, through successive "incarnations" in Seth, Noah, and Abraham, reached Moses. . . . This doctrine of migration is nowhere to be found systematically developed [in Jewish writings]. Wherever it occurs, it is tacitly assumed as well known . . . whenever referred to, it is always an ancient tradition. . . .
>
> All the beginnings of esoteric teachings are lost in the mist of antiquity, and, when such doctrines finally see the light of day, they have, as a rule, a long history behind them. It is, therefore, a fallacy to date the origin of metempsychosis among the Jews from the time when it becomes known publicly in the 9th or 10th century. The [Hebrew] masters of the occult science never doubted its Jewish character or its old origin. [They asked:] Was it not part of that heavenly mystery handed down from Adam on through all the great men of the past?[4]

THE CABALISTIC TRADITION IN JUDAISM

A few words first as to the man most responsible for the current revival of interest in this tradition, and our chief source of reference in the present discussion. He was Gershom Scholem (1897–1982), a towering figure in Jewish scholarship.

He left Germany in 1923 and joined the Hebrew University in Jerusalem, where he later became Professor of Mysticism and Kabbalah. Since 1968 he was president of the Israel Academy of Sciences and Humanities. Quoting from a special report from Tel Aviv to the *New York Times* at the time of his death,

> Professor Gershom Scholem, widely regarded as the world's foremost authority on Jewish mysticism, died Saturday night in Jerusalem. [He] is credited with elevating the esoteric subject of the Kabala to its proper place in Jewish studies. The Kabala is a system of interpreting the Scriptures that is said to have been handed down orally from Abraham. . . . Professor Scholem's discoveries of new manuscripts and writers gave the philosophy the perspective of history.
>
> Geoffrey Wigoder, an editor of the Encyclopedia Judaica, said in a tribute today that articles in the encyclopedia on Kabala had been derogatory and condescending, apparently under the impact of rationalism, until Dr. Scholem began contributing in the 1920's [February 22, 1982].

The long article on reincarnation, under *Gilgul*, in the *Encyclopedia Judaica* was written by Scholem.[5] (*Gilgul* is one of the Hebrew words for reincarnation.)

The American public first became aware of Dr. Scholem's work when he was invited by Rabbi Stephen Wise, then president of the Jewish Institute of Religion, to deliver the Hilda Strook Lectures in 1938. These have continuously been in print in Scholem's classic *Major Trends in Jewish Mysticism.*[6]

Scholem's recent work is *Kabbalah,* published in 1974 by the *New York Times* in their Library of Jewish Knowledge series. We will be quoting extensively from this source. The publishers state on the book jacket:

> Knowledge of the Jewish mystical tradition and its implications have been revolutionized in the course of this century thanks to the researches of one man, Professor Gershom Scholem. It is not long since most Jews looked upon mystical literature and study as an aberration outside the mainstream of Judaism. Now it is realized that throughout Jewish history there has been a strong mystical current in Judaism. It has profoundly affected many forms of religious expression as well as the course of Jewish history itself. Professor Scholem's studies on this subject have become classic. In this book he presents a summary of his life's studies. It covers the whole history of the Kabbalah.

Scholem's Eranos Lecture on Reincarnation. In 1955, Professor Scholem was invited to lecture on reincarnation at the prestigious Eranos conference series in Switzerland. As we will be referring frequently to his contribution, published in volume 24 of the *Eranos Yearbook,* some explanation as to the origin and sponsorship of the series seems appropriate. Quoting from *C. G. Jung: Word and Image,* edited by Aniela Jaffé (she is speaking):

> In 1928 the founder of the Eranos Conferences, Olga Frobe-Kapteyn, had the Casa Eranos constructed next to her villa on Lake Maggiore. . . . Since 1933, learned men and women from all over the world and a circle of listeners have been meeting annually in late August for these conferences or *Tagungen.*
>
> In ancient Greece the name Eranos meant a banquet at which each guest had to show himself worthy of having been invited by presenting an intellectual gift: a song, a poem, an improvised speech. . . .
>
> Over the years Eranos developed far beyond its original boundaries to become a center where ideas were exchanged on science and the humanities, on religion and myth, on psychology and gnosis. . . . Jung spoke fourteen times at the Eranos conferences. . . . In addition he played a leading role in planning the programs throughout those years.[7]

Each conference is organized around a particular theme, and in 1955, when Scholem spoke, it was Man and the Sympathy of All Things. His gift was titled "Transmigration and the Sympathy of Souls in Jewish Mysticism." This sixty-three-page presentation unfolds, stage by stage, the appearance of reincarnation in cabalistic literature. John Becker, who teaches German, translated the entire lecture for us, and our deep thanks are extended to him for his excellent work. We also express appreciation to Dr. Ian Stevenson, who originally sent us a copy of the lecture in German. It is doubtful we would have otherwise learned of its existence. It was rather awesome to the present writers that, while we were preparing this portion of the chapter, the great soul of Gershom Scholem left his body.

Source and Influence of the Cabala.   The Cabala is said to represent the hidden wisdom behind the Old Testament, derived by the rabbis of the Middle Ages from still older teachings. In *A Talmudic Miscellany,* Rabbi Paul Isaac Hershon explains that the word "Cabala" means "a thing received," or traditional law. This, he says, together with the written law, was received by Moses on Mount Sinai, "and we are distinctly told in the Talmud" (Rosh Hashanah fol. 19, col. 1) "the words of the Kabbalah are just the same as the words of the law." Hershom states further that, in another part of the Talmud, "we find the rabbis declare the Kabbalah to be *above* the law."[8]

The renowned Italian renaissance humanist and Cabalist Pico della Mirandola explained that Moses transmitted many of his ideas orally through the seventy wise men in unbroken tradition until they had been embodied in the written Cabala.[9]

During medieval times there were many celebrated Cabalists. Rabbi Isaac Luria—who will be considered separately—founded a Cabalistic school in Safed, Palestine, and Rabbi Hayyim Vital, the great exponent of Luria's teachings, wrote a widely circulated work on reincarnation, *The Tree of Life,* which the Christian Cabalist Baron von Rosenroth (1636–1679) used as the basis of his book on the revolutions of souls.

Cabalists played an important part in bringing to birth the Italian renaissance and the German reformation.[10] Among Western authors who made abundant use of the Cabala were Milton and Blake.[11] Isaac Myer's *Quabbalah* provides a long list of other Europeans similarly influenced, including Paracelsus, Jacob Boehme, Pope Sixtus IV, Spinoza, Leibniz, Francis Bacon, Isaac Newton, and the later German philosophers Schopenhauer, Hegel, and Schelling.[12]

In Judaism itself, the Cabala "achieved one very important result," says Professor Scholem. "For the three-hundred-year period roughly from 1500 to 1800 (at the most conservative estimate) the Kabbalah was widely considered to be the true Jewish theology, compared with which all other approaches were able at best to lead an isolated and attenuated existence. In the course of this period an open polemical attack on the Kabbalah was practically unheard of, and characteristically, when such an attack appeared, it was almost always in the guise of a rebuke addressed to the later kabbalists for having misrepresented and corporealized the pure philosophy of their predecessors, rather than an open criticism of the Kabbalah itself."[13]

In the nineteenth century, Jewish scholars were hostile to Cabalism. They sought to give Judaism a rationalistic tone, in conformity with the spirit of agnosticism and skepticism prevailing then in science. "The most astonishing thing in reading the works of these critics," says Scholem, "is their lack of adequate knowledge of the sources or the subjects on which in many cases they ventured to pass judgment." But in the twentieth century, he writes, "the profoundly altered approach to Jewish history that followed in the wake of the Zionist revival and the movement for national rebirth led, particularly after World War I, to a renewal of interest in the Kabbalah as a vital expression of Jewish existence."[14]

If one can judge by the number of books currently in print on the Cabala, there is a large and growing interest among the lay public, as well as scholars, in Jewish mysticism. The 1983–1984 *Subject Guide to Books in Print* lists seventy-four books currently available.

The Zohar—The Book of Splendor.   Owing to a series of misfortunes

besetting the Palestinian Holy Land, Jewish peoples emigrated to Western
Europe. Cabalism flourished in France and prospered in Germany. But
when Muhammadan Spain became an important center for Jewish learning,
the Jews "were no longer dependent for their religious instructions on the
schools of the East," writes Dr. M. Friedlander. "Henceforth the schools
in the West asserted their independence, and even surpassed the parent
institutes." The Islamic caliphs, "mostly opulent, gave every encouragement to philosophy and poetry; and being generally liberal in sentiment,
they entertained kindly feelings towards their Jewish subjects."[15]

"In the years immediately following 1275," writes Scholem in *Major
Trends in Jewish Mysticism,*

> a book was written somewhere in the heart of Castile which was destined
> to overshadow all other documents of Kabbalistic literature by the success and
> the fame it achieved and the influence it gradually exerted; this was the *Sefer
> Ha-Zohar,* or Book of Splendor. Its place in the history of Kabbalism can be
> gauged from the fact that alone among the whole of post-Talmudic rabbini-
> cal literature it became a *canonical* text, which for a period of several
> centuries actually ranked with the Bible and the Talmud. . . .
>
> It was undeniably a success, first among the Kabbalists and later, particu-
> larly after the exodus from Spain, among the whole Jewish people. For
> centuries it stood out as the expression of all that was profoundest and most
> deeply hidden in the innermost recesses of the Jewish soul.[16]

The author of the *Zohar* is unknown but is generally believed to be
Rabbi Moses de Leon, a Spanish Cabalist who died in 1305. However, the
medieval Cabalists and the volume itself attribute much of the teaching to
a renowned second-century religious teacher, Rabbi Simeon ben Jochai. In
this connection, Scholem has discovered in the writings of de Leon a most
significant passage that appears to apply to himself as the recorder not
originator of the *Zohar*:

> There are hidden mysteries and secret things which are unknown to men.
> You will now see that I am revealing deep and secret mysteries which the
> holy sages regarded as sacred and hidden, profound matters which properly
> speaking are not fit for revelation so that they may not become a target for
> the wit of every idle person. These holy men of old have pondered all their
> lives over these things. . . .
>
> One generation passes away and another generation comes, but the errors
> and falsehoods abide forever. And no one sees and no one hears and no one
> awakens, for they are all asleep . . . they do not question and do not read
> and do not search out. And when I saw all this I found myself constrained to

write and to conceal and to ponder, in order to reveal it to all thinking men, and to make known all these things with which the holy sages of old concerned themselves all their lives.[17]

Reincarnation in the Zohar and Other Cabalistic Texts. In his Eranos lecture, Professor Scholem observed that, among the Spanish Cabalists, reincarnation—which they now called *Gilgul* (the revolution of souls) —was first introduced as a mystery. Few explanations were offered. In the *Zohar*, it was stated:

> All souls are subject to the trials of transmigration; and men do not know the designs of the Most High with regard to them; they know not how they are being at all times judged, both before coming into this world and when they leave it. They do not know how many transformations and mysterious trials they must undergo; how many souls and spirits come to this world without returning to the palace of the divine king.[18]

During this period, Scholem indicates, reincarnation "served as a rational excuse for the apparent absence of justice in the world. . . . The entire Book of Job and the resolution of the mystery of his suffering, especially as stated in the words of Elihu, were interpreted in terms of transmigration (e.g., in the *Commentary on Job* by Nahmanides, and in all subsequent kabbalistic literature)."[19] Scholem describes Nahmanides as "a man of extraordinary authority, who could at this time speak with complete freedom on such subjects."[20]

Among certain sectarian Cabalists, Scholem remarks, rebirth was limited to the souls of Israelites, but "it was expressly taught by many others as a law for all people." Furthermore, "it was not merely a punishment for crimes, but to provide the opportunity to fulfil certain laws of the Torah, and this above all, for the good of the world."[21]

Moses de Leon offers still another need for being reborn and, in doing so, provides an illuminating answer to a question often raised. If the soul is perfect when originally descending from its spiritual source, and then returns to the same condition when the world ends, why bother to make the journey? What has really been gained if the alpha and omega are the same? Rabbi de Leon replies, as quoted by Scholem, "The purpose of the soul in entering the body is to exhibit its powers and abilities in the world. . . . And when it is in this world, it perfects itself and completes itself from this lower world. . . . Then it is in a state of perfection, which was not the case in the beginning before its descent. . . . Were it not composed in a mystic manner of what is above *and* below, *it would not be complete*."[22]

Perfected souls, however, no longer need to return for their own development. As Scholem puts this, "Only the completely pious—just as in the case of the enlightened Buddhas—are freed from this law [of rebirth]. Yet like the Buddhas and Bodhisattvas, as depicted in Mahayana Buddhism, they can out of compassion for the world repeatedly return to help it."[23]

Cabalists also spoke of the possibility that Great Souls can temporarily merge with and light up worthy mortals, to accomplish some great end. The name for this was *Ibbur*. Scholem quotes David Ibn Zimra as saying, "I have asked a wise man of the Kabbalah, what is the difference between *Gilgul* and *Ibbur*. He answered, that *Ibbur*, or spiritual pregnancy, refers to a mystery. As a woman becomes pregnant and gives birth, without losing anything from her nature, so also the souls of the pious and righteous become pregnant and give birth. From them sparks radiate out into this world, in order to assist the age, or for some other reason, and it is as if one light kindles that of another."[24]

Isaac Luria, The Lion of the Cabbalah.   In Spain under Islamic rule, the Jewish peoples prospered for a number of centuries, creating their greatest civilization since the dispersion from Palestine in the second century. However, Christian kingdoms slowly infiltrated into northern Spain where Islamic power was weak. They waged perpetual, relentless wars against the Moors, until, by the late 1200s, only the province of Granada on the Mediterranean Sea was under Muhammadan control. Then the Muslims were completely driven out in 1492, the same year Christian Spain launched its worldwide colonial empire by sending Columbus on his first exploratory voyage. But 1492 had a tragic significance for the Jews.

In a Columbus Day article, "Ill Winds Drove Columbus" (*New York Times*, October 8, 1979), historian William Loren Katz related that on March 31, 1492, Spain's Jews "were handed an Edict of Expulsion ordering them out in four months," and "one official suggested that 'the whole accursed race of Jews of twenty years and upwards, might be purified by fire.' "

> The Inquisition did force many Jews, stretched on the rack, over burning coals, or tied to the stake, to pay the ultimate penalty. But Spaniards were after something financially more sound than a Nazi-style holocaust.
> The wealth that slipped from tortured hands [and evicted Jews] helped pay for Columbus's expedition. . . . The second sentence of Columbus's "Diary" shows that the captain knew the connection between their expulsion and his departure: "After having turned out all the Jews from all your Kingdoms

and Lordships . . . your Highness [King Ferdinand] gave orders to me that with a sufficient fleet I should go." . . .

Some 150,000 refugees had trudged to seaports as time ran out for the Jews on the very day before Columbus left; on the day he weighed anchor at Paos, the last band of Jewish refugees huddled at Cadiz waited for a ship to rescue them.

A distinguished historian and former president of the Jewish Historical Society in England, Cecil Roth, continues the saga in an essay on Isaac Luria, "The Lion of the Cabbalah."

It was the darkest hour in Jewish history. As today, many of the exiles directed their footsteps towards Palestine, the Holy Land, there reestablishing the settlement which had been all but extinct since the period of the Crusades. From the crushing vicissitudes of this world, they sought refuge in the contemplation of the mysteries of the next.

With greater singleness of purpose than ever before, they turned their attention to the study of the *Zohar* and the kindred esoteric literature. Gradually, the choicer spirits became concentrated in the "Holy City" of Safed in Upper Galilee—the scene of the terrestrial activity, fourteen centuries before, of Rabbi Simeon ben Jochai, reputed author of the *Zohar,* The Book of Splendour.

Here there grew up the strangest, strictest, maddest, most amazing community in Jewish history; a veritable Congregation of the Saints, recruited by eager mystics from every corner of Asia and Europe, passing twenty-four hours of every day in the study of the Holy Cabbalah, and maintaining in perpetuity the spirit of a revivalist camp. This was the scene of the activity of the Lion of the Kabbalah—Rabbi Isaac Luria.[25]

Scholem calls this rabbi "the central figure of the new Kabbalah. . . . In the whole history of the Kabbalah only the influence of the *Zohar* can measure up to his."[26] The religious movement Luria instituted spanned more than three hundred years and had "a decisive and continuous influence on the Diaspora as a whole, in Europe, Asia, and North Africa."[27]

Luria's teachings, including reincarnation, says Dr. Roth, "speedily permeated the Jewish world through and through giving fresh life to old observances. . . . The modern rationalists who sneer at the tendency do not realize what comfort it brought to their fathers in the long nightmare of the Ghetto, how it consoled them for the vicissitudes of daily life, how it made mechanical observances instinct with beauty, with hope, even with divinity."[28]

The thought of reincarnation, in fact, helped the Jewish peoples in exile to cope with their condition. They saw an analogy between the wandering

Jew and the journey of the soul. In Judaism, one of the words for "reincarnation" is *seelenwanderung,* or soul-wandering, the soul in exile from its true home until it reunites with God. This as a symbol, says Scholem, was a "key to Israel's history and had a great popular influence for many generations."[29]

By the middle of the sixteenth century, and for the two ensuing centuries, "the religious message of the Kabbalah reached into every Jewish home," writes Scholem in *Major Trends in Jewish Mysticism.* In a short time, the doctrine of *Gilgul* "became an integral part of Jewish popular belief and Jewish folklore. . . . In the later development of the school of Safed, this remarkable doctrine has been elaborated in great detail, and Hayim Vital's *Sefer Ha-Gilgulim,* or 'Book of Transmigrations,' in which he gave a systematic description of Luria's doctrine of metempsychosis, is the final product of a long and important development in Kabbalistic thought."[30]

The pervasive presence of reincarnational views in Judaism at this time was emphasized in strongest language by Rabbi Manasseh Ben Israel. He was both a theologian and a statesman. Owing to his efforts, Oliver Cromwell removed the legal prohibition of Jews from England that had existed for 350 years, since the reign of Edward I. In *Nishmath Hayem,* this revered son of Israel wrote, "The doctrine of the transmigration of souls is a firm and infallible truth accepted by the whole assemblage of our religion with one accord, so that there is none to be found who would dare to deny it. Indeed there are a great number of sages in Israel who hold firm to this doctrine as a fundamental point of our religion . . . as the truth of it has been incontestably demonstrated by the *Zohar,* and all books of the Kabbalists."[31]

Some Controversial Questions. A difference of opinion arose among the Cabalists as to whether the human soul, as a punishment, could incarnate in animals and plants. Some held that they could. However, says Scholem, this opinion was "opposed by many Kabbalists." Moses de Leon, he says, "seems to have disapproved of the theory of transmigration into non-human forms."[32] Today, Western reincarnationists affirm that "once a human being always a human being."

Another controversy developed as to whether human beings are always born into the same sex. Some Cabalists said "yes," and others said "no." Before its descent into matter, the soul was believed to be hermaphroditic or perhaps sexless. "In its root," writes Scholem, "every soul includes both sexes." They later "separate into masculine and feminine souls."[33] According to one Cabalistic text, *Yalkut Reubeni,* to be reborn a woman is a disgrace and punishment. "If a man be niggardly either in a financial or a spiritual regard, giving nothing of his money to the poor or not imparting of his knowledge to the ignorant, he shall be punished by transmigration into a woman. . . . The soul of Rahab transmigrated into Heber the Kenite, and afterwards into Hannah; and this is the mystery of her words, 'I am a woman of a sorrowful spirit' (I Sam. i. 15), for there still lingered in her soul a sorrowful sense of inherited defilement.''[34]

Apropos of this, we return to the interview with Isaac Bashevis Singer, who was the son of a rabbi and himself studied to become one. Rabbi Berkowitz inquired: "Today there is a major question whether women should become rabbis. What do you think? Were you in effect trying to make that point in your story *Yentl?*" Singer answered, "Yes. I think that the Jewish people made a big mistake by keeping our women too far away from religion. . . . If this mistake would be corrected, it would be wonderful for the sake of religion and also for the sake of justice. I myself have seen young women who told me that they would like to study for the rabbinate. One woman even said to me that she would like to be a *chazzan!*"[35]

The Human Being as the Perfecting Agent in the Cosmos. As to agreement and unanimity among the Cabalists, Scholem notes that all of them concur in the belief that the human soul "originates on a plane higher than that of the angels, a doctrine that is referred to repeatedly in discussions of the human condition." For if a human being "is capable of plunging to indescribable depths of depravity, he also had the capacity, when he fulfils his true destiny, of rising even above the angelic realm. No angel has that potential power to restore the worlds which has been granted to man.''[36]

Scholem elaborates this in one of his most inspired passages:

At opposite poles, both man and God encompass within their being the entire cosmos. However, whereas God contains all by virtue of being its Creator and Initiator in whom everything is rooted and all potency is hidden, *man's role is to complete this process* by being the agent through whom all the powers of creation are fully activated and made manifest. *What exists seminally in God unfolds and develops in man. . . .*

Man is the perfecting agent in the structure of the cosmos. . . . He is also the "transformer" who through his own life and deeds amplifies these forces to their highest level of manifestation and redirects them to their original source. . . .

The crucial turning-point in this cycle takes place at the moment he begins to develop an awareness of his own true essence and yearns to retrace the path from the multiplicity of his nature to the Oneness from which he originated[37] [italics added].

In achieving this grand consummation, the teaching of what the Cabalists called "soul-sparks" played a crucial role. Such soul-sparks, Scholem says, radiate from an individual when he returns to incarnation. They may be thought of as "a spiritual aura which surrounds him." As the individual grows in sympathy with others "an expansion of the individual's power field" takes place, and "the soul-sparks are no longer bound to the corporeal, visible boundaries of the individual." With an advanced soul "the whole world of mankind becomes a cosmic power field of his soul." In Hasidism, of which we shall shortly speak, this doctrine reached its climax. They taught that the power field even of ordinary people extended far beyond the limits of their personal selves. This teaching is also linked to the homeless Jew ever on the move. Wherever he goes, it is his task to "use the sparks emanating from his soul to free the life imprisoned in that area."[38]

Cabalism Under a Cloud.   The rise and fall of religious movements is a universal phenomenon. Forces of decay enter; false prophets assume the mantle of the real; the gullible masses accept their claims; fanciful doctrines replace foundational truths; and a once promising movement is eclipsed. This happened among the Cabalists. By the nineteenth century, Jewish leaders were so convinced of its bad effects, that the movement was submerged.

Among the mystics, however, the movement never died, and deeply learned Cabalists continued their studies. To avoid the disastrous consequences that ensued from the excesses of messiah-hunting, says Scholem, such Cabalists

> tried to lead the Kabbalah back from the market place to the solitude of the mystic's semi-monastic cell. . . . The classical representative of this tendency has been found in Rabbi Shalom Sharabi, a Yemenite Kabbalist who lived in Jerusalem in the middle of the 18th century and founded a center for Kabbalists which exists to this day. . . . We are in possession of documents signed by twelve members of this group in which the signatories pledge themselves to build up, through their common life, the mystical body of Israel and to sacrifice themselves for each other "not only in this life but in all lives to come."[39]

HASIDISM AND THE TRANSFORMATION OF JEWISH LIFE

Although the perspective of reincarnation was lost to many Jews during the nineteenth century, the interest therein expanded rather than diminished in Hasidism. This influential movement began in the eighteenth century among Polish Jews. One of the particularly remarkable things about it says Scholem, "is the fact that within a geographically small area and also within a surprisingly short period, the ghetto gave birth to a whole galaxy of saint-mystics . . . a wealth of truly original religious types which, as far as one can judge, surpassed even the harvest of the classical period of Safed. Something like a rebellion of religious energy against petrified religious values must have taken place."[40]

Thus, Scholem adds, "in the shadow of the deep crisis in the spiritual world of the Kabbalah," in the wake of false messiahs, "the Hasidic movement came into existence."[41] "For all its present decay," he says, "it remains a living force in the lives of countless thousands of people. . . . The literature on Hasidism has grown enormously. Of thoughtful and scholarly writers on the subject there has been no lack."[42]

To illustrate how reincarnational ideas permeate the life of the Hasidic communities, two selections are offered: one from a Hasidic prayerbook, another from Ansky's drama *The Dybbuk.*

*

The prayer that follows is called "Prayer Before Retiring at Night" and is printed in the *Siddur Tehillat Hashem* of the great Hasidic teacher Rabbi Shneur Zalman. His prayerbook has been constantly in use ever since it was first published in 1803.

> Master of the Universe! I hereby forgive anyone who has angered or vexed me, or sinned against me, either physically or financially, against my honor or anything else that is mine, whether accidentally or intentionally, inadvertently or deliberately, by speech or by deed, in this incarnation or in any other.[43]

The author of *The Dybbuk,* S. Ansky (Solomon Judah Rapoport), is identified in the *Universal Jewish Encyclopedia* as a "unique figure in Yiddish literature." The play, called "his masterpiece, is mystical and symbolical yet taken from actual Hasidic life."[44] These passages are from a translation published in English in 1926.[45]

> It's not only the poor it pays to be careful with. You can't say for a certainty, who any man might have been in his last existence, nor what he is doing on earth. . . .

Through many transmigrations, the human soul is drawn by pain and grief, as the child to its mother's breast, to the source of its being, the Exalted Throne above. . . .

The souls of the dead *do* return to earth, but not as disembodied spirits [as spiritualists think]. Some must pass through many forms before they achieve purification. . . .

A young person inquires about a person who dies prematurely: "What becomes of the life he has not lived . . . ? What becomes of his joys and sorrows, and all the thoughts he had no time to think, and all the things he hadn't time to do . . . ?"

Then answering her own question, she observes: "No human life goes to waste. If one of us dies before his time, his soul returns to earth to complete its span, to do the things left undone and experience the happiness and griefs he would have known."

As the drama concerns a person who has become obsessed by a *dybbuk,* this explanation is offered: "It sometimes happens that a soul which has attained to the final state of purification suddenly [through pride?] becomes the prey of evil forces which cause it to slip and fall. And the higher it has soared, the deeper it falls. [Such] vagrant souls which, finding neither rest nor harbor, pass into the bodies of the living, in the form of a *dybbuk,* until they have attained purity."

Gershom Scholem writes in his *Kabbalah* that, in Jewish folklore and popular belief, a *dybbuk* is "an evil spirit or doomed soul which enters into a living person, cleaves to his soul, causes mental illness, talks through his mouth. . . . It is thus the equivalent of possession. . . . The power to exorcise *dybbukum* was given to the *ba'alei shem* or accomplished Hasidim. They simultaneously redeemed the soul by providing a *tikkun* ('restoration') for him, either by transmigration or by causing the *dybbuk* to enter hell" until purified.[46] In either case, there was hope for such unfortunates—and for the afflicted people possessed by them.

A Hasidic Story by Martin Buber. In introducing excerpts from Buber's remarkable book, *For the Sake of Heaven,*[47] it should be explained that the great Jewish mystics were accredited with the ability to see into the previous incarnations of those who came to them for help. Scholem reports that the Cabalists believed that "everybody carries the secret trace of the transmigrations of his soul in the lineaments of his forehead and his hands, and in the aura which radiates from his body. And those to whom it is given to decipher this writing of the soul can aid in its wandering [from life to life]. It is true that this power is conceded by Cordovero and Luria only to the great mystics."[48]

For the Sake of Heaven concerns two such mystics, both bearing the same name, Jaacob Yitzchak. In the *Journal of Bible and Religion,* Maurice Friedman calls the book "one of the crowning achievements of Buber's lifetime of significant work, a profound literary work which may properly be compared with Dostoevski's novel *The Brothers Karamazov* in its dialectic between types or religious figures and in the depths of its insight into the problem of evil and of human existence."[49] Here, in brief, is the story, the quoted parts being from the exquisite translation of Ludwig Lewisohn.

Four hundred years ago, high on a hill in the northeasterly part of the city of Lublin in Poland stood a proud castle and a church. Below the hill were swamps, and none had dreamed of living on those inhospitable lands until, in the sixteenth century, Jews who traded in the city but were forbidden to dwell therein took it into their heads to buy ground in the swamps. "Lot after lot around the hill was drained. Beside a house of prayer and study, rose first the houses of great rich Jews, next of the poorer and very poorest," and thus the castle became surrounded by a coil of Jewish lanes and homes.

Now, during the time of the Napoleonic wars, Rabbi Jaacob Yitzchak—called the "Seer"—dwelt in this ghetto among the poor, and prayed and studied with his disciples. "They took no part in the offices or studies of the Chief Synagogue; they were hasidim, the 'pious' ones. . . . The established order wanted no dealing with them nor they with it, yet from a distance they fought both subtly and powerfully for the souls of the rising generations."

It was told, says Buber, that, when this "Seer" was born, he had been able to see from the beginning to the end of the world. However, "he was so dismayed by the flood of evil which he beheld engulfing the earth, that he besought the gift to be taken from him and his vision to be restricted to a narrower span." Later, when he officiated as a rabbi and numberless people came to him with their problems, he looked upon their foreheads and saw the paths their souls had taken from the beginning. He gazed "into the depth of time and saw the origin and story of the soul of each suppliant, of which the mortal dwelling place, the body, stood before him. . . . He saw how often during its pilgrimage it had entered a human frame and how each time it had wrought ill or well at the great task which it was destined to accomplish."

His power to read former lives was once vicariously conferred upon a young promising disciple who also bore the name Jaacob Yitzchak, but was generally known as "the Yehudi." As told in the chapter called "The Shirt," the elder Jaacob Yitzchak—who was the Zaddick for the whole community of Hasidics—had to leave for a while on a mysterious journey. But, instead of leaving his oldest and most learned disciple in charge, he chose the young Jaacob, commanding the young man wear one of the rabbi's own shirts. The lad begged that another be appointed because he felt so inexperienced, but the teacher replied *"You are the right one."*

"On the very next morning after prayers the Yehudi, having donned the Rabbi's shirt, went dutifully to his house and took his stand in the ante-chamber in order to fulfill, as need arose, the functions of his office. At that very moment sundry strangers entered. . . . And now something came to pass which frightened him as nothing had done all his life long.

"He looked at one of those who had entered, a very ordinary person, and looked involuntarily upon the man's forehead. In the next instant it seemed to him as though a curtain were drawn apart. Yehudi stood at the brink of a sea, whose dark waves assaulted the very heavens. And now they, too, were split asunder as the curtain had been and thus gave space for a figure, totally unlike that visitor, but with the same seal upon its forehead that was to be seen upon [him now]. But already that figure was devoured by the waves; behind it stood another, different again but sealed with the same seal. It too vanished and farther and farther the depths revealed figures after figures.

"The Yehudi closed his eyes. When he opened them again nothing was to be seen but that ordinary man and the people about him and the room with its habitual furnishings.

"For a long time he did not dare to look at the next visitor. So soon as he did so, the same thing took place. . . . Again a curtain was torn asunder and again waves rolled in the abyss and again vision succeeded vision. At this point the Yehudi mastered the disturbance of his mind and decided to obey the plain and open bidding that had been given him. He observed and sought to grasp every figure. He let it sink into the depth of his memory; he forced his eyes to remain open as long as possible." [And suddenly, after the fourth and fifth visitor entered the Rabbi's home] "he noticed that a change had been accomplished within himself. His vision penetrated the depths independently; with inhuman swiftness it pierced those realms; it reached to the *background* of that row of figures and came upon the very being of the primordial."

And thus Martin Buber concludes this particular adventure of the Yehudi, leaving us with the thought that, although the soul may have many lives, what is needful is to fathom the divine primordial Source from which they emanate.

Rabbi Steinsaltz's The Thirteen Petaled Rose. This slender volume on Jewish theology was singled out for commendation in *Newsweek*'s featured article on this world-renowned rabbi who heads Israel's Institute for Talmudic Publications. His "extraordinary gifts as scholar, teacher, scientist, writer, mystic and social critic have attracted disciples from every faction in Israeli society" (May 26, 1980). The title of his book is taken from a symbol for the community of Israel as used in the opening lines of the *Zohar*. In the selections that follow, Rabbi Steinsaltz addresses the question of how each individual can attain the highest level of development, and how this in turn will lead to the redemption of the whole world.

> The destiny of a person is connected not only with those things he himself creates and does, but also with what happened to the soul in its previous incarnations. The encounters and events of life, its joys and sorrows, are influenced by one's previous existence. One's existence is therefore a continuity, the sustaining of a certain fundamental essence; and certain elements may arise to the surface which do not seem to belong to the present. These a person has to complete or fix or correct. It is a portion of the world which is his task to put in order so as to raise his soul to its proper level. And this struggle of the souls is also the struggle and way of the world toward its redemption.
>
> As the souls return and strive to correct the world and vindicate themselves, at a certain level they reach their highest peak. Then the greatest obstacles are behind the human race, and it can go forward towards its perfection with sure steps and without the legacy of suffering inherited from previous existences and previous sins. This is the beginning of Salvation, which is the time of the Messiah.
>
> In this manner human beings proceed until that stage is reached when all the souls return, each to its own self, when every self in the world will enter into a new life in complete fusion with the higher forces of the soul, manifesting all the potential powers it contains. This level of the perfection of all humanity is called "Heaven" or the "next world." It is the goal toward which all souls, in discharging their private and specific tasks in life, aspire and strive.[50]

Crisis in Judaism. A special report to the *New York Times* notes that numerous young Jews are deserting their faith for membership in other religions, many of the oriental variety. Among rabbis interviewed was James Rudin, assistant national interreligious director for the American Jewish Committee. He declared that in some of these groups 25 or 30 percent are Jewish. "We're talking about 8 or 9 times what it should be," he said, for whereas there are nearly 6 million Jews in the United States, they are only 2.7 percent of the nation's population. To counteract these outside influences, Jewish groups have been aroused to take strong measures. But another rabbi, Rubin Dobin, says the results are not encouraging—"We gain one and lose five" (November 22, 1981).

Most of the groups that interest young Jews teach reincarnation. This outlook gives themselves an identity that death cannot dissolve. Life to them has an enduring, elevated purpose, and they find this view substantiated by evidence uncovered in scientific research (see chapters 4 and 5).

Although many rabbis today privately hold to the many-lives view, it is not openly taught in the three main branches of Judaism: Orthodox, Conservative, and Reform. It is, as indicated, a cardinal doctrine in Hasidism, but the strict orthodoxy of the Hasidic communities, the old-world rabbinical attire of most of their male members, and the inferior place they allot women* are not attractive to the modern Jew. So the young seek elsewhere.

Need they seek elsewhere? Nobelists of the stature of Isaac Bashevis Singer and Saul Bellow, as well as leading Jewish scholars such as Rabbi Steinsaltz and Professor Gershom Scholem, to whom we have given much space, all believe that the time is eminently ripe for Jewish people to expand their horizons, by reexamining their religious heritage when rebirth was the dominant outlook in Judaism, and then adapt that vision to illuminate the problems of the modern world.

---

*An exception to discrimination against women is in the work of the Hasidic teacher Rabbi Salman Schachter, whose liberality and compassionate, wise counseling have attracted a wide following in this country. We are especially grateful to him for calling our attention to Martin Buber's story *For the Sake of Heaven*, from which we quoted earlier.

13
Jesus and the Christian Vision

Prove all things; hold fast that which is good.

SAINT PAUL, I Thessalonians 5:21

The mission of Jesus is undoubtedly of special importance for the West and for the world. The path to salvation, and of ethical living, he taught has remained a beacon light through the centuries. Many of Christ's early disciples saw no further than that the world would end soon after his death, but Jesus himself envisioned the far horizons beyond. His message of 2,000 years ago was not merely for the people of his time. It can never be dated.

The question before us is whether reincarnation is part of that vision and message. Or, to state the question in another way, is reincarnation compatible with Christian faith?

The question as thus framed, with possible answers, is the subject of two of Professor Geddes MacGregor's books. The first published in 1978, by Quest Books, is titled *Reincarnation in Christianity: A New Vision of the Role of Rebirth in Christian Thought.* The second, *Reincarnation as a Christian Hope,* was published in 1982 in London by Macmillan in its Library of Philosophy and Religion series, and later in the United States by Barnes & Noble, a division of Harper & Row.

As Professor MacGregor will be quoted frequently in the pages ahead, some background information is in order. He is an Anglican (Episcopalian) priest and author of numerous works on religious subjects. He is emeritus distinguished professor of philosophy at the University of Southern California, where, from 1960 to 1975, he taught the philosophy of religion. He was also dean of the university's School of Religion. Among the many honors showered on him was his appointment in England as special preacher at St. Paul's Cathedral (1969), and at Westminster Abbey (1970). MacGregor graduated from the University of Edinburgh and received his doctorate from Oxford. He has received two post-doctorate degrees: the French State *grand doctorat,* awarded *summa cum laude* from the Sorbonne in Paris; and Doctor of Divinity from Oxford. Hebrew Union in the United States has conferred on him the honorary degree of doctor of humanities. Among his many books are *He Who Lets Us Be, God Beyond Doubt, The Bible in the Making, The Nicene Creed Illumined by Modern Thought, The Vatican Revolution, The Coming Reformation,* and *The Hemlock and the Cross.*

MacGregor has given courses on reincarnation at the University of California (Berkeley) and at the University of Iowa. *Reincarnation in Christianity* grew out of his Birks Lectures at McGill University on "The Christening of Karma." The book is dedicated to the faculty of Religious Studies at McGill, and "to all my students there and everywhere in gratitude for their critical zest and most of all for the knowledge of their abiding love." Cardinal Manning, Archbishop of Los Angeles, says of the work: "Professor MacGregor's exciting thesis challenges our traditional orthodoxy." Dr. Ernest Gordon, Dean of Chapel, Princeton University, remarked that, "rather than his position detracting from the personal nature of the Christian life, he enhances it."

In the volume itself, Professor MacGregor writes,

> Reincarnation is one of the most fascinating ideas in the history of religion, as it is also one of the most recurrent themes in the literature of the world. It is widely assumed to be foreign to the Christian heritage, and especially alien to the Hebrew roots of biblical thought. That assumption is questionable. . . . It has persistently cropped up in various crannies along the Christian Way, from the earliest times down to the present. It has also flourished in Judaism. Wherever western thinkers have learned to love the Christian Way well enough to strip off dead dogma without destroying living tissue, it has found a place in the Church's life.[1]

In his later book, *Reincarnation as a Christian Hope,* he assures his readers: "I am immensely sympathetic to those of my fellow Christians who suspect reincarnationism as one of the extraneous weeds that has no place in the ongoing life of the Church," and that it is "as ill-fitting as a pagoda atop a Gothic church. . . . Nevertheless, I believe their fears on this particular score to be entirely unwarranted. Dangers, however, do abound; not all forms of reincarnationism are compatible with an authentic

Christian hope. That is why I stress so much the necessity of seeing in what form reincarnationism can properly be christened."[2]

*

Although, as we have seen from the 1981 Gallup poll, 23 percent of Americans acknowledge acceptance of reincarnation, it is certainly true, as Professor C. J. Ducasse remarks, that the idea "appears fantastic today to most adherents of the Judaeo-Christian religion. . . . But this is only because it diverges from the ideas of life and death to which they have been habituated from childhood. . . . For when these are viewed objectively, they are seen to be more paradoxical than that of reincarnation," an example being "the idea of 'resurrection of the flesh' notwithstanding the dispersion of the dead body's material by cremation or by incorporation of its particles into the living bodies of worms, sharks or vultures," or even cannibals![3]

At the outset, it can be stated without qualification that Jesus in the four Gospels and St. Paul in the books of the New Testament attributed to him say not one word against the teaching of reincarnation. In the Epistles to the Hebrews—which were once thought to be written by St. Paul and are now listed by authorities as anonymous—there is a short sentence that anti-reincarnationists frequently quote as ruling out rebirth. (Whether it really does will be discussed later.) On the other hand, when we come to the selections from the Gospels themselves, there are a number of places where reincarnation seems clearly expressed. But there are good reasons why the record is not more expansive. Christ's disciples expected the world to end shortly after his death. Hence there was no need to think of future lives, which would never be lived. The degree to which the disciples misunderstood Jesus and mistakenly expected doomsday is evident from the verses that follow from the New Testament.*

DOOMSDAY: THE END OF THE WORLD EXPECTATION

The end was first mentioned in Matthew 3:2, when John the Baptist, preaching in the wilderness of Judea, said, "Repent for the kingdom of heaven is at hand." After John was imprisoned, the ministry of Jesus

---

*The Revised Standard Version of the Bible is generally used in this chapter. This modern English bible was first published in 1952 and "has been approved by Roman Catholics, Eastern Orthodox and Protestants" (*New York Times,* June 13, 1980). "It makes use of the latest research into sources, and so is highly respected by scholars" (*Time,* April 20, 1981).

began. When Jesus sent his twelve disciples out to do missionary work, he told them, "Preach as you go, saying, 'The kingdom of heaven is at hand' " (Matt. 10:7). In the same chapter, he said to the disciples, referring to the second coming of Christ, "When they persecute you in one town, flee to the next, for truly, I say to you, you will not have gone through all the towns of Israel, before the Son of man comes" (Matt. 10:23).

In chapter 24 of Matthew, Jesus predicted that the end would come when the temple in Jerusalem was destroyed (it was destroyed in 70 A.D.). "Nations will rise against nations, and there will be famines and earthquakes, and the sun will go out, the stars will fall from heaven. Then will Christ appear in the heavens and his angels will gather the elect." In verse 35 of this chapter, Jesus said, "Truly, I say to you, this generation will not pass away till all these things take place. Heaven and earth will pass away, but my words will not pass away."

In Mark 9:1, Jesus indicated that some of those living then would see these cataclysmic events within their own lifetime. "And he said to them, 'Truly I say to you there are some standing here who will not taste of death before they see the kingdom of God has come with power.' "

In the last book of the New Testament, The Revelation to John, a prevision is given of what will transpire at the apocalypse. Among other marvelous sights, Jesus appears in the heavens upon his throne. In the closing lines, he is said to announce: "Surely I am coming soon." And John replies, "Amen. Come, Lord Jesus!" (22:20) Thus ends the New Testament.

Well, either Jesus was wrong, or, what is more likely, his disciples misunderstood the Master. (One wonders how many other of his teachings they may have misunderstood!) As to the verses just quoted, Dr. James Robinson, director of the Institute for Antiquity and Christianity at Clare-mont Graduate School in California, believes that Jesus "announced the end of the world *as we have known it* and its replacement by a quite new, utopian kind of life in which the ideal would be the real."[4] The disciples were mistaken about its imminence.

Professor MacGregor believes that the most powerful circumstance that "conspired to inhibit official acceptance of reincarnationism after Jesus died" was this "apocalyptic character of the primitive Christian temper."

> In such a climate of expectancy Christians could have little interest in speculations about pre-existence of the soul, and less still in reincarnationism. Indeed, when people feel the end of the world is at hand they have no interest in any kind of philosophical speculations. They are filled, rather,

with a sense of the urgency of the situation and of the need for repentance and preparation. . . . A man who sees himself engaged in a last, brief, ferocious duel with Satan, with the prize of paradise awaiting him at the end of his final ordeal, will treat metempsychosis as impatiently as a soldier in a bayonet charge would treat one of Spinoza's scholia. That is not to say, however, that he would necessarily be repudiating it, it is only to say he has no time for it.[5]

DOES NOT REINCARNATION ENCOURAGE PROCRASTINATION?

There was a good side to the sense of urgency that prevailed among the early and later Christians. It encouraged reforming one's life immediately and not putting it off until the future. Jesus always stressed the need for total and immediate commitment. It is then understandable that Christians today frequently object to reincarnation because they say it provides the excuse to be ever postponing one's salvation to the next life.

Here is a conversation on this subject taken from a diary entry in Loran Hurnscot's *A Prison, a Paradise*:

Had a rather irritable telephone conversation with my parsonical friend. I said that Buddhism was more Christian than Christianity; that in the end it promised salvation to all—it did not look on the multitudes as chaff to be burned eternally. He said that there had to be a certain urgency; that with endless lives in prospect, one would always put off making the effort until the next.

I said that to hinge eternal salvation on one single, confused and handicapped lifetime seemed to me a diabolical idea. He didn't agree; he said that everyone had their chance in this life, and if they wouldn't take it, "well, you've had it." If this is orthodoxy, then may God save me from it.[6]

The parson's argument is an excellent one, but only when reincarnation is divorced from the law of sowing and reaping, or karma. The wages of procrastination in one life are heavy enough, and if human beings have future lives, the karma of postponing obligations is likely to be increasingly painful. Who would wish to start his next life plagued with unnecessary handicaps?[7]

EARLY CHRISTIANS BECOME INTERESTED IN THE AFTERLIFE

"The first-century Christians," observes Dr. MacGregor, "were not interested in the *details* of the future life." Why? For the same reason they were not interested in reincarnation. "They expected daily the coming of Christ. Tomorrow may be the day the sky will darken and Jesus risen in glory will appear as the judge of all men. . . . They believed that when they laid down to sleep at night, tomorrow might be that day."[8]

However, only as they became increasingly aware that the duration of our world was much longer than anticipated did they begin to wonder what happens after death. Turning to the Gospels for information, they discovered nothing but bare hints and conflicting stories. The record was incomplete because, first, so long a time had elapsed between the recording of the Gospels and Christ's departure that his words on the subject were only dimly remembered.* Second, it is likely his words made little impression when uttered because the teaching of the afterlife was considered irrelevant to those about to experience the great happenings of Christ's Parousia or Second Coming.

The fragmentary record left the field wide open to speculation and conjecture in both filling in the picture of what had not been recorded and in interpreting what had been recorded. To this unenviable task the church fathers turned, and the theologians have been at it ever since.

Of all the church's teachings, MacGregor says, the doctrine of the future life is the most confused and complicated because contradictory ideas appear on this in the New Testament, and it takes a considerable amount of ingenuity to try to fit them all together. "The extraordinarily muddled state of traditional eschatology serves only to perplex those who live by the Christian faith." ("Eschatology" means "last things.") As a result, a large number of churchgoers have actually abandoned all belief in personal survival.

To compound the confusion, Protestants and Catholics are in serious conflict on one very important point respecting life after death. And each group bases its views on different statements in the New Testament.[10]

Protestant teaching is that, after death, the soul is asleep in the grave until Judgment Day. Those asleep in the grave include the millions of people who lived before Christ as well as after. When Jesus returns, the bodies of the saved are transformed and glorified. The bodies of sinners

---

*According to the latest studies of scholars, the Gospels were recorded from thirty to sixty years after the crucifixion. The earliest Gospel, that of Mark, was written thirty to forty years after Jesus departed. The disciples Matthew, Mark, and Luke did not write the books headed by their names; it is speculated that John may have been the author of his. The first three Gospels are based on oral reports as to what Jesus taught and may have been exaggerated, added to, deleted, or misquoted, the scholars say. The delay in recording the Gospels is understandable, because the general expectation was that the world was to end soon. Why bother![9]

become asbestoslike in nature, so that they can burn eternally without being consumed.

Some of the more sophisticated thinkers in Protestantism believe in the doctrine of total death, which affirms that between death and resurrection there is absolutely nothing. They say that "death as payment for sin concerns the whole man and casts him totally into nothingness. He exists only in the memory of God who will create him anew, as it were, on the Last Day."[11] But fundamentalists are particularly insistent about our sleeping in the grave. Until Judgment Day, "heaven is empty, hell is empty," is their unmovable belief.

Catholics have an entirely different teaching. Immediately after death, they say, damned souls go to hell. Those who merit salvation, but still require purification, go for a period to purgatory and then to heaven. The saintly go straight to paradise. However, here is an astounding fact of which most Catholics are not aware. (We have questioned many of them on this and know this to be true.) Catholic theologians teach, as Protestants do, that the bodies of all those who have died since Adam will be resurrected when our world ends. At this time the resurrected body rejoins the souls who are in heaven or hell.[12] If for thousands of years souls have been adequately functioning in heaven, what possible need could they now have for a resurrected body? In what way could it add to their bliss?

The puzzlement and confusion in the early church on the teachings of the afterlife became cumulative as the Christian sects multiplied over the centuries. And as to the state of Christendom in the twentieth century, what William Kingsland wrote in the 1930s in his much-reprinted book on Christianity is even more true today:

> Anyone who has taken the trouble to wade through even a small portion of the enormous mass of polemical writings or of Biblical exegesis which belong to modern scholarship, must very quickly come to the conclusion *that there is no hope of arriving at the real truth in that direction.* The most profound scholarship and the keenest critical faculty have been brought to bear upon the documents in our possession, with the result that hardly any two critics are in complete agreement, while many are diametrically opposed in their view. The general impression left upon us by these works is simply that nothing is known for certain.[13]

In this muddled situation, it is not surprising that the 1981 Gallup poll disclosed that 21 to 26 percent of American Protestants and 25 percent of Catholics have turned to a reincarnational explanation of the mysteries of life and death (see chapter 2).

REINCARNATION
IN THE NEW TESTAMENT

In view of our extended discussion concerning the apocalyptic tenor of thinking among the early orthodox Christians, the reader may anticipate that no affirmative reference to reincarnation could be expected to have survived in the New Testament as we now have it. Is this actually the case? Let us consider first whether reincarnation could possibly apply to the founder of Christianity himself.

DOES JESUS HAVE THE POWER TO BE REBORN?

Inasmuch as Christ, as the Son of God, has presumably all powers, why would he not have the power to be reborn again and again to save the world? Why only once? He himself said that he has this power and that he has other flocks than the one he came to as Jesus.

> I lay down my life for the sheep. *And I have other sheep, that are not of this fold;* I must bring them also, and they will heed my voice. So there shall be one flock, one shepherd. For this reason the Father loves me, because I lay down my life, that I may take it again. No one takes it from me, but I lay it down of my own accord. *I have power to lay it down, and I have power to take it again* (John 10:15–18) [italics added].

Did he have this same power before he appeared on earth as Jesus? In other words, had he been among human beings in previous times? In chapter 8 of the Gospel of John, Jesus was taunted by the Israelites for setting himself up as greater than Abraham. He replied: "Your father Abraham rejoiced that he was to see my day; he saw it and was glad." The astounded Israelites replied, "You are not yet fifty years old, and have you seen Abraham?" Jesus answered, "Truly, truly, I say to you, *before Abraham was, I am*" (John 8:56–58) (italics added).

Incidentally, the church fathers themselves were not in agreement about Christ's descending to earth only once. Origen, who is acknowledged to be the most learned biblical scholar in the early church, wrote in *Contra Celsum* (vi:78), "When God sent Jesus to the human race, it was not as though Christ had just awakened from a long sleep. Jesus had at all times been doing good to the human race."[14] If this be true, how glorious his sacrifice that he would be willing to undergo again and again for our sake the trials and tortures that humanity inflicts on its great saviors.

DO HUMAN BEINGS HAVE THE POWER TO REINCARNATE?

Some will say that what applies to Jesus can hardly apply to ourselves. Where in the New Testament is there any indication that beings other than Jesus have the power to return? Before presenting some statements of Jesus that appear to affirm such reincarnations, we consider a verse from the Epistle to the Hebrews (9:27) that appears to rule out the possibility of human rebirth. In the King James Version, the epistle is attributed to St. Paul, but scholars now reject this attribution, as do modern bibles. In the King James Version the verse reads, "It is appointed unto men once to die, but after this *the* judgment." The word italicized by the authors conveys the impression that this "judgment" refers to the Judgment Day at the end of our world. However, when the Bible was retranslated, it was discovered that "the" is an interpolation. The Revised Standard Version gives the verse this way: "It is appointed for men to die once, and after that comes judgment."

In the question period following a lecture on reincarnation, Dr. MacGregor was asked about the verse in Hebrews. He answered,

> I do not think that is a great difficulty really. Of course, there is judgment; there is judgment all the time, and the notion that there is a special judgment for the world—the whole of this planet—all that is perfectly comprehensible, and perfectly compatible with the notion of reincarnation. It is appointed for me, that is, the present me, once to die. I do not die anymore than once in my present incarnation, and I am also judged. The law of karma or however you like to put it, symbolizes the concept of judgment. We are all being judged if there is any moral law at all; we are being judged all the time, but there is a special judgment when I die.[15]

We had occasion to ask Anglican priest Thomas Strong in England about the statement in Hebrews. He replied, on April 28, 1980,

> I have frequently had Hebrews 9:27-28 put to me, and it appears to some as a kind of ace card [disallowing reincarnation]. I have examined the text in Greek and it appears to me that the passage is ambiguous. . . .
>
> Hebrews was written specifically for Jewish converts to convince them that the Temple ritual sacrifices were no longer relevant to the Jewish Christian. The author had no eschatological intention to put reincarnation out of court. He was subject to the common, but erroneous idea of his time (10:36-37) that Christ's return was near at hand. Questions of rebirth, etc. simply would not have occurred to him.

The Case of the Blind Man.   On one occasion, Jesus had the opportu-

nity to condemn reincarnation and warn all Christians it was untrue or
pernicious, but he did not. This concerned the man who had been born
blind, whose sight had been restored through Jesus. Interestingly enough,
the passage follows immediately after the part, already quoted, where
Jesus spoke of himself as having lived at the time of Abraham.

> [As Jesus] passed by, he saw a man blind from his birth. And his disciples
> asked him, "Rabbi, who sinned, this man or his parents, that he was born
> blind?" (John 9:1–2)

The disciples' question indicated there were only two possible explanations for the man's blindness—either he had sinned before he came into
incarnation, suggesting that he lived previously, or his parents had themselves been guilty of some transgression. That the idea of preexistence and
possible reincarnations had entered the minds of the disciples appears to
indicate it was a prevalent theory among the Jews of the time. It has been
suggested that, because it was so well known, Jesus felt no need to make a
special point of teaching it.

Now, how did Jesus respond to the question? He said only that the man
was afflicted because he was destined through Christ to have his sight
restored in a miraculous way, so that "the works of God should be made
manifest in him." It is not known how Jesus would explain the cause of
blindness in other cases where no supernatural healing is involved. In each
generation, there are thousands of children born blind. What explanation
would he offer?

The Case of Elijah and John the Baptist.   In the ninth century B.C., the
prophet Elijah is believed to have lived. According to scripture, when his
time came to die, a fiery chariot appeared with horses of fire and Elijah
went up in a whirlwind to heaven and was seen no more (II Kings 2:11).

Four centuries later, Malachi recorded in the closing lines of the Old
Testament, this prophecy made by God: "Behold I will send you Elijah
the prophet before the great and terrible day of the Lord comes" (Mal.
4:5). To the Jewish people this meant that, before their much-looked-for
Messiah would appear, the signal of his coming would be the return of
Elijah. Then, with the appearance of the Messiah, "the terrible day of the
Lord," or the last judgment would take place.

Because the disciples of Jesus identified Christ as the Messiah, they
naturally believed the prophecy recorded by Malachi should apply to him.
But where was the forerunner? Where was the returned Elijah? So they
asked Jesus to explain this. He made the astonishing reply that Elijah had

already returned, that he had come back as John the Baptist. The first reference to this appears in chapter 11 of Matthew.

> Now when John [the Baptist] heard in prison about the deeds of the Christ, he sent word by his disciples and said to him "are you he who is to come, or shall we look for another?" [Jesus then answers by telling of his own miracles.] As they went away, Jesus began to speak to the crowds concerning John. . . . "This is he of whom it is written, 'Behold I send my messenger before thy face, who shall prepare thy way before thee.' Truly, I say to you, among those born of women there has risen no one greater than John the Baptist. . . . *and if you are willing to accept it, he is Elijah who is to come. He who has ears to hear let him hear"* (Matt. 11:2–15) [italics added].

Another passage on this subject in the Gospel of Matthew is introduced in this way in Reverend Thomas Strong's *Mystical Christianity*:

> Jesus took his three most spiritually evolved disciples, Peter, James and John, up on to a mountain. There the three frightened disciples experienced an extraordinary phenomenon. Jesus began to glow as though lit by a brilliant inner light. He was transfigured so that his material body was changed and etherialized. Jesus was seen to talk with materializations of Moses and Elijah. The three disciples were extremely disturbed because they knew that Elijah should have been reborn as a forerunner of the Messiah. If Jesus had been talking to Elijah, how could he, Jesus, be the Christ? The troubled friends ask Jesus to explain the situation.[16]

"The incident is interesting," comments Reverend Strong, "for it indicates that belief in reincarnation was accepted by the disciples, and Christ's reply confirms that he also believed in it." The disciples asked Jesus, "Why do the scribes say that first Elijah must come?" Christ replied, "Elijah does come, and he is to restore all things; but I tell you that Elijah has already come, and they did not know him, but did to him whatever they pleased. [He was beheaded.] So also the Son of Man will suffer at their hands." Then the disciples understood that he was speaking to them of John the Baptist (Matt. 17:10–13; Mark 9:9–13).

In Matthew, there is still another pertinent reference. Here Jesus does not again identify John the Baptist as Elijah but, from the question he asks and the reply of the disciples, it is evident that the people of the time were not only expecting Elijah to return but other of their great prophets: "Now when Jesus came into the district of Caesarea Philippi, he asked his disciples, 'Who do men say that the Son of man is?' And they said, 'Some say John

the Baptist, others say Elijah, and others Jeremiah or one of the prophets.' ''
(Matt. 16:13; Mark 8:27–28; Luke 9:18–19).

In these three selections, there is no intimation that reincarnation was regarded as unusual or extraordinary. It seems to be taken for granted, the sole point of concern being the identity of the individual who was reborn. The reasoning seems to be that, if an individual was a seer, an inspired religious person, he must have been the return of a prophet that lived before. Jesus evidently understood that such was surmised about himself, hence his question to his disciples: "Who do men say that the Son of man is?"

Professor MacGregor observes that all these questions asked by the Jews regarding the return of their prophets suggest that the theory of rebirth was commonplace to them. "These are certainly not questions that the average churchgoer today would be likely to raise concerning a great saint or teacher that appeared on the horizon. . . . They are, however, characteristic of the way people were thinking at the time of Jesus."[17]

A question may arise concerning John the Baptist himself. Was he aware that he was Elijah? In the Gospel record, he was queried on this very matter by priests and others from Jerusalem. They asked, "Are you Elijah?" John replied "I am not." Again he is asked, "Are you that prophet," and again he answers "no." "Who are you?" they asked. "Let us have an answer for those who sent us. What do you say about yourself?" He responded, "I am the voice of one crying in the wilderness, 'Make straight the way of the Lord,' as the prophet Isaiah said" (John 1:21–23).

Whose view shall we accept—that of Jesus, who declared John was Elijah reborn, or John the Baptist's denial of the same? That John had limitations seems evident from the remark of Jesus that, "among those born of women there has risen no one greater than John the Baptist; yet he who is least in the kingdom of heaven is greater than he" (Matt. 11:11). That John himself recognized his limitations is evident from his words to the people of Judea who came to hear him in the wilderness: "After me comes he who is mightier than I, the thong of whose sandals I am not worthy to stoop down and untie. I have baptized you with water; but he will baptize you with the Holy Spirit" (Mark 1:7–8).

Tertullian, who wrote in the second century in defense of Christianity but later became a heretic, gives the view that many orthodox people take concerning the Elijah/John verses in the Gospels. In brief: *Elijah's body never died in the first place. God translated him directly to heaven.* Thus, Elijah's subsequent redescent was not a rebirth, but merely a return visit *in*

JESUS AND THE CHRISTIAN VISION 211

his old body.[18] Tertullian no doubt bases this on the statement already quoted from II Kings 2:11 that a chariot of fire appeared and Elijah went up in a whirlwind into heaven and was seen no more.

However, if Tertullian's reasoning is logically sustained, Elijah's return to earth as John the Baptist should have occurred in the same miraculous way he left. He should have appeared in the sky in his fiery chariot *and arrived on earth as a mature man.* Yet the scriptures indicate that John was born in the ordinary way. As quoted earlier, Jesus himself spoke of John as *"born of woman."* And, in Luke 1:13–17, an angel makes this prophecy to Zacharias, the father of John: "And your wife Elizabeth shall bear you a son, and you shall call his name John. . . . And he will go before him in the spirit and power of Elijah."

This last sentence is made much of to prove that John was merely under the control of Elijah and that Elijah therefore was not incarnated in him. But Jesus did not say this. He was quite explicit in regard to John: "This is Elijah. . . . *He who has ears to hear let him hear"* (Matt. 11:14–15). The words italicized here by the authors are repeated several times in the Gospels, but the first time they appear is in this passage. How many millions over the centuries have read the message but have not heard?

Discussing all the Bible verses on John as Elijah, nineteenth-century American philosopher Francis Bowen of Harvard remarked in his article "Christian Metempsychosis," "That the commentators have not been willing to receive, in their obvious and literal meaning, assertions so direct and so frequently repeated as these, but have attempted to explain them away in a non-natural and metaphorical sense, is a fact that proves nothing but the existence of an invincible prejudice against the doctrine of the transmigration of souls" (*Princeton Review,* May 1881).

It was an "invincible prejudice" perhaps in the last century, but it is appreciably lessening in this one.

The New Testament, a Missionary Book. It is natural to inquire why the New Testament as a whole does not say more on life after death and other metaphysical subjects. Professor MacGregor points out that it does not even say a word on the doctrine of the trinity, which "is the very touchstone of Christian orthodoxy: Protestant, Roman Catholic, Greek Orthodox, Anglican, whatever." To understand the trinity, he says, requires a deep philosophical and theological background, and the Gospels simply do not go into such questions. The question of reincarnation could present a similar case.[19]

If the New Testament is not a philosophical book, what was its original function? Werner George Kümmel in his noted *Introduction to the New Testament* refers to the Gospels as missionary writings. "The main concern is to evoke faith and strengthen it." The word "gospel," coming from the Greek, means "good news."[20] In this case, the good news was how to be saved before it was too late, before the world came to an end. So the Bible is not a treatise; it does not go into metaphysical thought.

THE UNDISCLOSED TEACHINGS OF JESUS

The Book of John, which concludes the four Gospels, ends with these astounding words: "There were also many other things which Jesus did; were every one of them written, I suppose the world itself could not contain the books that would be written" (John 21:25).

"Many other things which Jesus did"—would not this presuppose that there were also many other things he taught? Furthermore, the Gospels themselves clearly state that Jesus had two teachings, one for the multitudes and the other for his trusted disciples. The first were in the nature of parables, and these are recorded in the Gospels. But what happened to the inner or esoteric teachings?

Here are the passages in the Gospel of Mark referring to the inner and outer message of Christ.

[Jesus speaks] To you has been given the secret of the kingdom of God, but for those outside everything is in parables, so that they may indeed see but not perceive, and may indeed hear but not understand [Mark 4:11].

With many such parables he spoke the word to [the multitudes] as they were able to hear it, he did not speak to them without a parable, but privately to his own disciples he explained everything [Mark 4:33–34].

Explained everything? Yet the disciple John indicates that there were even some things Jesus never told his disciples. "I have yet many things to say to you, but you cannot bear them now. When the Spirit of truth comes, he will guide you into all the truth" (John 16:12–13). Also in that Gospel are Christ's famous words, "Ye shall know the truth, and the truth shall make you free" (John 8:32).

Saint Paul makes it clear why the mysteries were not as yet to be shared with all. In speaking to the Corinthians, he said,

I, brethren, could not address you as spiritual men, but as men of the flesh, as babes in Christ. I fed you with milk not solid food; for you were not ready for it; and even yet you are not ready, for you are still of the flesh. For while there is jealousy and strife among you, are you not of the flesh, and behaving like ordinary men? For when one says, "I belong to Paul," and another, "I belong to Apollos," are you not merely men? [I Corinthians 3:1–4].

What a lesson to Christians who have become divided into over 300 sects!

All the foregoing leads to one conclusion: In the New Testament, we do not have all that Jesus knew, or all that he taught to his disciples. Consequently, it would be unwise to insist that only those things are true that may be found in the Bible, and that one is not permitted to investigate further.

*

In the next section, it will become plain that the history of Christianity is not to be limited to the orthodox version of that story. There were numerous Christians who were totally dedicated to Christ as their teacher and savior but who disagreed with the conservative majority on many fundamental issues. As we shall see, it is among these peoples that reincarnation was taught as basic to Christianity.

REINCARNATION
IN CHRISTIAN GNOSTICISM

Recent unearthing of long-lost Gnostic writings has caused a furor of interest among scholars and theologians around the world. In consequence, the history of the beginnings of Christianity is being rewritten. "Scholars today recognize more than ever before," writes Geddes MacGregor, that "Gnosticism was a far more powerful force in the background of Christianity than formerly supposed. . . . No longer can anyone suppose, as was customary fifty years ago, that the Gnostic movement that troubled the church in the second century can be dismissed as a mere ideological oddity, the creation of wild and fuzzy-minded deviants." "That some Gnostic sects such as the Valentinians, used Gnostic notions in weird ways is not to be denied," MacGregor admits. "But it has been the fate of all religious movements to be ill represented by some of their votaries."[21]

That the views of the Gnostics were grossly distorted by the church—their bitterest theological enemy—is now well known. Furthermore, all Gnostic treatises that could be found were destroyed, and the views of their authors, it was hoped, were silenced forever. Professor Elaine Pagels notes in her renowned work, *The Gnostic Gospels,* that "the efforts of the majority to destroy every trace of heretical 'blasphemy' proved so successful that, until the discoveries at Nag Hammadi [which we will be considering], nearly all our information concerning alternate forms of early Christianity came from the massive attacks upon them."[22] Hence MacGregor adds, "the reputation of the Christian Gnostics has turned whole generations of people against the very word gnosis as if the term were plague-infested."[23]

One of the chief reasons for antagonism against Christian Gnosticism was its independence from such theological authorities as popes or bishops. There were no Gnostic temples. It was not a church. Gnosticism was rather, says MacGregor, "a climate of thought: an extremely pervasive one. It encouraged going beyond the symbols of popular religion to truths Gnostic teachers said were to be found underlying them. Transmigrationism found ready hospitality in such a climate."[24]

Although, he says, "Gnostic tendencies came under suspicion and eventually under the condemnation of the Church, Gnostic teachings were a live option for the earliest generation of Christians."[25] In fact, "the New Testament canon itself is saturated with Gnostic ideas, expressed discreetly rather than blatantly."[26]

As to the source from which the Gnostics of the second century claimed they derived their teachings, Smith and Wace in their *Dictionary of Christian Biography* write that they averred "to be in possession of genuine apostical traditions, deriving their doctrines, some from Saint Paul, others from Saint Peter, and others again from Thomas, Philip, and Matthew." These were supposedly secret teachings, "professed to have been received by oral tradition." The Gnostics also "appealed to alleged writings of the apostles themselves or their disciples."[27]

Jung believed that "the central ideas of Christianity are rooted in Gnostic philosophy."[28] Those acquainted with his writings know how deeply he studied Gnostic teachings and symbols. At a critical period in his life, he wrote a tiny volume called *Seven Sermons to the Dead* in Gnostic fashion, imagining the sermons to have been penned by the great Gnostic teacher Basilides himself. In the chapter "Gnostic Symbols of the Self," in Jung's volume *Aion,* he remarks that "the idea of the unconscious was not unknown" to the Gnostics, and that they "have a vast number of symbols for the source or origin" of our inmost self, "the center of being."[29]

In his closing address at the International Colloquium on Gnosticism in Stockholm in 1973, honorary president Hans Jonas, the distinguished authority on Gnostic beliefs, remarked, "Something in Gnosticism knocks at

the door of our Being and our twentieth-century Being in particular. . . .
And there is certainly something in Gnosticism that helps one to understand humanity better than one would understand if one had never known
of Gnosticism."[30]

STORY OF THE DISCOVERY OF LONG-LOST GNOSTIC MANUSCRIPTS

In 1945, on a cliff near Nag Hammadi, a town on the Nile about 300
miles from Cairo, an Arab farmer named Muhammad Ali, in company
with his brothers, made an astonishing discovery. Dismounting from their
camels, they sought to obtain special soil to fertilize their crops and,
digging around a massive boulder in an old Coptic cemetery, hit a red
earthenware jar almost three feet high. Muhammad hesitated to break the
jar, imagining a *jinn*, or spirit, might reside therein. But, thinking it might
contain gold, he smashed it, only to be disappointed to find thirteen books
bound in leather plus a mass of loose papyrus manuscript sheets. Returning
home, he dumped it all by the oven, and his mother used many of the loose
sheets to kindle the fire.

How the books finally came to the attention of the authorities in Egypt—
and of scholars around the globe—is a story of high drama, excitement,
intrigue, and, in the Christian academic world, jealous battles for who
would be first.[31] What Muhammad unearthed proved more precious than a
carload of gold—fifty-two papyrus Gnostic texts, including gospels and
various secret writings, some dating from the beginning of the Christian
era, the period when the New Testament Gospels themselves were written.
They were Coptic copies made some 1,500 years ago of original Greek
documents.

It is believed they were buried by nearby Christian Coptic priests during
one of the purges against the Gnostics. *The American Scholar* (Summer
1980) said that "the disappearance of the Gnostic literature is not hard to
explain. By the time of Irenaeus, bishop of Lyons about AD 180, Gnosticism had already been branded a heresy, and the Roman church worked
diligently to suppress it. After the conversion of Constantine, the church
militant had the power of the State behind it, and the suppression became
highly efficient. In a literary religion, the most effective way to extinguish
nonconforming ideas is by burning books." After Constantine, the death
penalty was often exacted for being a Gnostic.[32]

Professor Elaine Pagels, author of *The Gnostic Gospels,* writes that
"even the 52 writings discovered at Nag Hammadi offer only a glimpse of

the complexity of the early Christian movement. We begin to see that what
we call Christianity—and what we identify as Christian tradition—actually
represents only a small selection of specific sources, chosen from among
dozens of others.'' Before the Nag Hammadi discoveries, Pagels explains,
"scholars had known only a handful of original gnostic texts, none published before the nineteenth century.''[33]
    Distinguished scholars in many parts of the world are presently engaged
in studying these newly uncovered Coptic documents, separate teams of
specialists focusing on areas in their fields. Professor D. M. Scholer's *Nag
Hammadi Bibliography* lists over 4,000 books, editions, articles, and re-
views published in the last thirty-five years concerning research on the
texts.[34]
    In 1977, Harper & Row published *The Nag Hammadi Library in English,*
the product of years of work in translating the Coptic originals by a team
of select scholars. In the preface, various organizations are listed that
made major grants in support of the project. We list them to indicate the
scope of interest aroused by the findings: The National Endowment for the
Humanities, the Smithsonian Institute, the American Philosophical Society,
UNESCO, the John Simon Guggenheim Memorial Foundation, and Clare-
mont Graduate School—the sole Christian-oriented body that helped fi-
nance the work.

ELAINE PAGELS'S *THE GNOSTIC GOSPELS*

    Investigations of the Gnostic manuscripts went on for thirty years before
the mass media took much notice. It was not until Pagels's *The Gnostic of
Gospels* was published in 1979 that the discoveries became featured news
in periodicals and on television and radio everywhere. Reviewing the book
in the *New York Times*, Tom Driver, Paul Tillich Professor of Theology
and Culture at Union Theological Seminary in New York, called it ''the
first major and eminently readable book on gnosticism benefiting from the
texts at Nag Hammadi'' (April 16, 1980). He added that ''the contemporary relevance of Gnostic ideas, and Pagels' good historical sense, accounts for her book's fame and for some harsh attacks upon it,'' emanating
from conservative theologians. The volume received the National Book
Critics Circle Award and was a Book-of-the-Month-Club selection. *The
New Yorker* called it ''an intellectually elegant, concise study. . . . The
economy with which she evokes the world of early Christianity is a marvel''
(January 21, 1980).
    She does not write as a critic or debunker of church doctrine and

frankly admits to a passionate love for Christianity and its sacraments and ritual. This young, beautiful, and brilliant scholar became interested in the discoveries at Nag Hammadi as a result of entering the graduate program at Harvard University to study the history of Christianity. Her teachers encouraged her to learn Coptic in order someday to read the documents in the original. Such opportunity came when she received grants to go to Cairo to study them in the Coptic Museum. Once there, she was invited to join the team of scholars translating the texts. Since 1970 she has taught in New York at Barnard College, where she chairs the Department of Religion.

Elaine Pagels's book is quoted frequently in the remainder of this chapter, and we will not be citing page numbers for each selection. The reader is encouraged to consult the book itself.

Gnosticism as a Christian Movement. The Christian Gnostics were really Christians, emphasizes Pagels, though, up until the discoveries at Nag Hammadi, the effort from early Christian times onward had been to claim that they were not. Their orthodox contemporaries tried to say their teachings were founded on "Greek philosophy, astrology, mystery religions, magic, and even Indian sources." In modern times, some have pointed to Babylonia and Iran as their source, others to Jewish Gnosticism, and still others insisted the Gnostics were an independent religious movement. However, Pagels writes that "much of the literature discovered at Nag Hammadi is distinctly Christian."

There is the precious Gospel of Thomas—which the Jung Institute at Zurich was fortunate in acquiring, the Gospel of Philip, the Secret Book of James, the Apocryphon of John, the Apocalypse of Paul, the Letter of Peter to Philip, and the Apocalypse of Peter—all Christian in nature.

"Those who circulated and revered these writings," Pagels states, "did not regard themselves as heretics, but as Gnostics—that is Christians who possess knowledge (gnosis) of Jesus' secret teaching—knowledge hidden from the majority of believers" until they have "proven themselves to be spiritually mature." She cites the verse we previously quoted from the gospel of Mark, wherein Jesus said to his disciples, "To you has been given the secret of the kingdom of God, but for those outside everything is in parables" (Mark 4:11).

GNOSTIC INSTRUCTION OPEN TO WOMEN AND MEN ALIKE

According to the Gnostics, writes Dr. Pagels, "achieving *gnosis* involves coming to recognize the true source of divine power—namely, 'the depth' of all being. Whoever has come to know that source simultaneously comes to know himself and discovers his spiritual origin: he has come to know his true Father and Mother."

True Father *and Mother*? With many of the Gnostics, God is not exclusively masculine, but "embraces both masculine and feminine elements." The Supreme Source of all can hardly be a He or a She. In Pagels's *Gnostic Gospels,* an entire chapter—"God the Father/God the Mother"—is on this subject.

Now, consistent with this view and contrary to orthodox Christian doctrines and practices, both women and men were considered equal among the Gnostics. Tertullian angrily protests that women among the Gnostic heretics share with men positions of authority. "They teach, they engage in discussion; they exorcise; they cure." "He suspects," says Pagels, "that they might even baptize; which meant they also acted as bishops!" Furthermore, in their regular meetings, they had no priestly hierarchy and made no distinctions between the clergy and the laity. Tertullian complains that "they all have access equally, they listen equally, they pray equally— even pagans, if any happen to come. . . . They also share the kiss of peace with all who come." The renowned Gnostic teacher Marcion, says Pagels, "scandalized his orthodox contemporaries by appointing women as priests and bishops."

Pagels reports that, in the Gnostic manuscripts called *Pistis Sophia* (which we will be quoting extensively on reincarnation), Peter complains to Jesus because "Mary Magdalene is dominating the conversation with Jesus and displacing the rightful priority of Peter and his brother apostles. He urges Jesus to silence her and is quickly rebuked." Later, "Mary admits to Jesus that she hardly dares speak to him freely because, in her words, 'Peter makes me hesitate; I am afraid of him, because he hates the female race.' Jesus replies that whoever the Spirit inspires is divinely ordained to speak, whether man or woman."

This is of particular interest because, from the reincarnational viewpoint, souls are sexless and can alternately incarnate in male and female bodies, depending upon which type of experience is needed.

"In 1977," notes Pagels, "Pope Paul VI declared that a woman cannot be a priest 'because our Lord was a man'! . . . The Nag Hammadi sources, discovered at a time of contemporary social crisis concerning sexual roles, challenges us to reinterpret history—and to re-evaluate the present situation."

REINCARNATION IN GNOSTICISM

In *The Gnostic Gospels,* Elaine Pagels remarks that "ideas that we

associate with Eastern religions emerged in the first century through the
Gnostic movement, in the West, but they were suppressed and condemned
by polemicists like Irenaeus.'' Prominent among these ideas was reincarnation, although the source was not Eastern religions but, according to the
Gnostics, original Christianity itself. Geddes MacGregor mentions that
''reincarnational views were commonplace in the Gnostic climate in which
Christianity developed.''[35]
    An eminent Greek and Latin scholar, G.R.S. Mead, author of several
volumes on Gnosticism and a translator of Gnostic texts, observes in his
Fragments of a Faith Forgotten that the whole of Gnosticism ''revolved
round the conception of cyclic law for both the universal and individual
soul.'' ''Thus,'' he states, ''we find the gnostics invariably teaching the
doctrine not only of the pre-existence but also of the rebirth of human
souls. They held rigidly to the infallible working out of the great law of
cause and effect.''[36]
    Mead wrote at the turn of the century, at a time when scholars were not
especially kind to the concept of rebirth. Thus he took occasion to remark
that ''these two main doctrines of reincarnation and karma, which explain
so much in gnosticism and throw light on so many dark places, have been
either entirely overlooked or, when not unintelligently slurred over, despatched with a few hurried remarks in which the critic is more at pains to
apologize for touching on such ridiculous superstitions as 'metempsychosis'
and 'fate,' *than to elucidate tenets which are a key to the whole position.*''[37]
    But even now, when Gnosticism is receiving such widespread attention, and
reincarnational ideas are so very much in the air, the general public is not
made aware that the Christian Gnostics were reincarnationists and that
rebirth was a live option in early Christianity. The reluctance to mention
such subjects seems evident among scholars and writers reporting on the
Nag Hammadi documents. One of several exceptions is the French Egyptologist Jean Doresse, who happened to be in Cairo in 1947 when the first
manuscripts arrived there. Despite the apathy of others, he immediately
recognized their value and, together with Togo Mina, the eminent head of
the Coptic Museum, overcame monumental difficulties in tracing and col-
lecting for future generations these then widely scattered documents. In the
section on Gnostic eschatology in Doresse's *The Secret Books of the
Egyptians,* he writes that the Nag Hammadi texts disclose the Gnostics
believed ''man has to pass through successive births'' before reaching his
ultimate goal.[38]

Reincarnation in the Pistis Sophia. This eminently important collection of Gnostic manuscripts astonished the academic world when it first turned up in the last century. The words *Pistis Sophia* have been variously translated as "Faith-Wisdom" and "Knowledge-Wisdom," the knowledge being transcendental in nature. Our selections are from the translation of G.R.S. Mead.[39] In the introduction, he writes,

> Our Gnostics found no difficulty in fitting transcorporation [or reincarnation] into their plan of salvation, which shows no sign of the expectation of an immediate end of all things—that prime article of faith [of the orthodox Christian] of the earliest days. So far from thinking that reincarnation is alien to gospel-teaching, they elaborately interpret certain of the most striking sayings in this sense, and give graphic details of how Jesus . . . brought to rebirth the souls of John the Baptist and of the disciples, and supervised the economy of his own incarnation. In this respect the *Pistis Sophia* offers richer material for those interested in this ancient and widespread doctrine than can be found in any other old-world document in the West.

In one portion, Christ instructs the disciples as to how serious personal defects have repercussions in an ensuing life. A person who curses others will in the new life be "continually troubled in his heart." He wished trouble for others and is now himself troubled. "An arrogant overweening person" could find himself in a deformed body, which is looked down upon by others. And similarly, Christ indicated, each vice had its appropriate effect. Prior to incarnating, he further teaches, such persons—as do most people—drink of the waters of forgetfulness and therefore do not remember what transpired during the time between incarnations.

The disciple John then wonders if there is any hope for a person who "has committed all sins and all iniquities, but at last has found the mysteries of the Light, *is it possible for him to be saved?*" The Savior replies: "Such a man who has committed all sins and all iniquities, and finds the mysteries of the Light, performing and fulfilling them, and ceases to sin, will indeed inherit the Treasury of the Light."

John persists with still another question: What will happen to a person who has committed no sin, but has done good persistently, yet has not found the mysteries? Such a person before birth, says Christ, does not drink of the waters of forgetfulness. He receives rather "a cup filled with thoughts of wisdom, and soberness is in it." He is then reborn "into a body which can neither sleep nor forget because of the cup of soberness which has been handed to it. It will whip his heart persistently to question about the mysteries of the Light until he finds them, through the decision of the Virgin of Light, and inherit the Light forever."

Christ emphasizes again and again that the ultimate achievement is so stupendous that freedom from sin cannot by itself bring about this consummation. Knowledge of the Mysteries is essential. "Amen, Amen, I say to you: Even if a righteous man has committed no sins at all, he cannot possibly be brought into the Light kingdom, because the sign of the kingdom of the mysteries is not with him." On another occasion, the disciples are told by Jesus that "there is no mystery which is more excellent than these mysteries on which you question, in that it will lead your souls to the Light of lights, into the regions of Truth and Goodness, into the region of the Holy of all Holies, into the region in which there is neither female nor male, nor are there forms in that region, but a perpetual indescribable Light."

As to those advanced souls who are on the way to such illumination, Christ said to Mary Magdalene, "I have turned Elijah and sent him into the body of John the Baptist. The rest of the patriarchs and of the righteous from the time of Adam until now, I have through the Virgin of Light turned into bodies which will all be righteous—those which will find the mysteries, enter in, and inherit the Light-kingdom."

*

During this conversation with Jesus, Mary Magdalene is puzzled as to whether the prospect of many incarnations will not encourage putting off one's salvation. She uses a novel expression for rebirth, calling it "coming in at another circuit," and asks, "My Lord, if souls come into the world in many circuits and are neglectful of receiving the mysteries, hoping that, if they come into the world at any other circuit, they will receive them, will they not then be in danger of not succeeding in receiving the mysteries?" In reply, Christ addresses all the disciples. "Herald unto the whole world and say to men: Strive thereafter that you may receive the mysteries of the Light in this time of affliction and enter into the Light-kingdom. Join not one day to another, hoping that you may succeed in receiving the mysteries if you come into the world in another circuit."

He then warns that there is a time limit for attainment of perfection in any world. When "the number of the perfect souls shall be at hand, I will shut the gates of light and no one from that time onwards will enter in nor will any one hereafter go forth [into incarnation again] for the number of the perfect souls is completed, for the sake of which the universe has arisen."

When this happens and our world ends, there will be a purifying fire, says Christ. But this will not be the final end, because according to the Gnostics worlds too are reborn.[40]

GNOSTICISM DRIVEN UNDERGROUND

"The process of establishing orthodoxy," writes Professor Pagels in *The Gnostic Gospels,* "ruled out every other option." "To the impoverishment of Christian tradition, gnosticism, which offered alternatives to what became the main thrust of Christian orthodoxy was forced outside. The concerns of gnostic Christians survived only as a suppressed current, like a river driven underground. Such currents resurfaced throughout the Middle Ages in serious forms of heresy." Prominent among these heresies was reincarnation. Specialists in medieval history reveal that all over Europe there were hundreds of thousands of Christian reincarnationists who were eventually crushed through holy wars and inquisitions.[41] They were charged with the crime of succeeding the early Gnostics.* In their own view, they were carrying on the tradition of esoteric Christianity.

Why Was the Medieval Church Antagonistic to Reincarnation? Professor Geddes MacGregor addresses this important question in *Reincarnation as a Christian Hope:* "Wherein lay the threat of such a seemingly innocuous idea?" "It has a special tendency to cause those who believe in it to feel able to dispense with the *institutional* aspects of the Christian Way. . . . For reincarnational systems of belief particularly call attention to the role of the individual will. They stress freedom of choice and the individual's capacity to make or mar his or her own destiny. My destiny is up to me. The Church may be immensely helpful to me. I may deeply reverence its teachings and thirst for its sacraments. . . . Yet if I accept a reincarnationist view I recognize that in the last resort I can do without the Church, as a boy can do without his mother, deeply though he may love her.

"Few Church leaders are either humble enough or sufficiently mature in the spiritual life to be ready so to abdicate power. . . . We all know how jealously the leaders of any organization hold on to such power and authority as is conceded to them either by tradition or by acclamation. This has always been notably the case in the Church and has come to be widely

---

*These successors to the Christian Gnostics were also charged with violating a decree of the Fifth Ecumenical Council (A.D. 553), which it was believed anathematized the doctrine of the preexistence of the soul. This ruled out all possibility that souls had lived previously on earth. To henceforth believe in preexistence carried the penalty of excommunication from the church. Most Christian scholars today are convinced that the Council never *officially* passed this decree. The astounding story of what transpired at the Council and what led to it is told in *Reincarnation, the Phoenix Fire Mystery* (pp. 144–148, 156–160).

recognized as one of the Church's greatest weaknesses as a conduit of spirituality. . . .

"The Mediaeval Church could be generous, not to say indulgent, to those who followed the rules, assuring them of a relatively easy passage through this life, through purgatory, and into heaven. The price was, however, total reliance on the Church as the indispensable instrument of God. Once the paternalism of the Church was challenged, as it was by a doctrine such as reincarnation, people would become less dependent children and more independent adults in their pilgrimage towards salvation, and the mediaeval Church was not adaptable to such a state of affairs. It would have fatally injured priestly power."[42]

All the Old Questions Are Being Reopened. In the concluding chapter of *The Gnostic Gospels*, Elaine Pagels writes, "When Muhammed Ali smashed that jar filled with papyrus on the cliff near Nag Hammadi and was disappointed not to find gold, he could not have imagined the implications of his accidental find. Had they been discovered 1,000 years earlier, the gnostic texts almost certainly would have been burned for their heresy. But they remained hidden until the twentieth century, when our own cultural experience has given us a new perspective on the issues they raise. Today we read them with different eyes, not merely as 'madness and blasphemy' but as Christians in the first centuries experienced them—a powerful alternative to what we know as orthodox Christian tradition. Only now are we beginning to consider the questions with which they confront us. . . .

"Now that the Nag Hammadi discoveries give us a new perspective . . . we can understand why certain creative persons throughout the ages, from Valentinus and Heracleon to Blake, Rembrandt, Dostoevsky, Tolstoy, and Nietzsche, found themselves at the edges of orthodoxy. All were fascinated by the figure of Christ—his birth, life, teachings, death, and resurrection; all return constantly to Christian symbols to express their own experience. And yet they found themselves in revolt against orthodox institutions.

"An increasing number of people today share their experience. They cannot rest solely on the authorities of the Scriptures, the apostles, the church—at least not without inquiring how that authority constituted itself, and what, if anything, gives it legitimacy.

"All the old questions—the original questions, sharply debated at the beginning of Christianity—are being reopened: How is one to understand the resurrection? What about women's participation in priestly and episcopal office? Who was Christ, and how does he relate to the believer? What are the similarities between Christianity and other world religions?''

And, in light of all the foregoing, was reincarnation a teaching expounded by Jesus?

Something Optional or Something Lost? In a recent interview, Professor MacGregor spoke of the tremendous interest in reincarnation today. "It is the sort of thing the *clergy* should interest themselves in, and it seems to me that short of those who are extremely literalistic, like the so-called fundamentalist Protestants, it would be something thoughtful clergy would give a great deal of attention to.''

As to Christians generally, he added, such a study would enrich them very much. "It would show people that Christianity has all sorts of hidden riches within the tradition. Many people when talking about Christianity are thinking only of the particular kind of Christianity that they know about: Southern Baptist, Lutheran, Irish Catholic, or whatever it may be. When a Russian Orthodox, for example, thinks of Christianity, he thinks of Russian Orthodoxy and usually knows very little about anything else. The fact that a church of any importance in the Christian scheme of things held that reincarnation was at least a viable option would certainly show people what a much richer treasure Christianity has than they had supposed.''

A natural question that follows, says the professor, "is whether reincarnation is the sort of doctrine that can be regarded as optional, as a possible interpretation, or whether it may be more than that—*something that the Church has really lost and should recover*," and which "for various historical reasons has been overshadowed and pushed aside."[43] As we study the religions of the world, MacGregor remarked elsewhere, "We find over and over again the reincarnationist motif asserting itself just at those junctures in human history in which the institutional element in religion has become stultifying and the need for spiritualization enters. This indeed may be one of those periods in the long story of humanity."[44]

14
Krishna and
the Bhagavad-Gita

I owed—my friend and I owed—a magnificent day to The Bhagavad-Gita.
*It was the first of books; it was as if an empire spoke to us, nothing small
or unworthy, but large, serene, consistent.*

RALPH WALDO EMERSON, *Journals*

The lives of Jesus and Krishna, as recorded in the scriptures, were
so extraordinarily similar that the early Christian missionaries in India
concluded that the story of Krishna was plagiarized from that of the Christian savior. Even their names seemed similar, and as late as the 1880s
Western oriental scholars were spelling Krishna "Christna." It is now
known that the legends concerning Krishna were written long before the
time of Jesus. It may be that humanity's Great Teachers lived "symbol"
lives, following a similar paradigmatic pattern indicative of their spiritual
nature and mission.

Similarities in the lives of Krishna and Jesus include the following. Both
were of royal descent. Both were supposedly born of immaculate virgins.
Krishna was brought up by shepherds and has been called the Shepherd
God. Jesus was worshipped by shepherds and is called the Good Shepherd.
Krishna was an avatar, an incarnation of Vishnu, the second person of the
Hindu trimurti or trinity. Jesus is likewise believed to be an incarnation of
the trinity or the Godhead.

Krishna's birth and divine descent were kept secret from King Kansa,
tyrant of Madura. Once the secret was discovered, the king had thousands
of male babies slaughtered in the hope of destroying the child, but the
object of his wrath miraculously escaped. Jesus was persecuted by Herod

and escaped into Egypt under conduct of an angel. To assure his slaughter, the king ordered a massacre of innocents, and 40,000 were slain.

Krishna's story, as told in Hindu books such as the *Harivansa* and the *Vishnu Purana,* is largely mythological in nature. When the story was accepted literally, it gave rise to ridiculous tales that the missionaries were fond of repeating to discredit Hinduism. However, the story of Krishna as a spiritual teacher is to be found in *The Bhagavad-Gita. Bhagavad* is one of the names of Krishna, and *Gita* means "song." Thus the title translates as "The Song of Krishna."

The *Gita* has achieved such importance and status in India that it and the Upanishads are regarded as the Hindu bible. The renowned Indian scholar and former president of India, Dr. S. Radhakrishnan, observes that these texts "have inspired generations of Indians with vision and strength by their inexhaustible significance and spiritual power. . . . The fire still burns bright on their altars."[1] In introducing his translation of the *Gita,* he says it "represents not any sect of Hinduism but Hinduism as a whole, not merely Hinduism but religion as such, in its universality, without limit of space, embracing within its synthesis the whole gamut of the human spirit."

Probably for this reason it has transcended national and racial boundaries and has become so widely valued in the West. J.W.Hauer, a Sanskrit scholar who served for some years as a missionary, wrote in *The Hibbert Journal* that the *Gita* is "a work of imperishable significance," providing "profound insights that are valid for all times and for all religious life" (April 1940).

Before turning to a further consideration of the *Gita* and its influence, a few general thoughts on reincarnation in Hinduism are provided.

AN OVERVIEW OF REBIRTH IN INDIAN THOUGHT

"In the East," writes William Q. Judge, whose rendition of the *Gita* we will be using,

the life of man is held to be a pilgrimage, not only from the cradle to the grave, but also through that vast period of time, embracing millions upon millions of years, stretching from the beginning to the end of a *Manvantara,* or period of evolution, and as he is held to be a spiritual being, the continuity of his existence is unbroken. Nations and civilizations rise, grow old, decline and disappear; but the being lives on, spectator of all the innumerable changes of environment. Starting from the great All, radiating like a spark from the central fire, he gathers experience in all ages, under all rulers, civilizations and customs, ever engaged in a pilgrimage to the shrine from which he came. He is now the ruler and now the slave; today at the pinnacle of wealth and power, tomorrow at the bottom of the ladder, perhaps in abject misery, but ever the same being. To symbolize this, the whole of India is dotted with sacred shrines, to which pilgrimages are made.[2]

The acceptance of rebirth is so widespread in India that its philosophers and religious teachers felt no need to prove the doctrine, anymore than an instructor in our society would spend time demonstrating that day follows night, and night day. Thus Indian scriptures reflect the chief concern in the East—what kind of life releases a soul from unnecessary misery-causing involvement in the round of rebirths and leads it progressively through incarnation after incarnation to spiritual illumination, freedom, and ultimately Nirvana.

INFLUENCE OF THE *GITA* IN THE WEST

The idea of reincarnation pervades *The Bhagavad-Gita,* and when the scripture was translated into European tongues in the eighteenth and nineteenth centuries, it was effective in restoring to Western philosophical thought an appreciation for this long-lost teaching.[3]

The *Gita* has appealed to minds of diverse character. The atomic scientist Robert Oppenheimer not only studied the *Gita* but learned Sanskrit in order to read it and other Hindu works in the original (*Time,* November 8, 1948). A century earlier, a very different sort of man, Henry David Thoreau, had this to say in *Walden.*

In the morning I bathe my intellect in the stupendous and cosmogonal philosophy of the *Bhagvat Geeta,* since whose composition years of the gods have elapsed, and in comparison with which our modern world and its literature seem puny and trivial; and I doubt if that philosophy is not to be referred to a previous state of existence, so remote is its sublimity from our conceptions.

I lay down the book and go to my well for water, and lo! there I meet the servant of the Brahmin come to draw water for his master, and our buckets as it were grate together in the same well. The pure Walden water is mingled with the sacred water of the Ganges.[4]

In *The Orient in American Transcendentalism,* Arthur Christy relates that "no one oriental volume that ever came to Concord was more influential than *The Bhagavad-Gita.* This is evident from the manner and frequency in which the Concordians spoke of it.[5] Sanborn says that for years

Emerson was one of the very few Americans who owned a copy, and that his was even more widely used than that in the Harvard Library.''[6]

The edition they used—and the first to appear in the West—was that translated by Sir Charles Wilkins. When it was published in England in 1785, it was received with astonishment in Europe. Three years later, a Russian translation was published at the Moscow University Press through the agency of Nikolai Novikov, the eminent Russian journalist and writer.[7] William Blake was one of the early readers of the Wilkins's *Gita*.[8] One of Blake's lost paintings was titled *Mr. Wilkins Translating the Geeta.*

The preface to the Wilkins edition was written by Warren Hastings, the first British governor-general of India. Emerson in his essay "English Traits" made this superb comment: "I am not surprised to find an Englishman like Warren Hastings, who had been struck with the grand style of thinking in the Indian writings" offering his countrymen a translation of the *Gita*. "For a self-conceited modish life, made up of trifles, clinging to a corporeal civilization, hating ideas, there is no remedy like the Oriental largeness. That astonishes and disconcerts English decorum. For once, there is thunder it never heard, light it never saw, and power which trifles with time and space."[9]

GANDHI AND THE *GITA*

This scripture became the most important book in Gandhi's life, yet he did not discover its value until he went to England to study law as a young man. In his *Autobiography*, he wrote,

> Towards the end of my second year in England I came across two Theosophists, brothers. . . . They talked to me about the *Gita*. . . . They invited me to read the original with them. I felt ashamed, as I had read the divine poem neither in Sanskrit nor in Gujarati. . . . I began reading the *Gita* with them. . . . They also took me on one occasion to the Blavatsky Lodge and introduced me to Madame Blavatsky and Mrs. Besant . . . I recall having read, at the brothers' instance, Madame Blavatsky's *Key to Theosophy*. This book stimulated in me the desire to read books on Hinduism, and disabused me of the notion fostered by the missionaries that Hinduism was rife with superstition. . . .[10]

Professor James Hunt remarks in *Gandhi in London* that when Gandhi first came there he was more interested in fashion than his studies in law. He came there believing wholeheartedly that Indians should become like Englishmen. "It was through Theosophy that Gandhi was induced to study his heritage. This effect was generated in many Indians," and brought about a revival in India of appreciation for its ancient scriptures which had been neglected under the influence of the missionaries and Western science.[11] Gandhi informed his biographer, Louis Fischer, that "Theosophy is the teaching of Madame Blavatsky. It is Hinduism at its best." Twice he emphasized: "Theosophy is the brotherhood of man."[12]

Professor Michael Nagler speaks of the effect of *The Bhagavad-Gita* on Gandhi in his foreword to *Gandhi the Man* by Eknath Easwaran: "How did Gandhi manage to expand the narrow little personality of Mohandas K. Gandhi to become Mahatma, the immense force for human progress which has been described by countless biographers but accounted for by none?"[13] The answer, as found in Easwaran's book, says the professor, is that "the secret of Gandhi's power" was his philosophy, based on the *Gita*. He not only studied that scripture—he *became* the transformation it describes.

"When disappointments stare me in the face," wrote Gandhi, "and I see not one ray of light, I turn to *The Bhagavad-Gita* and I immediately begin to smile in the midst of overwhelming sorrow. My life has been full of external tragedies and if they have not left any visible and indelible effect on me, I owe it to the teaching of *The Bhagavad-Gita*" (*Young India*, August 6, 1925).

The *Gita*'s teaching of reincarnation sustained him in his herculean labors to free India from foreign domination thereby demonstrating to the world that "war without violence" could achieve peace and freedom. In *Young India* (April 2, 1931) he wrote, "Having flung aside the sword, there is nothing except the cup of love which I can offer to those who oppose me. It is by offering that cup that I expect to draw them close to me. I cannot think of permanent enmity between man and man, and believing as I do in the theory of rebirth, I live in the hope that if not in this birth, in some other birth I shall be able to hug all humanity in friendly embrace."

THE STORY OF THE *GITA*

The *Gita* forms a small but all-important part of the longest epic ever written, the *Mahabharata*. Elizabeth Seeger, in her young people's version of this classic, says that it "is three times as long as the Bible and eight times as long as the *Iliad* and the *Odyssey* put together." It contains "the storehouse of genealogy, mythology, and antiquity" of the Hindus.[14]

The *Gita* is in the form of a dialogue between Krishna and Arjuna, a prince who is waging war to regain his kingdom usurped by a hundred wicked cousins. Those unaware of the Hindu psychological system might view this in a literal sense as an actual armed conflict. The war theme as a symbol enhances the story rather than, as some think, disfigures it, because a battle demands supreme effort and commitment. Did not Jesus say that the Kingdom of Heaven is to be taken by violence and not by weakness of attack (Matt. 11:12)? "Know'st thou not," writes Walt Whitman, that "there is but one theme for ever enduring bards? And that is the theme of War, the fortune of battles, the making of perfect soldiers."[15]

Gandhi viewed the *Gita* in this light, as did India's great sages. "Even in 1888–89, when I first became acquainted with the Gita," Gandhi writes, "I felt that it was not a historical work, but that, under the guise of physical warfare, it described the duel that perpetually went on in the hearts of mankind, and that physical warfare was brought in merely to make the description of the internal duel more alluring" (*Young India*, August 6, 1931). "The war is the war between Jekyll and Hyde, God and Satan, going on in the human breast" (*Harijan*, January 21, 1939).

Thus in the opening chapter of the *Gita*, we find the hero Arjuna and his armies facing on the battlefield the assembled forces who have usurped Arjuna's kingdom. Although he has chosen Krishna for his charioteer and spiritual adviser, when Arjuna sees at close range just whom he has to "kill," his heart becomes overwhelmed with despondency, and he refuses to continue. Using the psychological key just mentioned, this means that, once any Arjuna—the hero in each of us—has resolved to live a higher life, his old selfish tendencies or "relatives," fighting for their very existence, throw up clouds of doubt, fear, and despondency to deter him from proceeding further.

In the selections that follow, the translation is that of William Q. Judge.[16] His companion work, *Notes on the Bhagavad-Gita*, is an illuminating and inspiring discussion of the psychological aspects of this dialogue.[17] In a letter to one of the authors dated October 6, 1977, I. B. Horner, the distinguished woman president of the Pali Text Society in London, wrote that this commentary "showed more insight into the teaching and understanding of this superb poem than I have ever seen elsewhere."

SELECTIONS FROM THE *GITA*

ARJUNA Now, O Krishna, that I have beheld my kindred thus standing anxious for the fight, my members fail me, my countenance withereth, the hair standeth on end upon my body, and all my frame trembleth with horror! Even Gandiva, my bow, slips from my hand, and my skin is parched and dried up. I am not able to stand: for my mind as it were, whirleth round, and I behold on all sides adverse omens. When I shall have destroyed my kindred, shall I longer look for happiness? I would rather patiently suffer that the sons of Dhritarashtra kill me unresisting in the field. I shall not fight, O Govinda.

KRISHNA Whence, O Arjuna, cometh upon thee this dejection in matters of difficulty, so unworthy of the honorable, and leading neither to heaven nor to glory? Abandon this despicable weakness of thy heart, and stand up. Thou grievest for those who may not be lamented. I myself never was not, nor thou, nor all the princes of the earth; nor shall we ever hereafter cease to be. As the Lord of this mortal frame experienceth therein infancy, youth, and old age, so in future incarnations will it meet the same. One who is confirmed in this belief is not disturbed by anything that may come to pass. As a man throweth away old garments and putteth on new, even so the dweller in the body, having quitted its old mortal frames, entereth into others which are new. . . .

This perishable body, O son of Kunti, is known as *Kshetra*; those who are acquainted with the true nature of things call the soul who knows it, the *Kshetrajna*. That knowledge which through the soul is a realization of both the known and the knower is alone esteemed by me as wisdom. Know, O chief of the Bharatas, that whenever anything is produced, it is due to the union of the *Kshetra* and *Kshetrajna*—body and the soul. The deluded do not see the spirit when it quitteth or remains in the body, nor when, moved by the qualities, it has experience in the world. But those who have the eye of wisdom perceive it, and devotees who industriously strive to do so see it dwelling in their own hearts. . . .

This exhaustless doctrine of Yoga I formerly taught to Vivaswat; Vivaswat communicated it to Manu and Manu made it known to Ikshwaku; and being thus transmitted from one to another it was studied by the Royal Sages, until at length in the course of time the mighty art was lost. It is even the same exhaustless, secret, eternal doctrine I have this day communicated unto thee because thou art my devotee and my friend.

ARJUNA Seeing that thy birth is posterior to the life of Ikshwaku, how am I to understand that thou wert in the beginning the teacher of this doctrine?

KRISHNA Both I and thou have passed through many births! Mine are known unto me, but thou knowest not of thine. I produce myself among creatures, O son of Bharata, whenever there is a decline of virtue and an insurrection of vice and injustice in the world; and thus I incarnate from age to age for the preservation of the just, the destruction of wickedness and the establishment of righteousness.

ARJUNA On account of the restlessness of the mind, I do not perceive any possibility of steady continuance in this yoga of equanimity which thou hast declared. For indeed, O Krishna, the mind is full of agitation, turbulent, strong, and obstinate. I believe the restraint of it to be as difficult as that of the wind.

KRISHNA Without doubt, O thou of mighty arms, the mind is restless and hard to restrain; but it may be restrained by practice and absence of desire. To whatsoever object the inconstant mind goes out [one] should subdue it, bring it back, and place it upon the Spirit. Supreme bliss surely cometh to the sage whose mind is thus at peace.

ARJUNA What end, O Krishna, does that man attain who, although having faith, has not attained to perfection in his devotion because his unsubdued mind wandered from discipline? Does he become destroyed, being deluded in the path of the Supreme Spirit?

KRISHNA Such a man does not perish here or hereafter. For never to an evil place goeth one who doeth good. The man whose devotion has been broken off by death goeth to the regions of the righteous, where he dwells for an immensity of years and is then born again on earth in a pure and fortunate family; or even in a family of those who are spiritually illuminated. But such a rebirth into this life as this last is more difficult to obtain. Being thus born again he comes in contact with the knowledge which belonged to him in his former body, and from that time he struggles more diligently towards perfection. For even unwittingly, by reason of that past practice, he is led and works on. Even if only a mere enquirer, he reaches beyond the word of the *Vedas*. But the devotee, who, striving with all his might, obtaineth perfection because of efforts continued through many births, goes to the supreme goal.

    There dwelleth in the heart of every creature, O Arjuna, the Master—*Ishwara*—who by its magic power causeth all things and creatures to revolve mounted upon the universal wheel of time. Take sanctuary with it alone, with all thy soul; by its grace thou shalt obtain supreme happiness, the eternal place. As a single sun illuminateth the whole world, even so does the One Spirit illumine every body. In those for whom knowledge of the true Self has dispersed ignorance, the Supreme, as if lighted by the sun, is revealed.

Have you heard all this with mind one-pointed? Has the delusion of thought which arose from ignorance been removed? I have made known to thee this knowledge which is a mystery more secret than secrecy itself; ponder it fully in thy mind; act as seemeth best.

REINCARNATION IN HINDUISM TODAY

Dr. Ian Stevenson reports that despite Christian and Muslim influences in India, the great majority of the inhabitants continue, strongly as ever, to believe in reincarnation, as did their ancestors millenniums ago.[18] The belief may be as strong, but it undoubtedly has undergone changes, for the India of recent times is far removed from the golden age of its culture. Many factors have contributed to India's later decline: economic conditions; political domination by foreign powers for many centuries; religious conflicts; and a rigid caste system instituted by the Brahmin priests, who imposed their brand of teaching on the masses. They often used reincarnation as a "big stick," falsely warning that nonconformance with the "rules" could mean demotion to an animal or insect in the next life.

A probing study of the prevailing trends in Hinduism appeared in India's *Illustrated Weekly* (September 26, 1971), under the title "Will Hinduism Survive?" The survey revealed that many Hindus are ignorant of their religion and indifferent to their basic scriptures. They practice rites without knowing their meaning, yet unconsciously they are influenced by certain persisting conceptions. Despite the confusion of the present, a substratum of timeless philosophy has recognizably survived. "It exists like a lotus in the mire. And it is conveyed by Hindus in numerous subtle, indescribable ways. Karma and reincarnation are to them more than a dogma, they are like the air that they breathe. And Hindus cannot help themselves feeling that they are part of a cosmic scheme that is perpetually in a whirl." As Krishna says in the *Gita,* "All worlds up to that of Brahma are subject to rebirth again and again."

The *Illustrated Weekly* envisions the possibility of a resurgence of spirituality in India. It continues:

There is a growing awareness of the challenges faced by Hinduism today. Many people want a break with the iniquities of the past and feel the need to accentuate the higher aspects of the religion. . . . This new awakening has touched even those who have been trained in modern science. . . . A new Hinduism may emerge in the days to come—that is, a Hinduism with all its lofty ideals of the past translated to the needs of modern man. Hinduism will survive as long as *The Bhagavad-Gita* is understood by people. The *Gita* has integrated a life of action with a life of renunciation. It has accomplished the impossible. And that is what life demands of us.

"No one who engages in a reverent study of that book," wrote Gandhi, "can help becoming a true servant of the nation and through it humanity. The *Gita* contains the Gospel of Work, the Gospel of *Bhakti* or Devotion, and the Gospel of *Jnana* or Knowledge. Life should be a harmonious whole of these three."[19] Of this harmonious whole, Gandhi himself was an exemplar. Albert Einstein said of him: "Generations to come will scarce believe that such a one as this ever in flesh and blood walked upon this earth."[20] But, if Gandhi's philosophy of rebirth is true, he will return, and so will we. Thus he said: "If for mastering the physical sciences you have to devote a whole lifetime, how many lifetimes may be needed for mastering the greatest spiritual force that mankind has known? For if this is the only permanent thing in life, if this is the only thing that counts, then whatever effort you bestow on mastering it is well spent."[21]

What is this spiritual force? In the teachings of Krishna in *The Bhagavad-Gita*, it is universal compassion and love, rooted not just in sentiment and emotional feelings but in spiritual knowledge. For such knowledge demonstrates the fundamental Oneness and eternality of all beings in their progressive march toward a higher life. In the fourth discourse of the *Gita,* Krishna explains how such spiritual knowledge may be obtained.

> Seek this wisdom by doing service, by strong search, by questions, and by humility; the wise who see the truth will communicate it to thee, and knowing which thou shalt never again fall into error. Even if thou were the greatest of all sinners, thou shalt be able to cross over all sins in the boat of spiritual knowledge. There is no purifier in this world to be compared to spiritual knowledge; and he who is perfected in devotion findeth spiritual knowledge springing up spontaneously in himself in the progress of time. The person of doubtful mind has no happiness either in this world or in the next or in any other. Wherefore, O Arjuna, having cut asunder with the sword of spiritual knowledge this doubt which existeth in thy heart, Arise!"[22]

*

Some concluding thoughts on reincarnation are taken from Albert
Schweitzer's *Indian Thought and Its Development*.

By reason of the idea of reincarnation, Indian thought can be reconciled to
the fact that so many people in their minds and actions are still so engrossed
in the world. If we assume that we have but one existence, there arises the
insoluble problem of what becomes of the spiritual ego which has lost all
contact with the Eternal. Those who hold the doctrine of reincarnation are
faced by no such problem. For them that non-spiritual attitude only means
that those men and women have not yet attained to the purified form of
existence in which they are capable of knowing the truth and translating it
into action. So the idea of reincarnation contains a most comforting explanation of reality by means of which Indian thought surmounts difficulties
which baffle the thinkers of Europe.[23]

15
The Life and Teachings of Buddha

Better than the life of a hundred years of a person who does not perceive the deathless state, is the short life of a single day of the person who senses that deathless state.

BUDDHA, *The Dhammapada*

When Buddha was born in India, there was an air of expectancy. A messiah was anticipated, one able to emancipate mankind from its misery and suffering. When Buddha, as Prince Siddhartha, was born to Queen Maya and King Suddhodana, many prophets and astrologers foretold that he was such a deliverer of the human race. It was prophesied that he would renounce his princely life when he saw four signs: an aged person, a sick person, a corpse, and a holy sage.

As the major events in the life of Buddha prior to his reaching enlightenment revolved around problems concerning life and death, birth and rebirth, the retelling of that story is appropriate in the present work. The text we will be using is *The Light of Asia* by Sir Edwin Arnold.[1] Prior to the large-scale Buddhist revival of recent years, the popularity Buddhism enjoyed in the West was due more to this memorable poem than to anything written before or since. As karma and reincarnation pervade this work, it may be credited with contributing to the growing Western interest in these ideas. The very first line after a stanza of introduction reads, "Then came he to be born again for men."

By way of introduction, we first turn our attention to some preliminary thoughts on Buddha's major teachings, and their influence in the modern world.

Buddha's Modern Message. ''After 2,500 years the teachings of Gotama Buddha are being regarded as 'really quite modern' '' states one writer in a foreword to Buddha's *Dhammapada*. ''This Indian sage, perhaps more than any other who has lived, provided a meeting-ground for all extremes of persuasion—agnosticism and gnosticism, belief and the skepticism of caution, appreciation of intuition and devotion to logic. While the world of the mind is still quivering from abrupt change—transition from too much other-world religion to too much physical science—a person who recognized, as parts of a larger whole, the valid emphases of each, is one whose thoughts are worth knowing today.''[2]

Lafcadio Hearn wrote, in *Gleanings in Buddha-Fields,*

> I remember that when I first attempted, years ago, to learn the outlines of Buddhist philosophy, one fact which particularly impressed me was the vastness of the Buddhist concept of the universe. The modern scientific revelation of stellar evolution and dissolution then seemed to me, and still seems, like a prodigious confirmation of certain Buddhist theories of cosmical law. By its creed the Oriental intellect has been better prepared than the Occidental to accept this tremendous [astronomical] revelation. And I cannot but think that out of the certain future union of Western knowledge with Eastern thought there must eventually proceed a Neo-Buddhism inheriting all the strength of science, yet spiritually able to recompense the seeker after truth.[3]

There has been for some decades a mounting interest in Buddhism among psychologists and psychiatrists. This was highlighted in the late 1950s when some fifty American psychologists met the distinguished Zen Buddhist teacher Dr. D. T. Suzuki and spent a week with him and his ideas. An outgrowth of the conference was the book *Psychoanalysis and Zen Buddhism* by Erich Fromm, D. T. Suzuki, and Richard DeMartino. Years earlier, Freud came to some degree under Buddhist influence. A student under his personal tutelage related that his mentor named Buddha the greatest psychologist of all time.[4]

How do we imagine Buddha would respond to such a statement? There is no need to imagine. A similar estimate was once made in his presence by the venerable monk Sariputta: ''There was not, will not be, and there is not now any teacher who has deeper knowledge respecting enlightenment than you, the Exalted One.''

The Buddha replied, ''Lofty, bold, and assured indeed are your words, a veritable lion's roar. Then Sariputta, you actually know those holy ones, fully enlightened, who lived in times past, and having encompassed all

these exalted ones in your mind could say: 'Such and such was their
virtues, teaching and wisdom?' And, Sariputta, what do you know about
the holy ones who will live in times to come? Do you know their virtues,
teaching and wisdom?'' To each question the monk was obliged to confess
ignorance.[5] How foolish, then, to imagine that one's own teacher is the
greatest.

From the foregoing it is obvious that Buddha did not consider himself
unique. Nor do Buddhists regard him as unique. The noted Buddhist
scholar, Edward Conze, remarks that while

> it is easy to see that we could not have any "Buddhism" unless a Buddha
> revealed it, we must, however, bear in mind that "Buddha" is not the name
> of a person, but designates a type. "Buddha" is Sanskrit for someone who
> is "fully enlightened" about the nature and meaning of life. Numerous
> "Buddhas" appear successively at suitable intervals. Buddhism sees itself
> not as the record of the sayings of one man who lived in Northern India
> about 500 B.C. His teachings are represented as the uniform result of an
> often repeated irruption of spiritual reality into this world. The state of a
> Buddha is one of the highest possible perfections [in this world]. It seems
> self-evident to Buddhists that an enormous amount of preparation over many
> lives is needed to reach it.[6]

BUDDHA ON THE REINCARNATING SOUL

Much misunderstanding exists as to what Buddha taught about reincarnation and about the soul. This is because the Buddhist texts first available in
the West were chiefly those of Theravada or Southern Buddhism. In this
school, Buddha's teachings are interpreted to mean that there is no soul to
be reborn; only the qualities and attributes of a person are reincarnated.
However, when Buddhist scholars went back to early Buddhist texts, these
limiting views were shown to be erroneous.[7] Even while Buddha was
alive, such misconceptions were circulating, and he exclaimed to his disciples:
"And I, O monks, am accused wrongly, vainly, falsely, and inappropriately by some ascetics and Brahmans: 'A denier is the ascetic Gotama, he
teaches the destruction, annihilation, and perishing of the being that now
exists.' These ascetics accuse me of being what I am not, O monks, and of
saying what I do not say.''[8]

The original Buddhist scriptures, known as the Pali Canon, were recorded in that language several hundred years after Buddha's death. The

most celebrated of these is *The Dhammapada*. Here Buddha plainly speaks of two selves within each human being, the lesser self and the greater self, the former being perishable, the latter enduring from life to life. Here are a few selections:

> The SELF is the Lord of Self; what higher Lord could there be? When a man subdues well his self, he will find a Lord very difficult to find. . . . Rouse your self by your Self, examine your self by your Self. Thus, Self-guarded and mindful you will live happily. . . .
>
> Knowing that this body is like froth, knowing that its nature is that of a mirage, the disciple passes untouched by death. Death bears off the man whose mind is intent on plucking the flowers of sense, as a flood sweeps away a sleeping hamlet. . . . He in whom the desire for the Ineffable has arisen, whose mind is permeated by that desire, whose thoughts are not distracted by lower desires, he is named "Bound upstream." . . .
>
> The craving of a thoughtless man grows like the Maluva creeper that eats up the tree on which it fastens. From life to life he is like a monkey seeking fruits in a forest. . . . Vigilance is the path to Life Eternal. Thoughtlessness is the path to death. The reflecting vigilant die not. The heedless are already dead. . . . Rejoice in wakefulness. Guard well your thoughts . . . at one time this mind of mine would wander as it liked, as it desired, as it pleased. Now I control it completely. . . .
>
> Him I call a Brahmana [a true Brahmin] who has destroyed his doubts by knowledge and has plumbed the depth of the Eternal. . . . Him I call a Brahmana who knows the mystery of death and rebirth of all beings, who knows his former lives, who is a sage of perfect knowledge and who has accomplished all that needs to be accomplished. . . .[9]

THE MAHAYANA SCHOOL OF BUDDHISM

Thus far we have mentioned Theravada or Southern Buddhism, that of Burma, Sri Lanka, Cambodia, Thailand, and parts of Vietnam. The Mahayana or Northern Buddhism prevails in Tibet, China, Japan, and Korea. In this school the belief in a reincarnating soul is definitely taught.

Thus, when the Dalai Lama on his first visit to the United States lectured at Harvard University's Center for the Study of World Religions on October 17, 1979, he affirmed that "by our own experience it is established that the self exists." "If we did assert total selflessness," he said, "then there would be no one who could cultivate compassion." Even in Nirvana, he added, "the continuum of consciousness goes on; one has not ceased the continuum of mind and body." Furthermore, "if the continuum of mind and body did cease when one attained Nirvana, then there would not be anybody to attain Nirvana."[10]

Two years later, the Dalai Lama again visited America. Addressing the Theosophical Society at its American headquarters in Wheaton, Illinois (July 21, 1981), he said, "According to the Theravada school of thought, when a person reaches Nirvana then there is no more person, he completely disappears, but according to *the higher school of thought* the person still remains, the being itself still remains."[11]

*

Dr. D. T. Suzuki, speaking on behalf of that form of Mahayana called Zen Buddhism—of which he was the leading exponent in the West— elaborates, in several of his writings, on the need for an immortal, reincarnating self in each of us.

> Without self there will be no individual; without an individual there will be no responsibility. Without the idea of responsibility morality ceases to exist . . . human community becomes impossible. We must in some way have a self.[12]

> We can never get rid of a self—we somehow always stumble over it. . . . Can this ego be really such a ghostly existence, an empty nothing . . . ? If it is really such a non-existent existence, how does it ever get into our consciousness or imagination? The Self then is not a thing or an emptiness and something incapable of producing work. It is much alive in our innate feeling of freedom and authenticity. When it is stripped of all its trappings, moral and psychological, and when we imagine it to be a void, it is not really so.[13]

> When the self thus stands in its native nakedness, it beggars all description. . . . The emptied self is no other than the psychological self cleansed of its ego-centric imagination. It is just as rich in its contents as before; indeed it is richer than before because it now contains the whole world in itself instead of having the latter stand against it. Not only that, it enjoys itself being true to itself. It is free in the real sense of the word because it is the master of itself, absolutely independent, self-relying, authentic, and autonomous.[14]

The historian Lynn White declares in his *Frontiers of Knowledge in the Study of Man* that the publication of Dr. Suzuki's first series of *Essays in Zen Buddhism* in 1927 "will seem to future generations as great an intellectual event as William of Moerbeke's Latin translations of Aristotle in the thirteenth century or Ficino's of Plato in the fifteenth."[15]

While occidental scholars usually accord Suzuki the credit of first popularizing Mahayana teachings in the West, he himself shared the honor with Helena Blavatsky. In reviewing the biography *The Real H.P. Blavatsky* by

William Kingsland,[16] Suzuki wrote, "Undoubtedly Madame Blavatsky had in some way been initiated into the deeper side of Mahayana teaching. . . . There is no doubt whatever that the Theosophical Movement made known to the general world the main doctrines of Mahayana Buddhism, and the interest now being taken in Mahayana in the Western World has most certainly been helped forward by the knowledge of Theosophy. . . . As Mr. Kingsland says, 'She did more than any other single individual to bring to the West a knowledge of Eastern religious philosophy.' "[17]

DID BUDDHA BELIEVE IN GOD?

Gandhi wrote, in his foreword to *The Way of the Buddha*,

> I have heard it contended times without number and I have read in books claiming to express the spirit of Buddhism, that the Buddha did not believe in God. In my humble opinion such a belief contradicts the very central fact of the Buddha's teaching. Confusion has arisen over his rejection, and just rejection, of the base things that passed in his generation under the name of God. He undoubtedly rejected the notion that a being called God could be actuated by malice, could repent of his actions, and like the kings of the earth could possibly be open to temptations and bribes, and could have favorites. The one thing that the Buddha showed India was that God was not a God who can be appeased by sacrificing innocent animals. His whole soul rose up in mighty indignation against such a belief.[18]

A valuable volume on deity in Buddha's teaching is *The God of Buddha* by Jamshed K. Fozdar (New York: Asia Publishing House, 1973). The author reveals that what Buddha sought to eradicate was "the widespread acceptance of a multitude of gods, big and small, personalized and semi-human, which had become the central preoccupation of the Hindus" and were "far removed in time from their own pure doctrinal sources," when the emphasis was on the Supreme Spirit or Brahma as the source of all life.

I. B. Horner, president of The Pali Text Society and a renowned Pali scholar herself, points out that the union of the higher self with Brahma, was often mentioned in the first recordings of Buddha's teachings. In her article "Atta or Anatta,"[19] she discloses that, just as the Theravadists overlooked an immortal soul as taught by Buddha, they ignored his teaching on God. Yet a frequent expression used by him was *brahmacariya*, which Horner defines as "the Walk to or with Brahma, the Sublime." She quotes him as stating in the *Anguttara-Nikaya* (11 206): "The person who torments neither himself nor others, lives with a self become Brahma."

THE LIFE OF BUDDHA

Sir Edwin Arnold's *The Light of Asia.*   This work will be our main source on Buddha's life. According to the British *Dictionary of National Biography,* there were sixty editions of this work in England and eighty in America, and translations were numerous.[20] In America, almost a million copies were sold.[21] In a twenty-six-page review, Oliver Wendell Holmes wrote, "Its tone is so lofty there is nothing with which to compare it but the New Testament."[22] It was not Buddha's ethical teachings that astounded Arnold's readers—the Sermon on the Mount teaches these—but the fact that five hundred years before Jesus another savior had gloriously lived and taught the Christ life. Arnold's book also arrested the attention of Gandhi, and in his *Autobiography* he said, "My young mind tried to unify the teachings of the *Gita,* the *Light of Asia* and the Sermon on the Mount."[23]

As a drama, *The Light of Asia* was successfully produced in New York in 1927 by the great Shakespearean actor Walter Hampden and architect Claude Bragdon, who designed the costumes for 100 different characters. Ruth St. Denis staged the Dance of the Maidens in the temptation scene.[24]

In *Buddhism, Its Essence and Development,* Dr. Conze lists the publication of *The Light of Asia* in 1879 as one of the important events in the history of Buddhism.[25]

Arnold, who was knighted by Queen Victoria, also rendered *The Bhagavad-Gita* into English verse under the title *The Song Celestial.* When Britain's poet laureate Tennyson died in 1892, the queen favored Sir Edwin as his successor. However, Prime Minister Gladstone wanted a fundamentalist, and as they both could not agree, the coveted office remained vacant for several years.[26]

As a young man, Arnold lived for three or four years in India where he was principal of Deccan College in Puna. There he learned Sanskrit and studied oriental philosophy. Owing to the frail health of his wife, he returned to England. As a poet can hardly raise a family with remuneration from published verse, Arnold was obliged to build a dual career and for many years was chief editor of London's *Daily Telegraph.* Under his management, the paper rose to world prominence. "The forty years which Arnold spent on the staff of the *Telegraph,*" writes a biographer, "span the era which was the high-watermark of Britain's greatness. It was Arnold's fortune and that of his paper to chronicle and in some measure to guide the course of those decades."[27]

Arnold's older son Lester wrote of his father, "In the case of great poets one is usually forced to the conclusion that they were born, not made, and my father was apparently no exception to this rule. I have before me a pedigree of his family going back into the mists of the middle ages, and in that long array of sturdy Kentish esquires and of comely wives who devoted their lives to the management of store cupboards and the production of numerous offspring, there is no hint of poetic tendencies in the race. Sir Edwin's genius came into being unexpectedly, unaccountably.''[28]

Arnold's youngest son Emerson, a medical doctor, had an intriguing explanation. But first, it is interesting to learn how this son acquired his name. It was bestowed by his father when Ralph Waldo Emerson, on a visit to the Arnold family in Kent, prayed over and blessed the baby. This is mentioned in Brooks Wright's biography *Interpreter of Buddhism to the West: Sir Edwin Arnold.*[29] Wright comments that, with such an auspicious beginning to the child's career, it is not surprising that he later became a theosophist. Incidentally, Dr. Conze also identifies Sir Edwin as a theosophist.[30] Here, now, are Emerson Arnold's thoughts on the source of his father's genius:

> I hold the view very strongly myself that the explanation lies in previous Indian incarnations. My father, although very patriotic and intensely British in many ways, was always a semi-Oriental; in outlook, tastes, manners and thoughts, and even in appearance. I believe that his brief visit to India resuscitated the subconscious memories of former lives spent there and that these gave him his wonderful knowledge and insight and his love for and attraction to Eastern life and philosophy.
>
> A prominent Hindu pandit and philosopher, whom I had the honor of meeting quite recently, said to me that in reading my father's Indian works he always felt as if it was a fellow-countryman writing, so natural and native was the tone and so perfect and penetrating the insight and descriptions.
>
> To anyone who, like myself, is a convinced student of Theosophy and Oriental Occultism the phenomenon is all the more striking. For his works reveal an expert and deep knowledge of Eastern philosophy which is amazing.[31]

Introducing the volume, Sir Edwin Arnold writes in the preface, ''In the following poem I have sought, by the medium of an imaginary Buddhist votary, to depict the life and character and indicate the philosophy of that noble hero and reformer, Prince Gotama of India, the founder of Buddhism. A generation ago little or nothing was known in Europe of this great faith of Asia, which had nevertheless existed during twenty-four centuries, and at this day surpasses, in the number of its followers and area of its prevalence, any other form of creed. Four hundred and seventy millions of our race live and die in the tenets of Gotama; and the spiritual dominions of this ancient teacher extend, at the present time, from Nepal and Ceylon, over the whole Eastern Peninsula, to China, Japan, Tibet, Central Asia, Siberia, and even Swedish Lapland.

"India itself might fairly be included in this magnificent Empire of Belief; for though the profession of Buddhism has for the most part passed away from the land of its birth, the mark of Gotama's sublime teachings is stamped ineffaceably upon modern Brahmanism, and the most characteristic habits and convictions of the Hindus are clearly due to the benign influence of Buddha's precepts."

The Light of Asia has never been out of print, but in recent years tiny pocket-size, small-print editions have not been inviting to read. This difficulty has now been remedied by the publication of a new, lovely inexpensive clothbound edition.[32]

We turn now to the story of Buddha's life as recorded in Arnold's poem, and all quotations, unless otherwise indicated, are from that work. The poet's exquisite portrayal of Indian life and landscapes has been regretfully omitted. Also, to conserve space and overcome the difficulties people often experience in reading poetry, we have, in most cases, taken the liberty of running the verses together as if they were prose, while endeavoring to preserve the power and beauty of the original.

BUDDHA'S EARLY YEARS

When Buddha was born as Prince Siddartha, a wise man by name Asita visited the palace and prophesied that the child would become a great and holy teacher: "Know, O King! this is that Blossom on our human tree which opens once in many myriad years—but opened, fills the world with Wisdom's scent and Love's dropped honey: From thy royal root a Heavenly Lotus springs. Ah, happy House! yet not all-happy, for a sword must pierce thy bowels for this boy." Asita also foretold that the queen, "dear to all gods and men for this great virgin birth," in seven days time would die, being now too sacred for life on earth.

The king was deeply dismayed by the news that his son would become a holy Buddha, for he planned that the boy would someday reign "a king of kings and be the glory of his time." Extraordinary measures were therefore taken to nullify Asita's prophecy by surrounding the prince with wealth and luxury, isolating him from all knowledge of sorrow, sickness, and death. Each morning before dawn, the gardeners were ordered to remove every sign of dying vegetation from the palace gardens. Among the boy's retinue all must be young and beautiful. When signs of graying hair appeared, the attendants were dismissed.

One day the king took his growing son to see the beauties of the spring and his farms where peasants toiled. "All things spoke peace and plenty, and the prince saw and rejoiced. But, looking deep, he saw the thorns which grow upon this rose of life; how the peasant sweated for his wage, how lizard fed on ant, and snake on him, and kite on both. Everywhere each slew, and in turn was slain, life living upon death. So the fair show veiled one vast, savage, grim conspiracy of mutual murder. 'Is this,' he said, 'that happy earth they brought me forth to see?' " Thus did Buddha learn of death in nature's kingdoms, but of human death he knew naught.

The prince then seated himself "under a Jambu tree with ankles crossed—as holy statues sit—and first began to meditate this deep disease of life, what its far source and whence its remedy." All through his youth and amid the play of sports came these periodic musings and withdrawals, so that the king surrounded him more and more with pleasures and luxury beyond description.

Marriage of Prince Siddartha. When the lad reached eighteen, the king's ministers said that love will cure his sadness, will "weave the spell of woman's wiles about his idle heart." And so his father commanded that a festival be held where all the kingdom's loveliest maids would compete in youth and grace, and to those most fair the prince will give the prizes. As they passed before him, he sat so passionless, gentle, but so beyond them, their eyes were fixed upon the ground.

The last to come was young Yasodhara, "and those that stood nearest Siddartha saw the princely boy start, as the radiant girl approached. A form of heavenly mold, a face so fair words cannot paint its spell." She alone with full gaze looked into his eyes, her stately neck unbent. " 'Is there a gift for me?' she asked, and smiled. 'The gifts are gone,' the prince replied, 'yet take this for amends, dear sister.' Therewith he loosed the emerald necklet from his throat, and clasped its green beads round her dark and silk-soft waist; and their eyes mixed, and from the look sprang love."

Long after, when enlightenment was full, Lord Buddha was asked why his heart thus took fire at first glance of the Sakya girl. He answered, we were not strangers, we had been husband and wife in another life.

After the marriage, "love was all in all, yet not to love alone trusted the king; love's prison house stately and beautiful he bade them build, so that in all the earth no marvel was like the prince's pleasure-place. Thus Siddartha lived forgetting."

Intimations of the World's Sorrows. In this calm home of happy life and love, "Lord Buddha, knowing not of woe, nor want, nor pain, nor plague, nor age, nor death, save as when sleepers roam dim seas in dreams."

Thus oftentimes on waking "he would start up and cry, 'My world! Oh, world! I hear! I know! I come!' " And Yasodhara would ask with large eyes terror-struck, "What ails my Lord?" Then he would smile again to stay her tears.

To wile away the time, an attendant told a tale "of love and of a magic horse, and lands wonderful, distant, where pale peoples dwelled." And the prince inquired of his wife: "Is there so wide a world where hearts dwell like ours, countless, unknown, perhaps not happy, whom we should love? Now have I in this hour an ache, at last, thy soft lips cannot kiss away. Why have I never seen and sought?"

And of his courtiers he asked: "Tell me what lies beyond our brazen gates?" One answered: "The city first, fair prince! And next King Bimbasara's realm, and the vast flat world, with crores on crores of folks." "Good," said Siddartha, "let the word be sent that Channa yoke my chariot—at noon tomorrow I shall ride and see beyond."

BUDDHA LEARNS OF OLD AGE

When the cautious king heard of this, he said, "Yes, it is time for him to see, but let the criers go about and bid my city deck itself, so there be met no noisome sight; and let none blind or maimed, none that is sick or stricken deep in years, no leper, and no feeble folk come forth."

When Siddartha arrived, he found a city full of smiles, joyous to see their prince. "Fair is the world," he said, "it likes me well! And gentle and kind these men that are not kings, and sweet my sisters here, who toil and tend; what have I done for these to make them thus?"

"Drive, Channa! through the gates, and let me see more of the gracious world I have not known." So on he went, a joyous crowd surrounding him. Then deep consternation! "What is that?" Midway in the road, slow tottering from the hovel where he hid, crept forth a wretch in rags, haggard and foul. Bent was his back with the load of many days, his eyepits red with rust of ancient tears, his toothless jaws wagging with palsy and the fright to see so many and such joy. "Alms!" moaned he, "give, good people! for I die tomorrow or the next day!"

The crowd wrenched the man away to hide him from the prince, but Siddartha cried: "Let be! let be! Channa! what thing is this who seems a man, yet surely only seems, being so bowed, so miserable, so horrible, so

sad? Are men born sometimes thus? What meaneth he moaning 'tomorrow
or next day I die?' Finds he no food that so his bones jut forth? What woe
hath happened to this piteous one?''

The charioteer answered: ''Sweet Prince! this is no other than an aged
man. Some fourscore years ago his back was straight, his eyes bright, and
his body goodly. Now the thievish years have sucked his sap away, pil-
lared his strength. His lamp has lost its oil, the wick burns black. Such is
age. Why should your Highness heed?''

Then the prince spoke: ''But shall this come to others, or to all? Or is it
rare that one should be as he?'' ''Most noble,'' answered Channa, ''even
as he, will all these grow if they live so long.'' ''But,'' said the prince, ''if
I shall live as long shall I be thus; and if Yasodhara live fourscore years, is
this old age for her?'' ''Yea, great Sir!'' the charioteer replied. Siddartha
said, ''Turn back, drive me to my house again! I have seen that I did not
think to see.''

That evening he ate not at all. The finest delicacies could not tempt his
palate, ''nor once looked he up when the best palace-dancers strove to
charm.'' And his wife sank to his feet weeping: ''Hath not my Lord
comfort in me?'' ''Ah, sweet!'' he said, ''such comfort that my soul
aches, thinking it must end, *for it will end*, and we shall both grow old,
Yasodhara! Loveless, unlovely, weak, and bowed.'' Through that night he
sat sleepless, uncomforted.

LEARNS OF SICKNESS AND DEATH

''Once again the spirit of the prince was moved to see the world beyond
his gates,'' but this time he asked to pass unknown among the people and
see their lives not in gay holiday attire but as they really were.

All day Channa and he wandered around the town and viewed the busy,
noisome sights of the townfolk at work, but one experience blanked out all
the rest. ''From the roadside moaned a mournful voice. 'Help, masters! lift
me to my feet; oh, help! or I shall die before I reach my house!' A stricken
wretch it was, whose quivering frame, caught by some deadly plague, lay
in the dust writhing. The wild eyes swam with inward agony. 'Good
people help!' '' Siddartha ran and tenderly lifted the man and laid his sick
head on his knee. ''Why is it, Channa,'' he asked, ''that he pants and
moans?''

''Great prince! this man is smitten with some pest; in his veins the
blood, which ran a wholesome river, leaps and boils a fiery flood. His
heart, which kept good time, beats like an ill-played drum-skin, quick and

slow, and all the grace and joy of manhood fled. This is a sick man with the fit upon him. Oh, sir! it is not good to hold him so! The harm may pass, and strike thee, even thee.''

"Come such ills unobserved?" the prince inquired. And Channa replied, "Like the sly snake they come that stings unseen." "Then all men live in fear," asked the Prince, "and none can say, 'I sleep happy and whole tonight, and so shall wake?' " "None say it," came the answer.

"But if they cannot bear their agonies, or if they bear, and be, as this man is, too weak except for groans, what happens then?" "They die, Prince." "Die?" "Yes, at the last comes death. Some few grow old, most suffer and fall sick, but all must die—behold, behold, where comes the Dead!''

A funeral procession passes by, a band of wailing people, carrying to the river bank a grim corpse, stark and stiff. Soon the lighted flames feed on the flesh "with swift hissing tongues, and crackle of parched skin, and snap of joint.''

"Is this the end which comes to all who live?" exclaims the prince. "This is the end that comes to all," answers Channa. "He upon the pyre, ate, drank, laughed, loved, and lived, and liked life well. Then came— who knows?—some gust of jungle-wind, a stumble on the path, a taint in the tank, snake's nip, half a span of angry steel, a chill, a fishbone, or a falling tile, and life was over and the man is dead. Those whom he loved wail desolate, for even that must go, the body, which was lamp unto life, or worms will have a horrid feast of it. Here is the common destiny of flesh: The high and low, the good and bad, must die.''

Siddartha turned eyes gleaming with divine tears to the sky, eyes lit with heavenly pity to the earth. From sky to earth he looked, from earth to sky, as if his spirit sought in lonely flight some far-off vision, linking this and that, lost—past—but searchable, but seen, but known, then cried he:

"Oh! suffering world, oh! known and unknown of my common flesh, caught in this common net of death and woe, and life which binds to both! I see, I feel the vastness of the agony of earth, the vainness of its joys, the mockery of all its best, the anguish of its worst. For pleasures end in pain, and youth in age, and love in loss, and life in hateful death, and death in unknown lives, which will but yoke men to their wheel again to whirl the round of false delights and woes that are not false.

"Me too this lure has cheated, so it seemed lovely to live, and life a sunlit stream forever flowing in a changeless peace. The veil is rent which blinded me! I am as all these men who cry upon their gods and are not heard or are not heeded—yet there must be aid! For them and me and all there must be help! Perchance the gods have need of help themselves being so feeble that when sad lips cry they cannot save! I would not let one cry whom I could save! Channa! lead home again! It is enough! Mine eyes have seen enough!''

BUDDHA MEETS A SAGE

It will be recalled that it was prophesied that Buddha would not leave home until he saw an aged person, a sick person, a dead man, and finally a wise ascetic. Three of these experiences have come to him; only the fourth remains. Edwin Arnold does not record it, but Asvaghosha, who lived in the first century A.D., did so in his famous life of Buddha, rendered into English by Samuel Beal.[33]

The story goes that, before the prince returned home after his latest visit to the city, he stopped to meditate under a tree on the cause of woe. While he was lost in contemplation, ''a Deva of the Pure Abode, transforming himself in the shape of a monk, came to the place where the prince was seated. The prince rose to meet him, and asked who he was. 'I am a Shaman, depressed and sad at thoughts of age, disease, and death; all things hasten to decay and there is no permanency. Therefore I search for the happiness of something that decays not, that never perishes, that never knows beginning, that looks with equal mind on enemy and friend, that heeds not wealth nor beauty.' ''

''As the Shaman stood before the prince, gradually rising up, he disappeared in space,'' and the prince was reminded of ''former Buddhas, established thus in perfect dignity of manner; with noble mien and presence.''

This wondrous vision brought to Siddartha a burning conviction that he must fulfil the quest set by this heavenly visitor and thereby free humanity from misery and suffering.

CHOICE TO SAVE THE WORLD

Resuming the tale as told in *The Light of Asia,* we find Siddartha resolved to leave the pleasure-palace and princely life that encaged him. He secretly plans to escape. On the night of his departure, his wife, now expecting a child, has troubled dreams her Lord will go away. She wakes terrified at the thought.

With tender smile, the prince bent over his weeping wife and softly said, ''Though thy dreams may be shadows of things to come, and though the gods are shaken in their seats, yet whatsoever falls to thee and me, be sure I loved and love Yasodhara. But if my soul yearns sore for souls unknown, and if I grieve for griefs which are not mine, judge how my high-winged thoughts must hover here. Ah, thou mother of my babe! whose body mixed with mine for this fair hope, of this be sure, always I loved and always love thee well, and what I sought for all sought most for thee. Now Princess! rest, for I will rise and watch,'' and so she falls asleep.

In her sleep, she sighed as if the vision passed again before her eyes and from her sleeping lips came the words, "The time! The time is come!"

> Siddartha turned, and, lo! the moon shone by the Crab! the stars in that same silver order long foretold, stood ranged to say, "This is the night! —choose thou the way of greatness or the way of good; to reign a king of kings, or wander lone, crownless and homeless, that the world be helped." And surely Gods were round about the place watching our Lord, who watched the shining stars.
>
> "I will depart," he said; "the hour is come! Oh, mournful earth! for thee and thine I lay aside my youth, my throne, my joys, my golden days, my nights, my happy palace—and thine arms, sweet Queen! harder to put aside than all the rest!" Thrice around the bed in reverence, as though it were an altar, he softly stepped, with clasped hands laid upon his beating heart, "for never," said he, "lie I there again." And thrice he made to go, but thrice came back, so strong her beauty was, so large his love.
>
> "Wife! child! father! and people! you must share a little while the anguish of this hour that light may break and all flesh learn the Law. Now am I fixed, and now I will depart, never to come again till what I seek be found—if fervent search and strife avail. Therefore farewell, friends! while life is good to give, I give, and go to seek deliverance and that unknown light!"

Then strode he forth into the night.

BUDDHA'S ENLIGHTENMENT

Seven long years passed by, the object of Buddha's search still unfound. He goes then to Gaya where he feels enlightenment will at last be reached. There in the sylvan solitudes, Buddha lived pondering on the woes of the world. But so long and deeply did he meditate that he often forgot to eat. His beauty and grace faded. More withered than a dry leaf became this "princely flower of all his land."

One day a gay band of nautch-dancers and musicians passed through the forest, and one of the girls sang this song: "Fair goes the dancing when the sitar's tuned. Tune us the sitar neither low nor high, and we will dance away the hearts of men. The string over stretched breaks, and the music flies; the string over slack is dumb, and music dies; tune us the sitar neither low nor high.''

So sang the nautch-girl, fluttering like some vain, painted butterfly from glade to glade along the forest path, never dreaming her light words echoed on the ear of that holy man, who sat so rapt under the fig-tree by the path. But Buddha lifted his great brow as the wantons passed, and said: ''The foolish ofttimes teach the wise; I strain too much this string of life, meaning to make such music as shall save. My eyes are dim now that they see the truth, my strength is waned now that my need is most; would that I had such help as man must have, for I shall die, whose life was all men's hope.''

Partaking of food of wondrous virtue prepared by a grateful woman upon whose life Buddha had conferred a special blessing, his strength was renewed. The World-Honored One arose ''and bent his footsteps where a great Tree grew, the Bodhi-Tree (thenceforward in all years never to fade), beneath whose leaves it was ordained that Truth should come to Buddha. Wherefore he went with measured pace, steadfast, majestical, unto the Tree of Wisdom. Oh, ye Worlds! Rejoice! The hour is come; this is the Night the ages waited for.''

Mara's Hosts Battle with Buddha. ''Then fell the night as our Master sat under that Tree. But he who is the Prince of Darkness, Mara—knowing this was Buddha who should deliver men—gave unto all his evil powers command. Wherefore there trooped from every deepest pit the fiends who war with Wisdom and the Light, seeking to shake his mind.''

The ten chief sins came, Mara's mighty ones, Angels of Evil, *Attavada* first, the Sin of Self who in the universe as in a mirror sees her fond face shown, and crying ''I'' would have the world say ''I,'' and all things perish so long as she endures.

Then came Doubt, subtlest of man's foes, he that denies, and this hissed in the Master's ear, ''All things are shows, thou chasest but the shadow of thyself. There is no better way than patient scorn, nor any help for man.''

After doubt, came she who gives dark creeds their power, a sorceress, draped fair in many lands as lowly Faith, but ever juggling souls with rites and prayers. ''Wilt thou dare,'' she said, ''put by our sacred books, dethrone our gods, unpeople all the temples, shaking down that law which feeds the priests and props the realms?'' But Buddha answered, ''What thou biddest me keep is form which passes, but the free Truth stands; get thee unto thy darkness.''

Next there drew gallantly nigh a braver Tempter, he, *Kama,* the King of passions, who hath sway over the gods, themselves, Lord of all loves, ruler of Pleasure's realm.

After *Kama* came Hate, then *Tanha,* thirst and greed for life, and next came Lust for Fame. Also, to tempt the Buddha, came the Fiend of Pride, followed by smooth Self-Righteousness, with many a hideous band of vile and formless things, which crept and flapped toadlike and batlike. The last to come was Ignorance—source of all fears—"*Avidya,* hideous hag, whose footsteps left the midnight darker, while the mountains shook, the wild winds howled."

"But Buddha heeded not, sitting serene, with perfect virtue. And the Sacred Tree—the Bodhi-tree—amid that tumult stirred not, for all this clamor raged outside the shade spread by those cloistered stems."

In the third watch, the earth being still, the hellish legions fled, Buddha attained *Samma-sambuddh.* He saw the line of all his lives in all the worlds, far back and farther back and farthest yet. Five hundred lives and fifty. He saw as one, at rest upon a mountain-summit, marks his path wind up by precipice and crag, past thick-set woods shrunk to a patch; through bogs glittering false-green; down hollows where he toiled breathless; on dizzy ridges where his feet had well-nigh slipped. Thus Buddha beheld life's upward steps from levels low to higher slopes and higher whereon the ten great Virtues wait to lead the climber skyward.

Also, Buddha saw how new life reaps what the old life did sow, and how in each life good begets more good, evil fresh evil; death but casting up debit or credit, whereupon the account in merits or demerits stamps itself by sure arithmetic, certain and just, on some new-springing life.

In the middle watch, Buddha saw the law of reincarnation operating on a cosmic scale. "He attained *Abhidjna,* insight vast ranging beyond this sphere to spheres unnamed, system on system, countless worlds and suns moving in splendid measures, the silver islands of a sapphire sea." And from each and all flashed "the ceaseless radiance of life." All this and much more "he beheld with unsealed vision, cycle on epicycle."

But beyond all worlds, "immutable, unspeakable, supreme, was a Power which builds, unbuilds, and builds again, ruling all things according to the rule of virtue, so that all things do well which serve the Power, and ill which hinder. The worm does well obedient to its kind. The dewdrop and the star shine sisterly, globing together in the common work. And man lives well if he guides his ways by blamelessness and earnest will to hinder not but help all things both great and small which suffer life. These did our Lord see in the middle watch."

Lo! the dawn sprang with Buddha's victory, and so holy was its influence that, far and near, there spread an unknown peace. The slayer hid his knife; the robber laid his plunder back; all evil hearts grew gentle, kind hearts gentler. Kings at fierce war called truce; the sick leaped laughing from beds of pain; the dying smiled. And over the heart of sad Yasodhara, sitting forlorn at Prince Siddartha's bed, came sudden bliss. The priests stood with the wondering people in the streets watching the golden splendors flood the sky, saying "There hath happened some mighty thing!"

BUDDHA RETURNS TO HIS FATHER'S KINGDOM

"Sorrowful dwelt the King Suddhodana all those long years lacking the speech and presence of his son. Sorrowful sat the sweet Yasodhara, knowing no joy of life. Messengers from the king had gone and come bringing account of many a holy sage lonely and lost to home; but nought of him, far wandered now, forgetful, changed, or dead."

One day as Yasodhara walked in the palace grounds with her son Rahula, now seven years old, her attendants enter with great excitement. "He is seen! Thy Lord—our Lord—the hope of all the land—Siddartha. Merchants just arrived have seen him face to face. He is become a teacher of the wise, world-honored, holy, wonderful; a Buddha who delivers and saves all flesh."

The king sent nine ambassadors, one at a time, to bring Siddartha back, while Yasodhara sent nine horsemen. But each, in turn, arriving where Buddha spoke became so enraptured by his words, forgot their mission and did not return. Then the King ordered Udayi to go, "Chiefest in all the Court, and faithfulest, Siddartha's playmate in the happier days." As he approached the Bamboo-Garden where the Buddha taught, he sealed his ears with wool, and thus safely delivered the King's invitation.

Then spoke Buddha. "Surely I shall go! Let no man miss to render reverence to those who lend him life. Let the King know and let the Princess hear I take the way forthwith."

Eager to be the first to see him, Yasodhara rode in her litter to the city walls. Long she waited, expecting a grand procession with much fanfare. Then "she beheld one slow approaching with his head close shorn, a yellow cloth over his shoulder cast, and in his hand an earthen bowl. Two followed him wearing the yellow robe, but he who bore the bowl so lordly seemed, slowly, group by group, children and men and women drew behind, whispering with covered lips, 'Who is he? who? when looked a Rishi thus?' "

Suddenly, "all unveiled, Yasodhara stood in his path crying 'Siddartha!

Lord!' then sobbing fell upon his feet, and lay." Afterwards, when this weeping lady passed into the Noble Eightfold Path, a disciple of Buddha asked why, having taken the vow of chastity, he suffered such embrace. The Master said: "The greater beareth with the lesser love so it may raise it to easier heights."

But when the king heard how Siddartha came as a beggar, wrathful sorrow drove love from his heart. He climbed upon his war-horse and dashed angered until he found Buddha walking alone, followed by a mighty crowd, so huge the roadway could nowhere be seen. As the eyes of Buddha met his father's, all wrath melted, and he knelt before his son. "So dear it seemed to see the Prince, to know him whole, to mark that glory greater than of earthly state crowning his head." Nonetheless, the king burst forth, "Ends it in this, that great Siddartha steals into his realm, shorn, sandalled, craving food of lowborns, he whose life was as a god's? Son! why is this?"

"My Father!" came reply, "it is the custom of my race." "Thy race," answered the King, "counteth a hundred thrones, but no deed like this." The Master said, "Not of mortal line, I speak, but of descent invisible, the Buddhas who have been and shall be: of these am I, and what they did I do."

BUDDHA PREACHES TO HIS OWN

Though soon to depart, Buddha set himself that evening to teach the truth in hearing of his own, all the earnest throng catching the opening of his lips to hear these words of wisdom.

> Behold, I show you Truth!
> > Higher than heaven, outside the utmost stars,
> Farther than Brahm doth dwell,
>
> Before beginning, and without an end,
> > As space eternal and as surety sure,
> Is fixed a Power divine which moves to good,
> > Only its laws endure.
>
> This is its touch upon the blossomed rose,
> > The fashion of its hand shaped lotus-leaves;
> In dark soil and the silence of the seeds
> > The robe of Spring it weaves;
>
> That is its painting on the glorious clouds,
> > And these its emeralds on the peacock's train;

It hath its stations in the stars; its slaves
  In lightning, wind, and rain.

This is its work upon the things you see,
  The unseen things are more; men's hearts and minds,
The thoughts of peoples and their ways and wills,
  Those, too, the great Law binds.
Unseen it helpeth you with faithful hands,
  Unheard it speaketh stronger than the storm.

Seek nought from the helpless gods by gift and hymn,
  Nor bribe with blood, nor feed with fruit and cakes;
Within yourselves deliverance must be sought;
  Each one his prison makes.

I, Buddha, who wept with all my brother's tears,
  Whose heart was broken by a whole world's woe,
Laugh and am glad, for there is liberty!
  Know you who suffer! know you suffer from yourselves.

The Books say well, each one's life
  The outcome of his former living is;
The bygone wrongs bring forth sorrows and woes
  The bygone right breeds bliss.

Who toiled a slave may come next life a Prince
  For gentle worthiness and merit won;
Who ruled a King may wander earth in rags
  For things done and undone.

You reap the things you sowed,
  Sesamum, corn, so much cast in past birth;
And so much weed and poison-stuff, which mar
  You and the aching earth.

If you shall labor rightly, rooting these,
  And planting wholesome seedlings where they grew,
Fruitful and fair and clean the ground shall be,
  And rich the harvest due.

This is the Law that moves to righteousness,
Which none at last can turn aside or stay;
The heart of it is Love, the end of it
Is Peace and Consummation sweet, Obey!

All that night Buddha spoke "and on no eyes fell sleep—for they who heard rejoiced with tireless joy. Also the King, when this was finished, rose upon his throne—bowed low before his son kissing his hem; and said, 'Take me, O Son! lowest and least of all thy Company.' Sweet Yasodhara, all happy now, cried 'Give to our son Rahula the Treasure of the Kingdom of thy Word for his inheritance.' Thus passed these Three into the Path."

To all his disciples, Buddha said, "Enter the Path! There is no grief like Hate! No pains like passions, no deceit like sense! Enter the Path! Far has one gone whose foot treads down one fond offence."

> Enter the Path! There spring the healing streams
> Quenching all thirst! There bloom the immortal flowers
> Carpeting all the way with joy! There throng
> Swiftest and sweetest hours!

This, however, is no selfish bliss, for the one who so travels has the obligation from life to life to share his happiness and wisdom with others. Such is Buddha's great message, as revealed in the Mahayana Buddhist school. In *The Teachings of the Compassionate Buddha,* Dr. Edwin Burtt, Sage Professor of Philosophy at Cornell University, observes that the Mahayanist "wants to overcome craving and obstructions not just to achieve his own perfection but for the sake of a deeper oneness with others, and for the greater power to serve them."[34] This is called the bodhisattva ideal, bodhisattvas being one step away from complete Buddhahood. The traditional pledge made by them, as well as by all earnest students of Mahayana, is:

> *Never will I seek nor receive private, individual salvation; never will I enter into final peace alone; but forever, and everywhere, will I live and strive for the redemption of every creature throughout the world.*[35]

It is interesting that the word "Mahayana" symbolizes this great sacrifice. It means "the Great Vehicle," in contradistinction to Hinayana, "the Small Vehicle," an uncomplimentary synonym for Theravada Buddhism. The Small Vehicle is so named because, like a bicycle, it accommodates only oneself on the path to Nirvana. The Great Vehicle, however, is likened to a large train that compassionately takes on many others as well.

Dr. Burtt raises an important problem concerning the Mahayana ideal. It would appear to mean, he says, that

> the Bodhisattva, who most deserves the bliss of perfect attainment, never enjoys it, because he turns back and shares the suffering of those still caught in the stream of life and death, in loving concern for their salvation. [However]

as the Bodhisattva goes through the various stages leading toward Buddhahood, he comes to realize that the essential meaning of Nirvana is [that of] spiritual perfection. Thus, the perfected Bodhisattva becomes aware that just by being a Bodhisattva *he is already in Nirvana* as it is truly understood. For him Nirvana, and Samsara (the world of reincarnations) are not two different realms. Nothing is outside Nirvana. Paradoxically put, the spiritual insight here is that to renounce Nirvana for oneself, in love for others, *is to find oneself in Nirvana in its real meaning.*[36]

Up to a certain point, it is said, all those who travel on the path toward enlightenment and perfection travel together. But there comes a time when the path divides, and it is motive alone that determines the division. As described in the Tibetan Buddhist text, *The Voice of the Silence,*

> The Path is one, Disciple, yet in the end twofold. At one end, bliss immediate, and at the other bliss deferred. Both are of merit the reward: the choice is thine. The [selfish] path leads to Nirvana, the glorious state of Absoluteness, the bliss past human thought. Thus the first Path is Liberation. But Path the second is Renunciation. It leads also to Paranirvanic bliss—but at the close of cycles without number; Nirvanas gained and lost from bound-less pity and compassion for the world of deluded mortals. But it is said "The last shall be the greatest." Buddha, the Teacher of Perfection, gave up his SELF for the salvation of the world by stopping at the threshold of Nirvana—the pure state.
>
> Now bend thy head and listen well. Compassion speaks and says: "Can there be bliss when all that lives must suffer? Shalt thou be saved and hear the whole world cry?" If thou would'st be Buddha follow upon thy predecessor's steps, remain unselfish till the endless end.[37]

Every human being on the path of rebirths will someday have to make that choice. But such final choice is the product of numerous small ones. Thus even now we may be choosing the direction we will ultimately take. Of the nobler path, the Christs, Buddhas, and Messiahs of all ages are the supreme examples.

*

We now approach the concluding section of this work. Here the major problems confronting the individual and society will be viewed in the light of reincarnational psychology and philosophy. The problems that will briefly engage our attention include health and therapy; liberation of women—and men; crime in our culture; education of children; and acute global issues such as wars and the ecology crisis. One chapter will treat of the popula-tion explosion in relation to rebirth, another, of the heart-rending problem of suicide, accelerating today as more and more individuals hopelessly resort to this tragic means of "resolving" their difficulties.

On the affirmative side will follow a consideration of the influence reincarnation has exerted on the careers of noted people who became trailblazers in our modern world. The last chapter, "Horizons Far and Horizons Near," concerns the present and immediate future and what may lie in store for humanity and planet Earth in the far, far beyond.

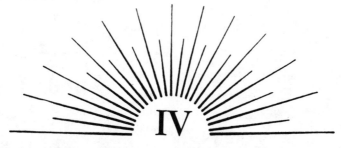

IV
TRANSFORMATION
OF LIFE
AND SOCIETY

Let us stamp the impress of eternity upon our lives. Live so that you may desire to live again—that is your duty—for in any case you will live again.

This doctrine is lenient toward those who do not believe in it. It speaks of no hells and contains no threats. He who does not believe in it has but a fleeting life in his consciousness. Let us guard against teaching such a doctrine as if it were a suddenly discovered religion! It must percolate through slowly, and whole generations must build on it and become fruitful through it—in order that it may grow into a large tree which will shelter all posterity.

From the moment when this thought begins to prevail all colors will change their hue and a new history will begin.

FRIEDRICH NIETZSCHE, *Eternal Recurrence*

16
War and Its
Transcendence

The old question posed by the Gnostics, "Whence comes evil?" has been given no answer by the Christian world. Today we are compelled to meet that question; but we stand empty-handed, bewildered, and perplexed. As the result of the political situation and the frightful, not to say diabolic triumphs of science, we are shaken by secret shudders and dark forebodings; but we know no way out, and very few persons indeed draw the conclusion that this time the issue is the long-since-forgotten soul of man.

CARL JUNG, *Memories, Dreams, Reflections*

At the time of the 1982 war in the Falklands, an essay, "The Metaphysics of War," by Lance Morrow appeared in *Time,* from which we quote:

> Watching the war in the South Atlantic—remote and ominous and obscurely disgusting—we keep telling ourselves that we cannot do that sort of thing anymore. Since the bomb fell on Hiroshima, mankind has fought roughly 125 wars (of one sort or another), including the longest one in U.S. history.
>
> Especially since World War I destroyed an entire generation of Western Europe's best men, the West has tended to call war futile, the kind of thing that brown rats do to each other in a locked room. Seeing its horrors, we conceive of it as history gone mad. If man by some inconceivable grace were to give up war, it would be an evolutionary step almost equivalent to his primordial emergence from the sea.
>
> War sometimes serves civilization and freedom. But it is the sheer technology today that tears loose the wiring of our consciences—the knowledge that

TRANSFORMATION OF LIFE AND SOCIETY

in another year or two or three, almost any country with a backyard pluto-
nium kit will be dealing in apocalypse [May 17, 1982].

World War II took some 60 million lives, many of them civilians. To
even dimly portray such a horrendous tragedy would take a master pen—
that of a Dostoevsky or a Tolstoy. In one of Tolstoy's little known essays,
"Christianity and Patriotism," he wrote of the senseless repetition of the
war habit.

"The bells will peal, the drums will sound, the priests will begin to pray
for successful slaughter—and the old, well-known and terrible story will
begin all over again. The editors of the daily press will start virulently to
stir up men to hatred and manslaughter in the name of patriotism.
Manufacturers, merchants, contractors of military supplies, will hurry joyously about their business, expecting double profits. And smothering despair within their souls by songs, debauches and liquor, hundreds of thousands
of simple-minded, good-natured people, torn away from peaceful labor,
from their wives, mothers and children, will march, with weapons of
murder in their hands, anywhere they may be driven. They will march to
freeze, to starve, to be sick, or die from disease, and finally they will
arrive at the place where they will be killed by the thousands, or kill other
thousands themselves—men they have never seen before and with whom
they have no quarrel. And again will men become infuriated, brutalized,
and bestialized, and love will wane in the world, and the incipient
Christianization of humanity will be delayed for decades and centuries."[1]

*

To dramatize this, playwright Peter Ustinov, star of stage and screen,
used the theme of reincarnation in his play *The Unknown Soldier and His
Wife*. Its first performance was at the Chichester Festival in England, and
this summary appeared in the London *Daily Telegraph*.

The play is an anti-war allegory. Its purpose is to show by a survey
extending over 2,000 years how the human lust for fighting has persisted
until it has brought us to the point where total extinction of the race is not
only a possibility but a threat. . . . Through Ustinov's pageant of history
move a number of stock figures who reincarnate in each episode, in relationships which vary only slightly. There is the General (the war maker) and his
opponent, the Enemy Leader; there is the Sergeant, the eternal worshipper
of discipline, and the Rebel, the eternal breaker of discipline; the Archbishop,
the eternal priest who tries to make war seem a holy duty [May 23, 1968].

Ustinov, himself, opens the play as a high priest of Jove, then becomes
a Benedictine abbot, an eighteenth-century divine, and a modern television-

conscious archbishop. "There is also the Unknown Soldier, a pathetic and ineffectual figure, who in each episode dies an untimely and usually unnecessary death, always leaving his young wife pregnant with a child he is destined never to see." Without his obedient, unquestioning participation, none of the wars could ever have been fought. Will the Unknown Soldier ever wake up?

Is there a part of him that is *already* awake and clear-seeing? Ustinov apparently believes there is. In an interview reported in *Life* magazine he observed, "A newly born child is striking by its expression of immense old age and omniscience, whereas the face of a man engaged in dying peacefully is remarkable for its serenity and the smiling tolerance of the human activities he still dimly sees. There is a mystic link between the margins of life, a cool majesty in which some secret is shared, a secret far removed from the high summer of love, sex, ambition and fretful jockeying for position. I am endlessly jealous of this secret" (April 19, 1963).

However, the problem here is how that which now manifests at the *margins* of life, and in occasional intuitive insights *during* life, can become a practical, actualizing power to prevent humanity from ceaselessly embroiling itself in conflicts that no side ever wins.

The war syndrome is also considered in another reincarnation play, *I Have Been Here Before*, written by no less a man of letters than J. B. Priestley. The noted author André Maurois wrote of it in his article "Tragic Decline of the Humane Ideal."

> The subject of this play was the Eternal Return, the idea that the same events occur over and over again, that people find themselves, after millions of years, in situations which they have previously encountered, and that, each time, they make the same mistakes which cause the same tragedies. But the author of the play admits that certain individuals, at the moment when they find themselves on the threshold of their drama, *remember confusedly their previous misfortunes and find in this memory the strength to thwart destiny by a free action which breaks the fatal chain* [*New York Times*, June 19, 1938].

Maurois sees an application of this to the suicidal wars in which mankind is repeatedly involved, and which are based, he says, on the erroneous belief that "after a period of violence a new golden age will dawn for mankind because a particular class or race has triumphed. In the name of this false ideal men cut one another's throats, asphyxiate one another, willingly undergo the most horrible torments. Such is the cycle which humanity has already traversed a great many times. *May we hope that it will at last say to itself,* 'I HAVE BEEN HERE BEFORE' *and that it will eventually find the wisdom to renounce self-destruction''* (italics added).

To be able to say, with authenticity, "I have been here before," could that not in itself help us "to find the wisdom to renounce self-destruction"? We would then declare, when viewing the mistakes as well as the glories of the past: "These are *our* footsteps on the sands of time, not someone else's." When wars and holocausts are perpetrated against the human race, instead of repeating the cliché "see how history repeats itself," we would say: *"We are repeating ourselves."* How unnecessary, how dreadfully stupid, how boring, how catastrophic in its consequences—the wasted lives, the nullification of humanity's noblest dreams, and now the destiny of the planet hangs in the balance.

When we stop to think, we realize a major factor in producing wars is the fear of death, the fear that the enemy can kill you. It is therefore imperative to stockpile thousands of nuclear bombs and build a gigantic war machine to be ready, if necessary, to kill him first. The premise of such thinking needs reexamining. In the light of rebirth, we cannot destroy our enemies. They will only reincarnate and be our enemies again. But, if we destroy the entire earth in a nuclear holocaust, what then? If reincarnation is true, humankind will not be destroyed—it will only have committed suicide. It will have to start all over, in a new world, with all the old problems awaiting resolution. In the light of such possibilities how wise these words of Jesus: "Do not let the sun set before you make peace with your adversary."

A Peaceful Mind Ensures a Peaceful World. In his memoirs, *My Land and My People,* the Dalai Lama expressed the opinion that a deep-seated conviction in rebirth "should engender a universal love," because all living beings in the course of their numberless lives and our own, have probably been our friends, or may have been our beloved parents, children, brothers or sisters. This, he affirmed, should encourage "tolerance, forbearance, charity, compassion." Furthermore, he added, "If belief in afterlife is accepted, religious practice becomes a necessity, which nothing else can supplant, in the preparation for one's future incarnation. . . . By whatever name religion may be known, its understanding and practice are the essence of a peaceful mind and therefore of a peaceful world. If there is no peace in one's mind, there can be no peace in one's approach to others, and thus no peaceful relations between individuals or between nations."[2]

When the Dalai Lama made his historic first visit to the United States, he spoke further along these lines at an interfaith service in his honor at St. Patrick's Cathedral in New York. We quote from the *New York Times* report.

"Without inner peace, it is impossible to have world peace," the Dalai Lama told nearly 5,000 people. The exiled leader, who puts his followers at about six million Tibetan Buddhists, spoke of "compassion and love" while standing at the sanctuary of the huge Roman Catholic cathedral, as rabbis, priests, ministers and lamas sat behind him.

As a leader of a religion that seeks inner enlightenment and harmony with the world, the Dalai Lama shared his vision of how to face our problems. "Inner development, sufficient development—very important," he said. "At this moment, in the field of science and technology, we are still progressing. But we must balance external development with internal development, then we will have true value and advance world peace. Through compassion, through love, it is possible to become a true human family. We can solve many problems, we can have true happiness, real disarmament. We cannot buy compassion in one of New York City's big shops. You cannot produce it by machines. But by inner development, yes" [September 6, 1979].

The overflow crowd gave him a standing ovation before and after his talk. Cardinal Cooke called the gathering "one of the dramatic 'movements of the Spirit' in our time." "This is a miracle," said Ines Fileppo of Manhattan, who gave a gold carnation to the stranger next to her, "I worship here at this altar every morning, and I'm telling you, a stronger hand than man has produced this evening. The soul of the world is here. It is a miracle."

Interviewing the Dalai Lama in India on the sad affairs in Tibet as a result of the brutal occupation by the Chinese, the *New York Times* reported his views on this horrendous tragedy in the light of karma and reincarnation.

[The Lama's] hope for his country was not that the current instability in China would enable Tibet to shake loose from Peking's domination. Rather, he said, it was a long-range conviction that the next generation of Chinese leaders would be "more reasonable." Then he proceeded to show just how long-range his judgments were. As a Buddhist, he said, he believes that present events are determined by intricate sets of causes stretching back into the previous lives of those who are affected by them. Thus, he said, it was only an "outward appearance" that the Tibetans were suffering today because of the Chinese aggression. "The aggression must have come because we did something bad."

Similarly, he went on, it is only an "outward appearance" that Chinese rule in Tibet is now permanent. The chain of causes that will eventually undermine it, must already be lengthening, even if it cannot be seen. "Cause and effect, cause and effect, cause and effect," he said cheerfully in English, his fingers darting in the air to join the links on the imaginary chain. Then his hands dropped to his lap and he said, "There will certainly be change" [November 12, 1967].

It was six years later that the Dalai Lama first touched soil in the Western world. This was in Europe in 1973, where he visited eleven countries. (The U.S. government would not permit his entry here.) His first stop was at the Vatican. At the unprecedented meeting with Pope Paul, the latter said, "Your Holiness comes to us from Asia, the cradle of ancient religions and human traditions which are rightly held in deep veneration." One needs to respect "these ways of conduct and those teachings of other religions which mirror the ray of eternal truth enlightening all men."[3]

Christ's Sermon on the Mount. Christians do not have to look to a Buddhist holy man for the compassionate advice he proffered on world peace. They need but turn to the Sermon on the Mount in the Book of Matthew, where Jesus said:

Blessed are the peacemakers; for they shall be called the children of God (5:9).

You have heard that it has been said "An eye for an eye, and a tooth for a tooth." But I say to you, That you resist not evil, but whosoever shall smite you on your right cheek, turn to him the other also (5:38–39).

You have heard that it has been said "You shall love your neighbor and hate your enemy." But I say to you, Love your enemies and pray for those who persecute you (5:43–44).

Nations in the West, professing to be Christians, have not taken such advice seriously because they lack conviction it will work. They wait for the other fellow to start. Yet Jesus said that, if we had the faith of even a mustard seed, we could move mountains. Not physical mountains, perhaps, but mountains of selfishness, prejudice, and hate.

It took an oriental—a Hindu and reincarnationist—to demonstrate practically the power of the Sermon on the Mount. In Gandhi's *Autobiography,* he acknowledged the inspiration he received as a young man from that sermon and its love-thy-enemy teaching. "It went straight to my heart."[4] It became a major influence in the formulation of his revolutionary plan of satyagraha, first in South Africa, then in India, where his country successfully freed itself—without arms, without blood—from British domination. His vision has since captivated women and men of good faith to such a degree that more books in the West have been written about this peaceful proponent of "war without violence" than have appeared concerning our own hero, Abraham Lincoln. Millions of viewers were awed and inspired by Sir Richard Attenborough's Academy-Award-winning film on Gandhi.

Be assured, this Indian leader was no impractical dreamer. He was acutely aware that his plan was not likely to be accomplished in a few short years. As we learned earlier (chapter 14), he was sustained in his dream for world peace by the philosophy of rebirth. "Having flung aside the sword, there is nothing except the cup of love which I can offer to those who oppose me. It is by offering that cup that I expect to draw them close to me. I cannot think of permanent enmity between man and man, and believing as I do in the theory of rebirth, I live in the hope that if not in this birth, in some other birth I shall be able to hug all humanity in friendly embrace" (*Young India,* April 2, 1931).

If we are all here just for a season and then disappear—die forever or go to an everlasting heaven or hell—this ideal of universal peace seems nebulous and unrealistic. We are all transients, here today, gone tomorrow. But, if it can be appreciated that we spring from the same spiritual source, that we are one human family who has been incarnating together for ages, and with whom we will be working in many cycles to come, the power of fraternal thoughts and feelings could be strengthened and deepened a hundredfold.

In a little known address delivered in Boston in 1838, Ralph Waldo Emerson expressed concern regarding the war buildup and armament stockpiling in his day—a child's arsenal compared to what we have today. "It is really a thought that built this portentous war-establishment," he said. "And a thought shall also melt it away."[5]

My Race, My Religion, My Country, My Status

17

It seems to me that I have always lived! And I possess memories which go back to the Pharaohs. I see myself very clearly in different professions and in many sorts of fortune. My present personality is the result of my lost personalities. Many things would be explained if we could know our real genealogy. Thus heredity is a just principle which has been badly applied.

GUSTAVE FLAUBERT, Letter to George Sand (1866)

The problem in this chapter is one of exclusiveness. Carried to extremes, it leads to the conflicts and wars previously discussed. Now, how would this sense of separateness and superiority be transcended were the individual—and masses of individuals—to say, "I have been here before. I will be here again"?

"It becomes clear," observes psychologist Gina Cerminara in *The World Within,* "that anyone who accepts the idea of reincarnation cannot, with impunity, despise at wholesale any alien race or nation; for if he does so, *he runs the risk of despising his own past or future self.*" In the past we may have been a member of other nations and races; so, too, perhaps in the future. This is also true of religions. We may have been Buddhists, Hindus, Moslems, Jews, and in the future may rebecome such or become members of religions yet unborn. How then can a person be so narrow-mindedly assured that his or her present religion is the best—*the only true one*?

Furthermore, Dr. Cerminara suggests, if one accepts the reincarnational view that the human being *is* a soul and *has* a body, instead of the reverse, as usually believed, other insights emerge. "Here is the first intellectual

268

step towards a tolerance that shall be thorough and scientific rather than superficial and sentimental.''

When one recognizes that the body is merely the transitory expression and vehicle of the soul, one must of necessity see that to despise a man for his race, nationality, or color, is as absurd and unreasonable as to despise an actor for the costume he is wearing.

The longer one reflects upon the matter, in fact, the more does one's sense of separativeness and self-importance tend to dissolve. For if my soul has incarnated in black bodies and white, in red bodies and brown bodies, and yellow; if each of these peoples has at one time or another been the creator of great civilizations equal to, comparable to, or even superior to our own; if I participated in those colors and those civilizations, whether as an inferior or a superior member, whether as peasant or prince, whether as moron or as mastermind—how then can I remain smugly convinced of the unique importance and superiority of the race or nation to which I happen to belong in the present?[1]

All this could apply to one's present position in society or the business world, to one's wealth, possessions, and family background, etc. Such divisive status symbols with which people so tenaciously identify themselves and others seem immature when considering the implications of the following thoughts of Professor C. J. Ducasse on reincarnation.

There can be no doubt that each of us, on the basis of his same enduring individuality, would have developed a more or less different mind and personality if, for instance, he had been put at birth in a different family, or had later been thrust into a radically different sort of environment, or had had a different kind of education, or had met and married a very different type of person. Reflection on this fact should cause one *to take his present personality with a large grain of salt,* viewing it no longer humorlessly as *his absolute self,* but rather, in imaginative perspective, as but one of the various personalities which his individuality was equally capable of generating had it happened to enter phenomenal history through birth in a different environment[2] [italics added].

As a Person Thinketh So He Becomes. Among Dr. Stevenson's cases is one where a reborn child remembered a previous life as a member of a clan that its present parents were feuding against. He had been reborn among his former enemies![3] *Think of the implications!* If a person hates the Russians, he may be born one. If he despises the Jews, he may be born one. If he has only contempt for the blacks, he may find himself in that race, and vice versa.

This could apply to all partisanships, such as attachment to political parties. In another of Stevenson's cases, he reports an argument among some Lebanese reincarnationists who are members of the Druse religion, and prefaces it thus:

> The Druses sometimes permit themselves to conjecture about the turn of events that might see a wealthy and boastful man die in his mansion and be instantly reborn in a hut. One can hear cautionary tales of this type from time to time. For example, in an argument between two Druses reported to me, one was advocating the merits of his political party so fervently that his adversary remarked: *"Be careful! You may be reborn in our party next time."* To this the first man replied with some insight: "Well, if that happens, I shall be an equally fanatical supporter of it!"[4]

All the more reason, then, if individuals wish to become enlightened and compassionate, they should eliminate biases of every description now. If not, such impediments will surely be reborn with them.

The celebrated author of *The Way of All Flesh,* Samuel Butler, in his reincarnation poem "Life After Death," humorously notes that, when we meet our opponent in the ensuing life,

> We shall not argue saying " 'Twas thus" or "Thus,"
> Our argument's whole drift we shall forget;
> Who's right, who's wrong, 'twill be all of one to us;
> We shall not even know that we have met.
> Yet meet we shall, and part, and meet again,
> Where dead men meet, on lips of living men.[5]

Butler writes in quite another vein respecting those who deeply love each other, and penned this moving tribute in honor of a just-departed friend.

> We have been three lights to one another and now we are two,
> For you go far and alone into the darkness;
> But the light in you was stronger and clearer than ours.
> Out, out into the night you go,
> So guide you and guard you Heaven and fare you well!
>
> Yet for the great bitterness of this grief
> We three, you and he and I,
> May pass into the hearts of like true comrades hereafter,
> In whom we may weep anew and yet comfort them,
> As they too pass out, out, out into the night,
> So guide them and guard them Heaven and fare them well![6]

NO INFERIOR RACES

It should not be imagined that, because in a future life one may be reborn among peoples presently despised, this means the individual is downgraded. A new learning experience is imperative, but he is not being born in a lower condition. Some years ago Charles Johnston, who later taught Sanskrit at Columbia University, interviewed Helena Blavatsky in London, and this very subject arose. He was inquiring about the views of the theosophists, and she spoke of universal brotherhood. "Don't let us get vague and general," he said. "Tell me exactly what you mean by this." To illustrate, she spoke of how badly the British treat the Hindus. The interviewer objected: "I have always understood that they have done a good deal for India in a material way." Here is her reply, as recorded by Johnston.

What is the use of material benefits, if you are despised and tramped down morally all the time? If your ideals of national honor and glory are crushed in the mud, and you are made to feel all the time that you are *an inferior race*—a lower order of mortals—pigs, the English call them, and sincerely believe it. Well, just the reverse of that would be universal brotherhood. No amount of material benefit can compensate for hurting their souls and crushing out their ideals.

They are our wards, entrusted to us; and what do we do? We invade their lands, and shoot them down in sight of their own homes; we outrage their women, and rob their goods, and then with smooth-faced hypocrisy we turn round and say we are doing it for their good?

Besides there is another side of all that, which we as Theosophists always point out. There are really no "inferior races," for all are one in our common humanity; and as we have all had incarnations in each of these races, we ought to be more brotherly to them.[7]

18
Our Plundered Planet and Disregard for Its Creatures

The "control of nature" is a phrase conceived in arrogance, born of the Neanderthal age of biology and philosophy, when it was supposed that nature exists for the convenience of man. It is our alarming misfortune that so primitive a science has armed itself with the most modern and terrible weapons, and turned them against the earth.

RACHEL CARSON, *Silent Spring*

"Dramatic pictures of ecological disasters are now as common in the world press as reports of sensational crimes or political scandals," notes *Culture and Life*. "Behind these particular incidents there emerges the stark truth: our planet is chronically ill and the illness is worsening."

Every year the general secretary of the United Nations Environment Program publishes a bulletin on its state of health and the bulletin is becoming more and more alarming.

Just consider. Every minute an average 44 hectares (108 acres) of land are turned into barren desert. A thousand species of animals and about 25,000 plants are facing extinction. The area under forests is shrinking catastrophically. The Earth's mineral resources are being depleted, with 100 million tons of fuels and raw materials extracted every year. Large parts of the world ocean, not to speak of inland waters, are turned into dumps. Some countries consume more oxygen than the plants on their territories are capable of producing. The carbon dioxide concentration in the atmosphere has reached 16 percent and is rising at an annual rate of 130 million tons. As a result, global climactic processes are disrupted. There is a shortage of drinking water in 75 countries of the world.

"In concerning ourselves with nature's health," the article continues, "we are concerning ourselves with our own health, the health of the whole mankind. . . . For nature recognizes no state boundaries. Winds, clouds, and rivers do not need visas. The world ocean and the atmosphere belong to the whole mankind. A wound inflicted on nature on one continent will surely make other continents feel pain" (November 7, 1980). From all such reports, humankind is being confronted with the truth that the world is *one*.

Jonathan Schell in *The Fate of the Earth* suggests that if we cannot find a way to save the world for love of ourselves and of nature, we may be able to do so for love of distant descendants.[1] But suppose those distant descendants are ourselves. How does the picture change? The world we will then be born into is the world we are making now. Lacking this perspective, the effects of our actions on future generations can be shrugged off in the fierce struggle to live *now,* to enjoy ourselves *now.* This is our only time here, and we must make the most of it. Let the future generations take care of themselves. We will not be around to know or care what happens.

However, is there another aspect to this picture? Our concern thus far has been with the ecological mismanagement of the earth, with only incidental mention of the extinction of animal and plant life. Is there something more at stake in the lower kingdoms than the annihilation of precious species that have been healthfully surviving for millions of years and now are being wiped out never to be replaced? From the reincarnational outlook, the answer is "yes." For if reincarnation should prove to be a universal law, it would apply to all life, not just human life. All life is on its way upwards and onwards. The life in the other kingdoms is reborn again and again. If one species is destroyed, it will find others to incarnate in—but meanwhile it has been denied a valuable learning experience. But there are other ways, dreadful ways, in which millions of animals are being exploited and their development cruelly hindered.

In the House of Lords, on July 18, 1957, Lord Hugh Dowding delivered a memorable speech on "Painful Experiments on Animals" from which we will be quoting. Dowding, a national hero in Britain, was air chief marshal during World War II and saved England from invasion by the Nazis. Winston Churchill said of him: "We must regard the generalship here shown as an example of genius in the art of war." Lord Dowding, however, was not a warrior by nature. Although he shared with General Patton[2] of the American forces a belief in many lives, he was a very different sort of person. As to his belief in rebirth, he said in his book

Lychgate "I am personally convinced beyond any shadow of a doubt that reincarnation is a fact."[3]

In his speech before the House of Lords, he applied that philosophy to the practice of vivisecting animals. But first he described the types of experimentation currently being conducted, often without anesthetics or adequate sedatives: tearing out the eyes of animals; smashing their legs with 80 to 100 blows of a hammer; exposing them to radioactive material, cosmic rays, poison gases, blasts from high explosives; performing brain operations and displacement of other organs; inducing epilepsy by injections into the brain; projecting them into space in rockets; producing in their bodies cancer, dropsy, eye diseases, ulcers, polio, pneumonia, rheumatism; exposing them to severe shock from injury or prolonged fatigue—and so the list went on. In some countries, an animal is paralyzed so it cannot interfere with the experiment by struggling or crying out, yet is left with its other sensations unimpaired.

Dowding reported that 2.5 million experiments were currently being performed in Britain each year in about 520 laboratories. (In the United States, the annual total is 64 million, including 400,000 dogs, 200,000 cats, 33,000 apes and monkeys, and thousands of horses and ponies [*New York Times Magazine,* December 31, 1979].) A physician who believed Dowding was exaggerating visited seven medical laboratories at Oxford University, his alma mater, and was so horrified, he declared Dowding had *understated* the case.

In the concluding part of the air marshal's speech, he drew attention to what he called the esoteric side of the subject and the bearing reincarnation has on the lower kingdoms.

I firmly believe that painful experiments on animals are morally wrong, and that it is basically immoral to do evil in order that good may come— even if it were proved that mankind benefits from the suffering inflicted on animals. . . . I cannot leave this subject without some reference to its esoteric side—to the place of the animal kingdom in the scheme of things, to man's responsibility to animals, and to the results of man's failure to meet this responsibility.

As the human race evolves, it becomes ready for fresh revelation, and the defect in most of the world's religions is that they fail to realize this very important fact. The priests are inclined to say "everything that is necessary for salvation is contained in *this* Book. It is unnecessary and indeed impious, to search elsewhere." It is I think, this aspect of our childhood's teaching which leads to the idea that animals have no continuing life after physical death. That phrase in the 49th Psalm, "The beasts that perish," has much to answer for, for it is a fact that the beasts do not perish anymore than do men.

All life is one, and all its manifestations with which we have contact are climbing the ladder of evolution. The animals are our younger brothers and sisters, also on the ladder but a few rungs lower down than we are. It is an important part of our responsibilities to help them in their ascent, and not to retard their development by cruel exploitation of their helplessness.[4]

Lord Dowding's wife, Lady Muriel, is also noted for work on behalf of animal welfare. She founded the widespread movement called "Beauty Without Cruelty," aimed at eliminating experiments on animals to test cosmetics and outlawing the yearly trapping of millions of animals—an incredibly torturous experience that causes slow, lingering deaths. In her autobiography, *Beauty—Not the Beast*, she tells of her work.[5] The book indicates that Lord Dowding, now deceased, was a theosophist, as is Lady Muriel.

Dowding's compassion for our younger friends came to public attention in the United States in a long article in the *New York Times Magazine* of December 31, 1979. It was titled "New Debate Over Experiments with Animals" and was written by Patricia Curtis, author of *Animal Rights*. Dr. Curtis spoke of alternatives to animal experimentation that are successfully being developed and of the work in this direction of the Lord Dowding Fund for Humane Research, which has granted $400,000 to dozens of scientists.

Saint Francis's Teaching of the Animal Soul. Although the ecclesiastical teaching has been that animals have no souls, the great lover of nature, Saint Francis of Assisi, disagreed with church authorities on this. Lynn White, historian and professor, writes of this in *Science*. In opposing the arrogance of man as king of creation and seeking a democracy of all creatures, the professor says, this saint was "the greatest radical in Christian history since Christ. . . . But what Sir Steven Runciman calls 'the Franciscan doctrine of the animal soul,' was quickly stamped out." Quite possibly, White adds, the teaching that animals have souls "was in part inspired, consciously or unconsciously by the belief in reincarnation held by the Cathar Christian heretics who at that time teemed in Italy and southern France" (March 10, 1967).

The elimination of Saint Francis's teaching of the animal soul henceforth gave an excuse for the masses in Europe to overwork domesticated animals, and for the elite to kill in sport untold millions of wild animals. Even refined, delicate ladies enjoyed such pastimes.

The Bible Does Teach Animals Have Souls. Despite the ecclesiastical ruling to the contrary, the Bible indicates that animals are immortal. Dr. Lian Brophy was surprised to discover this by reading an article "Have Animals Souls?" by H. P. Blavatsky. He featured her article in his paper published in the October 1982 *AV Magazine* (the journal of the American Anti-Vivisection Society). Dr. Brophy calls her monograph "one of the most erudite and convincing pronouncements on the subject of animal spirits ever published," ranging "through the Bible, the Fathers of the Church, the Sacred Books of the East, Scholastic philosophy and modern literature. . . . That some of the highest Christian authorities, such as Saints Paul and John Chrysostom, also believed in the resurrection of the souls of animals was proved by Helena Blavatsky." The magazine quoted her:

> No Hindu could plead more earnestly for animal life than St. Paul in writing to the Romans. Hindus indeed claim mercy to the dumb brute on account of the doctrine of transmigration, and hence of the sameness of the principle or element that animates both man and brute. St. Paul goes further: he shows (Rom. viii, 21) the animal hoping for, and living in the expectation of the same deliverance "from the bondage of corruption" as any good Christian.

"She cites several other Pauline texts as evidence that the Apostle to the Gentiles believed in an after life for animals, and held that man and animal are on a par on earth as to suffering ('the whole creation *omnis creatura,* groaneth') in their evolutionary efforts towards the goal." "It may surprise some," says Brophy, "that the eminent theosophist produced evidence to show that Pope Benedict XIV believed in the miracles of the specific resurrection of animals, and held them to be as well authenticated as 'the Resurrection of Christ.' "

A last quote from Blavatsky's article concludes the *AV* discussion: "When the world feels convinced that animals are creatures as eternal as ourselves, vivisection and other tortures daily inflicted on the poor brutes," after calling forth indignant protests from society generally, "will force all Governments to put an end to those barbarous and shameful practices."[6]

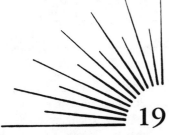

19

Reincarnation and the Population Explosion

My grandfather's rule: Don't never prophesy—unless you know.

JAMES RUSSELL LOWELL, *The Biglow Papers*

Since way back in Roman times, the specter of a world with too many people in it—too many mouths to feed, too many people to clothe and shelter—has haunted the minds of the people of this earth. Church father Tertullian was disturbed by the alarming increase of population in Roman countries in the early centuries A.D. And so, in his arguments against reincarnation, he discounted the doctrine because he claimed it could not explain where all these extra people came from. He need not have worried about the population problem, for soon thereafter, in the middle ages, the numbers of people in Europe dwindled to a low level.

In recent years, demographers have been projecting disastrous pictures of stupendous increases in population. This is also turning out to be a false alarm. Based on current statistics, *New York Post* columnist Ben Wattenberg headed his April 28, 1981 column, "Population 'Boom' is Going Bust" and writes,

Three hundred million people have disappeared during the past decade. Most of those missing persons were from the poor countries of the world. They are gone. Lost forever.

These people were victims neither of a cruel famine nor of a tyrant's repression—but of plunging birthrates. The missing 300 million Third Worlders are, of course, only a statistical artifact. They were people who, back in 1968, UN demographers predicted would be born by the year 2000. But by

1970, as birthrates kept falling, the same demographers predicted that those 300 million people would *not* be born by the turn of the century.

These changing projections point up a fact of our modern circumstance that has received very little attention. It is that around the world, the so-called "population explosion" is receding—and quite rapidly in most places. . . . The often-bizarre "Global 2000 Report" commissioned by President Carter cites a harum-scarum projection dealing with a world population of almost 30 billion in the next 120 years. Today, the low end of the moderate projections comes in at about 10 billion while the low-ball demographers are talking about 8 billion. . . .

What we see, then, is a pattern that is observable elsewhere in our society: we trumpet and politicize bad trends that may not be bad and may not be trends.

An article in the *New York Times* headed "World Fertility in Rapid Decline According to Vast New Study" reports on the returns "of the World Fertility Survey, a multinational endeavor begun in 1972 and recognized as the largest social science research project ever launched." The *Times* writes that the survey concluded that its "worldwide survey of 400,000 women in 61 countries shows that the population explosion that has plagued much of the world is easing. Fertility and birthrates in the third-world countries and in the developed nations have significantly diminished in the past decade, the survey concluded" (July 15, 1980).

The science editor of the *New York Daily News*, Edward Edelson, writes that in the United States "the declining birth rate in recent years is one of the most striking trends in American history" (May 10, 1980).

Two years earlier the U.S. Census Bureau released a report (November 19, 1978) that the world population growth has reversed itself in an unprecedented turnaround. While the population is still increasing, the *rate* thereof has substantially decreased. At the United Nations Fund for Population Activities, a spokesman said the new figures show "the downward trend is sufficiently impressive to remove any doubt that fertility is falling sharply." Demographers say there is no pat explanation why the growth rate has reversed itself. "No one knows the real reasons," says information director of the fund, Tarzie Vittachi. He adds, "no one should imagine that the population problem is solved. It is still a question of apportioning world resources. But there is light at the end of the tunnel" (*The Star-Ledger*, November 20, 1978).

How Many People Have Lived on Earth? That the world population has increased enormously during the present century is beyond question, and so the argument against rebirth raised earlier by Tertullian as to where all these extra people came from, appears on the surface to be valid. Dr. Ian Stevenson, in his reincarnation researches, once addressed himself to this problem.[1] This was in 1974 before the downward trend in the world's population became evident. He wrote in answer to the question "If reincarnation occurs, how do you account for the 'population explosion'?'':

Since many persons seem to have mistaken ideas about the number of human beings who have lived on the earth, I feel justified in going a little deeper into this question. The recent great increase in the world's population, if it continues, could bring difficulties for the reincarnation hypothesis, but they have not reached us yet. Furthermore, we have only rough estimates of the number of human beings who have lived on the earth since the origin of man.

Such calculations, says Stevenson, depend on various assumptions, such as estimates of the date of man's origin. In recent years you could choose any figure from 600,000 to 1,600,000 years. However, owing to startling discoveries in 1976 the figure increased to 3.75 million years,[2] while subsequent excavations reported in 1984 by an expedition sponsored by Harvard University and the National Museums of Kenya in Africa, disclosed that our remote ancestors lived five million years ago, and projections are made that eight million years may be the most likely figure.[3]

Who, then, can say as a fact how many people lived during this stupendous span of time? Great civilizations have risen and fallen, with no records left behind as to population statistics. "We have little reliable information about population growth rates," notes Stevenson, "for periods before the beginning of modern demography in the seventeenth and eighteenth centuries. And the farther we extend our inquiries into the remote and protohistoric past the more we replace facts by guesses." Demographers have produced estimates of total world population that range between 69 billion (Keyfitz, 1966) and 96 billion (Wellemeyer, et al., 1962).[4] For discussion purposes, Stevenson draws an average between these figures, and uses as a conservative base 80 billion people. He writes:

The population of the world today is about four billion. Therefore, conservatively assuming 80 billion human lives altogether, each human soul (to use a convenient expression) could have had, on the average, opportunities for twenty incarnations. The foregoing estimate—appallingly crude as it is—makes the further quite unjustified assumption that the interval between death and rebirth has remained constant throughout man's existence. But perhaps the "intermission" between lives was once very much longer than it is today. In such a period many souls would exist in the state (whatever that may be) between terrestrial lives and few would be incarnated. In recent centuries conditions could have altered so that now more souls are incarnated and fewer remain in the discarnate condition.

"In this way," says Stevenson, "we can, if we wish, think of a finite number of souls" connected with this earth, "which are now reincarnating more rapidly after death than formerly."

That the intermission between lives was once quite lengthy is in accord with the views of the ancients. Plato avers in *The Phaedo* that save for certain exceptions "many revolutions of ages" ensue between lives. In *The Republic* he mentions a thousand-year cycle of rebirth. Vergil does likewise in the *Aeneid*. Krishna in *The Bhagavad-Gita* also speaks of an "immensity of years" between lives.[5] Daily life in those early times proceeded at a much slower pace than today. Everything is speeded up in our modern world. Even children mature faster. Perhaps, then, it is only natural that the time between incarnations is much shorter than previously.

But even these speculations do not exhaust the possibilities, for as Stevenson points out: "we can at least conceive that human souls evolved and 'graduated' to human bodies from subhuman animals, even though we have no evidence that directly supports this conjecture. And finally—here we approach science fiction—human souls may also have 'emigrated' from other solar systems to our planet."

One factor yet to be mentioned should be considered as contributing to the present rise in population: *People are living longer on earth than previously.* A UPI dispatch reported that "the average human span in the United States has increased twenty-six years in this century from forty-seven years to seventy-three. Statistics on life expectancy over the last eight decades indicates that by the year 2000 the average life span would be 82.4 years" (*The New York Times,* July 18, 1980).

Intelligence at Work in Leveling Off Population Rise? A report concerning the "astounding turnabout in the world's demographic fortunes," quotes Jonas Salk as stating that the new trend might be the result of an evolutionary imperative. "He gave as an example fruit flies whose populations may shoot up at what seems an exponential rate, but then levels off" (*The Saturday Review,* March 3, 1979). If flies can do this, is it not reasonable that in human evolution there is a similar leveling off?

That there may be some intelligent regulatory factor in the births of human beings preventing extraordinary excesses, may possibly be inferred from the fact that demographers have noted that in countries after a war, more male babies are often born than female. Ordinarily it is the other way around. "These figures," says Stevenson, "have been interpreted as indicating the capacity of Nature to compensate for the increased numbers of men dying during wars." "The concept of reincarnation," he adds, "provides an explanation of how such a process might work through more male personalities seeking to be reborn after wars in which more men than women had been killed."[6]

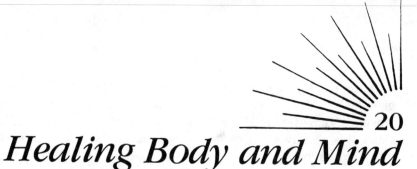

20
Healing Body and Mind

When we have come to better terms with death, we'll wear a different expression; we human beings. Our looks will change, when we come to terms.

SAUL BELLOW, *Herzog*

Our concern in this chapter is with how the unnatural state of imbalance called disease can be eliminated and what effectual part the philosophy and psychology of rebirth and karma may play in the process.

In Marilyn Ferguson's widely discussed book *The Aquarian Conspiracy,** she mentions that

> in the 1920s, Jan Christian Smuts formulated a brilliant concept that antici-
> pated many scientific breakthroughs of the late twentieth century. In *Holism
> and Evolution,* Smuts called attention to an invisible but powerful organiz-
> ing principle inherent in nature. If we did not look at *wholes* [holism and
> holistic come from whole], if we failed to see nature's drive toward ever
> higher organization, we would not be able to make sense of our accelerating
> scientific discoveries. There is a whole-making principle in mind itself,
> Smuts said. Just as living matter evolves to higher and higher levels, so does
> mind. . . . Wholeness, Smuts said, is a fundamental characteristic of the
> universe. . . . "Evolution has an ever deepening, inward spiritual character."[1]

In recent decades these ideas have taken hold and the idea of holism has been adapted to the health of the body in its relatedness to the total human

---

*In a favorable writeup on *The Aquarian Conspiracy,* the *New York Times Book Review* under the caption "The Plot Quickens," reports that as of then 300,000 books were in print, and foreign translations in French, German, Dutch, Swedish and Japanese were doing well (November 21, 1982).

being, including mind and spirit. The body is seen as a dynamic system, a field of energy, within other, ever finer, invisible energy fields. "Within a few short years," remarks Ferguson, "without a shot being fired, the concept of holistic health has been legitimized by federal and state programs, endorsed by politicians, urged and underwritten by insurance companies, co-opted in terminology (if not always in practice) by many physicians, and adopted by medical students. Consumers demand 'holistic health,' a whole new assortment of entrepreneurs promise it, and medical groups look for speakers to explain it."

In 1975, Malcolm Todd, then president of the American Medical Association, endorsed the concept of "humanistic medicine" that deals with the "body/mind," and he urged doctors to integrate these holistic approaches into the system. Wisely used, he said, "the spectrum of components might range from biofeedback and the psychology of consciousness to paranormal phenomena, psychic healing."[2] In 1976, the Rockefeller Foundation sponsored a meeting in New York attended by two hundred top policymakers who were introduced to these alternative health approaches. The importance of the "*inner* physician" was stressed.

The "inner physician"—what about the professional physician? Despite the brilliant technological achievements in modern medicine today, it no longer enjoys the public esteem it once had. The doctors themselves are sick, "thirty to a hundred times likelier than the general population to be addicted to drugs. Likelier to suffer from coronary disease. Likelier to be a problem drinker. . . . More often sued—and suicidal." Lacking the holistic, humanistic, approach, as one physician himself bitterly complained, "physicians are left with their diagnostic requisition slip, and their prescription pads to pursue their increasingly automated, slick, scientific, impersonal art." As William Steiger, chairman of the department of medicine of a Virginia Hospital, told a group of physicians: "when a medical problem persists, the doctor usually pursues *more lab tests,* when what is needed at that point is a deeper human understanding."[3]

In 1977, the National Institute of Mental Health received federal grants to prepare an annotated bibliography on holistic medicine. In its request for the grant, it eloquently defined the need.

During the last two decades many physicians and mental health professionals have begun to discover the limitations in the paradigms and practices of western allopathic medicine. Its focus on pathology and disease rather than prevention, the destructiveness of so many pharmaceutical and surgical remedies, the too-rigid separation of physical and emotional problems, the

assumption of an asymmetrical relationship between an all-powerful physician and a submissive patient have all prompted clinicians and researchers to
look for answers in other traditions and techniques.[4]

TREATING THE WHOLE PERSON

Holistic health as a science is not new. It has been practiced for centuries,
especially in the East where reincarnational teaching prevails, and where
the whole person, body-mind-soul, and its prelife history is taken into
account. In *Harper's* (January 1976) an American surgeon, Richard Selzer,
wrote of Yeshi Donden, the personal physician to the Dalai Lama. Upon
making rounds in an American Hospital, the Tibetan doctor did a pulse
diagnosis on a patient. "For the next half hour he remained suspended
above the patient like some exotic golden bird with folded wings, holding
the pulse of the woman beneath his fingers, cradling her hand in his. All
the power of the man seems to have been drawn into this one purpose. . . .
And I know that I, who have palpated a hundred thousand pulses, *have not
truly felt a single one*" (January, 1976).

The surgeon reported that Yeshi Donden accurately diagnosed a specific
type of congenital heart disorder solely on the basis of the pulse. However,
his purpose was not merely diagnostic, but healing and deep empathy with
the patient.

In Tibetan and other reincarnational cultures, there is not a doctor for
the body and another for the mind and soul. But in Western medicine,
body and mind are separate. If a doctor considers a patient's illness to be
psychosomatic he feels helpless and must refer the patient to a psychiatrist.
In the new paradigm of health called holistic medicine, psychosomatic
illness is the province of all health-care professionals, and they are so
trained.

Psychiatrists of the orthodox schools might well remember that the word
"psychiatry" means, by derivation, "doctoring the soul." Forgetting this,
psychiatrists have been least successful in producing cures. Norman Mailer
spoke of this in his biography of Marilyn Monroe and had the unforgivable
presumption—according to some reviewers—to consider reincarnation as a
possible tool for healing.

> If we want to comprehend the insane, then we must question the fundamen-
> tal notion of modern psychiatry—that we have but one life and one death.
> The concept that no human being has ever existed before or will be reincar-
> nated again is a philosophical rule of thumb which dominates psychiatry; yet
> all theory built upon the concept has failed—one is tempted to say

systematically—in every effort to find a consistent method of cure for psychotics.

Even the least spectacular processes of reasoning may therefore suggest that to comprehend psychosis, and the psychology of those who are exceptional (like our heroine), it could be time to look upon human behavior as possessed of a double root. While the dominant trunk of our actions has to be influenced by the foreground of our . . . life here and now . . . the other root may be attached to some karmic virtue or debt some of us (or all of us) acquired by our courage or failure in lives we have already lived.

Mailer adds that "if such theory is certainly supported by no foundation"—he is apparently unaware of the reincarnational researches of Ian Stevenson— "nonetheless it offers some immediate assistance for comprehending the insane, since it would suggest we are not all conceived in equal happiness or desperation," but have a karmic past prior to birth. He proposes an intriguing definition of karma—"Double-entry bookkeeping on a celestial level!"

Applying this to his subject, he remarks, "If we are to understand Monroe, and no one has, why not assume that she may have been born with a desperate imperative formed out of all those previous debts and failures of her whole family of souls." The imperative was to improve her record, but when she gave up trying, she sought the "easy" way out and took her life. "To explain her at all," said Mailer, "let us hold to that karmic notion as one more idea to support in our mind while trying to follow the involuted pathways of her life."[5]

*

Reincarnationists hold, as did the founder of the mental hygiene movement, Clifford Beers, that the real "we," the Inner Self, is never insane or psychotic. It is only the brain-mind that has become confused and irrational. The Real Self, being blocked, cannot get through. Beers himself had been in a mental institution and later told of his constant awareness that *he* was all right. He could watch the actions of his crazed mind, but was helpless to control it. He records the story in *A Mind That Found Itself*. The minds of many mental cases, unfortunately, never find themselves. Is there no hope for them? Walt Whitman wrote of this in relation to reincarnation. In his poem "Faces," he tells of visiting a mental institution:

> I saw the face of the most smear'd and slobbering idiot
>   they had at the asylum. . . .
> And I shall look again in a score or two of ages,
> And I shall meet the real landlord perfect and unharm'd,
>   every inch as good as myself.[6]

Must we wait for ages to bring harmony and healing into our lives? Would it not help *right now* to realize there is a wholeness within that is never sick, that can be our base for healing? Ferguson quotes an anatomist: "The healer inside us is the wisest, most complex, integrated entity in the universe." It became so wise, perhaps, because it is the efflorescence of numerous lives of experience. If so, "there is always a doctor in the house."[7] When physicians are convinced of this, and become partners with that power, they may be more successful healers of both mind and body.

Further ways will now be considered in which reincarnational philosophy may aid in uncovering a new horizon for human health.

COPING WITH AND OVERCOMING STRESS

A lead article in the science section of the *New York Times* quotes in its headline Sir William Osler, the father of modern medicine: "The Care of Tuberculosis Depends More on What the Patient Has in His Head than What He Has in His Chest." The article reports that, up until recently, the medical establishment, "despite physicians like Dr. Osler had scorned or ignored previous suggestions of a strong mind-body link. . . . Although the influence of mind on body was well known to ancient healers and has dominated folklore to the present day, 'scientific' medicine has until recently focused almost exclusively on physical causes for bodily illness. The new studies strongly indicate, however, that virtually every ill that can befall the body—from the common cold to cancer and heart disease—can be influenced, positively or negatively by a person's mental state" (May 24, 1983).

In a paper on "Coping with Stress," a British physician, Dr. Ian Pearce, provides a rather ominous picture of what stress does to our bodies. Stress-producing causes such as irritation, frustration, impatience, resentment, jealousy, worry, doubt, anxiety, cause the body to mobilize in the blood stream stored cholesterol to cope with the problem.

> Since the body is unable to convert the cholesterol back into the storage stage, it tends to remain in the blood stream, and eventually to be deposited in the arterial linings. This leads first to a narrowing of the lumen of the artery, and then to rise in blood pressure which is needed to force the blood through the narrowed vessel.
>
> The arterial walls then thicken so as to resist the added pressure, and lose their elasticity, thus still further reducing the blood flow. Pressure rises still further and the heart enlarges to keep up with the increased work load. Eventually, calcium becomes laid down in the arterial walls as a result of the

continued pressure; they become hard and brittle, and the stage is set for catastrophe: there follows a heart attack or a stroke.

Of course there are other damaging effects of stress. The body's mechanism for repair and defence against invasion, the immune system, becomes impaired, so that people under stress are more likely to fall victim to infections in the surrounding environment. Physical wear and tear is less readily made good, so that there is a heightened incidence of rheumatic disease in people under stress, and so on; the list is endless. . . .

Many people tend to believe that "if only they could get away from it all"—to some place where the sun always shone, where there was no noise and no traffic, where the telephone did not ring and the taxman did not write—they would be free of the demon stress. This escapist way of thinking is a complete illusion. . . . There is just as much stress in the quiet confines of many a nunnery or monastery as there is in a business office— indeed the writer said as much to a group of nuns recently, and was rewarded with nods of agreement from all sides. Because stress is a state of mind [*The New Humanity Journal*. December 1982].

A prevalent state of mind that causes sickness is described in a startling new book by Dr. Larry Dossey, *Time, Space and Medicine*.[8] He calls the mental attitude "hurry sickness" or "the time syndrome." Dossey is chief of staff at the Medical City Dallas Hospital and adjunct professor of psychiatry at North Texas State University. His book was featured in the *Science Digest* of October 1982, and these extracts were offered (italics have been added).

Pavlov, the Russian physiologist, conditioned dogs to salivate by ringing a bell while simultaneously presenting food to them. After awhile he could make them salivate by merely ringing the bell, regardless of whether food was presented. Just as Pavlov's dogs learned to salivate inappropriately, *we have learned to hurry inappropriately*.

Our sense of urgency is set off not by a real need to act quickly but through learned cues. Our "bells" have become the watch, the alarm clock, the morning coffee, and the hundreds of self-inflicted expectations that we build into our daily routine. *The subliminal message from the watch and the clock is: time is running out; life is winding down; please hurry*. . . .

[This causes] our internal clocks to run faster. The end result is frequently some form of "hurry sickness"—expressed as heart disease, high blood pressure, or depression of our immune function leading to an increased susceptibility to infection and cancer.

The time syndrome plays further havoc "as the severity of a disease increases." "The temporal aspects of being ill begin to influence our perceptions profoundly. The more severe an illness, *the greater the likeli-hood that we will be reminded of our mortality, of death.* Serious illnesses force us to confront the end, the final state, the forever." Dr. Dossey continues:

> In some situations heightened time awareness can be fatal. In a 1968 study of a series of patients who were admitted to a coronary care unit in a major hospital following an acute myocardial infarction, one group was observed to be generally unruffled in comparison to another group. *Those patients who seemed intensely anxious and worried survived the coronary care unit in fewer numbers.* Time awareness—expressed as fear of death, that time may run out—seemed to represent an increased risk of dying in the acute phase following a heart attack.

Elongating the Time Sense. What is novel about Dossey's book is that he suggests an unusual way to counteract stress that will " 'elongate' the time sense." Thus "time sick individuals can alter many of the devastating effects of the time syndrome." He asks "what might happen to our regard for death if we use various methods to expand our sense of time? . . . As we learn to see a friendlier face of time, death itself becomes transformed." Among the methods he suggests are meditation and biofeedback. "We develop a familiarity with a new sense of time," and "begin to feel at home with time."

Reincarnational philosophy would offer a more effective method for extending time. For if rebirth is a reality, time can never run out nor can we. Carl Jung speaks of this in *Memories, Dreams and Reflections:* "We must not forget, that for most people it means a great deal to assume that their lives will have an indefinite continuity beyond their present existence. They live more sensibly, feel better, and are more at peace. One has centuries, one has an inconceivable period of time at one's disposal. What then is the point of this senseless mad rush?"[9]

But lacking this perspective, it is understandable why so many people burn themselves out long before their demise. They are victims, we might say, of the "you-only-live-once" syndrome. This disease not only intensi-fies the fear of death, it heightens the competitive struggle for existence with its devastating effects on the individual and society. It also results in the greedy scramble to crowd all experiences into the narrow span of one short life. No time to fully enjoy and learn from each moment as it comes. One must feverishly rush on to the next, and the next. And when life ends, the sad realization dawns—*one never really lived at all!*

Relax, Relax, You Must Relax. This refrain is heard on all sides. Books on the subject are best-sellers. Yet all the advice somehow does not bring desired results. Doctors warn that muscular tension interferes with the circulation of the life fluids in the body and deprives the organs and limbs of their needed quota of nutrients. Prolonged tension thus results in disease or in malfunctioning of the "favorite" areas of stress. When the tension seems unbearable people use such expressions as "I'm in a bind," "I am tied up in a knot." More than metaphors, these affirmations are *facts.*

Can the horizon of more lives than one help here? It can help the individual to relinquish his viselike grip on the body. Tense persons identify themselves completely with their bodies, holding on to them every waking moment of the day, with nightly aftereffects of rigid, distorted bodily sleep habits. If they could appreciate that they are *not* those bodies, but the indwelling entity temporarily using them, then it would be foolish to so identify. And when they are sick, they will say, "I am not sick. It is my body that is ill and needs fixing."

Even undesirable habits can be overcome by ceasing to identify with the body. A person can overcome any habit if he knows that *he* is not the habit. But let him identify with it—I *am* a smoker, I *am* an alcoholic, I *am* a glutton—and then the task seems insuperable.

As to other virtues of relaxation, Professor Eugen Herrigel, in his little gem *Zen and the Art of Archery,* tells of the master archer who draws the strongest bow with arms and shoulders totally at ease. Almost invariably the arrow hits target center. Let the novice, however, be strained, overanxious, and he places upon himself the handicaps that make success difficult. So likewise in all other sports. So likewise in playing a musical instrument. And above all in playing *the human instrument.*

"Our Looks Will Change." Have you ever observed the graceful bearing of Buddhist monks? Their peaceful eyes, brows unfurrowed, jaws unclenched, the full, smiling lips. Saul Bellow was perhaps right: "When we have come to better terms with death, we'll wear a different expression; we human beings. Our looks will change, when we come to terms."

The beautiful Balinese, from all reports, have come to terms. As we learned earlier, anthropologist Margaret Mead saw a relationship between their way of life and their belief in reincarnation. This, she said, seemed to explain why "the Balinese believe you can learn at any age—the very young and old learn with great relative effortlessness, beauty lasts into old age." She discovered that another people, the Manus, who had no such belief, "were finished at forty."

The Balinese are also held up as an example by Harvard theologian Harvey Cox, who is cited on this in an article titled "Visions of a New Faith." The author of the article observes that "a model for the religions of the future may come from the past," and quotes Dr. Cox. "The Balinese claim they have no art. They just do everything beautifully. There was a time not too long ago when one would have been hard put to discover anything separate and distinct in human societies that could be called 'religion.' People just 'did everything' with awe or joy or with a sense of mystery" (*Science Digest*, November 1981).

This, surely, is a lost horizon worthy of recovery. (The prevalence of reincarnational teaching among these older peoples is the focus of chapter 11.)

PAST-LIFE READINGS OF EDGAR CAYCE

We have been considering health problems arising from actions and attitudes in *this* life and how the rebirth philosophy might help. Now we turn to medical and psychological difficulties that may have their antecedents in other lives. Our base for discussion will be the life readings of Edgar Cayce (pronounced "Casey"). Innumerable people have been awakened to reincarnation and the workings of karma from life to life through the work of this one man. Despite the many books and articles on this "miracle man of Virginia Beach," we keep meeting people who never heard of him. So a brief resumé of his background seems in order.

Cayce was born in 1877 in Kentucky of uneducated farming parents. As a young man, he worked as an insurance salesman until, owing to a throat ailment, he lost his voice for a year. The cure came when, under hypnosis, he diagnosed his own case. It was then discovered that, in self-induced trance, Cayce could also diagnose the ills of others. Although he had only a ninth-grade education and never read a medical text, reports one writer, he was startled to learn that in trance he could give "medical counsel to an Italian in fluent and flawless Italian." "Nor was the complicated medical terminology that rolled off his tongue any more intelligible to him in his waking state than was the fluent Italian."[10]

A group of physicians in Kentucky used his talents to assist in diagnosing their own patients. One doctor, Dr. Wesley Ketchum, submitted a report on this unorthodox procedure to a clinical research society in Boston. As a result, on October 9, 1910, the *New York Times* carried two-page headlines and pictures. From then on, sick people from all over the world sought Cayce's help.

One of his early cases was a young girl in Selma, Alabama, who suddenly lost her reason and was committed to a mental institution. Her deeply concerned brother requested Cayce's help. The latter revealed that she had an impacted wisdom tooth that was pressing on a nerve leading to the brain. The tooth should be extracted. Upon removal, the girl's sanity returned.

As Cayce's fame spread, he was deluged by long-distance calls and telegrams from people appealing for help. He then discovered that he could give readings at a distance by merely knowing the name and location of the person. In *Many Mansions,* Dr. Gina Cerminara tells of a personal touch. Often he would begin these distant readings with some comment in an undertone on the surroundings of the person for whom he was giving the reading: "Pretty rough wind here this morning." "Winterhur, Switzerland. Isn't it pretty! Nice, beautiful stream." "The body is just leaving—going down in the elevator now." "Not bad-looking pajamas." "Yes. We find the mother praying." These descriptions invariably proved accurate and provided one more piece of evidence for the validity of his clairvoyance.

The essayist Nora Ephron wrote about Cayce in an article in the *New York Times Book Review.* She related how Thomas Sugrue's biography of Cayce, *There is a River,* found a publisher in William Sloane. A unique tale in publishing, it turned out to be! Sloane, in an interview, told her,

> Now there isn't any way to test a manuscript like this. So I did the only thing I could do. A member of my family, one of my children, had been in great and continuing pain. We'd been to all the doctors and dentists in the area and all the tests were negative and the pain was still there.
>
> I wrote Cayce, told him my child was in pain and would be at a certain place at such-and-such a time, and enclosed a check for $25. He wrote back that there was an infection in the jaw behind a particular tooth. So I took the child to the dentist and told him to pull the tooth. The dentist refused—he said his professional ethics prevented him from pulling sound teeth. I told him he would have to pull it. One tooth more or less didn't matter. So he pulled the tooth and the infection was there and the pain went away. I was a little shook. I'm the kind of man who believes in X-rays.
>
> About this time, a member of my staff, who thought I was nuts to get

involved with this, took even more precautions in writing to Cayce than I did, and he sent her back facts about her own body only she could have known. So I published Sugrue's book [August 11, 1968].

Hugo Munsterberg, a psychologist from Harvard, personally investigated Cayce, expecting to find ''a cabinet, a darkened room, and the other usual paraphernalia of mediumistic charlatans. He was surprised to discover that Cayce needed none of these things, that he simply lay down on a couch in full daylight, and that, after receiving a simple hypnotic suggestion, he began to talk coherently in his sleep.'' Munsterberg went away convinced that, whatever Cayce was, he was not a charlatan.[11]

CAYCE DISCOVERS REINCARNATION

For twenty years, Edgar Cayce gave medical readings. Then one day in October 1923, a man named Arthur Lammers, a well-to-do printer from Ohio came to see him. He had no medical problems but was curious to check out the authenticity of Cayce's clairvoyance. Convinced on that score, ''he began to think that a mind able to perceive realities unavailable to normal sight should be glad to shed light on problems of more universal significance than the functioning of a sick man's liver or the intricacies of his digestive tract.''[12] So he spoke to Cayce about undertaking an investigation along those lines. Thomas Sugrue reports.

> Lammers asked questions Edgar did not understand—what were the mechanics of the subconscious, what was the difference between spirit and soul, what were the reasons for personality and talent? He mentioned such things as the cabala, the mystery religions of Egypt and Greece, the medieval alchemists, the mystics of Tibet, yoga, Madame Blavatsky and theosophy, the Great White Brotherhood, the Etheric World. *Edgar was dazed.*
> ''You ought to find out about these things,'' Lammers said. ''There are hundreds of philosophic and thousands of theological systems. Which are right and which are wrong? What is the real nature of the soul and what is the purpose of this experience on earth? Where do we go from here? What were we doing before we came here? *Haven't you asked any of those questions?*''
> ''No.'' Edgar said. He couldn't think of another word to say. He didn't dare tell the truth; that he had always considered such an idea sacrilegious, because God was revealed in the Bible, and to suppose that [Cayce through his readings] could answer the mysteries of the universe would be an open invitation for Satan to speak through him. That was what he had felt. Now, as he heard Lammers speak, he knew the feeling had passed.[13]

With the foregoing program in mind, Lammers invited Cayce to be his guest for a week or two at his home in Dayton. The initial reading there began with a request for the sleeping Cayce to give Lammers's horoscope. This came through in brief staccato sentences, but toward its close came the astounding words: "HE WAS ONCE A MONK!"

This electrified those present, but the one who was most amazed—in fact, *deeply disturbed*—was Cayce himself when he awoke. Owing to his strong Christian upbringing—his early ambition was to be a preacher—he underwent torturous doubts, when such past-life readings came through, and it was only after much study and searching of the Bible that he finally reconciled himself to reincarnation.

THE SOURCE OF THE CAYCE READINGS

Lammers later asked the sleeping Cayce, "Where was the information coming from that revealed the past lives of people?" The answer came, that the first source was Cayce's subconscious mind, but at a deeper level than psychologists usually tap. The second source, as Cerminara reports it,

had to do with what the readings called "Akashic Records." As always, with unfamiliar words, the sleeping Cayce spelled out the term—*Akasha,* the noun; *Akashic,* the adjective. In brief, Cayce's explanation was this:

Akasha is a Sanskrit word that refers to the fundamental etheric substance of the universe, electro-spiritual in composition. Upon this *Akasha* there remains impressed an indelible record of every sound, light, movement, or thought since the beginning of the manifest universe.

The *Akasha* registers impressions like a sensitive plate, and can almost be regarded as a huge candid-camera of the cosmos. The ability to read these vibratory records lies inherent within each of us, dependent upon the sensitivity of our organization, and consists in attuning to the proper degree of consciousness much like tuning a radio to the proper wavelength.

Of all the strange statements that had come from his sleeping lips, this, to Cayce, seemed the most utterly strange. Yet by repeated incredulous questioning the same explanation always came through. Frequently the readings indicated that the "*Akashic* Records" could also be called "The Universal Memory of Nature" or "The Book of Life."[14]

The *accuracy* with which these records could be read would naturally depend upon the inner development of the seer. They can only reach the conscious mind by filtering through the subconscious, and consequently can become tinged or even distorted by its religious and philosophical outlook. In Cayce's case, the readings have a strong Christian coloring and are steeped in the language of the Bible. (He read the Bible through once a year.)

What is especially constructive about Cayce's work is its ethical tone. In one reading, addressed to a man who had written several times for help, this advice was offered.

> Yes, we have the body here, this we have had before. As we find, there have been *physical* improvements in the body, yet there is much, much to be desired. As already indicated, this is a karmic condition and there must be measures taken by the entity to change its attitude toward things, conditions, and its fellow man. So long as mechanical things were applied for physical correction, improvements were seen. But when the entity becomes so self-satisfied, so self-centered, as to refuse spiritual things, and does not change its attitude, so long as there is hate, malice, injustice, jealousy; so long as there is anything within at variance with patience, long suffering, brotherly love, kindness, gentleness, there cannot be a healing of the condition of this body. What does the entity want to be healed for? That it may gratify its own physical appetites? That it may add to its own selfishness? Then, if so, it had better remain as it is. . . . Will you accept, will you reject? It is up to you. We are through—unless you make amends.[15]

THREE KINDS OF KARMA

Cayce's past-life readings have been divided into three categories: (1) boomerang karma, (2) organismic karma, and (3) symbolic karma.

An example of boomerang karma is that of a college professor who had been born totally blind. Having heard of Cayce on a radio program, "he applied for a physical reading and experienced conspicuous improvement in health and vision in his left eye, which had been considered hopeless by eye specialists. . . . It was in Persia that he had set in motion the spiritual law which resulted in his blindness in the present. He had been a member of a barbaric tribe whose custom was to blind its enemies with red-hot irons, and it had been his office to do the blinding.[16]

Organismic karma involves the misuse of the organism in one life with an appropriate affliction in a succeeding life. A man suffering from digestive weakness since infancy was revealed as having been a glutton in a previous life.

Symbolic karma is the most intriguing. It can be explained best by examples. A person, who in another life "turned deaf ears" to pleas for help, was born deaf in the present. (Deafness in other cases could have other causes.) One individual suffered extreme feelings of inferiority in this life owing to smallness of stature. This had its source in another life of haughtiness, superiority, and condescension. "Through a curious reversal objectification, the attitude of having once 'looked down' on other people, and the behavior of having *used* one's own superior physique to take advantage of others," now made this person—though not everyone who is short— "subject to being literally looked down on by other people."[17]

*

All such negative karma, the Cayce readings disclosed, was not punitive in character but provided invaluable learning experience. As Shakespeare phrased it in *As You Like It,*

> Sweet are the uses of adversity,
> Which, like the toad, ugly and venomous,
> Wears yet a precious jewel in his head.

This reminds us of a story told about some students who came to a nineteenth-century Hasidic Master, Reb Zusya, hoping he could explain the enigma of evil in a world created by a good God. He should surely know, they thought, for he was good and pious, yet sick and poverty stricken. "How do you explain evil?" they asked. "What evil?" replied the rabbi, with wide wondering eyes. The amazed students reminded him that he was ill, and suffered pain and poverty. "Oh that," he answered, "that is just what my soul needs."[18]

Concluding this chapter with an overview of the value of reincarnational philosophy in the midst of trials and difficulties—mental, emotional, and physical—we turn to some observations of Professor Geddes MacGregor. The awareness of reincarnation, he suggests, radically changes the quality of life when it is realized that our present existence is only a portion of a long journey. This enormously "increases our adaptability to circumstances."

When people's circumstances are made to appear as once-for-all arrangements, then impotent rebellion and revolt against them are natural. For then people feel like permanently square pegs in permanently round holes. When our circumstances are seen, by contrast, to be so very temporary, we chafe much less under the difficulties they put in our path, knowing as we then do that they belong to but one little phase in our long pilgrimage through the ages.[19]

21
The Liberation of Women—and Men

The living soul is not a woman. It is not a man. Whatever body it takes, with that it is only temporarily joined.

Gems from the East

In his paper "The Explanatory Value of the Idea of Reincarnation" (see chapter 4), Dr. Ian Stevenson reports that he has "investigated numerous cases of the reincarnation type in which the subject claims to remember a previous life as a person of the opposite sex."[1] Many reincarnational cultures concur that such sex exchanges do occur. If this assumption is correct, then all human beings could have equal rights to incarnate as male or female. Do they willingly wish to exercise those rights? We have inquired of numerous men whether they would like to come back as women, and they said "no." Women, too, despite the indignities, exploitations, and downgradings they often experience, have become attached to their role and prefer to keep it. So why bother to change places?

According to reincarnational philosophy, the one who exercises the right of choice prior to incarnation is not the previous personality, with its likes and dislikes, but the indwelling permanent individuality. Its choice is not based on personal preferences but on *needs*. What needs? It is the need to be a totally balanced human being, with all its powers and faculties harmoniously developed. It seems significant that the advanced members of the human race, such as Jesus, Buddha, and Krishna, embody both male and female qualities. Dynamic strength and power are equally blended with gentleness, tenderness, and compassion; wisdom with humility; extraordinary abilities as leaders and reformers with patience, persistence, and endurance.

The harmonizing of feminine and masculine qualities in society as a whole is becoming appreciated in the women's movement itself. Marilyn Ferguson writes, in *The Aquarian Conspiracy*,

> The shift from militant feminism is evident in recent statements like that of Patricia Mische in a monograph, *Women and Power*. Instead of asking for a piece of the pie men have had all along, she said, "we should be trying to create quite another pie." Human affairs will not be advanced by the assimilation of more and more women into a literally man-made world. Rather, women and men *together* can create a new future. . . . Just as individuals are enriched by developing both the masculine and feminine sides of the self (independence and nurturance, intellect and intuition), so society is benefiting from a change in the balance of power between the sexes.[2]

There are other imperatives for exchanging sex roles than those mentioned. When one sex dominates another he or she may incarnate next time in that very sex—not as a punishment but as a learning experience. If, for example, one marriage partner mistreats the other, the only way he or she may appreciate what it means to undergo such abuse may be to endure a similar situation. But, according to two poets of note, this could occur without changing sex.

In John Masefield's reincarnation poem, "A Creed," there is this stanza:

> I know that in my lives to be
> My sorry heart will ache and burn,
> And worship unavailingly
> The woman whom I used to spurn,
> And shake to see another have
> The love I spurned, the love she gave.[3]

William Ernest Henley wrote in his poem, "To W.A.",

> Or ever the knightly years were gone
> With the old world to the grave,
> I was a King in Babylon
> And you were a Christian slave.

> I saw, I took, I cast you by,
> I bent and broke your pride. . . .
> And a myriad suns have set and shone
> Since then upon the grave
> Decreed by the King of Babylon
> To her that had been his slave.

The pride I trampled is now my scathe,
For it tramples me again.
The old resentment lasts like death,
For you love, yet you refrain.
I break my heart on your hard unfaith,
And I break my heart in vain.[4]

Conversely, a good relationship between partners will bring mutual benefit and blessing in future lives. Goethe wrote of this concerning his friend
Frau von Stein: "I cannot explain the significance to me of this woman or
her influence over me, except by the theory of metempsychosis. Yes, we
were once man and wife. Now our knowledge of ourselves is veiled, and
lies in the spirit world. I can find no name for us—the past, the future, the
All!"[5]

DOES INCARNATION IN ANOTHER SEX CREATE PROBLEMS?

It is probably a mistake to imagine that in one life one is a woman and
the next a man. More likely a series of lives would be lived in one sex,
and when too much maleness or femininity exists in an individual's psyche,
a changeover is required to establish balance. The transition is not likely to
be easy. In some cases, it could result in what psychiatrists call "gender-
identity confusion" or "gender dysphoria," an uncertainty as to which sex
one belongs.

In reporting a case in the *Journal of Mental and Nervous Disease* Dr.
Stevenson comments: "In Southeast Asia (among Hindus and Buddhists),
numerous cases of gender dysphoria occur. They generally receive less
attention than they do in the West and evoke relatively little concern on the
part of the persons affected, and the members of their families. The condition is attributed to residues of a previous life as a member of the opposite
sex" (September 1977). (Stevenson's case is reported in chapter 5, under
the heading "A Case of Gender Dysphoria.") Extreme cases of this order
are medically termed transsexualism, which refers to the individual's fixed
belief that she is a female "trapped" in a male body, or vice versa. If this
is not overcome, it can lead to homosexual tendencies in adult life.

The liberated person, however, is not enslaved by such thoughts as "I
am a man," "I am a woman." These are useful roles played by the
sexless soul in its journey to spiritual freedom, but they are not for keeps.

THE TROUBLED SCENE OF MARRIED LIFE

In a survey conducted by the psychologist Dr. Joyce Brothers, marriage was found to be a "quiet hell" for about half of American couples. Speaking before a convention of the American Hospital Association, she said four out of twelve marriages are likely to end in divorce, while another six become loveless "utility" relationships to protect children, property, shared careers and other goals. Thus only two out of twelve are loving, joyful relationships.[6] What is the cause for failure?

In Erich Fromm's classic work, *The Art of Loving: An Inquiry into the Nature of Love,* this eminent psychoanalyst spoke of the confusion that exists

> between the initial experience of *"falling"* in love, and the permanent state of *being* in love, or as we might better say, of "standing" in love. . . . If two people who have been strangers suddenly let the wall between them break down, and feel close, feel one, this moment of oneness is one of the most exhilarating, most exciting experiences in life. It is all the more wonderful and miraculous for persons who have been shut off, isolated, without love. . . . The two persons become well acquainted, their intimacy loses more and more its miraculous character, until their antagonism, their disappointments, their mutual boredom kill whatever is left of the initial excitement.

Each learns the other's secrets, ideas, experiences, and when everything is told, the mystery ceases, the magic is gone, and from then on it is a broken record which repeats over and over again the same tune.

But do they really know all about each other? And what do they know of the depths within themselves? "The longing to know ourselves and to know our fellow companion," observes Dr. Fromm, "has been expressed in the Delphic motto 'Know Thyself.' It is the main spring of all psychology." At present we are an "enigma to ourselves" and others "remain an enigma to us."[7]

If we can appreciate that all of us have had many lives, the fruit of those lives being buried somewhere within, we could be challenged to unearth these resources in ourselves and others. Relationships will then be an endless source of surprises and delights. With our children, we can experience the same joyful task of uncovering the hidden treasures within them. As Nobelist Saul Bellow writes in *Herzog,* "Three thousand million human beings exist, each with some possessions, each a microcosm, *each infinitely precious; each with a peculiar treasure."*[8]

The word "treasure" brings to mind some deep-stirring thoughts on love contained in *The Treasure of the Humble* by the celebrated author of *The Blue Bird,* Maurice Maeterlinck.

We parted and not a word was spoken, but at one and the same moment had we understood our inexpressible thought. We know now that another love had sprung to life, a love that demands not the words, the little attentions and smiles of ordinary love. We have never met again. Perhaps centuries will elapse before we ever do meet again, before we shall again find ourselves in the same movement of the soul as on that evening; but we can well afford to wait.

Perhaps human beings do not yet know what the word to love means. It is a thing that lies a thousand fathoms deeper, where our softest, swiftest, strongest words cannot reach it. At moments we might believe it to be a recollection, furtive but excessively keen, of the great primitive unity.

The souls of all our brethren are ever hovering about us, craving for a caress, and only waiting for the signal. But how many beings there are who all their life long have not dared make such a signal! It is the disaster of our entire existence that we live thus away from our soul, and stand in such dread of its slightest movement. Did we but allow it to smile frankly in its silence and its radiance, we should be already living an eternal life.[9]

The Aching Problem of Suicide, and a Remedy That Works

To be, or not to be: that is the question. To die: to sleep and end the heartache. To die, to sleep, perchance to dream; ay, there's the rub.

SHAKESPEARE, *Hamlet*

Several years ago, a friend of one of the authors phoned her in a state of acute alarm. She had just discovered a suicide note written by her daughter, but the girl had yet to take her life. Something must be done fast! On two previous occasions, the girl had slashed her wrists. This time she was disconsolate over a severed love affair. A copy of Raymond Moody's *Life After Life,* with the parts on suicide marked for attention, was rushed over to her house. The mother later reported that, not only did her daughter change her mind about destroying herself, she was so enthralled by other parts of this book on near-death experiences, she kept reading parts aloud to her mother.

It was with a gratifying surprise that we subsequently learned that the remedy we offered was being employed by a professional psychologist. Dr. Kenneth Ring reports this in his book *Life at Death: A Scientific Investigation of the Near-Death Experience.*[1] "Exposure to near-death research findings can apparently be helpful in reducing the likelihood of suicide. Psychologist John McDonagh practices what he calls 'bibliotherapy' with his suicidally-minded patients. He simply has them read Moody's book *Life After Life.* His findings? It works."

Now what did Dr. Moody say in *Life After Life* on suicide? He says he has frequently been asked, ''Have you ever interviewed anyone who has had a near-death experience in association with a suicide attempt? If so, was the experience any different?''

He replied, ''I do know of a few cases in which a suicide attempt was the cause of the apparent 'death.' These experiences were uniformly characterized as being unpleasant. As one woman said, 'If you leave here a tormented soul, you will be a tormented soul over there, too.' In short, they report that the conflicts they had attempted suicide to escape were still present when they died, but with added complications. In their disembodied state they were unable to do anything about their problems, and they also had to view the unfortunate consequences which resulted from their acts. A man who was despondent about the death of his wife shot himself, 'died' as a result, and was resuscitated. He states: 'I didn't go where [my wife] was, I went to an awful place. . . . I immediately saw the mistake I had made. . . . I thought, 'I wish I hadn't done it.'

''Others who experienced this unpleasant 'limbo' state have remarked that they had the feeling they would be there for a long time. This was their penalty for 'breaking the rules' by trying to release themselves prematurely from what was, in effect, an 'assignment'—to fulfill a certain purpose in life.''[2]

In his subsequent volume *Reflections on Life After Life,* Dr. Moody had more to say:

> At the time I completed the manuscript of my first book I had encountered very few significant cases of near-death resulting from attempted suicide. I think this is understandable in that persons who have had such experiences might be more reluctant to talk about them because of possible residual guilt feelings about the attempt. Since that time, however, I have come upon some additional cases. All of these people agree on one point: they felt their suicidal attempts solved nothing. They found that they were involved [in the other world] in exactly the same problems from which they had been trying to extricate themselves by suicide. Whatever difficulty they had been trying to get away from was still there on the other side, unresolved.
>
> One person mentioned being ''trapped'' in the situation which had provoked her suicide attempt. [It was] repeated again and again, as if in a cycle. [She said:] ''This problem I was telling you about, you know, well, looking back on it now, of course, it doesn't seem so important, from a more adult way of looking at it. But at the time . . . it really seemed very important. . . . Well, the thing was, it was still around, even when I was 'dead.' And it was like it was repeating itself, a rerun. I would go through it

once and at the end I would think, 'Oh, I'm glad that's over,' and then it would start all over again, and I would think, 'Oh, no, not this again.' "[3]

According to psychiatrist George Ritchie, one of the worst fates of a suicide is that after death he can see the misery caused others by his act of self-destruction. Among the places Dr. Ritchie was taken by his celestial guide during his own near-death experience (see chapter 8) was a house where a younger man was following an older one from room to room. "I'm sorry, Pa!" he kept saying. "I didn't know what it would do to Mama! I didn't understand." But though Ritchie

> could hear the young man clearly, it was obvious that the man he was speaking to could not. The old man was carrying a tray into a room where an elderly woman sat in bed. "I'm sorry, Pa," the young man said again. "I'm sorry, Mama." Endlessly, over and over, to ears that could not hear. In bafflement I turned to the Brightness beside me. But though I felt His compassion flow like a torrent into the room before us, no understanding lighted my mind.
>
> Several times we paused before similar scenes. A boy trailing a teenage girl through the corridors of a school. "I'm sorry, Nancy!"

Then there was a middle-aged woman begging a gray-haired man to forgive her. Ritchie turned pleadingly to his guide: " 'Why do they keep talking to people who can't hear them?' Then from the Light beside me came the thought: *They are suicides, chained to every consequence of their acts.* This idea stunned me, yet I knew it came from Him, not me, for I now saw no more scenes like these, as though the truth He was teaching had been learned."[4]

There is an apparent healing message for those left behind in these experiences of people who have taken their lives. By understanding the miserable state in which such loved ones *temporarily* exist—for it does not last indefinitely—survivors can shorten its period by sending the victims thoughts of love and forgiveness, thus helping them overcome the guilt feelings that chain them to their former deed.

There are many factors—some quite ameliorating—that contribute to persons taking their lives. Dr. Kenneth Ring made a study of these when interviewing suicidal near-death survivors. But, whether the act seemed justified or not, he discovered that "the most striking feature of suicide-related near-death experiences that sets them apart" from other NDEs is

> among our suicide attempters, no one reported the tunnel phenomenon as such, or saw a brilliant but comforting light, or encountered a presence, or

was temporarily reunited with loved ones who had died, or entered into a transcendent world of preternatural beauty. Instead the suicide-related core experience tends to be truncated, aborted, damped down.

It does begin with a feeling of relief or peace and continues with a sense of bodily detachment to the same degree as other categories. But it tends to end, if it gets this far at all, with a feeling of confused drifting in a dark or murky void—a sort of "twilight zone."[5]

Because they were revived, these people had an opportunity to complete their natural life. What, then, was the effect of their NDE experience? Dr. Bruce Greyson, assistant professor of psychiatry at the University of Michigan Medical Center (Ann Arbor), reports on this. He has studied more than 150 NDEs in his area, and his current focus is on attempted suicides. Those who have been resuscitated, he says, "come out with a real sense of purpose in their lives. Although death is no longer fearful, life has become more meaningful."[6]

Why has it become more meaningful? They are now convinced that life on earth, despite its difficulties, is a continuing, growing process; death is not a dead end. Do they now believe that death leads ultimately to rebirth? The 1981–82 Gallup poll survey of religious beliefs in the United States disclosed that 31 percent of those who had near-death encounters thereafter "believe in reincarnation, as opposed to 23 percent of the general public."[7] (The intimate relationship between near-death experiences and reincarnation has been discussed in chapter 8.)

Thoughts of Reincarnation Can Prevent Self-Destruction. The life of Richard Wagner holds an example of this. After years of struggle and failure, he wrote to Hans Bülow on September 27, 1858: "I cannot take my life, for the Will to accomplish the Object of Art would draw me back into life again until I realized that Object, and so I would only be re-entering this circle of tears and misery."[8] At another time, speaking of the discouraging contrasts in human development—some people being so very much less advanced than others—he said, "Only the profoundly conceived idea of reincarnation could give me any consolation, since that belief shows how all at last can reach complete redemption. . . . Thus all the terrible tragedy of life is seen to be nothing but the sense of separateness in Time and Space."[9]

Another aborted suicide came to the attention of one of the present writers when we were speaking at the Findhorn Foundation in northern Scotland several years ago. A woman introduced herself after the lecture and confided that, as a child and young adult, she had a persistent vision of a rope around her neck. She was certain she had previously hung herself. Although she was strongly suicidal in this life, the vision warned her against repeating the act. Now she has conquered this tendency.

In chapter 1, we learned of Tolstoy's struggle with suicidal thoughts at the height of his literary fame and prosperity. Later, on February 13, 1896, he wrote in his diary, "How interesting it would be to write the story of the experiences in this life of a man who killed himself in his previous life; how he now stumbles against the very demands which had offered themselves before, until he arrives at the realization that he must fulfil those demands. Remembering the lesson, this man will be wiser than others."[10]

I Do Not Want to Come Back. The suicide-prone do not always take kindly to the thought of reincarnation—in fact, understandably, they may furiously oppose it. Their consuming desire is to blot out consciousness forever in the sleep of death and thereby annihilate all their problems. That is how the leading character in J. B. Priestley's play *I Have Been Here Before* felt.

ORMUND If I'd any sense I'd use [my revolver to kill myself]. No more questions that can't be answered, twisting like knives in your guts. Sleep, a good sleep, the only good sleep.

DR. GÖRTLER I am afraid you will be disappointed. It will be a sleep full of dreams—like this. And the questions will still be there. You cannot blow them to bits with a pistol.

ORMUND I suppose you believe that if I take the jump into the dark, I'll find myself back again on the old treadmill. Well, I don't believe it, I can find peace.

DR. GÖRTLER You can't. Peace is not somewhere just waiting for you. . . . You have to create it. . . . Life is not easy. It provides no short cuts, no effortless escapes. . . . Life is penetrated through and through by our feeling, imagination and will. In the end the whole universe must respond to every real effort we make. We each live a fairy tale created by ourselves.

ORMUND What—by going around the same damned dreary circle of existence as you believe?

DR. GÖRTLER We do not go round a circle. That is an illusion, just as the circling of the planets and stars is an illusion. We move along a spiral track. It is not quite the same journey from the cradle to the grave each time. Sometimes the differences are small. Sometimes they are very important. We must set out each time on the same road but along that road we have a choice of adventures.[11]

The Likeliest Candidates for Suicide. "Life is not easy," observed Dr. Görtler. We should add that it is *purposely* not easy, for without challenges people would never grow or acquire the stamina to face and overcome all difficulties. It seems significant, therefore, that where children are denied such challenges, they are among the group where the suicide rate is highest. Psychiatrist Mary Griffin reports that young adults in upper middle class and rich families account for the disastrous increase in the suicide rate today. "We can only conclude," she says, "that we are raising children who have very fragile personalities, kids who can be devastated by the slightest setback" (*Wall Street Journal,* May 14, 1981).

More on this appears in an article, "Cries for Help, Adolescent Suicide," by educator Mary Susan Miller. She reports that "among adolescents, suicide has increased more than 200 percent in recent years." "In fact, it has risen so sharply that some call it epidemic."* As to suicide attempts, she says, they outnumber successful suicides by as much as 50 to 1. One of several major causes, says the teacher, is that "parents strive to give their children happiness, not by a search for what is fulfilling, but by an avoidance of what presents difficulties. They eliminate boredom by crowding a year round schedule with activities . . . they eliminate effort by doing things for their children. Children grow up then, not only self-indulgent, but lacking in confidence. Their overprotective parents have instilled in them a feeling of 'I can't cope.' Therefore, when trouble arises, they are ill-prepared to face it" (*Independent School,* December 1977).

---

*Later figures indicate an even greater increase in suicides among the young. According to *USA Today* (April 18, 1984): "The National Center for Health Statistics reports that suicides among 15- to 24-year-olds have more than quadrupled—from 1,239 in 1960 to 5,239 in 1980—and the rate per 100,000 has jumped from 5.2 in 1960 to 12.3 in 1980. The actual number of suicides, experts believe, *is at least double that.* 'We believe many single motorcar accidents, especially in the younger population, may indeed be suicides,' says Dr. Susan Blumenthal, director of suicide research at the National Institute of Mental Health."

In contrast, the philosophy of reincarnation can inspire the conviction that we can endure anything. Surely, if we have had other lives, we may have gone through far worse trials than presently experienced, and here we are, still alive, still surviving, still going on with our evolution.

An Amazing Case of Endurance. The power to endure impossible situations is not the exclusive possession of special people, endowed with special gifts. The humblest person can live a heroic life, as this true story movingly illustrates. It is related by Dr. Ritchie in *Return from Tomorrow*.

While stationed in France during World War II, his medical unit was ordered to a concentration camp near Wuppertal, Germany. The war in Europe had just ended. "This was the most shattering experience I had yet had; I had been exposed many times by then to sudden death and injury, but to see the effects of slow starvation, to walk through those barracks where thousands of men had died a little bit at a time over a period of years, was a new kind of horror. For many it was an irreversible process: we lost scores each day in spite of all the medicine and food we could rush to them."

Ritchie was drawn to one Polish Jew who had obviously not been an inmate of the concentration camp very long. "His posture was erect, his eyes bright, his energy indefatigable. Since he was fluent in English, French, German and Russian, as well as Polish, he became a kind of unofficial camp translator. We came to him with all sorts of problems; the paper work alone was staggering in attempting to relocate people whose families, even whole hometowns, might have disappeared." But, though this Polish man "worked fifteen and sixteen hours a day, he showed no signs of weariness. While the rest of us were drooping with fatigue, he seemed to gain strength. 'We have time for this old fellow,' he'd say. 'He's been waiting to see us all day.' His compassion for his fellow-prisoners glowed on his face, and it was to this glow that I came when my own spirits were low."

One day Ritchie was astounded to learn from the man's papers *that he had been in Wuppertal since 1939!* "For six years he had lived on the same starvation diet, slept in the same airless and disease-ridden barracks as everyone else, yet without the least physical or mental deterioration." During that period many inmates had taken their lives; it was a daily occurrence.

Here is the man's story. "We lived in the Jewish section of Warsaw, my wife, our two daughters, and our three little boys. When the Germans reached our street they lined everyone against a wall and opened up with machine guns. I begged to be allowed to die with my family, but because I spoke German they put me in a work group. I had to decide right then whether to let myself hate the soldiers who had done this. It was an easy decision, really. I was a lawyer. In my practice I had seen too often what hate could do to people's minds and bodies. Hate had just killed the six people who mattered most to me in the world. I decided then that I would spend the rest of my life loving every person I came in contact with.''[12]

In contrast to this man's tragedy, how exceedingly small seem the troubles most of us endure each day. Yet we have the same powers to endure he had. It was by forgetting himself and his problems, by learning to radiate love to everyone he met, that he was able to transcend intolerable conditions.

If, then, the suicidally minded person wants to escape life because ''other people do not understand or love me; because they abuse me; because I am in bad health; because I am out of work''—all reasons offered in suicide notes—the cure may lie in reversing the situation. ''Now, that I have experienced how miserable a person can be, let me look around and help other people having similar problems.'' Then there is little time to become morbid about one's own fate. Also, something else happens, something quite wonderful—the person finds surging up from within the power to transform the lives of others as well as his own. And for the first time—in this life at least—true joy and happiness are known.

Columbia University Lectures on Reincarnation

On December 21, 1976, the United Nations General Assembly passed a resolution proclaiming 1979 the International Year of the Child. Appropriate to this, a three-day symposium on "The Child and Death" was held at Columbia University's College of Physicians and Surgeons in January of that year. Doctors, nurses, and teachers from many parts of the United States participated. The departments at Columbia that hosted the event were the Department of Psychiatry; School of Nursing; Cancer Research Center; and The Foundation of Thanatology, whose director, Dr. Austin Kutscher of Columbia, was chiefly responsible for coordinating the symposium.

Among persons invited to speak were four who offered the perspective of reincarnation. Their papers form the content of this chapter and are given in order of presentation. The first, by Sylvia Cranston, is now in updated form.

THE CHILD AND DEATH

Thus far at this conference, there has been much anguished speech as to how to cope with the experience of death and dying when a young person is mortally ill, or has lost a parent, or a school companion has died in an accident. One teacher told how an entire school went into shock when a boy, running to class, was mangled beyond recognition by a truck. Another teacher reported that she entered the field of death education twelve years ago because a parent of one of her students jumped out of a window, and the teacher could not answer the questions raised by her frightened class. We heard earlier that the suicide rate among young adults is highest where they have lost a parent through illness or accident.

Up to now, however, there has been little attempt to explain *why* premature deaths occur, except in the moving speech of Rabbi Steven Moss. Among other responsibilities, he has been chaplain for seven years at the Memorial Sloan-Kettering Cancer Center in New York City. He spoke of his heart-rending experience in the children's ward. Judaism offers the possible explanation that the children have sinned. This, he said, some rabbis fiercely reject. How could young children have had time to sin? It must be the parents who have sinned. His own answer is that "God gives life and God takes it away." If this is true, one must ask, why does that beneficent power do so in such a cruel way? But is it really necessary to blame God in the first place?

Several years ago, the Reverend Billy Graham was interviewed in England on the BBC, and the moderator asked him, "How do you account for an all-merciful God allowing children to be born blind, maimed, retarded, or otherwise afflicted?" He did not know what to say and finally offered this weak response: "The Bible says there are mysteries."

Morey Bernstein included such problems in his famous book on reincarnation *The Search for Bridey Murphy*. He explains therein why, during his youth and early manhood, he was a soul-denying atheist.

> This pattern of thinking had started as early as the first grade. If I hadn't noticed it before, then I surely observed during my first year at school that there were glaring inequalities among the kids in the class. Keith, for instance, was brilliant; he knew all the answers. He was taller and huskier than the others; any girl would willingly tell you that he was the best-looking boy in the class. And he was the best all-around athlete, could play anything. To top it all, his parents seemed to have plenty of money; he dressed better, lived in the biggest house, and his father drove the biggest car.
>
> Orlando, on the other hand, had been short-changed in every department. The poor lad was so dull that the most elementary exercise was beyond him. On the playground he was so clumsy that he soon picked up uncomplimentary nicknames. And there was no denying that he was unattractive to look upon, really an ugly kid. His clothes, because his family lived in poverty, were so shabby and ill-fitting as to draw derision. Then one day a truck ran over Orlando, and he died in pain a few weeks later.
>
> I would ask my mother the "why" of these things. Why did the Keiths have everything while the Orlandos had been blessed with nothing but misery? My poor Mother did her best to answer, but it was clear that she was

bewildered too. And as for my father he was so busy working night and day, making it possible for me to wear clothes like Keith's, that I was sure he had no time to think about any kind of philosophy. I came, therefore, to my own conclusion: Religion and immortality are fables. Life is an accident—an accident that begins at birth and ends in death.[1]

It was not until Morey was exposed to reincarnational thinking, and was challenged to investigate this "ridiculous" subject, that his philosophical outlook changed, and he began to find rational answers.

Although, as we have seen, Rabbi Moss provided various Judaic views to explain the suffering and death of children, he failed to mention the strong current in Judaism of belief in the doctrine of many lives (see chapter 12). The distinguished author of *The Zohar,* Rabbi Simeon ben Jochai, wrote:

> All souls are subject to the trials of transmigration [or reincarnation]: and people do not know the designs of the Most High with regard to them; they know not how they are being at all times judged, both before coming into this world and when they leave it. They do not know how many transformations and mysterious trials they must undergo. . . .
> The souls must re-enter the absolute substance whence they have emerged. But to accomplish this end they must develop all the perfections, the germ of which is planted in them; and if they have not fulfilled this condition during one life, they must commence another, a third, and so forth, until they have acquired the condition which fits them for reunion with God.[2]

Applying all this to our subject and viewing the difficult experiences in life as trials, are children with terminal illnesses capable of handling them? In the experience of the world-renowned author of *On Death and Dying,* Dr. Elisabeth Kübler-Ross, they are, and they often express an innate conviction in their own immortality. This is evident in the pictures they draw, often of a butterfly emerging from its chrysalis.

*

For those unfamiliar with the work of Dr. Kübler-Ross, we present excerpts from an excellent introductory summary that appeared in *Playboy*'s featured seventeen-page interview with this psychiatrist (May 1981). In the interview itself, conducted by Marcia Seligson, Dr. Ross spoke openly of her conviction in reincarnation as an opportunity for unfolding the spiritual potentials within each human being. As to her amazing career, *Playboy* wrote:

> Elisabeth Kübler-Ross altered the consciousness of the world in her area of work: death and dying. Before this Swiss-born physician and psychiatrist

began lecturing all over the globe, working with thousands of terminally ill patients and writing [on the subject] . . . the topic of death was, in our Western culture, the ultimate taboo.

Doctors, nurses, and medical personnel, well-trained in the science of life, but lacking in the capacity to deal with death, frequently could not tell patients the truth, could not listen to them, ignored their emotional needs and truly abandoned them. Families, too, were ill-equipped to handle a loved one's impending death. So terminal patients were left to face the last, most profound act of their lives in a nightmare of loneliness and pretense.

Kübler-Ross has transformed all that; she has revolutionized the care of the dying. . . . For the past 12 years, she has traveled more than 250,000 miles a year, lecturing to health professionals and laymen, visiting dying patients, spreading her credo that "dying can be one of the most beautiful, incredible experiences of life if it is shared with loved ones," conducting five-day workshops called Life, Death and Transition for the terminally ill and their families.

Her pioneering work is also responsible for the thousands of courses in death education conducted each year in our schools. As the president of the Foundation of Thanatology here at Columbia, Dr. Austin Kutscher, has remarked to one of the authors: "Ross started the entire movement rolling."

I turn now to one of the cases described in Dr. Ross's book *To Live Until We Say Good-Bye.* It concerns a little girl named Jamie who died of a brain tumor at the age of five. When Dr. Ross first visited the child and her mother, Linda, the latter had prepared in advance the kind of dialogue she anticipated she would have with a psychiatrist. However, "she was stunned and surprised when she was asked *not to talk,* but to sit with her daughter and to draw a picture of her own. She used the same explanations that most adults use. 'I cannot draw. I haven't drawn in a long time.' But no excuse would do. She had to draw a picture, no matter what it revealed."

And while she drew a picture of her own desolate, sad and lonely house, which revealed far more of the pain that she lived through, Jamie happily used all the conceivable colors, making figure after figure, connected and disconnected at times, except for the left upper quadrant where there was a free-floating purple balloon—a spiritual color—free-floating up into the sky, unattached and unencumbered.

Little did Jamie know how we used this technique developed by Susan Bach, a Jungian analyst from London, a famous but not enough recognized authority. It is a method that reveals the inner meaning of spontaneous drawings of dying children. In the spontaneous drawings, where there is a free choice of form, color, and design, these children very often reveal their knowledge of their own impending death and are able to share with those who understand the symbolic language the meaning of their illness, their life, and their future. The upper left quadrant usually reveals the far future and death.

"In Jamie's drawing," Dr. Ross continued, "the upper left quadrant showed that the concept of death was different from the remainder of the picture; it revealed an absence of fear and attachment and a high spiritual quality. Yes, Jamie had an awareness of death and of life after death and was not afraid of it, and Linda gradually became aware of that fact and took consolation in the knowledge that if Jamie could have the courage to face her own transition with peace and equanimity, then she, too, would be able to mobilize enough strength to make it."[3]

Some months before Jamie died, although only five years old, she managed to write this letter to her mother:

When Dr. Ross first worked with the terminally ill at the University of Chicago, she was very skeptical about an afterlife, but now envisions that the soul is reborn on earth. Several years ago she wrote me: "I think it would be marvelous if more and more people would become aware of the fact that there are many lives we have to live in order to learn all the lessons" (November 16, 1977).*

PERIOD OF BEREAVEMENT

I have known several parents with a reincarnational outlook who underwent the dreadful tragedy of losing a child. However deep the personal loss, the time of bereavement was lessened owing to their conviction that the child was not permanently cut off from life's opportunities for growth and experience but would return to continue its evolution. Where such

---

*Since this time, Dr. Ross has spoken publicly on many occasions about reincarnation. She wrote the foreword to the paperback edition of Head and Cranston's *Reincarnation, the Phoenix Fire Mystery*.[4] In Christmas of 1981, Carey Williams visited the doctor at her home in California. Dr. Ross disclosed that when she first mentioned reincarnation in lectures, some of the audience visibly bristled with resentment, but now wherever she goes there is no resistance at all!

conviction is lacking, the period of grief is often much longer, and confusedly bitter, as well.

To illustrate, take this case reported in the October 1981 monthly newsletter of Forum for Death Education and Counseling: A couple lost their eldest son on the eve of his nineteenth birthday in a motorcycle accident. The parents were on the verge of collapse. "Nineteen years of love and extra-special caring wiped out, gone just like that." They finally went for help to a thanatologist, Sister Clarisse of Holy Cross Hospital in Silver Springs, Maryland, who gave them loving support. She warned them: "It takes a minimum of two years to work through the grieving process emotionally"—a fact that nearly sent the husband to the door. They learned that "grieving takes every ounce of energy; there is little left for anything else. Even the smallest task becomes monumental." This is "very normal and natural," they were told. After eight months of counseling, the couple were able to begin the rebuilding process, but "we still ask why, we still question, feel cheated, and vent our anger now and then." Though they believed in immortality, their ideas thereon were too vague to bring them healing or understanding.

WHEN A CHILD LOSES A PARENT

The pain experienced by children when they lose a parent is often equally excruciating. Dave Hirshey, a staff writer for the *New York Sunday Daily News Magazine*, tells of his own experience in "Something's Happened to Your Mom," an article published in the June 10, 1979, issue. His story opens with this scene:

> There were so many toys, he didn't know which to choose. The housekeeper held his hand and pointed to a row of baseball mitts. He looked at bats, dump trucks, airplanes. He took a fire engine to the counter, unsure of how much he was allowed to spend.
>
> "Why don't you take it home and show it to your mother?" the saleswoman said kindly. "She'll tell you if it's all right."
>
> He threw down the fire engine, tore his hand away and ran out onto the sidewalk. He was crying. *His mother was dead.* Didn't they know? Why did they keep reminding him he didn't have one? Dead, dead, dead. The kids at school teased him. No mommy. Dead mommy. He never went back to that store. Never.
>
> I was 6 when I tore out of that toy store on Broadway. My mother had died a few months before. She had been sick for nearly all my memories of her. Hodgkins disease, they explained to me later. Much later. I found out once I grew the courage to ask.

Children who have borne the death of a parent retain vivid memories of the moment they find out. One out of 20 children experience that moment before they enter high school. It becomes the day the earth stood still, the day things got all queer and off key, as in these three examples: *He* was called to the principal's office in the middle of recess. *Her* uncle was waiting after school, and his face was all funny. *His* father took him to buy an ice cream cone and when he was biting off the end, there were the awful words:

"Something's happened to your mom."

"But what is 'something'?" Hirshey asks. He then tells the story of Bernard, age eleven, who responded in this way after his father died: "Aunt Kathy said he was sleeping up in heaven but I know my daddy got kilt. Kilt on the road in the car. Squished up squirrels got kilt on the road and they didn't look like they were sleeping. I ran away from seeing the squirrel that time with all the blood and the tongue out. And anyhow, if God is so good how come he let my daddy get kilt and squished like that?"

If that boy could learn to appreciate that it was only the bodily house his father lived in that got smashed, not daddy himself, and that he is still living—housed perhaps in an invisible, spiritual body—the lad's feelings would be less bitter, and his grief lessened. If, furthermore, he could realize that his father still loves him and some day will return to earth in a new physical body, when the boy may be back in his own new house or body, then the feeling of loss would not be so absolute.

This is not just a bedtime story to quiet a child's anxieties. Serious research into reincarnation is being conducted by scientists of repute (see chapter 4). One of these, Dr. Ian Stevenson, has five large volumes of case histories of children who provide considerable evidence of past-life recall. Many of them died prematurely of illness, or accident; some were even murdered. *Yet here they are alive again, going on with their evolution!*

A HOLOCAUST VICTIM

If the foregoing be fact, it must likewise apply to collective deaths. The grief arising from such inhumanly dreadful tragedies becomes unbearable when it is believed that this was the *only* chance the sufferers had to live on earth, and now it is gone forever.

One of Stevenson's cases involves a holocaust victim. It was reported, in brief, in an article in *Look* magazine on his research (October 20, 1970). The case concerned an American girl "Gail Habbyshaw, aged 18, a friendly brunette, somewhat small for her age, who is one of a pair of identical twins. Since early childhood, her attraction to Judaism has been so strong that she quit Christian Sunday school and has since been driven fifteen miles to the nearest synagogue on the Sabbath. . . . Pork and certain shellfish revolt her, and she is converting to Judaism. Her twin sister Susan feels none of this.'' Gail is convinced that she was killed in Nazi Germany in the thirties. The experience apparently did not embitter her, and she is grateful to have another chance to go on with her life.

In closing, I offer these moving lines from Walt Whitman's *Leaves of Grass:*

I wish I could translate the hints about the dead young men and women.
And the hints about old men and mothers, and the offspring taken soon out of their laps.
What do you think has become of the young and old men?
And what do you think has become of the women and children?
They are alive and well somewhere. . . .
No doubt I have died myself ten thousand times before.[5]

REINCARNATION IN THE CLASSROOM

This presentation to "The Child and Death" symposium was by Myrra Lee, who in 1977 was selected, from among 140,000 nominees, for the coveted position of America's Teacher of the Year. She was personally honored at the White House by President Carter, the New York Times *featuring a picture of them together. While each year there is a new Teacher of the Year, somehow one does not hear too much about them. However, when Mrs. Lee was selected, many magazines and newspapers carried stories about this unusual teacher and her innovative methods. The major area of her work is in social studies and history. She also conducts classes in death education.*

Teaching is a challenging profession. Teaching a course for which there is no accepted curriculum or methodology is exceptionally challenging. A teacher who institutes a course on death and dying must be an individual who both accepts this challenge and is prepared to deal with the unknown and unexpected.

The unknown is what aspects of death and dying will interest the students; the unexpected may be the desire of students to investigate those aspects of the subject that have come into public prominence in recent years. One of these is reincarnation, which has become very popular with all aspects of media, from popular song to film.

The idea of previous existences is widely discussed by students. It would seem that these topics must be considered by the death-and-dying teacher in addition to all the more conventional aspects of the subject. They must be considered because they will inevitably be brought up by at least one student in each class.

For the past five semesters, I have taught courses which included units on death and dying. Each semester we have discussed the idea of reincarnation. The question raised by students may be, "What do you think about reincarnation?" or "Can we talk about reincarnation?" It may be a statement, "I believe in reincarnation." Whatever it be, students are eager to discuss it.

Since a classroom should be the place where ideas can be openly discussed and investigated, teachers should not be reluctant to pursue this interest. I would not recommend that the teacher *initiate* the discussion, but recommend that she not deny student interest. The reason that I suggest teacher reticence is that, in some communities, teacher initiation of the topic of reincarnation may be considered as infringing upon religious beliefs.

However, if the teacher produces material on after-death states that has been medically ascertained, she cannot be accused of stepping on the toes of religion. A discussion of reincarnation inevitably follows such a presentation.

*

How can a teacher handle this subject so that it proves to be beneficial to both the students and the teacher? How can the teacher deal with the concern that it may be a religious issue? How can students be answered who may confront the teacher with statements that reincarnation is denied by Western religion?

The first step is to have made sure that students feel free to express their opinions in a supportive atmosphere. Work toward producing such an atmosphere must have gone on from the beginning of the semester. It cannot just happen at this point in time. The second step is to have confidence that such a subject is appropriate for the classroom. If students have been made to feel free to discuss many different ideas and concepts prior to this time, there will be no problem. The third step is to become familiar with the subject and references that will support any statements the teacher may make.

Frequently, the students will carry the discussion by themselves. The only role the teacher will play will be as moderator. Challenge to the concept may also be handled by the students. However, student support generally will be on a feeling or intuitional basis.

The teacher must direct investigation in several ways: Draw up lists of arguments pro and con reincarnation; relate the findings of death-and-dying experts like Elisabeth Kübler-Ross in relation to reincarnation, out-of-body experiences, and after-death states. Have available for students, to take out, copies of Dr. Raymond Moody's *Life After Life,* and *Reflections on Life After Life.* They are inexpensive and available usually wherever paperback books are sold. Acquaint the students with the results of Dr. Ian Stevenson's studies of reincarnation and children; correlate the studies of Cranston and Head in their book, *Reincarnation, the Phoenix Fire Mystery,* with the arguments concerning Western religions.

In this connection, it is necessary when discussing reincarnation that the teacher be aware of the fact that such a concept has been an integral part of Western as well as Eastern religions, and that it was taught by many of the early Christians. This is where the Cranston and Head book is so invaluable. It provides sources which substantiate statements made by the teacher on the subject. In addition, it has chapters on reincarnation in Western philosophy, literature, art, and the latest findings in science and psychology. Students who have questioned statements made by me have been satisfied to use this reference as a start for their own investigations.

Although the word "reincarnation" has become widely known, there are many misconceptions about what it actually means. If we are going to discuss reincarnation in the classroom, we teachers had better be sure of our facts. We need to know who and what is supposed to reincarnate. We need to understand the purpose of rebirth. We need to realize that a majority of people in the world believe and accept it as part of their philosophy of life. Isn't it valid to consider a concept in which so many people believe?

If we are sure of ourselves, our facts, and our duty to expand the minds of our students, if we have established the right to freedom of expression for our students, then we teachers need not fear making reincarnation an integral part of our death-and-dying courses.

If we could realize how meaningful the entire study of death and dying can be to our students, we would not hesitate to institute such a course of study. It can be done just as objectively as when various religious ideas are considered in a course in comparative religion, and the students are left free to come to their own conclusions.

My students progress from fear and trepidation about death to an understanding and acceptance of the process. They no longer feel fear because much of the unknown is dispelled. They have lost their trepidation about how to relate to the dying or those who grieve because they understand what is being experienced. They learn how to relate because they develop confidence and empathy. Fear generally exists when we confront the unknown. Death and dying no longer are part of that realm.

JUVENILE CRIME AND BELIEFS IN THE HEREAFTER

The author of this paper, Caren M. Elin, M.S., has had wide experience in teaching and also in death education. In the latter capacity, she was invited to speak at the Columbia University symposium on "The Child and Death."

She has visited many colleges and universities where classes in death and dying are conducted and has surprisingly discovered that some colleges have two or more departments simultaneously teaching this same subject! Such departments may be any of the following: Health and Physical Education, Humanities, Philosophy, Psychology, Religion, and Social Studies. In universities having medical and/or nursing schools, the subject is often in the curriculum. Can we think of any other topic that could be taught in so many different areas of learning? Obviously, the need for enlightenment in this field is urgent in our time.

In "The Human Situation," the Gifford Lectures of W. Macneile Dixon, that distinguished educator observed: "To live is by universal consent to travel a rough road. And how can a rough road which leads nowhere be worth the traveling? Mere living, what a profitless performance; mere painful living, what an absurd!" In this view, he said, "there is nothing to be hoped for, nothing to be done save to await our turn to mount the scaffold and bid farewell to that colossal blunder, the much-ado-about-nothing world."

However, he continued, "give assurance that what death appears to proclaim is not so, and the scene is changed. The sky brightens, the door is left open for unimagined possibilities, things begin to fall into an intelligible pattern."

"What kind of immortality is at all conceivable?" he asked. "Of all doctrines of a future life, palingenesis or rebirth, which carries with it the idea of pre-existence, is by far the most ancient and most widely held, 'the only system to which,' as said David Hume, 'philosophy can hearken.' ''[6]

It is not only philosophers like Hume and Dixon who are preoccupied with such thoughts on the meaning of life and death. Young adults frequently dwell on the problem, but often not in a hopeful way. This was clearly demonstrated to a visiting teacher in a special type of California school. She offered each class this choice—to go on with their regular curriculum, or to discuss the subject of death. They unanimously chose the latter. The students were then asked to draw a picture of their concept of death and elaborate their ideas in writing. In the selections that follow, the grammar and spelling of the pupils is used. To protect the identity of the students pseudonyms are used.

> *Allen Lewis:* Death is . . . what is death? Is there life after death, or do they just put you six feet under? I do indeed sometimes wonder. Is there a heaven high in the sky? Is there even a hell far below? Or do you just go in the ground when you die?
>
> I think there is a heaven and a hell. It depends on whether your naughty or nice or whether you tell lies or the truth. I think I will go to hell. What is hell. Hell is certainly not heaven. I think hell is a bunch of hoods who don't know their if's and but's from their could's. Hell is eternal fire. With all these hoods, gambling, drinking and doing dope. Let's face it, when you die there is just no hope.

At this point you may be wondering where is this special classroom. Ron Lacey's answer to the assignment makes this clear.

> What death means to me. Death is when your locked up and you don't have your freedom like being here, when you hear that door shut your throat gets dry and you feel like you just swallowed a clump of flour and it won't go down, then you feel like beating your head against the wall wondering why you are here and why you did what you did to get here. Every so often I ask that question and wonder [where] I will go next. To me death does not mean you have to be killed. One person can die many times in his lifetime.

Yes, these students are all in prison and attend schools within the juvenile court system of California, and the teacher was myself. Over a period of several months, as a substitute teacher, I taught a number of their classes, grouped by age and sex.

A question that continually plagued me is, why do so many of these young adults feel that life is already over for them? For Shawn Hayes (age fifteen), ''being locked up is the first step of death. And after that there is no hope." But why did the students of Juvenile Hall feel so convinced they were doomed? It is because, now they were caught and imprisoned, the stigma of such incarceration made them feel outcasts in society. They had ruined their life. Never again could they have a clean slate in either their own eyes or in the eyes of the people "out there."

A contrasting picture of how prisoners who believe in karma and reincarnation feel is told by H. Fielding Hall who, as a British government official, lived for some years in Burma. It is to be found in his beautiful book *The Soul of a People*. He wrote:

"Not very many years ago an officer in Rangoon lost some currency notes. He had placed them upon his table overnight, and in the morning they were gone. The amount was not large. It was, if I remember rightly, 30 rupees; but the loss annoyed him, and as all search and inquiry proved futile, he put the matter in the hands of the police.

"The possession of the notes was traced to the officer's Burmese servant. The boy was caught in the act of trying to change one of the notes. He was arrested, and he confessed. He was very hard up, he said, and his sister had written asking him to help her. He could not do so, and he was troubling himself about the matter early that morning while tidying the room, and he saw the notes on the table, and so he took them. It was a sudden temptation and he fell.

"When the officer learnt all this, he would, I think, have withdrawn from the prosecution and forgiven the boy; but it was too late. In our English law the accused must be tried before a magistrate. His master asked that the punishment might be light. The boy, he said, was an honest boy, and had yielded to a sudden temptation. But the magistrate did not see matters in the same light at all. It was a serious matter, and he felt himself obliged to make an example of such as were convicted to be a warning to others. So the boy was sentenced to 6 months' rigorous imprisonment; and his master went home, and before long had forgotten all about it.

"But one day, as he was sitting on his veranda reading before breakfast, a lad came quickly up the stairs and knelt down before him. It was the servant. As soon as he was released from jail, he went straight to his old master and begged to be taken back again into his service. But the master doubted. 'How can I take you back again?' he said. 'You have been in jail. I could forgive the theft, but the being in jail—how can I forgive that?'

"And the boy could not understand. 'If I have stolen, I have been in jail for it. That is wiped out now,' he said again and again. But to the Englishman punishment was a degradation. It seemed to him far more disgraceful that his servant should have been in jail than that he should have committed theft.''

Fielding Hall commented: The boy "had committed theft. That he admitted. He was prepared to atone for it. The magistrate was not content with that, but made him also atone for other men's sins. He was twice punished, because other men who escaped did ill. That was the first thing the boy could not understand. And then, when he had atoned both for his own sin and for that of others, when he came out of prison, he was looked upon in a worse state than if he had never atoned at all. The boy was proud of having atoned in full, very full, measure for his sin; the master looked upon the punishment as inconceivably worse than the crime.

"So the officer went about and told the story of his boy coming back, and expecting to be taken on again, as a curious instance of the mysterious working of the Oriental mind. 'Just to think,' he said, 'he was not ashamed of having been in prison!' ''

The Buddhists believe, says Fielding Hall, "in absolute justice—always the same, eternal and unchangeable as the laws of the stars. We purposely make punishment degrading; they think it should be elevating, that in its purifying power lies its sole use and justification. We believe in tearing a soiled garment; they think it ought to be washed. Almost the only confirmed criminals have been made so by punishment, by that punishment which some consider is intended to uplift them, but which never does aught but degrade them. Instead of cleansing the garment, it tears it, and renders it useless for this life.''[7]

In the East, the people believe, as we know, that if the actions engendered in one life, whether good or bad, are not paid off in that life, such compensation will be made in a future life. There is no doctrine of an everlasting hell. But my students in Juvenile Hall certainly believed such a place exists, and their minds were full of horrid, grotesque images that they drew pictures of. Eddie Hayes wrote, "If I were dead I would go to hell and bern at the stake at the fire place.'' His picture showed himself stretched out on a revolving spit, perpetually roasting over burning hot coals. From his mouth came the word "HELP!''

During the discussion periods it became evident that most of the students— whether they had committed serious offenses or not—had one feeling they could neither draw nor write about, and that was their hopeless conviction that it was impossible for them to alter their own lives. And when they were asked, "Do you want to stop getting into trouble?'' a mumbled reply

COLUMBIA UNIVERSITY LECTURES

so often came. "Why should we change when we're going to hell anyway?" With such an attitude, it is easy to see how a first offender could become a second and a third offender, and finally a hardened criminal.

Cannot we find a way as teachers, psychiatrists, psychologists, or social workers, to instill some hope and purpose into these students who feel their lives have already ended? There must be a way to help such a student as Connie who wrote,

> Your born, you live and you die . . . what can I say. A lot of people are afraid to die. I'm not afraid to die. I'm just afraid how and when I'm gonna die. I'll admit this though, I'm not gonna be a little Angel so that God will look down on me and pull me up to heaven—cause I already messed my life up. Thats why I'm in the Hall cause I stabbed my stepdad, and at that moment I felt death for him. Its a terrible feeling knowing that you almost killed some one. [Her drawing of death was a sharp knife dripping with blood!]

In my classes in the Juvenile Halls, the words of humanity's great teachers were frequently quoted—words imbued with hope and courage, conveying a sense of self-worth and responsibility. When the subject of reincarnation arose and the class desired to know more about this, these words of Buddha in the poem *The Light of Asia* by Sir Edwin Arnold were sometimes read.

> The books say well, each person's life
> The outcome of his former living is:
> The bygone wrongs bring forth sorrows and woes
> The bygone right breeds bliss.
> That which you sow you reap.

> By this the slayer's knife did stab himself,
> The unjust judge has lost his own defender,
> The false tongue dooms its lie; the creeping thief
> And spoiler rob, to render.

> Know you who suffer! know
> You suffer from yourselves.
> Within yourselves deliverance must be sought;
> Each person his prison makes.
> Each has such lordship as the loftiest ones.
> You are not bound; the Soul of things is sweet.
> Stronger than woe is Will.[8]

I frequently looked up as I read, to see if the students understood what was being said, for in our modern age, poetry is not easy even for adults to comprehend. I was often amazed and deeply moved to observe their faces beaming with hope, as if a light had been turned on within their usually dim and lightless selves.

What is meant by "each has such lordship as the loftiest ones," I would ask. The reply came at times in the form of another question: "Are we divine, too?" The verses elicited such remarks as, "It just may pay off to cease a life of crime and drugs." Some responded by asking whether the path they had chosen in this life may have been the same they chose in another life. I replied that if reincarnation is a fact, then this is possible. However, it was emphasized that tendencies can always be changed in *this* life. We are always free to choose a better way.

Crime Rate in the West and East Compared. One grave concern today is the mounting criminal violence within the schools themselves, as well as in society at large. Does the latter occur among populations where reincarnation is the fundamental outlook? The percentages of crime among the people living in India and Ceylon (Sri Lanka) were once taken by the British government. This was a hundred years ago, when Western materialistic influences were not so strong there as today, and consequently the effect of the Hindu and Buddhist philosophy was more manifest in people's conduct. Here are the statistics for convictions for criminal offences of people living in India and Ceylon:

Europeans	1 in 274
Moslems	1 in 856
Hindus	1 in 1,361
Buddhists	1 in 3,787
Natives converted to Christianity	1 in 799

Commenting on the last item, a London periodical, *The Tablet,* wrote, "It appears from these figures that, while we effect a very marked moral deterioration in the natives by converting them to our creed, their natural standard of morality is so high, that however much we 'Christianize' them, we cannot succeed in making them altogether as bad as ourselves."[9] These converts, however, had given up their conviction in reincarnation and karma in exchange for the church doctrine of forgiveness of sins. It is easier to do wrong, if you feel somebody can forgive you, or you can go to confession and receive absolution.

It is doubtful that such escapist teachings can be attributed to Jesus. In

Matthew 7:2 he said, "The measure you give will be the measure you get." And in Luke 12:59, using the example of a man in prison for his debts, Jesus declared this general law as applying to all of us: "I tell you, you will never get out till you have paid the last copper." Similarly, St. Paul said, "Be not deceived, God is not mocked. Whatever you sow that shall you also reap" (Galatians 6:7). There is also evidence that Jesus taught reincarnation, as Judaism does (see chapters 12 and 13).

Note that Jesus and St. Paul affirm that you will pay up only the *exact* amount you owe; you will reap only the *exact* amount you sow—not everlasting punishment. It was the eternal damnation idea that so confused and warped the minds of the students in my classes.

When people are convinced there is a law of exact compensation in the universe, and it will operate whether the authorities catch up with them or not, they are not likely to commit crimes against society. The theosophist Helena Blavatsky once wrote, "The most fertile source of all crime and immorality is the belief that it is possible for people to escape the consequences of their own actions. Once teach them reincarnation and karma, and besides feeling in themselves the true dignity of human nature, they will turn from evil and avoid it as they would a physical danger."[10]

Karma, the law of cause and effect—be assured—is not a harsh, punitive law, as many think, but healing and educational, because we learn to do better by seeing the exact results of our actions. Using an analogy, a young, immature violinist can learn from the screeching, disharmonious effects he produces just what he is doing wrong, and correcting this, can in time play beautiful music.

In closing, I will share one more paper written by students at Juvenile Hall. Here a fifteen-year-old lad spontaneously expressed in his own way the philosophy of reincarnation and karma:

> *Phil Murray:* With me life is only a testing ground for my basic emotions and if I prove to myself that love, joy, peace and being human is the way to be, then when my existence on this plane is ended I will step to a higher one and after that the next higher one. But if at any time I fail to see myself and those around me as loving beings and hurt anyone, I come back here to try again till I get it right.

EDUCATION TRANSFORMED

The author of this paper, Professor George Baird, was for a number of years instructor in education at New York University. Since his retirement, he has been conducting a series of evening seminars at NYU on some of the great philosophical issues of our time, including reincarnation.

Although this paper is addressed primarily to teachers and the problems of education in the schools, it applies equally to the full-time teachers known as parents, as well as to each of our readers desirous of functioning more creatively in the greatest school of all, the School of Life.

One would have to be intellectually blind not to be aware of the major changes that are presently taking place in our beliefs about the nature of life and death, about what a human being really is and, of course, what a child is. One would have to be equally blind to be unprepared for the major reorientation of educational aims, methods, and objectives that these basic philosophic shifts are likely to create.

If looked at from this vantage point, the history of education clearly shows that educational methodology and philosophy have followed obediently in the footsteps of the prevailing beliefs about the nature of human beings, and more specifically about the endowments that the newborn child brings with it. As these ideas have changed, so the public schools and the demands made on them have changed.

The other side of the picture seems just as clear, and it would not be difficult to demonstrate that, where there is little or no change in the concept of the human being, there is little or no change in what goes on in the classroom. With few exceptions our noble experiments in education sooner or later settle back into the timeworn grooves of standard practice. They all fail, and they will all fail, until there is an understanding of the true nature and history of the one basic ingredient in education—*the child.*

THE QUESTIONS THAT SURROUND US

The inevitable questions that arise about this magical being, this child, this possible visitor from another life, from a thousand lives, are these: If there is no death for the Real Being, for the Soul, or whatever we choose to call this Eternal Pilgrim, then who or what is this entity, what has it been, what has it been doing, what does it know? If it has lived through countless experiences and that knowledge is in some way its—then how can this wisdom be brought to bear on its present life? How can the school and the teacher aid in the process?

The answers to the question of how to help are not too different nor too foreign for those teachers who have learned the value of honestly listening in the classroom. And there are many, many teachers who have intuitively come not only to accept but to count on the child as an endless number of things trying to happen—as a vortex of feelings and half-formed ideas waiting to be expressed—as somebody inside trying to come through and be counted.

What teachers have yet to accept and to understand is the possibility that an ancient, immortal, self-conscious being has *once more* taken on a form, a personality, an unbelievably complex instrument for the purpose of carrying on its evolution—and that the teacher and child have to become partners in the process of control and unfoldment.

The cumulative results of the individual's efforts in past lives, if they exist, are bound to shine through to any teacher who is sincerely interested. It will mean that each child is unique, and brings its own set of talents, problems, judgments, and drives, that deep within there are marvelous insights, interesting points of view, and ethical standards that cannot be the product of these few years.

Interestingly enough, support for the idea of the unique nature of each child has recently come as a result of research into the learning processes of the brain. In an article in *Phi Delta Kappan*, entitled "The New 'Brain' Concept of Learning," Leslie A. Hart wrote,

> The brain was long thought to be passive, a *tabula rasa*, a blank on which instruction could be inscribed. This notion gave rise to the structure we try to employ—of subjects, courses, and curriculum—all expressions of the belief that if X and Y are taught, X and Y will be learned.
>
> Mountains of evidence tell us that doesn't happen. Now we can see more clearly why: The human brain is intensely *aggressive*. Each brain is highly individual, unique; it seeks out, demands, and will accept only what *it* needs next to "make sense" of surrounding reality, as *it* perceives that reality. This means that group instruction in an elementary subject is certain to fail. It is grossly brain-incompatible [February 1978].

In this passage, Dr. Hart does not give us any reasons for the uniqueness of each brain, reasons that would become clear if each child has lived and learned many times before and is not merely an accidental combination of genetic material that can be manipulated by teacher or society. But what this educator says adds one more acknowledgment of the fact that our educational philosophy could use a new basis.

SOMEONE HAS TO LIGHT THE FIRES

Anyone who has been around schools and children is cognizant of two truisms: one, that the child's concept of itself sets the limits of its growth; and two, that the teacher's concept of the child becomes either a pigeon hole or a wide open window for it. There is no limit to the potentiality of the Inner Being, and once the teacher is convinced of that, we have a true teacher.

The task of the educator is to awaken in the student the desire to know. The teacher must light the fires of interest in learning. The classroom has to be comfortable and friendly and safe for that private being who sometimes peeks out and sometimes blurts out with the most amazing discoveries. There has to be someone who is capable of practicing the fine art of listening. Someone has to be interested enough to want to hear more, whatever it is. Someone has to be there who understands that if it is real it is going to be unique, it is going to fit no pattern and will answer no prescription. That someone is *the teacher*. But again, it will all depend upon what the teacher thinks a child is, and what he thinks *this* child is. He may know all about "children" and ethnic groups and the sociology of the urban child, but it won't help him much with *this* child. It is only putting new names on the problem and putting it back on the shelf. *This* child is like no other, will learn and develop like no other. This child may even be wiser than the teacher. It just needs help and understanding in bringing this wisdom out. The teacher therefore has to be a midwife and help the child give birth to a unique human being. He has to give faith and warmth and encouragement, and then step aside and watch it happen.

Plight of the Elderly

This presentation was given at a symposium on "The Thanatological Aspects of Aging," held at Columbia University's College of Physicians and Surgeons in October 1978. The conference was attended by doctors, nurses, and other professional workers in the field of geriatrics. Sylvia Cranston was invited to speak on reincarnation in relation to problems confronting the elderly. This chapter is an abbreviated form of that talk, but includes a few additional observations. Her original paper is being published with other papers from the conference in a book on geriatrics edited by Dr. Austin H. Kutscher, to be published in New York in 1985 by Praeger.

Let anyone walk observantly through the streets of our large cities, and day after day he will see the hopeless, frightened looks of those who, afraid to die and afraid to live, push themselves to the last limit rather than spend their final days in a nursing home. A friend of mine has a responsible position in one of the newest and best equipped homes in New York. "When I get old," she told me, "let them take me out and shoot me rather than end my days in this kind of place."

Doctors and social workers in geriatrics are constructively testing alternate ways of providing for the aged. However, such solutions leave untouched the root fears that eat into the minds and hearts of their patients. Dr. Elisabeth Kübler-Ross revealed in an interview that 80 percent of the elderly approach their last years in bitterness and depression. They feel themselves a drag and burden on others. One by one, their friends die, and they feel increasingly isolated and alone. In a society that worships bodily beauty, they see themselves more and more like dried-up mummies. All the experience gained during their long life now seems useless and futile, soon to be swallowed up by death. And death itself, despite religious beliefs, is often fearfully dreaded as a plunge into an abyss of nothingness.

If reincarnation were demonstrated to be true—and there is serious scientific investigation being conducted in this area—such fears and worries would cease or be greatly diminished. I have personally known dozens of reincarnationists who despite infirmities, approached death serenely and without the slightest fear. They are mentally alert and interesting—not boring to themselves, or others, nor full of self-pity. They look much younger than their peers in appearance. Life is viewed on a scale vaster than the narrow confines of one short existence and consequently does not revolve so exclusively around a small circle of friends and relatives. Death is welcomed as a time for rest and spiritual renewal.

Reincarnationists believe that the cycle of life and death is analogous to that of waking and sleeping. Who of us is afraid to go to sleep at night? Some few individuals are, but the great majority welcome nightly rest and refreshment. They go to sleep assured that in the morning they will awake and continue their previous day's activities. For the reincarnationist, the same applies to death. All that they have learned in this life can be put to use in their next "day" or incarnation. Even to the last moments of this earthly existence, they can learn lessons that will count as a harvest for the future. Appropriate to these thoughts are some words from a Buddhist funeral service. "When the day's work is ended, night brings the blessing of sleep. So death is the ending of a larger day, and in the night that follows, every person finds rest, until of his own volition he returns to fresh endeavor and to labors anew. So has it been with this our friend, so will it be for all of us."

Let us turn to a country like India, where acceptance of reincarnation is universal among the Hindus, and ascertain the effect of this belief upon the dying. Count Hermann Keyserling wrote in his *Travel Diary of a Philosopher*, "Benares is overflowing with the diseased and the infirm. No wonder: a great number of the pilgrims come here in order to die on the shores of the Ganges. . . . These sufferers suffer so little; they have above all, no fear whatever of death. Most of them are superlatively happy; and as to their infirmity—well that must be endured; it will not take very long anyhow. And some old sin is no doubt scored off in the process. The faith of the Indians is said to be pessimistic. I know of none which is less so."[1]

These people come to terms with death long before they die. In the West, we tend to postpone thinking about death until faced with the possibility and then are ill prepared to meet it. Freud wrote of this in "Thoughts for the Times of Death and War." "To anyone who listened to us, we were prepared to maintain that death was the necessary outcome of life. In reality, however, we showed an unmistakable tendency to put death to one side, to eliminate it from life. The complement to this cultural and conventional attitude towards death is provided by our complete collapse when death has struck down someone whom we love."[2] But our collapse is even more complete when it is our own death that seems imminent, as Dr. Lewis Thomas observes in *The Lives of a Cell*.

> Death on a grand scale does not bother us. We can sit around a dinner table and discuss war, involving 60 million volatilized human deaths, as though we were talking about bad weather; we can watch abrupt bloody death every day, in color, on films and television, without blinking back a tear. It is when the numbers of dead are very small, and very close, that we begin to think in scurrying circles. At the very center of the problem is the pending naked cold deadness of one's own self, the only reality in nature of which we can have absolute certainty, and it is unmentionable, unthinkable.[3]

In closing, I would like to share some inspiring words from a letter of Gandhi to Madeleine Slade, a British admiral's daughter who renounced position and comfort to work with this world leader. What he wrote was in reply to a letter about the deteriorated condition of her sick mother, and it seems equally helpful to the elderly who approach death as to those left behind to mourn.

> [Your] mother is slowly going. It will be well if the end comes soon. It is better to leave a body one has outgrown. To wish to see the dearest ones as long as possible in the flesh is a selfish desire and it comes out of weakness or want of faith in the survival of the soul after the dissolution of the body. . . .
> The more I observe and study things, the more convinced I become that sorrow over separation and death is perhaps the greatest delusion. To realize that it is a delusion is to become free. There is no death, no separation of the real substance. And yet the tragedy of it is that although we love friends for the substance we recognize in them, we deplore the destruction of the insubstantial that covers the substance for the time being.
> The form ever changes, ever perishes. The informing spirit neither changes nor perishes. True love consists in transferring itself from the body to the dweller within, and then necessarily realizing the oneness of all life inhabiting numberless bodies. You seem to have got the truth for the moment. Let it abide forever.[4]

25

Careers of Famous People Influenced by Reincarnation

Human genius in a lightning flash of recollection can discover the laws involved in producing the universe, because it was present when those laws were established. I am certain I have been here a thousand times before, and I hope to return a thousand times more. Man is the dialogue between nature and God. On other planets this dialogue will doubtless be of a higher and profounder character. What is lacking is Self-Knowledge. After that the rest will follow.

GOETHE, *Conversations with Johannes Falk*

In the present chapter our attention focuses on individuals whose careers were not only influenced by the philosophy of rebirth, but who in turn influenced society as a whole, or one or more of its cultural expressions.

TRANSFORMATIONS IN TWENTIETH-CENTURY LIFE

HENRY FORD AND THE AUTOMOBILE ERA

A radio interview at the American University in Washington, D.C., brought one of the writers to that city in the spring of 1980. Passing by the Smithsonian Institution, she stopped in to see their new exhibit on the Model T Ford. It disclosed that Ford had built his first motor vehicle in

1896 when he was thirty-three years old, that the automobile era which
changed the whole of Western society opened in 1900, and that on October
1, 1908, Ford introduced his first Model T. The foregoing time schedule is
pertinent when reading the selections that follow from two interviews with
Ford. Therein we learn that he was twenty-six when he first discovered
reincarnation, and what effect this had on his overall career. The first
interview appeared in the Hearst newspapers for April 27 and 28, 1938.

> When I was a young man, I, like so many others, was bewildered. I
> found myself asking the question, "What are we here for?" I found no
> answer. Without some answer to that question life is empty, useless. Then
> one day a friend handed me a book. . . . That little book gave me the
> answer I was seeking. It changed my whole life. From emptiness and
> uselessness, it changed my outlook upon life to purpose and meaning. I
> believe that we are here now for a reason and will come back again. . . . Of
> this I am sure . . . that we are here for a purpose. And that we go on. Mind
> and memory—they are the eternals.[1]

The second interview appeared ten years earlier in the *San Francisco
Examiner*.

> I adopted the theory of Reincarnation when I was twenty-six. . . . Reli-
> gion offered nothing to the point. . . . Even work could not give me com-
> plete satisfaction. Work is futile if we cannot utilize the experience we
> collect in one life in the next. When I discovered Reincarnation it was as if I
> had found a universal plan. I realized that there was a chance to work out
> my ideas. Time was no longer limited. I was no longer a slave to the hands
> of the clock. . . . Genius is experience. Some seem to think that it is a gift
> or talent, but it is the fruit of long experience in many lives. Some are older
> souls than others, and so they know more. . . .
> The discovery of Reincarnation put my mind at ease. . . . If you preserve
> a record of this conversation, write it so that it puts people's minds at ease. I
> would like to communicate to others the calmness that the long view of life
> gives to us" [August 28, 1928].

ERNEST THOMPSON SETON—FOUNDER OF THE BOY SCOUTS OF AMERICA

Since the inception of the movement, there have been millions of Boy
Scouts, many of whom grew up to hold responsible positions as leaders in
our society. We wonder how many of them were aware of the *real story*
that led to the founding of the organization in this country and the part
reincarnation played therein, as we shall see.

In addition to his work with the Scouts, Seton wrote and exquisitely illustrated some forty books on nature. Creatively active into his late eighties, he was on the eve of a ten-thousand-mile lecture tour when he died at Seton Village in New Mexico. At the time he was characterized by *Time* magazine as "a man who, in an age of sweeping mechanization, had loved the natural earth, its seasons and its creatures with rare intensity and an unusual power to communicate his vision to others" (November 4, 1946). His daughter is the novelist Anya Seton.

Seton did much for the American Indian, and together with his wife Julia Seton—an authority on Indian life—wrote the small volume *The Gospel of the Redman.* She tells in the foreword of a crucial event that occurred in the life of Seton five years before he founded the Boy Scouts of America in 1910. She refers to him in the story that follows as "the Chief," a name by which he became known around the world. The title came into public use only after Seton headed the Boy Scouts, yet it is significant to the story his wife tells of this earlier time in his life.

"In March, 1905, we were in Los Angeles on a lecture tour. The morning after the lecture, we were met at the Van Nuys Hotel by some Eastern friends who, addressing the Chief, said: 'We have a message for you. There is a strange woman in the Hills who wishes to see you.' Accordingly, we took the tram to the end of the track, then set out on foot to climb what, I think, are now called the Beverly Hills. On the green slope higher up was a small white cottage; in front of this, a woman dressed like a farmer's wife. . . .

"She was introduced to us as a Mahatma from India, although born in Iowa. She had left her home as a small child, had spent many years studying under the Great Masters, and was now back on a mission to America. She was a strange-looking person. We could not tell whether she was thirty or a hundred and thirty years old. . . . Her eyes had the faraway veiled look of a mystic. Her talk was commonplace as she served coffee and cakes. We wondered why she had sent the summons. Finally, after an hour, we rose to leave.

"Then, suddenly, she turned on the Chief with a total change of look and demeanor. Her eyes blazed as she said, in tones of authority: '*Don't you know who you are?*' We were all shocked into silence as she continued: 'You are a Red Indian Chief, reincarnated to give the message of the Redman to the White race, so much in need of it. Why don't you get busy? Why don't you set about your job?'

"The Chief was moved like one conscience-stricken. He talked not at all on the road back, and the incident was not mentioned for long after.

But I know that the strange woman had focussed his thoughts on the mission he had been vaguely working on for some years. He has never since ceased to concentrate on what she had termed 'his job.' "[2]

LINDBERGH'S MYSTICAL FLIGHT ACROSS THE ATLANTIC

When Charles Lindbergh began his epic journey spanning two continents and opened the era of international air travel fifty years ago, he had no inkling he was on the eve of an occult adventure that would not only transform his own thinking but ensure the success of his venture. The public was unaware of this until the publication in 1956 of *The Spirit of St. Louis.*

When Lindbergh's plane skimmed the runway at Roosevelt Field, he was an agnostic and an atheist. If, in those days, there had been a Chapel of the Sky at the airport, he would not have entered to pray for success. His views were solidly based on the scientific revelations of his time. If his voyage ended in a watery grave, that would be the final chapter in his life. In his *Autobiography of Values,* he wrote shortly before he died, "In Missouri, at age twenty I was a disciple of the rising deity of Science, prepared to make daily sacrifices toward a mechanistic future that seemed to hold great benefits for men."[3]

Now, during the night and day preceding the Atlantic flight, Lindbergh slept hardly at all. Consequently, keeping keenly awake for the thirty-four-hour trip was a superhuman feat. In fact, he informs the reader *that he did go to sleep for long periods on that flight.* Why did his plane not plunge into the ocean?

A strange dissociation of states of consciousness took place within him. First, a separation was observed to take place between mind and body— aspects of himself he usually regarded as indivisible. Overwhelmed with drowsiness, the senses and organs sought sleep, though obviously it meant certain death. But the mind entity, standing "apart," held firm. In turn, the mind became unable to preserve wakefulness, and gave way to a transcendent power Lindbergh never suspected was within him. Finally, in mid ocean, the conscious mind fell fast asleep, and this third element, this new "extraordinary mind," which at first he feared to trust, now directed the flight. Here, in brief, is what he says occurred.

In the eighteenth hour of the journey, he felt himself as "an awareness spreading through space, over the earth and into the heavens, unhampered by time or substance." There was no weight to his body, no hardness to the stick in his hands. The fuselage behind became crowded with ghostly human presences, transparent, riding weightless with him in the plane. No surprise is experienced at their arrival, and without turning his head he sees them all, for his skull has become "one great eye, seeing everywhere at once." They seem able to disappear or show themselves at will, to pass through the walls of the plane as though no walls existed. Sometimes voices from afar off resound in the plane, familiar voices, advising him on his flight, encouraging him, conveying messages unattainable in normal life.

What connection exists between all these "spirits" and himself? It is more like a reunion of friends after years of separation, "as though I've known all of them before in some past incarnation." "Perhaps," he said, "they are the products of the experience of ages, dwellers of a realm presently closed to the people of our world." He feels himself in a transitional state between earthly life and a vaster region beyond, as if caught in the magnetic field between two planets and propelled by forces he cannot control, "representing powers incomparably stronger than I've ever known." Only when his *conscious* direction of the plane's course seems imperative does he find himself momentarily wakened, to be soon followed by these long, strange interludes of "sleep" with eyes wide open.

Values are changing within his consciousness. For twenty-five years, it has been imprisoned in walls of bone, and he had not recognized the endlessness of life, the immortal existence that lies outside. Is he already "dead" and about to join these "phantoms"? Death ceases to be the final end he thought it was. Simultaneously, he lives in the past, the present, and the future. Around him are "old associations, bygone friendships, voices from ancestrally distant times." Yes, he is flying in a plane over the Atlantic, but he is also living in ages long past.[4]

Owing to dense clouds, Lindbergh was flying blind much of the time. His plane was equipped with only primitive navigational instruments compared with what fliers have today. Yet, when land was finally spotted, he was astounded that he was only a few miles off course! His celestial guides—these possible friends from previous incarnations, now advanced beyond our realm—had certainly not misled him. We can understand now, why in 1936 he modestly titled his first book on the flight *We*.

*

In *Autobiography of Values*—Lindbergh's last testament—he included thoughts on his reincarnational philosophy. At one point, he told of a brief furlough he had on a Pacific island during World War II, after dangerous combat flight missions nearly took his life. The thoughts that follow occurred while he was lying in a mountain pool and felt no need for any object made by man.

"No luxury could have added to the peace, the beauty, the contentment I experienced. There, in that pool, was the essential 'I,' escaped from the outer framework of my life as the Buddhist's soul must escape the body between its incarnations. Does the soul look back upon its body as I looked back upon my fighting plane, as an outer shell, as a convenient tool for material accomplishments?" He wonders about what power an individual life can exercise to so "manipulate his life stream to revolutionize his race or temperament" in future lives and how "he can shape successive incarnations as a sculptor shapes his clay." Excesses should be avoided, he observed, for in that next life he may wish to do differently. Later, in speaking of human awareness, he remarks that "intuition tells us it will continue to evolve," for its potentialities are unconfined. "The farther we penetrate the unknown, the vaster and more marvelous it becomes."[5]

METAMORPHIC CHANGES IN MUSIC

RICHARD WAGNER

Wagner's interest in reincarnation began when he was first exposed to Oriental philosophy as a young man in his twenties. At this time, he lived with his brother-in-law, Herman Brockhaus, a Sanskrit teacher and scholar. Later, in 1855, he was to write to his friend Mathilde Wesendonck, advising her to procure the Indian Legends edited by Holtzmann. "All are beautiful, but if you wish to find out my religion, read *Usinar*. How shamed stands our whole culture by these purest revelations of the noblest humanism in the ancient East!"[6] In 1857 he confided to her that he had "unconsciously become a Buddhist."[7] His love for Buddhism was also evoked by his enthusiastic study of Schopenhauer, and he was inspired to compose a reincarnation opera, *Die Sieger (The Victors)*, based on a Buddhist tale. Granville Pyne, a Wagnerian specialist and chairman of the Wagner Society in England, wrote regarding *Die Sieger,* "Wagner found great underlying beauty in this material and saw the possibility of dealing with reincarnation through the special techniques of music-drama, in which the music could describe the past while the words spoke of the present. He thought that this greatly influenced his subsequent development."[8]

Wagner wrote, concerning this opera, "To the mental eye of Buddha the past life of any being he meets is like an open book. . . . The simple story [of *Die Sieger*] assumed significance by having the previous life of the leading characters merge into the present existence by means of an accompanying musical reminiscence. Having immediately realized how to present clearly this double life through simultaneously sounding music, I applied myself to the execution of the poem with particular devotion."[9] Pyne adds that "*The Victors* continued to haunt Wagner's imagination for twenty years, but it never came to fruition. The emotional and metaphysical impulse aroused in Wagner by *The Victors* was discharged in *Tristan and Isolde,* and the rest of this thought on the subject found a natural outlet in his last work, *Parsifal.* . . . One thing is certain: Buddhism laid a hand on the volcanic genius and tempestuous personality of Richard Wagner, whereby his works are different from what they otherwise would have been."[10]

In a letter to Mathilde Wesendonck, the inspirer of *Tristan and Isolde,* Wagner wrote, "In contrast to reincarnation and karma all other views appear petty and narrow."[11] In another letter he revealed to her how this philosophy gave him comfort when viewing the disparities of development among human beings.

> A prose translation of the four operas, *Hollander, Tannhauser, Lohengrin,* and *Tristan,* is soon to be issued. I have just gone through these translations and in so doing I was obliged to recall clearly to mind all the details of my poems. Yesterday *Lohengrin* touched me very much, and I cannot but hold it to be the most tragic poem of all, since only an immensely wide outlook upon life can provide a reconciliation between Lohengrin and Elsa.
>
> Only the profoundly conceived idea of Reincarnation could give me any consolation, since that belief shows how all at last can reach complete redemption. According to the beautiful Buddhist belief, the spotless purity of Lohengrin finds a simple explanation in the fact that he is the continuation of Parsifal, who had to fight for his purity. Even so Elsa in her rebirth would reach the height of Lohengrin. Thus all the terrible tragedy of life is seen to be nothing but the sense of Separateness in Time and Space.[12]

Higher on the scale of development than a Lohengrin or a Parsifal would be humanity's Great Teachers. Of them, Wagner wrote to August Roeckel in 1855: "From all time the minds that have attained to a clear perception, have turned to the minds of the multitude still in bondage and, having compassion on them, have sought a means of communication with them. Foremost among these enlightened spirits have been the founders of religions. Certainly the Indian Prince Buddha spoke the language which most nearly gives expression to that lofty enlightenment. . . . If we are to speak of this highest perception in terms understood by the people it can only be done under the form of pure and primitive Buddhist teaching. Especially important is the doctrine of the transmigration of souls as the basis of a truly human life.''[13]

Wagner's last opera *Parsifal* would indicate that in the end it was the Christian vision, as presently taught, that predominated in his philosophy. This may be, but it still included Buddhist teaching, and the composer held firm to his reincarnational outlook. As already mentioned, Wagner's uncompleted Buddhist opera, *Die Sieger,* found an outlet in *Parsifal.* Thus certain elements from Buddha's life were transposed, such as the well-known episode in which a swan is shot by Buddha's cousin. The dance of sexual enticement of the flower maidens in Act II of *Parsifal* comes straight from The Dance of Temptation scene when Buddha on the night of his enlightenment fought off the hosts of Mara. Also, the evil magician Klingsor, hurling at Parsifal a spear that remains suspended in the air, is from the old Buddhist tales, where Mara, the tempter, does the same thing.

As to reincarnation and karma, in Act I the knight Gurnemanz sings about Kundry, the only woman character, "Here she lives today—perhaps anew to suffer penance for debts incurred in former life, for which forgiveness still is due." Kundry is told in Act II, "You were Herodias—and what else? Gundryggia there Kundry here." Herodias, it will be recalled, was the wife of Herod, and according to the Gospels, she caused the beheading of John the Baptist. According to the opera, she also mocked Christ on the cross and was condemned to a tormented existence for centuries. "Now I try," says Kundry, "from world to world to find Him again."

Here the thought is that even the most miserable and degraded of human beings has other chances in this and future lives to become redeemed.

GUSTAV MAHLER

Until his death in 1911, Mahler received little attention as a composer. It was as a conductor that he was renowned in Europe and later in America. His symphonies and other compositions were in advance of their time and were received with puzzlement rather than acclaim. He prophesied "my time will come," and that it has. He is now universally regarded as a great master.

In a biography of the composer by his close friend Richard Specht, the latter records a conversation with Mahler in Hamburg in 1895.[14] Mahler said with great conviction: "We all return; it is this certainty that gives meaning to life and it does not make the slightest difference whether or not in a later incarnation we remember the former life. What counts is not the individual and his comfort, but the great aspiration to the perfect and the pure which goes on in each incarnation."

In this same year, Mahler began his third symphony. Although his earlier symphonies are tragic in character and disclose bitter disillusionment with life, the third was titled "The Joyful Knowledge," and according to the noted Mahler authority Deryck Cook indicated "a new-found optimism, or rather a kind of mystical revelation of the validity and purpose of existence." The symphony depicts the reincarnation of life through the kingdoms and beyond.

Cook quotes a letter in which Mahler states that he wanted to express in the work an evolutionary development of nature that hides "within itself everything that is frightful, great, and also lovely." "Of course no one ever understands this," he added. "It always strikes me as odd that most people when they speak of 'nature' think only of flowers, little birds, and woodsy smells. No one knows the god Dionysus, the great Pan. There now! You have a sort of program—that is, a sample of how I make music. Everywhere and always, it is only the voice of nature!" The vast first movement represented "nature in its totality . . . awakened from fathomless silence that it may ring and resound." The subsequent movements portray the stages of reincarnational ascension from vegetable and animal through mankind, back to the omniscient, omnipotent Divine Source.[15]

It was another reincarnationist, the distinguished conductor Dr. Bruno Walter[16]—a protegé and intimate friend of Mahler—who was the first to appreciate the latter's music, and by frequently programming it, eventually convinced the musical world of Mahler's true stature.

JEAN SIBELIUS

On the occasion of Sibelius's ninetieth birthday, the music critic for the *New York Times* wrote,

> The interrelationship between life and art is one of Sibelius' chief con cerns. . . . Sibelius' identification with the fields, the woods, the sea and the sky is so profound that it has always permeated his music. . . . As a boy, Sibelius wandered in the wilderness of his native province of Häme. Birds always fascinated him. "Millions of years ago, in my previous incarnations," he once told Jalas [his son-in-law], "I must have been related to swans or wild geese, because I can still feel that affinity" [December 4, 1955].

A friend and neighbor of the Sibelius family, Mrs. Ida Sohlman (who lived in New York in the 1960s), informed one of the writers that Sibelius spoke openly with intimate associates of his conviction in reincarnation and also of his previous lives.

Independent confirmation of this came in January 1982, in a chance meeting with Harrio Kallio in Santa Barbara, California. Kallio teaches in the schools there, and we met him at the Institute of World Culture with which he is actively associated. He told of spending some time in Finland and of a special visit made to the Sibelius family and to Yryo Paloheimo, an archaeologist who lived next door. He learned from the latter that the composer and the circle of artists surrounding him, were much involved in the study of theosophy. As we indicated in the Harvard talk (chapter 3), reincarnational ideas permeate theosophical philosophy.

INFLUENCES IN THE WORLD OF LITERATURE

JAMES JOYCE AND OUR ULYSSIAN JOURNEY

The works of Joyce, however distasteful to some, have become classics, influencing several generations of writers. It's estimated that thirty-five to forty doctoral dissertations are written on Joyce in America every year, and a bibliography of Joyce studies published in 1975 lists 8,000 items ("After Joyce, There's No World Without Joyce," *New York Times*, January 31, 1982).

On the occasion of the centennial of his birth, some 550 scholars assembled in Dublin for the eighth international James Joyce symposium. Under the headline "Happy Birthday: Dublin Jumps for Joyce," *Time* wrote, "In Dublin's fair city, a new plaque adorns a dingy, red brick house at 52 Upper Clanbrassil Street. It identifies the birthplace of someone who never lived and who, as long as there are readers will never die. . . . [The plaque reads] Here in Joyce's imagination was born in May, 1866, Leopold Bloom—citizen, husband, father, wanderer, reincarnation of Ulysses" (July 12, 1982).

Speaking of Joyce's exploration of the soul's underworld in *Ulysses*, the Irish author, George Russell, wrote, "The great deeps in us all must be dredged before our natures can truly be purified. . . . If Joyce would write a Purgatorio and a Paradiso to the Inferno which is his *Ulysses*, there would be one of the greatest works in literature."[17]

Ulysses is a formidable book to read without clues as to its inner

significances. The first of many volumes to attempt this was one prepared
in Paris with Joyce's constant help. It is Stuart Gilbert's noted *James
Joyce's Ulysses*. In the section amusingly headed "MET-HIM-PIKE-
HOSES," Gilbert writes,

> In the first episode of Mr. Bloom's day ("Calypso") several themes are
> stated which will recur frequently throughout Ulysses, and it is characteristic
> of the Joycean method that one of the most important of these leitmotifs
> should be presented in a casual manner and a ludicrous context. Mrs. Bloom
> has been reading in bed *Ruby: The Pride of the Ring*. . . . She asks her
> husband what that word in the book means—"met him pike hoses." He
> leaned downward and read near her polished thumbnail. "Metempsychosis?"
> . . . Mr. Bloom explains. "Some people believe that we go on living in
> another body after death, that we lived before. They call it reincarnation.
> That we all lived before on the earth thousands of years ago or on some
> other planet. They say we have forgotten it. Some say they remember their
> past lives."

Gilbert quotes several more selections on rebirth and comments: "The
passages indicate the persistence of the idea, or, rather, word 'metempsychosis,' in Mr. Bloom's memory." "But," adds Gilbert, "it is not
only as one of Mr. Bloom's possessions that the doctrine of reincarnation
is mentioned in *Ulysses*. Allusions, direct or indirect, to it are frequent,
and it is, in fact, one of the directive themes of the work. . . . References
to the eternal recurrence of personalities and things abound in *Ulysses* and
many of the obscurer passages can be readily understood if this fact be
borne in mind."[18]

Gilbert traces the source of Joyce's interest in reincarnation to contact
with theosophy and the Irish theosophists.[19] Quoting from the preface:
"When we chanced to be discussing Mme. Blavatsky's entertaining *Isis
Unveiled*, Joyce asked me if I had read any of Sinnett's work. (A. P.
Sinnett, a cultured and intelligent man, was a member of Mme. Blavatsky's
circle in India, and her biographer.) Naturally I took the hint and procured
his [volumes on theosophy] *Esoteric Buddhism* and *Growth of the Soul*,
well-written books from which Joyce certainly derived some of his
material."[20]

The reincarnation theme abounds in Joyce's other works. In *Finnegans
Wake*, writes the American poet Eugene Jolas, Joyce has "painted the
rotations of the wheel of life. He has made a hero out of Time: incessant
creation and return. He rebuilt the city across the ages in Finn's multiple
metamorphoses."[21] In James Atherton's *The Books of the Wake*, the
author writes that Joyce "believed that rebirth was the recompense for

death; not the result of ignorance and unsatisfied desire, and the cause of sorrow."[22]

Joyce's *A Portrait of the Artist as a Young Man*—which the *New York Times* reports (December 26, 1982) has sold over 23 million copies—ends with these stirring words, as the young hero Stephen Dedalus ventures forth into the world.

> Welcome, O life! I go to encounter for the millionth time the reality of experience and to forge in the smithy of my soul the uncreated conscience of my race. . . .
> Old father, old artificer, stand me now and ever in good stead.[23]

WILLIAM BUTLER YEATS—"POET OF THE CENTURY"

Since 1923, when Yeats received the Nobel Prize for literature, an incredible number of books have been published on this "poet of the century," as many regard him.

A *Newsweek* reviewer of Yeats's *Collected Poems* reports that his "perception of reincarnation did not come in intuitive flashes, but was the result of study and reflection. . . . As a youth, he was fascinated by the Russian theosophist Madame Blavatsky, and he went on to explore other aspects of Eastern mysticism."[24]

Tracing Yeats's use of reincarnation in his writings, Professor Richard Ellmann (the famed biographer of James Joyce) reports in *The Identity of Yeats:* The many-life theme pervades the poem "Kanva on Himself," and speaks out against fearing death, for "death cometh with the next-life key." In another poem, "An Image from a Past Life," a note by Yeats explains that the verses are based on the idea that our lives are haunted by memories of past incarnations.[25]

In *Later Phase in the Development of W. B. Yeats,* Shankar Mokashi-Punekar remarks that a comparison of the chapter on the after-death states "in Blavatsky's *Key to Theosophy* with Yeats' 'A Soul in Judgment,' would convince even a casual reader that Yeats was indeed continuing the same wisdom. . . . How much Yeats owes to the popular texts of Theosophy can hardly be missed by an unprejudiced observer."[26]

Yeats's last poem, "Under Ben Bulben," written three months before his death, gave instructions for his burial. One stanza reads:

> Many times man lives and dies
> Between his two eternities,
> That of race and that of soul,

TRANSFORMATION OF LIFE AND SOCIETY

And ancient Ireland knew it all.
Whether man die in his bed
Or the rifle knocks him dead,
A brief parting from those dear
Is the worst man has to fear.
Though grave-diggers' toil is long,
Sharp their spades, their muscles strong,
They but thrust their buried men
Back in the human mind again.[27]

THREE CELEBRATED ARTISTS

PAUL GAUGUIN

In 1898, Gauguin finished a large picture titled *Whence Do We Come, What Are We, Where Do We Go?* In a book he was then writing, he opened with the same questions and took considerable pains to provide answers. The work appeared posthumously as *Modern Thought and Catholicism*, from which we will be quoting.

An art critic, the Reverend Thomas Buser, observes in "Gauguin's Religion" in the *Art Journal* of Summer 1968 that "Gauguin was by no means a creative or a systematic theologian," but that "nevertheless his religious belief went beyond the ordinary anticlericalism and apologists of his time. His faith was easily more mystical than that prevalent in the Church at the time." Where did he derive it? "Quite simply," the priest answers, "Gauguin seems to have been enamored by theosophy. . . . The human soul, in Gauguin's theosophy, is destined to metempsychosis," and fits into a definite framework of evolution.

Here is how Gauguin explained reincarnation and the journey of the soul in *Modern Thought and Catholicism*, written during his years in Tahiti, where the most creative of his artworks were produced. The soul

constitutes the generating center of its organism, the pivot around which everything gravitates. . . . It is the soul which has formed its organism; it is the soul which has produced the evolution of living organisms constituting species. . . . The materialists smile when one speaks to them of an embodied or disembodied soul, saying that no one has ever been able to see one of them with a magnifying-glass or the naked eye, forgetting that no one has ever been able to see an atom of air or of matter, however much it may be volatilized. . . .

The soul, residing temporarily in a special organism, develops therein its animal faculties . . . and when this special organism breaks up, inasmuch as the soul survives, it becomes a germ [which is] qualified from metamorphosis to metamorphosis to ascend to a general life.

Thus, says Gauguin, "the idea of metempsychosis, recognized in the Hindu religion, and which Pythagoras, deriving it from the Hindus, taught in Greece," contains within it "the principle of graduated ascension."

Gauguin thought that "the parable of Jacob's ladder extending from earth to heaven, which the angels of God ascend and descend by steps," resembles the process of reincarnation. Through this means there is a gradual ascent "from the lowest to the highest life," during which the entity is "degraded or elevated according to merit or demerit."

"God as a symbol of the pure eternal spirit is the principle of all harmonies, the end to be attained, as represented by Christ, and before him by Buddha. All human beings will some day become Buddhas."[28]

KANDINSKY'S LEAP INTO ABSTRACTION

"Abstract art of one kind or another has changed the face of the modern world," writes the distinguished art critic Hilton Kramer in an article in the *New York Times* commemorating the centennial of one of abstract art's principal founders, Wassily Kandinsky.

In tracing Kandinsky's development, Kramer discusses the crucial period when the artist studied theosophy, enabling him "to make his revolutionary leap into abstraction. . . . Kandinsky needed a theoretical framework for carrying painting beyond the realm of representation. . . . With a mind like his—at once intellectual and mystical, seeking 'laws' and principles before committing itself to practice—the idea must always precede its realization." His "commitment to theosophy guaranteed—to him, at least— that abstract art would attain a higher spiritual meaning" (December 18, 1966).

Three of the other principal founders of modern art, Mondrian, Paul Klee, and Malevitch, were also seriously interested in theosophy. These artists "sought through theosophy deeper and more universal values, meaning behind meaning, new dimensions to understanding."[29]

What has this to do with reincarnation as related to abstract or nonrepre sentational art as conceived by its founders? Reincarnation implies that material forms and appearances are impermanent, ephemeral, constantly transformed, and when no longer usable, replaced by other forms or bodies. Hence the instinctive resort of these artists to symbolic devices and their disdain for copying fixed models. It was the intangible, but immortal, spirit behind forms that drew their interest.

The ultimate goal was to reach the "higher nirvanic world," and Kandinsky believed that many cycles of evolution and many incarnations would be required to reach this consummation.[30]

MONDRIAN "PERFECTED A VISION"

The most highly regarded of the founders of abstract art today is the Dutch artist Piet Mondrian. Recently one of his paintings sold for over two million dollars, the highest ever paid for a work of modern art. In "Mondrian: He Perfected Not a Style but a Vision," an article that appeared in the *New York Times*, Hilton Kramer observes that his work has grown with the passage of time. One of the reasons for this is precisely the relation that obtains—and is seen to obtain—between his art and its metaphysical foundations.

> We do not feel, in the presence of a Mondrian, that we are being offered a "merely" esthetic delectation. We feel ourselves in the presence of a larger struggle—indeed, a larger world—in which mind grapples with eternal threats to its fragmentation and dissolution. . . . [Today, in art,] what were once problems of metaphysical debate and social redemption are reduced to problems of style and taste. Inevitably, the requisite tension—the inner drama of a protagonist perfecting not a style but a vision—is missing [February 24, 1974].

Art historian Robert Welsh devoted an article to the "metaphysical foundations" of Mondrian's work, titled "Mondrian and Theosophy." It was featured as the opening contribution in *Piet Mondrian Centennial Exhibition,* published by the Guggenheim Museum in New York in 1972, where the exhibition was held. Welsh explains that "the ideas relevant to [his] . . . discussion were proliferated in numerous texts, lectures, and discussions undertaken by Madame Blavatsky and her followers. . . . However, for the sake of convenience, and because its role as a source for other quotations often has been overlooked, her monumental, two volume *Isis Unveiled* of 1877 will provide the exclusive text upon which our discussion is based," a Dutch translation of *Isis* having been available to Mondrian.

In relating several of Mondrian's paintings to the theosophical view of evolutionary growth through reincarnation, Welsh points particularly to one called *Metamorphosis,* and another, the celebrated triptych *Evolution.* He comments:

Evolution is no less than the basic tenet in the cosmological system predicated by Madame Blavatsky and, as such, replaces the Christian story of Creation as an explanation for how the world functions. This cosmology is analogous to Hindu and other mythologies which stress a perpetual cosmic cycle of creation, death and regeneration.

It also has much in common with the Darwinian scientific theory of evolution. Darwin's only essential mistake, in Blavatsky's opinion, was to substitute matter for spirit as the motivating force in the universe. In her own world view, matter, though constituting a necessary vehicle through which the world of spirit was to be approached, clearly stands second in importance to the latter phenomenon. . . .

This view of evolution, continues Welsh, "pervades the art theoretical writings of Mondrian." In his *Sketchbooks* of 1912–1914 "he specifically alludes to the Theosophical Doctrine of Evolution as a determining factor in the history of art." "In short," adds Welsh, "Mondrian could not have chosen as the theme of his monumental triptych a doctrine which was more central to Theosophic teaching than this."

In assessing his own achievements, Mondrian wrote in a letter to his friend Michel Seuphor, "It is in my work that I am something, but compared to the Great Initiates, I am nothing."[31] What did he mean by "the Great Initiates"? He referred to the flower of humankind, the perfected souls such as Christ and Buddha, who became such through many cycles of rebirth. But as to the expression itself, Mondrian likely borrowed it from a book widely influential among artists, composers, and writers bearing that title. Published in 1889, the volume went through 220 editions in French alone and was translated into a number of European languages. The English edition is still in print.

The author, Edouard Schuré, was a noted journalist and music critic, a friend of Wagner, Nietzsche, and other celebrities of the time. His name is frequently mentioned in works on the history of modern art. Schuré wrote *The Great Initiates* under the influence of a vision he experienced while residing in Florence: "In a flash I saw the Light that flows from one mighty founder of religion to another. These Great Initiates, those mighty figures whom we call Rama, Krishna, Hermes, Moses, Orpheus, Pythagoras, Plato, and Jesus, appeared before me in a homogeneous group." They all seemed to belong to One Fraternity.[32]

As to the reincarnational perspective, Schuré wrote these words, pondered over by innumerable artists and writers since they were written almost a hundred years ago.

The doctrine of the ascensional life of the soul through series of existences is the common feature of esoteric traditions and the crown of theosophy. I will add that it is of the utmost importance to us. For the person of the present day rejects with equal scorn the abstract and vague immortality of philosophy and the childish heaven of an infant religion. And yet he abhors the dryness of nothingness of materialism. Unconsciously he aspires to the consciousness of an *organic* immortality responding at once to the demands of his reason and the indestructible needs of his soul. . . .

Though each life has its own law and special destiny, the succession of incarnations is controlled by a general law, which might be called the repercussion of lives. "There is not a word or action which has not its echo in eternity," says a proverb. According to esoteric doctrine, this proverb is literally applied from one life to another.[33]

Horizons Far and Horizons Near

Births have brought us richness and variety,
And other births will bring us richness and variety. . . .
This day before dawn I ascended a hill and looked at the crowded heaven.
And I said to my spirit, When we become enfolders of those orbs, and the
  pleasure and knowledge of everything in them, shall we be filled and
  satisfied then?
And my spirit said, No, we but level that lift to pass and continue beyond.

WALT WHITMAN, *Leaves of Grass*

A horizon is a powerfully suggestive symbol, because it never ends. As we approach it, it ever recedes, beckoning us on and on. In regard to knowledge and goals, we know it represents the truth that there is always more to learn, to achieve, to encompass.

The final chapter of our book is about horizons, horizons close at hand and horizons that may lie far, far beyond, involving even the birth and rebirth of the universe as a whole, and of planets and solar systems as well. Reincarnational thinking invites such considerations. Surprisingly, the scientific community, particularly the astronomers and astrophysicists, often think in such terms.

REBIRTH OF THE UNIVERSE

"Two rival theories about the ultimate fate of the universe are running neck and neck just now," writes *New York Times* science essayist Malcolm W. Browne. "The excitement of the race has spurred astronomers, mathematicians, particle physicists, chemists and theorists to search their specialties for clues that might contribute something to the outcome." The question, he continues, is whether the universe is "open" and will continue forever its present apparent expansion, or whether it is "closed," destined one day to stop expanding and fall back on itself, to be then reborn. If the universe is "open" and ever expanding, then, of course, the energy needed to sustain life would eventually become so dispersed as to be unusable, and everything would die.

"Some scientists," Browne says, "develop personal preferences for one kind of *Götterdämmerung* or another. There are those who would prefer an open, one-shot universe, considering it to be consistent with biblical scripture. Some others would prefer a closed, oscillating universe, esthetically akin to the Hindu wheel of death and rebirth" (February 10, 1981). They would thus be in accord with the universal law of cycles manifest everywhere in nature. The Oriental theory is well described by Blavatsky in *Isis Unveiled*.

> The esoteric doctrine teaches, like Buddhism and Brahmanism, and even the *Kabala,* that the one infinite and unknown Essence or God exists from all eternity, and in regular and harmonious successions is either passive or active. In the poetical phraseology of Manu [the ancient Hindu lawgiver] these conditions are called the "day" and the "night" of Brahma. Brahma is either "awake" or "asleep."
>
> Upon inaugurating an active period, an expansion of this Divine essence, *from within outwardly*, occurs in obedience to eternal and immutable law, and the phenomenal or visible universe is the ultimate result of the long chain of cosmical forces thus progressively set in motion. In like manner, when the passive condition is resumed, a contraction of the Divine essence takes place, and the previous work of creation is gradually and progressively undone. The visible universe becomes disintegrated, its material dispersed; and "darkness," solitary and alone, broods once more over the face of the "deep."
>
> To use a metaphor which will convey the idea still more clearly an outbreathing of the "unknown essence" produces the world and an inhalation causes it to disappear. *This process has been going on from all eternity, and our present universe is but one of an infinite series which had no beginning and will have no end.*[1]

Another analogy—one used by some of our leading astronomers—is that of the rhythmic beat of the heart. These scientists, writes *The New Yorker,* "are coming around to the view that the universe has a heartbeat. The cosmos expands and contracts much as a heart does, bringing to life a succession of universes with each lub-dub." The magazine comments: "We congratulate science on finally beginning to discover its true identity, as an agency for corroborating ancient wisdom. Long before our century, before the Christian era, and even before Homer, the people of India had arrived at [such a] cosmogony" (July 17, 1965).

REINCARNATION OF INDIVIDUAL STARS

This is a well-known law in stellar development. Stars have their birth, youth, maturity, death, and rebirth. The different stages of a star's growth can often be identified, and each stage has its name. The ceaseless rebirth of worlds was portrayed several years ago in the Planetarium in New York by means of a fascinating flashing light exhibit. *Science Digest* mentions that "astrophysicist William Fowler received the Nobel prize for his work on how dying stars explode as supernovas and spew newly synthesized elements, including carbon, oxygen, and iron, into space—material with which new solar systems capable of supporting life are formed. . . . 'It is precisely this knowledge that gives us confidence that Earthlike planets probably exist throughout the galaxy,' astronomer Dr. Robert Jastrow says" (January 1984).

Even in the last century astronomers were aware that worlds reincarnate and speculated as to the process, as this story from Dostoevsky's *The Brothers Karamazov* dramatically portrays in its conclusion.

"This legend is about Paradise. There was, they say, here on earth a thinker and philosopher. He rejected everything, 'laws, conscience, faith,' and above all, the future life. He died; he expected to go straight to darkness and death and he found a future life before him. He was astounded and indignant. 'This is against my principles!' he said. And he was punished for that . . . he was sentenced to walk a quadrillion kilometres in the dark . . . and when he had finished the quadrillion, the gates of heaven would be opened to him and he'll be forgiven. . . . Well, this man who was condemned to the quadrillion kilometres, stood still, looked round and lay down across the road. 'I won't go, I refuse on principle!' . . . He lay there almost a thousand years and then he got up and went on.

" 'What an ass!' cried Ivan, laughing nervously. . . . 'Does it make any difference whether he lies there forever or walks the quadrillion kilometres? It would take a billion years to walk it!'

" 'Much more than that. . . . But he got there long ago. . . .'

" 'What, he got there? But how did he get the billion years to do it?'

" 'Why, you keep thinking of our present earth! But our present earth may have been repeated a billion times. Why, it's become extinct, been frozen; cracked, broken to bits, disintegrated into its elements, again "the water above the firmament," then again a comet, again a sun, again from the sun it becomes earth—and the same sequence may have been repeated endlessly and exactly the same to every detail.' "[2]

*

Furious speculations in books and articles as to whether there is life in these other worlds seem unending. Professor Harlow Shapley, the famed director of the Harvard Observatory, believed that there are "ten billion planets suitable for organic life something like that on earth."[3] Another well-known astronomer, Dr. Ernest J. Öpik states, "Many planets may carry life on their surface. Even if there were only one inhabited system in every million, there would be 10,000 million million abodes of life in the universe. What a variety of forms and conditions this implies!"[4]

AN INTERVIEW WITH FOUR PRINCETON COSMOLOGISTS
The interview appeared in *Intellectual Digest* of June 1973, with this headline: "Four Princeton Scientists Fire a Starburst of Ideas About Ends, Beginnings, Transformations and Reincarnations: Cycle After Cycle, Not Only of Man but of the Universe Itself."

The interviewer, Florence Helitzer, opened with this introduction

> The language of modern physics is alluring. Such words as "birth," "death" and "rebirth" and phrases like "cycles of creation and destruction" constantly recur. These words have been encountered before in other contexts; in myth and fairy tale, in oriental religion and in the Bible, in literature and in philosophy. . . . In an attempt to find a bridge between past culture and current physics, now reaching into an immense universe, questions drawn from religion, mysticism and philosophy were put to four eminent cosmologists who teach and do research at Princeton University.

One of the scientists was Dr. John Wheeler, now director of the Center for Theoretical Physics at the prestigious astrophysics and space research center at the University of Texas (Austin). He is noted for his investigation of the "black holes" that result in space from the gravitational collapse or death of stars. Wheeler was a colleague of Niels Bohr and one of the first scientists to concentrate on nuclear fission. The interviewer said to him: "The end of the world is anticipated by the existence of the black hole, a star having undergone gravitational collapse. This phenomenon is an invisible omen of our future, you've said, because gravitational collapse is the ultimate destiny of the universe. But you have also suggested that this end will become a new beginning—that something else, something new and different, will be reborn from the ashes." Dr. Wheeler replied: "I am thinking of the oriental concepts of reincarnation and of cycle after cycle, not only of man, but of the universe itself."

One of the scientists interviewed, Jeremiah Ostriker, who recently won the American Astronomical Society's Warner Prize, stated, "There are a lot of similarities between the mystic's view of the world and Einstein's. I don't know whether it's coincidental that currently the best cosmology is a 'big bang' cosmology and that the best potential rival is a cyclic one, which is more like the Eastern view. I am intrigued. I suspect that I could learn a lot just from thinking and talking about it." Dr. Wheeler added, "One has to be very humble in the face of people who have dealt with these eternal issues over so many generations."

The other Princeton scientists interviewed agreed in principle with Dr. Wheeler's views. Several years later, the *New York Times* quoted one of them, Dr. Robert H. Dicke, as suggesting "a model of successive universes, reincarnating themselves in changing forms 'almost suggestive of Hindu beliefs' " (March 12, 1978).

It is immensely interesting that the black holes of space, "originally thought to be the most 'passive' objects in the universe now appear to be the most active." At an international symposium at Cornell University, Dr. Dennis Sciame of Oxford made the foregoing statement based on five years of analyzing their characteristics. He described this new concept as a "conceptual revolution," to which theorists "are still trying to adjust." Sciame and other scientists at the meeting considered the possibility that the black hole in its final stages radiates out again into space and starts a new cycle going (*New York Times,* October 12, 1980).

CAN THE INDIVIDUAL SOUL SURVIVE THE PERIODIC DEATH AND REBIRTH OF THE UNIVERSE?

Astronomer Ernest J. Öpik addresses this question in his widely commended book *The Oscillating Universe.*

"The whole cosmos is performing a giant oscillation. At present it expands, shot out of the chaos of the primeval focal point, and while in flight, sheltering the wondrous metamorphoses of life. After many thousands of millions of years, expansion will cease, and the world will collapse into its former focus, the primeval atom, where material individuality will melt and disappear; only to rebound and precipitate itself into new expansion, creating new worlds, with new metamorphoses and dreams.

"Material things are born, vanish, and are born again. This is the rhythm of the physical world. All that can be measured, weighed, and timed obeys the rhythm. Yet there is something in us which has neither measure, weight, nor time: our consciousness—the "I," individually different from, yet similar to other "I"'s. Is it not a droplet or atom of the Great Cosmic Consciousness? Does it upon death rejoin the Great Consciousness? . . . [Does it later] awaken elsewhere with the same feeling of identity and individuality? Being outside space and time, time intervals would not matter to it; when awakening somewhere after [these] great cosmic oscillations, would it not be filled with the same fresh sense of individuality that it has now . . .?

"Maybe this consciousness is only the superficies of subconscious depths reaching to the root of all things. Maybe there is analogy with chemical affinity, an element of consciousness (or soul) combining with a suitable organism." Dr. Öpik concludes by observing, "Only from such a standpoint would it not seem strange and believable that we exist."[5]

Turning to ancient wisdom, a correlative passage from *The Bhagavad-Gita* appropriately reads,

> All the worlds, and even the heavenly realm of Brahma, are subject to the laws of rebirth. [When a new world is born] day dawns, and all the beings that lay hidden asleep come forth and show themselves, mortally manifest. Night falls, and all are dissolved into the sleeping germ of life. Thus they are seen and appear unceasingly, dissolving with the dark, and with day returning back to the new birth, new death.
>
> But behind the manifest there is another Existence, which is eternal and changeless. *This is not dissolved in the general cosmic dissolution.* It has been called the unmanifest, the imperishable. To reach it is said to be the greatest of all achievements.[6]

Closely related to this discussion there is also the teaching of the causal body in Hinduism, which the research physicist and teacher Professor Roger S. Jones correlates with current scientific views in his remarkable book *Physics as Metaphor,* published in 1982 by the University of Minnesota Press. He writes: "Modern spacetime is very reminiscent of the causal body in the Hindu spiritual hierarchy. . . . The causal body includes all of what we today should call space and time, past, present, and future. It contains the historic record of all individuals and cultures. It holds the *akashic* record of all past incarnations and acts like a sort of cosmic mediator of past and future karma. . . . It has an organic, living quality, so that causal body rather than something like causal plane is a particularly apt term for it. The causal body permeates space and time and forms a continuum with all beings, creatures, and things. We all participate in the causal body at some subconscious or, better, superconscious level." It is not destroyed when the material world disintegrates.

THE HORIZON BEFORE US NOW

The prospect of some day being reborn in more advanced worlds than our own is viewed with impatience by some reincarnationists. They say, "Why not go there now?" The German philosopher Friedrich Von Schlegel gave the answer in his nineteenth-century work *The Philosophy of Life*.

> Inasmuch as the true Indian teaching of metempsychosis, as we now know it correctly from the sources, is too serious and solemn to find much credence and applause in our time, the attempt has been made recently to carry it entirely into the realm of romanticism and to paint the future life in glowing colors as a sort of astronomical excursion from one star to another. . . . Would it not be more advisable, and more appropriate to human intellect, if we would first turn our gaze upon ourselves and our present dwelling place, the earth, instead of at once disappearing into the starry skies? May we not find that which we seek so often in the distance far closer at hand?[7]

Matthew Arnold believed that there is no "disappearing into starry skies" until people have reached a certain stage of inner development. In the lines that follow from his poem "Empedocles on Etna," he movingly encapsulates the whole drama of human life as it exists today on planet earth, and tells why we must incarnate again on earth.

> And then we shall unwillingly return
> Back to this meadow of calamity,
> This uncongenial place, this human life;
> And in our individual human state
> Go through the sad probation all again,
> To see if we will poise our life at last,
> To see if we will now at last be true

To our own only true, deep-buried selves,
Being one with which we are one with the whole world;
Or whether we will once more fall away
Into some bondage of the flesh or mind,
Some slough of sense, or some fantastic maze
Forged by the imperious lonely thinking-power.[8]

William Blake portrays the same epic story in his poem *Vala, or The Four Zoas* (the lines are run together as if they were prose).

Man rises to the Sun, and to the Planets of the Night. He touches the remotest pole, and in the center weeps, that he should labor and sorrow, and learn and forget, and return to the dark valley whence he came, and begin his labor anew. In pain he sighs, in pain he labors in his universe. And in the cries of birth and in the groans of death his voice is heard throughout the Universe; wherever a grass grows, or a leaf buds, The Eternal Man is seen, is heard, is felt, and all his sorrows, till he reassumes his ancient bliss.[9]

One distinguished philosopher who has put together all these thoughts in inspiring perspective is Dr. S. Radhakrishnan. During the latter's lifetime, Professor Charles Moore spoke of him as "a versatile genius, universally recognized and acclaimed for his remarkable ability as teacher, lecturer, scholar, and administrator, as philosopher, statesman, and India's cultural ambassador throughout the East and West." Not only has "his absolute tolerance brought him recognition as the greatest living interpreter of Indian philosophy, religion, and culture, but also as an original and creative thinker of the first order."[10] He became the first Indian to hold a chair at Oxford University, where he was Spalding Professor of Eastern Religions and Ethics. In 1931 he was knighted by King George V. In 1959 he received the Goethe Plaquette, and later became president of India. We quote now from Radhakrishnan's *An Idealist View of Life,* written when he taught at Oxford.

*

"The way to realization is a slow one. Hindu and Buddhist thought, the Orphic mysteries, Plato and some forms of early Christianity maintain that it takes a long time for realizing the holy longing after the lost heaven. The Hindu holds that the goal of spiritual perfection is the crown of a long patient effort. Man grows through countless lives into his divine self-existence. Every life, every act, is a step which we may take either backward or forward. By one's thought, will and action one determines what one is yet to be. According to Plato, the wise man turns away from the world of the senses, and keeps his inward and spiritual eye ever directed to the world of the eternal idea, and if only the pursuit is maintained, the individual becomes freed from the bonds of sensualism.

"Our feet are set on the path of the higher life, though they wander uncertainly and the path is not seen clearly. There may be the attraction of the ideal but no assent of the whole nature of it. The utter self-giving which alone can achieve the end is not easy. But no effort is wasted. We are still far from realizing the implications of the spiritual dignity of human beings in matters of conduct, individual and social. . . . If only we can support this higher life, the long labor of the cosmic process will receive its crowning justification and the evolution of centuries unfold its profound significance.

"The world process reaches its consummation when every person knows himself to be the immortal spirit. Till this goal is reached, each saved individual is the center of the universal consciousness. To be saved is not to be moved from the world. Salvation is not escape from life. The individual works in the cosmic process no longer as an obscure and limited ego, but as a center of the divine or universal consciousness, embracing and transforming into harmony all individual manifestations. It is to live in the world with one's inward being profoundly modified. The soul takes possession of itself and cannot be shaken from its tranquillity by the attractions and attacks of the world.

"If the saved individuals escape literally from the cosmic process, the world would be forever unredeemed. It would be condemned to remain for all time the scene of unending strife and darkness. Mahayana Buddhism declares that Buddha standing on the threshold of Nirvana took the vow never to make the irrevocable crossing so long as there was a single undelivered being on earth. *The Bhagavata Purana* [a Hindu scripture] records the following prayer: 'I desire not the supreme state with all its eight perfections nor the release from rebirth; may I assume the sorrow of all creatures who suffer and enter into them so that they may be made free from grief.' This respect for the individual as individual is not the discovery of modern democracy."[11]

*

In the closing pages of this chapter, "Horizons Far and Horizons Near," we turn to some thoughts on the future of one who has been called a Confucius for the West, the Scottish philosopher W. Macneile Dixon. The selections are from his celebrated Gifford Lectures, "The Human Situation."

*

"Many things are hard to believe, and a future life, some say, is quite incredible, and the mere thought of it a sort of madness. But what hinders if we have already found a present? Well, I should myself put the matter rather differently. The present life is incredible, a future credible. To be alive, actually existing, to have emerged from darkness and silence, to be here today is certainly incredible. A future life would be a miracle, and you find it difficult to believe in miracles? I, on the contrary, find it easy. They are to be expected. The starry worlds in time and space, the pageant of life, the processes of growth and reproduction, the instincts of animals, the inventiveness of nature, they are all utterly unbelievable, miracles piled upon miracles. If there be a skeptical star I was born under it, yet I have lived all my days in complete astonishment.

"Our interest in the future, how strange it is if we can never hope to see the future. That interest rarely seems to desert us, and in itself appears inexplicable were we not possessed of an intuition which tells us that we shall have a part in it, that in some sense it already belongs to us, that we should bear it continually in mind, since it will be ours. So closely are all human ideals associated with futurity that, in the absence of the faith that man is an immortal being, it seems doubtful whether they could ever have come to birth. 'In the further depths of our being we are secretly conscious of our share in the inexhaustible spring of eternity, so that we can always hope to find life in it again.'

"If things as they are have not a feature in common with things as they will be, we have no basis for thought at all regarding that future. As Leibniz said, 'a leap from one state to another infinitely different state could not be natural!' The experiences of time and of our present condition could, one feels, only be valuable in an existence not wholly unlike it; and any doctrine which insists upon a totally dissimilar existence, an indescribable spiritual life as a sequel to the present, makes of the present an insoluble enigma." [Although the idea that human beings return to earth life] "has for Western thought a strangeness, it is in fact the most natural and easily imagined, since what has been can be again. This belief seems, indeed, to be in accordance with nature's own favorite way of thought, of which she so insistently reminds us, in her rhythms and recurrences, her cycles and revolving seasons.

"It is Plato's doctrine, and none more defensible, that the soul before it entered our world—the realm of Becoming—existed in the universe of Being. [When death comes it is released from] the region of time and space and returns to its former heavenly abode into communion with itself. Then after a season of quiet, of assimilation of its earthly experiences and memories, refreshed and invigorated, it is seized again by the desire for further trials of its strength, further knowledge of the universe, the companionship of former friends, by the desire to keep in step and on the march with the moving world. There it seeks out and once more animates a body, the medium of communication with its fellow travellers, and sails forth in that vessel upon a new venture in the ocean of Becoming.

"Our lives are part of the universe and will last as long, but we must wait for the secrets of the history to come. And before we can attain to that final harmony between the universe and ourselves, to which we look forward as the consummation of existence, how much we have to learn about both! Nor can any boundary be set, any 'Thus far and no farther' to the expansion of the mind.

"As to our true natures, of what in truth we are and are capable of becoming, to what heights in knowledge, wisdom, power, the soul can climb, of all this science and philosophy have so far hardly yet spoken. In our present life we have acquired at the most the alphabet of this knowledge. The philosophers of the future will, I think, allow to the self or soul its unique status, its standing as a factor, a primary factor and an organizing factor in the universal whole. Human beings may be more interesting and important than our modern teachers suppose, possibly even a star of some magnitude in the celestial universe.

"As for the universe, itself, the modes of existence and happiness of which it permits, its possibilities as an abode for progressive beings like ourselves, we know less than nothing, and no single life could teach us what they may be. Nor can any reason be advanced why we should not in the end become its masters, mold it to our hearts' desires, and make of it a home, the natural and happy estate of the immortal spirits to whom it indefeasibly belongs."[12]

Notes

PREFACE

1. David Lloyd George, *Lord Riddell's Intimate Diary of the Peace Conference and After*. London: Victor Gollancz, 1933, pp. 122–23.
2. *Journal of Nervous and Mental Disease*, May 1977, p. 308.
3. *Time*, April 7, 1980.
4. Charles Darwin, *The Life and Letters of Charles Darwin*, ed. Francis Darwin. New York: Appleton, 1887, I: 282.
5. Geddes MacGregor, *Reincarnation in Christianity*. Wheaton, Illinois: Quest Books, 1978, pp. 67–68.
6. Joseph Head and S. L. Cranston, *Reincarnation, the Phoenix Fire Mystery*. New York: Crown, 1977; 1984 (paper). See index under "Animals, can people return as."

1 THE CRY FOR MEANING

1. Henry Pickering, *The Ruins of Paestum, and Other Compositions in Verse*. Salem, Massachusetts: Cushing & Appleton, 1822, p. 63.
2. Corliss Lamont, *The Illusion of Immortality*. New York: Philosophical Library, 1959, p. 146 fn.
3. Viktor Frankl, *The Unheard Cry for Meaning*. New York: Simon & Schuster, 1978, pp. 20–21.
4. Erich Fromm, *Zen Buddhism and Psychoanalysis*. New York: Harper & Row, 1960, pp. 85–86.
5. George Gallup, Jr., *Adventures in Immortality*. New York: McGraw-Hill, 1982, p. 2.
6. W. Macneile Dixon, *The Human Situation*. London: Edward Arnold, 1937, pp. 425, 428.
7. *The New York Times*, June 13, 1972, obituary for Edmund Wilson.
8. Leo Tolstoy, *My Confessions*. New York: Thomas Crowell, 1887, pp. 28–30, 35.
9. W. Macneile Dixon, *The Human Situation*, p. 423.
10. *Manas* (Los Angeles), June 20, 1979, p. 2.
11. *The Voice of Universal Love* (Moscow) 1908, No. 40, p. 634.
12. Leo Tolstoy, *Diary of Leo Nickolaevich Tolstoy*, ed. V. G. Chertkov. Moscow: 1906, I: 17.
13. Corliss Lamont, *The Illusion of Immortality*, p. 22.
14. Gottfried Wilhelm von Leibniz, *Philosophische Schriften*, ed. Gerhardt, IV: 300.
15. Geddes MacGregor, *Reincarnation in Christianity*. Wheaton, Illinois: Quest Books, 1978, pp. 107–8.
16. M. K. Gandhi, *Gandhi's Letters to a Disciple*. New York: Harper, 1950, p. 87.
17. John Ellis McTaggart, *Human Immortality and Pre-Existence*. London: Edward Arnold, 1915, pp. 105–13.
18. G. Lowes Dickinson, *J. McT. E. McTaggart*. Cambridge: Cambridge University Press: 1931, p. 37.
19. *Sunrise* (Pasadena, California), August 1959, p. 333.

2 CURRENT WESTERN BELIEF IN MANY LIVES

1. *Puzzled People*. London: Victor Gollancz, 1948.

360

2. Geoffrey Gorer, *Exploring English Character*. London: Cresset Press, 1955, pp. 259–60, 262.
3. George Gallup, Jr., *Adventures in Immortality* (cited in chapter 1), pp. 192–93.
4. Ibid., pp. 137–38, 192–93.
5. U. S. Bureau of Census, *Statistical Abstract of the United States 1982–83*, 103rd edition, Washington, D.C., 1982, p. 30.
6. *Journal of Nervous and Mental Disease*, September 1977, p. 172.
7. Harold Loukes, *Teenage Religion*. London: SCM Press, 1961.
8. Michael Paternoster, "Reincarnation—a Christian Critique," *The Christian Parapsychologist* (London), September 1979.

3 LECTURE AT HARVARD UNIVERSITY

1. Geddes MacGregor, *Reincarnation in Christianity* (cited in chapter 1), p. 5.
2. C. G. Jung, *Dreams, Memories, Reflections*. New York: Pantheon, 1963, pp. 318–19, 332–33.
3. Carl Van Doren, *Benjamin Franklin*. New York: Viking, 1952, p. 123.
4. Benjamin Franklin, *The Papers of Benjamin Franklin*, ed. Leonard W. Labaree. New Haven, Connecticut: Yale University Press, I: 310. L. H. Butterfield, "B. Franklin's Epitaph," *New Colophon*, 1950, III: 9–30.
5. Benjamin Franklin, letter to George Whatley, May 23, 1785 from *The Works of Benjamin Franklin*, ed. Jared Sparks. Boston: 1856, X: 174.
6. Ralph Waldo Emerson, *The Journals of Ralph Waldo Emerson*. Boston: Houghton Mifflin, 1909, I: 320.
7. John McTaggart, *The Nature of Existence*. Cambridge: Cambridge University Press, 1927, II: 397.
8. G. Lowes Dickinson, *J. McT. E. McTaggart* (cited in chapter 1), p. 128.
9. Ibid., p. 122.
10. *Rubaiyat of Omar Khayyam*, trans. Edward Fitzgerald. New York: Heritage Press, 1946, quatrain 51.
11. Huston Smith, *The Religions of Man*. New York: Harper & Row, 1958, pp. 35–37.
12. "Aphorisms on Karma," *Path* magazine (New York), March 1893, pp. 366–69. Reprinted in booklet "Karma." Los Angeles: Theosophy Co. n.d.
13. William James, *Talks to Teachers on Psychology*. London and New York: Longmans Green, 1899, pp. 77–78.
14. John Hick, *Death and Eternal Life*. London: Collins, 1976, pp. 351–52; Harper & Row, 1980 (paper).
15. Ralph Waldo Emerson, *The Selected Writings of Ralph Waldo Emerson*, ed. Brooks Atkinson. New York: Modern Library, 1950, p. 342.
16. Ibid., pp. 187–88.
17. Ibid., p. 445.
18. Henry David Thoreau, *The Writings of Henry David Thoreau*. Cambridge, Massachusetts: Houghton Mifflin, 1894, XI: 215, 253.
19. Ibid., p. 110.
20. Henry David Thoreau, *Walden and Other Writings*. New York: Modern Library, 1950, p. 122.
21. J. Paul Williams, "Belief in a Future Life," *Yale Review*, Spring 1945.
22. *Science Digest*, July 1982.
23. *Saturday Evening Post*, May 26, 1951.
24. Ernest Hemingway, *A Farewell to Arms*. New York: Charles Scribner's, 1929, p. 58.
25. Malcolm Cowley, *A Second Flowering: Works and Days of the Lost Generation*. New York: Viking, 1973, p. 224.

26. Raymond Moody, *Life After Life*. Covington, Georgia: Mockingbird Books, 1975. New York: Bantam, 1976 (paper), p. 119.

27. *The Journal of San Diego History*, San Diego Historical Society, Summer 1974, See also *Reincarnation, the Phoenix Fire Mystery*, p. 603, note 56.

28. H. P. Blavatsky, *The Secret Doctrine*. Los Angeles: Theosophy Co., 1968, reprint of original 1888 edition, II: 306, 424. Currently printed.

29. Huston Smith, *The Religions of Man*. New York: Harper & Row, 1958, chapter II, "Hinduism."

30. Eugene O'Neill, *The Great God Brown*. New York: Modern Library, 1959, p. 377.

31. Joseph Campbell, *Hero With a Thousand Faces*. New York: Pantheon, 1949.

32. Joseph Campbell, *The Masks of God: Oriental Mythology*. New York: Viking, 1962, p. 137.

33. Edwin Arnold, *The Light of Asia*. Los Angeles: Theosophy Co., 1977, Book the Eighth.

34. Lewis Thomas, *The Medusa and the Snail*. New York: Viking, 1979. Our selection is a condensed extract as published in *The Reader's Digest*, October 1979, pp. 98–99.

35. Ronald Duncan and Miranda Weston-Smith, eds., *The Encyclopedia of Ignorance*. Oxford: 1977.

36. William R. Corliss, *Mysterious Universe: A Handbook of Astronomical Anomalies*. Glen Arm, Maryland: The Sourcebook Project, 1979.

37. Gregory Bateson, *Mind and Nature*. New York: Dutton, 1979, pp. 27–29.

38. Harold M. Schmeck, Jr., "Exploring the Inside of a Cell," *The New York Times*, December 11, 1979.

39. "A Game of Cosmic Roulette," *The New York Times*, November 8, 1971.

40. Jacques Monod, *Chance and Necessity*. New York: Knopf, 1971, p. 138.

41. "A Game of Cosmic Roulette."

42. Joseph Wood Krutch, *More Lives Than One*. New York: William Sloane, 1962, pp. 322–23.

43. Will Durant, *The Story of Philosophy*. New York: Simon and Schuster, 1926, pp. 489–90.

44. *Manas* (Los Angeles), September 23, 1981, pp. 1–2.

45. Lewis Thomas, *The Medusa and the Snail*, pp. 15–16.

46. *Encyclopedia Britannica*, Macropaedia, XVIII: 276–78.

47. C. G. Jung, *Psychology and Religion: West and East*. New York: Pantheon, 1958, p. 529.

48. Theodore Roszak, "Madame Blavatsky's Secret Doctrine," *The Unfinished Animal*. New York: Harper & Row, 1975, pp. 117–25.

49. Theodore Roszak, "Where Is Evolution Going?" *Manas*, June 16, 1982, p. 1.

50. Alfred Russel Wallace to H. P. Blavatsky, letter dated January 1, 1878. *The Theosophist* (Adyar, India), April 1906, p. 559.

51. Blavatsky, *The Secret Doctrine*, I: vi.

52. Ibid., I: 477–78.

53. Walt Anderson, "In Search of Shunyata," *American Theosophist* (Wheaton, Illinois), Spring 1980, p. 102.

54. *The Yoga Aphorisms of Patanjali*, rendition of William Q. Judge. Los Angeles: Theosophy Co., 1930, pp. xvii, 48, currently printed.

55. Morey Bernstein, *The Search for Bridey Murphy*. New York: Pocket Books, 1978, p. 78.

56. Sir James Jeans, *The Mysterious Universe*. New York: Macmillan, 1931, p. 158.

57. Chapman Cohen, *Materialism Restated*. London: Pioneer Press, 1927.

58. Bertrand Russell, "Introduction," in Frederick A. Lange, *History of Materialism*. New York: Harcourt Brace, 1925.

59. James Freeman Clarke, *Ten Great Religions*. Boston: Houghton Mifflin, 1887, II: ix, 190.
60. Thomas Huxley, *Evolution and Ethics*. New York: Appleton, 1894, pp. 60–61.
61. Thomas Huxley, *Essays on Some Controverted Subjects*. New York: 1892, pp. 27, 171, 178.
62. Horace Meyer Kallen, "William James," *Encyclopedia Britannica*, 1959 edition, XII: 883.
63. William James, *The Will to Believe, and Human Immortality*. New York: Dover, 1956, pp. 17–18.
64. Ibid., pp. v–ix.
65. William James, *The Varieties of Religious Experience*. New York: Longmans Green, 1925, pp. 522–23.
66. Membership log in archives of Theosophical Society International, Pasadena, California. William James applied for membership in The Theosophical Society June 18, 1891. Diploma issued July 29, 1891.
67. Erich Fromm, *Psychoanalysis and Religion*. Yale University Press, 1950, p. 6.
68. Ludwig Binswanger, *Being-in-the-World*, trans. and ed., Jacob Needleman. New York: Basic Books, 1963, pp. 4, 183.
69. Ernest Jones, *Life and Work of Sigmund Freud*. New York: Basic Books, 1953–1957.
70. Bruno Bettelheim, *Freud and Man's Soul*. New York: Knopf, 1983.
71. Herbert Fingarette, *The Self in Transformation*. New York: Basic Books, pp. 171–237.
72. Benjamin Nelson, "Foreword," in Herbert Fingarette, *The Self in Transformation*, Harper Torchbook, 1965.
73. C. G. Jung, *The Secret of the Golden Flower*. London: Routledge, Kegan Paul, 1938, p. 124.
74. C. G. Jung, *Dreams, Memories, Reflections*, p. 319.
75. Eric Erikson, *Gandhi's Truth*. New York: Norton, 1969, pp. 35–36.
76. Thomas Hanna, *Explorers of Humankind*. San Francisco: Harper & Row, 1979.

4 THE RESEARCH OF IAN STEVENSON, M.D.

1. Tom Zito, "The Doctor Studies Reincarnation," *New York Post*, November 18, 1978.
2. "Will You Live Again?" *National Enquirer*, December 17, 1967. (Interviewer falsely posed as representing a reputable London paper; letter of Ian Stevenson to Joseph Head, December 21, 1967.)
3. *Family Circle*, June 14, 1978, p. 36.
4. Tom Zito, "The Doctor Studies Reincarnation."
5. Alton Slagle, "Reincarnation: A Doctor Looks Beyond Death," New York *Sunday News*, August 4, 1974.
6. Tom Zito, "The Doctor Studies Reincarnation."
7. J. Gaither Pratt and Naomi Hintze, *The Psychic Realm: What Can You Believe?* New York: Random House, 1975.
8. Ibid., p. 243.
9. Ian Stevenson, "Some Questions Related to Cases of the Reincarnation Type," *Journal of the American Society for Psychical Research*, October 1974, pp. 396–97.
10. Ian Stevenson, "Research into the Evidence of Man's Survival After Death," *Journal of Nervous and Mental Disease*, September 1977, p. 164.
11. Ian Stevenson, *Cases of the Reincarnation Type*. Charlottesville, Virginia: University Press of Virginia, 1980, III: 351.
12. Ian Stevenson, "Reincarnation: Field Studies and Theoretical Issues," *Handbook of Parapsychology*, ed. Benjamin B. Wolman. New York: Van Nostrand, 1977, p. 637.

13. Ibid., p. 650.
14. Ian Stevenson, *Twenty Cases Suggestive of Reincarnation*. Charlottesville, Virginia: University Press of Virginia, 2nd ed., 1974, p. 333.
15. Ibid., pp. 365, 368.
16. Stevenson, *Cases of the Reincarnation Type*, III: 346–48.
17. Ibid., p. 349.
18. Ibid., p. 359 fn.
19. Stevenson, *Twenty Cases Suggestive of Reincarnation*, p. 347.
20. Ibid., pp. 343–44.
21. Ian Stevenson, "The Evidence for Survival from Claimed Memories of Former Incarnations," *Journal of the American Society for Psychical Research*, April 1960.
22. Stevenson, *Twenty Cases Suggestive of Reincarnation*, p. 356.
23. Ibid., p. 380.
24. Ibid., p. 358.
25. Stevenson, "Reincarnation: Field Studies and Theoretical Issues," p. 637.
26. Stevenson, "Explanatory Value of the Idea of Reincarnation," *Journal of Nervous and Mental Disease*, May 1977, p. 317.
27. Stevenson, "Reincarnation: Field Studies and Theoretical Issues," pp. 637–38.
28. Stevenson, "The Possible Nature of Post-Mortem States," *Journal of the American Society for Psychical Research*, October 1980, p. 417.
29. Stevenson, "Reincarnation: Field Studies and Theoretical Issues," p. 654.
30. Stevenson, *Family Circle* interview, p. 39.
31. Stevenson, lecture at United Engineering Center, April 2, 1980, unpublished.
32. Stevenson, *Twenty Cases Suggestive of Reincarnation*, p. 259.
33. Stevenson, "Explanatory Value of the Idea of Reincarnation," p. 321.
34. Ibid., p. 314.
35. Stevenson, "Research into the Evidence of Man's Survival After Death," p. 182.
36. Stevenson, "The Evidence for Survival from Claimed Memories of Former Incarnations." Eugene Kinkaid, "Is There Another Life After Death," *Look*, October 20, 1970, p. 87.
37. Stevenson, "Explanatory Value of the Idea of Reincarnation," op. cit., pp. 318–20.
38. Stevenson, *Twenty Cases Suggestive of Reincarnation*, pp. 91–105.
39. Stevenson, *Cases of the Reincarnation Type*, I: 96.
40. Stevenson, "Some Questions Related to Cases of the Reincarnation Type," p. 407.
41. Stevenson, *Family Circle* interview, p. 41.
42. Alton Slagle, "Reincarnation: A Doctor Looks Beyond Death," New York *Sunday News*, August 4, 1974.

5 CASES OF THE REINCARNATION TYPE FROM AROUND THE WORLD

1. H. P. Blavatsky, *The Secret Doctrine* (cited in chapter 3), I: 149, 154–55, 171–73, 179–81; II: 64.
2. Stevenson, *Twenty Cases Suggestive of Reincarnation* (cited in chapter 4), pp. 181–203.
3. "Professor Recalls Life as a Doctor in 1620," *The Star* (New York), April 1, 1980.
4. *National Enquirer*, Dec. 28, 1969.
5. Ibid.
6. Arthur Guirdham, *The Cathars and Reincarnation*. London: Spearman, 1970, pp. 88–89.
7. Lecture of Dr. Guirdham before the College of Psychic Science, London, March 25, 1969.
8. C. J. Ducasse, *A Critical Examination of the Belief in a Life After Death*. Springfield, Illinois: Charles C. Thomas, 1961, pp. 232–33.

9. Raynor Johnson, *A Religious Outlook for Modern Man.* London: Hodder & Stoughton, 1963, p. 184.
10. Stevenson, *Twenty Cases Suggestive of Reincarnation* (cited in chapter 4), pp. 357–58, 358 fn.
11. Ibid., pp. 270–320.
12. Stevenson, *Cases of the Reincarnation Type* (cited in chapter 4), I: 70–106.
13. Ibid., I: 176–205.
14. Stevenson, "Research into the Evidence of Man's Survival After Death," (cited in chapter 4); complete report in Stevenson's *Cases of the Reincarnation Type,* IV: 229–41.
15. Stevenson, *Twenty Cases Suggestive of Reincarnation,* pp. 171–80.
16. Stevenson, *Cases of the Reincarnation Type,* III: 189 fn.

6 DID THEY SPEAK A PAST-LIFE LANGUAGE?

1. Ian Stevenson, "The Evidence for Survival from Claimed Memories of Former Incarnations" (cited in chapter 4), p. 25.
2. Ian Stevenson, *Xenoglossy.* Charlottesville, Virginia: University Press of Virginia, 1974, p. 5.
3. Ibid., p. 19.
4. Frederick Lenz, *Lifetimes.* Indianapolis: Bobbs-Merrill, 1979, pp. 37–38.
5. Our informants stated that Dr. McDuffie and his wife joined the United Lodge of Theosophists. Upon investigation, the latter's membership list disclosed that the doctor joined on November 28, 1928, and his wife on December 9, 1928.
6. Stevenson, *Xenoglossy,* pp. 16–17.
7. *Modern Screen,* April 1932.

7 HYPNOTIC REGRESSION EXPERIMENTS

1. Stevenson, "Some Questions Related to Cases of the Reincarnation Type" (cited in chapter 4), pp. 411–12.
2. Jeffrey Iverson, *More Lives Than One? The Evidence of the Remarkable Bloxham Tapes.* London: Souvenir Press, 1976.
3. Ibid. p. 25.
4. Ibid., chapter 11.
5. Ibid., chapters 4 and 5.
6. Ian Stevenson, "The Evidence for Survival from Claimed Memories of Former Incarnations," *Journal of the American Society for Psychical Research,* July 1960, p. 115.

8 NEAR-DEATH AND BEYOND-DEATH ENCOUNTERS

1. Lewis Thomas, *The Lives of a Cell.* New York: Viking, 1974, pp. 51–52.
2. Mary Ann O'Roark, "Life After Death: The Growing Evidence," *Reader's Digest,* August 1981, p. 53.
3. George E. Burch, *American Heart Journal,* 76:438 (1968).
4. Raymond Moody, *Life After Life* (cited in chapter 3).
5. Kenneth Ring, *Life at Death.* New York: Coward, McCann & Geoghegan, 1980.
6. Frederick Leboyer, *Birth Without Violence.* New York: Knopf, 1978, pp. 11–12.
7. Raymond Moody, *Reflections on Life After Death.* New York: Bantam, 1978, pp. 109–10.
8. George G. Ritchie, *Return From Tomorrow.* Lincoln, Virginia: Chosen Books, 1978. George G. Ritchie, "To Live Again and Again," A.R.E. tape 9120, n.d., Association for Research and Enlightenment, Virginia Beach, Virginia.

9. Ritchie, *Return From Tomorrow*, p. 81.
10. Raymond Moody, *Life After Life*, pp. 141–42.
11. Ian Stevenson, *Twenty Cases Suggestive of Reincarnation* (cited in chapter 4), p. 47. Ian Stevenson, *Cases of the Reincarnation Type* (cited in chapter 4), I: 63; II: 105.
12. Stevenson, *Cases of the Reincarnation Type*, IV: 6–7.
13. Ritchie, "To Live and Live Again."
14. Shirley MacLaine, *Out on a Limb*. New York: Bantam, 1983.
15. *Sunday Express* (London), May 26, 1935.
16. H. P. Blavatsky, *Isis Unveiled*.
17. H. P. Blavatsky, *The Secret Doctrine* (cited in chapter 3), I: 555.
18. Kenneth Ring, *Life at Death*, pp. 226–27.
19. Isaac Bashevis Singer, *Shosha*. New York: Farrar, Straus & Giroux, 1978, p. 145.

9 HEREDITY: PROBLEMS AND PUZZLES IN GENETICS
1. Julian Huxley, *What Dare I Think?* New York: Harper, 1931, pp. 82–83.
2. William Q. Judge, *The Ocean of Theosophy*. Los Angeles: Theosophy Co., 1971, pp. 72–73.
3. John McTaggart, *Some Dogmas of Religion*. London: Edward Arnold, 1906, p. 125.
4. C. J. Ducasse, *Nature, Mind and Death*. LaSalle, Illinois: Open Court, 1951, chapter 21.
5. James Ward, *The Realm of Ends*. Cambridge: Cambridge University Press, 1911, pp. 402–5.
6. H. P. Blavatsky, *The Secret Doctrine* (cited in chapter 3), I: 157.
7. Ian Stevenson, "Some Questions Related to Cases of the Reincarnation Type" (cited in chapter 4), p. 407.
8. Harold S. Burr, *Blueprint for Immortality: The Electric Patterns of Life*. London: Neville Spearman, 1972.
9. Thelma Moss, *The Body Electric*. Los Angeles: J. P. Tarcher, 1979, chapter 11, "The Mystery of the Phantom Leaf."
10. H. P. Blavatsky, *The Secret Doctrine*, II: 149.
11. Ibid., I: 219.
12. Lecture of Sir Fred Hoyle, reported in *The Theosophist* (Adyar, Madras), April 1982, p. 249.
13. E. Lester Smith, ed., *Intelligence Came First*. Wheaton, Illinois: Quest Books, 1975, p. 123.
14. Lewis Thomas, *The Medusa and the Snail* (cited in chapter 3), pp. 156–57. Our selection is a condensed extract as published in *The Reader's Digest*, October 1979, pp. 98–99.
15. James Ward, *The Realm of Ends*.
16. Julian Huxley's contribution to book *Where Are the Dead?*, quoted in *The Middle Way* (London), August 1969, p. 71.
17. Joseph Wood Krutch, *More Lives Than One*. New York: William Sloane, 1962, pp. 322–23.

10 UNEXPLAINED CASES OF GENIUS
1. *The Times of India* (Bombay), February 4, 1978.
2. *The Ottawa Citizen* (Ottawa, Canada), January 3, 1974.
3. Ian Stevenson, "The Explanatory Value of the Idea of Reincarnation" (cited in chapter 4), p. 310.
4. Leslie D. Weatherhead, lecture "The Case for Reincarnation," The City Temple Literary Society (London), 1957. Published as booklet by M. C. Peto, 4 Oakdene, Burgh Heath, Tadworth, Surrey, England KT20 6BN.

11 EARLY INSTRUCTORS OF THE HUMAN RACE

1. Carl Jung, *Collected Works*. New York: Pantheon, 1959, IX: Part I, "Archetypes and the Collective Unconscious," pp. 113, 116–17.
2. Isaac de Beausobré, *Histoire Critique de Manichée et du Manicheisme*. Amsterdam: 1734–1739, II: 491.
3. Edward Tylor, *Primitive Culture*. London: 1873, reprinted as *Religion in Primitive Culture*, Harper Torchbook, 1958.
4. See our chapter 3, section "Only Two Options or a Third Alternative?"
5. *The Listener* (London), January 21, 1954, p. 137.
6. Lord Fitzroy Raglan, *The Temple and the House*. London: 1964, pp. 3–4.
7. Ernst Cassirer, *An Essay on Man*. New Haven: Yale University Press, 1962, pp. 83–84.
8. Giorgi de Santillana, *Hamlet's Mill: An Essay on Myth and the Frame of Time*. Boston: Gambit, 1969, pp. 4–6, 310.
9. Joseph Head and S. L. Cranston, *Reincarnation, the Phoenix Fire Mystery* (cited in Preface), pp. 198–201.
10. Geddes MacGregor, *Reincarnation in Christianity* (cited in chapter 3), p. 31.
11. James Hastings, ed., *Encyclopedia of Religion and Ethics*. New York: Scribners, 1955, XII: 440.
12. Richard Wagner, *Gesammelte Schriften und Dichtungen (Collected Writings and Poetry)*, R. Wagner, ed. Leipzig: 1872, VI: 362–63.
13. Thomas Carlyle, *On Heroes, Hero-Worship, and the Heroes in History*. Philadelphia: Henry Altemus, 1893, pp. 55–56.
14. Julius Caesar, *Gallic War*, trans. William A. MacDevitt. London: 1853, Book VI.
15. Alfred Nutt, *The Voyage of Bran*, ed. Kuno Meyer. London: 1895–1897, II, "The Celtic Doctrine of Rebirth."
16. M. F. Cusack, *A History of the Irish Nation*. Kenmore, Ireland: Irish Publications Office, 1877, pp. 53–55.
17. Bryher, *Ruan*. New York: Pantheon, 1960, pp. 8–9.
18. Janheinz Jahn, *Munti—The New African Culture*. New York: Grove Press, 1961, p. 190.
19. E. G. Parrinder, "Varieties of Belief in Reincarnation." *The Hibbert Journal*, April 1957.
20. *The Canadian Theosophist*, January-February 1962.
21. D. Amaury Talbot, *Woman's Mysteries of a Primitive Culture*. London: Cassell, 1915, pp. 4–5, 39–40.
22. P. G. Bowen, "The Ancient Wisdom in Africa," *The Theosophist* (Adyar, Madras), August 1927.
23. Baldwin Spencer and F. J. Gillen, *Northern Tribes of Central Australia*. London: Macmillan, 1904, p. 145.
24. James Frazer, *The Belief in Immortality and the Worship of the Dead*, London: Macmillan, 1913, I: 127 (Gifford Lectures 1911–1913).
25. Vergilius Ferm, ed., *Ancient Religions*. New York: Philosophical Library, 1950, pp. 283–84.
26. Eduard O. Schmidt, *Doctrine of Descent and Darwinism*. New York: Appleton, 1875, pp. 300–301.
27. James Bonwick, *The Wild White Man and the Blacks of Victoria*. Melbourne: 1863, 2nd. ed., p. 57.
28. Margaret Mead, *Male and Female*. New York: William Morrow, 1949, pp. 389–90.
29. Max Freedom Long, *Introduction to Huna*. Cottonwood, Arizona: Esoteric Publications, 1975, p. 4, 35, 44–45.

30. *Theosophy* (Los Angeles), September 1946, pp. 437–38.
31. Daniel Brinton, *Myths of the New World*. Philadelphia: David McKay, 1896, p. 295.
32. Robert Adams, "Once Upon a Time," *Hudson Dispatch* (Jersey City, New Jersey), January 20, 1968.
33. Ernest Thompson Seton, *The Gospel of the Redman*. Los Angeles: Willing Publishing Co., 1948, p. 24.
34. Margaret Mead, *Male and Female*, pp. 389–90.
35. *Redbook*, March 1946.
36. *Algic Researches*. New York: Harper, 1839, I: 172–73.
37. Daniel Brinton, *Myths of the New World*, pp. 220–23.
38. *The New York Times*, June 19, 1966.
39. D. H. Lawrence, *The Plumed Serpent*. New York: Vintage, 1959, p. xi.
40. Ibid., p. 295.
41. Margaret Murray, *The Splendour That Was Egypt*. New York: Philosophical Library, 1949, pp. 210–11.
42. *The Book of the Dead*, trans. E. A. Wallis Budge. Chicago and London: 1901, III: 598.
43. J. B. Priestley, *Man and Time*. New York: Doubleday, 1964, pp. 147–48.
44. *Select Works of Plotinus, and Extracts from the Treatise of Synesius on Providence*, trans. Thomas Taylor. London: 1817.
45. *The Sayings of Mohammed*, from Nadarbeg K. Mirza, *Reincarnation and Islam*. Madras: 1927.
46. *Theosophy in Pakistan* (Karachi), October–December 1965.
47. Chapters on the Ismailis and other esoteric schools of Islam.
48. Mirza, *Reincarnation and Islam*.
49. *Theosophy in Pakistan*, op. cit.
50. Idries Shah, *The Sufis*. New York: Doubleday, 1964, pp. 115–16.
51. Mirza, *Reincarnation in Islam*, pp. 55–56.
52. Translators Shea and Troyer. London: 1843, III, chapter "Religion of the Sufis."
53. *The Bhagavad-Gita*, trans. W. Q. Judge. Los Angeles: Theosophy Co., 1971, p. 31, currently printed.
54. Chuang Tzu, *Taoist Philosopher and Chinese Mystic*, trans. Herbert A. Giles. London: Allen & Unwin, 1926, pp. 110, 121. "Lao Tzu and the Taoists," *Theosophy* (Los Angeles), November 1926, p. 20.
55. Dalai Lama, *My Land and My People*. New York: McGraw-Hill, 1962, p. 51.
56. James Hastings, ed., *Encyclopedia of Religion and Ethics*, XII: 437.
57. Gershom Scholem, "Man and the Sympathy of All Things," *Eranos Yearbook*. Zurich: 1956, p. 74.
58. Gershom Scholem, *Kabbalah*. New York: New York Times Book Co., 1974, p. 346.

12 JUDAIC TEACHERS AND PROPHETS

1. Isidore Epstein, *Judaism*. Penguin Books, 1959, p. 29.
2. Gershom Scholem, *Kabbalah* (cited in chapter 11), p. 333.
3. Gershom Scholem, "Man and the Sympathy of All Things" (cited in chapter 11), p. 68.
4. James Hastings, ed., *Encyclopedia of Religion and Ethics* (cited in chapter 11), XII: 435–40.
5. *Encyclopedia Judaica*. Jerusalem, Israel: Macmillan.
6. Gershom Scholem, *Major Trends in Jewish Mysticism*. New York: Schocken Books, 1961.
7. C. G. Jung, *Word and Image*, ed. Aniela Jaffé. Princeton: Princeton University Press, 1979, pp. 181–82.

8. Rabbi Paul Isaac Hershon, *A Talmudic Miscellany*. London: Trübner's, 1880, p. 318.
9. Lewis W. Spitz, *The Religious Renaissance of the German Humanists*. Cambridge, Mass.: Harvard University Press, 1963, p. 67.
10. *Reincarnation, the Phoenix Fire Mystery*, p. 129.
11. Denis Saurat, *Milton, Man and Thinker*. New York: Dial Press, 1925, "The Zohar and the Kabbalah." Saurat, *Blake and Modern Thought*. New York: MacVeagh, 1929.
12. Isaac Myer, *Qabbalah*. Philadelphia: 1888, p. 171. Reprinted, New York: Weiser, 1970.
13. Scholem, *Kabbalah*, pp. 190–91.
14. Scholem, *Major Trends in Jewish Mysticism*, p. 2.
15. Moses Maimonides, *The Guide to the Perplexed*, trans. M. Friedländer. New York: Dover, 1956, pp. xv, xvi.
16. Scholem, *Major Trends in Jewish Mysticism*, p. 156.
17. Ibid., pp. 201–2.
18. Quoted in E. D. Walker, *Reincarnation, A Study of Forgotten Truth*. Boston: Houghton, Mifflin, 1888, p. 212. Another translation in Isaac Myer, *Qabbalah*. Philadelphia: 1888, p. 413.
19. Scholem, *Kabbalah*, pp. 345–46.
20. Scholem, "Man and the Sympathy of All Things," p. 68.
21. Ibid., p. 73.
22. Scholem, *Kabbalah*, p. 159.
23. Scholem, "Man and the Sympathy of All Things," p. 104.
24. Ibid., p. 88.
25. *Aryan Path* (Bombay), April 1935.
26. Scholem, *Kabbalah*, p. 74.
27. Ibid., p. 68.
28. *Aryan Path*, April 1935.
29. Scholem, "Man and the Sympathy of All Things," p. 107.
30. Scholem, *Major Trends in Jewish Mysticism*, p. 281.
31. *The Path* (New York), February 1894, p. 359.
32. Scholem, *Kabbalah*, p. 347; *Major Trends in Jewish Mysticism*, p. 243.
33. Scholem, *Kabbalah*, p. 157.
34. Hershon, *A Talmudic Miscellany*, pp. 323–26.
35. *Jewish-American Examiner*, December 24, 1978.
36. Scholem, *Kabbalah*, p. 157.
37. Ibid., pp. 152–53.
38. Scholem, "Man and the Sympathy of All Things," pp. 104, 105, 113–14, 117.
39. Scholem, *Major Trends in Jewish Mysticism*, pp. 328–29.
40. Ibid., pp. 337–38.
41. Scholem, "Man and the Sympathy of All Things," p. 108.
42. Scholem, *Major Trends in Jewish Mysticism*, pp. 325–26.
43. Shneur Zalman, *Siddur Tehillat Hashem*, trans. Rabbi Nissen Mangel. Brooklyn: Merkos L'Inyonei Chinuch, Inc., p. 118.
44. *Universal Jewish Encyclopedia*. New York: Ktav Publishing, 1969.
45. S. Ansky, *The Dybbuk*, trans. H. Alsberg and W. Katzin. New York: Boni & Liveright, 1926, pp. 71–72, 78–79, 81, 82, 101.
46. Scholem, *Kabbalah*, pp. 349–50.
47. Martin Buber, *For the Sake of Heaven*, trans. Ludwig Lewisohn. New York: Atheneum, 1981.
48. Scholem, *Major Trends in Jewish Mysticism*, p. 283.

49. Quoted on the jacket of *For the Sake of Heaven*.
50. Rabbi Adin Steinsaltz, *The Thirteen Petaled Rose*. New York: Basic Books, 1980, pp. 64–65.

13 JESUS AND THE CHRISTIAN VISION
1. Geddes MacGregor, *Reincarnation in Christianity* (cited in chapter 3), p. ix.
2. Geddes MacGregor, *Reincarnation as a Christian Hope*. London: Macmillan, 1982.
3. C. J. Ducasse, 1960 Garvin Lecture, "Life After Death Conceived as Reincarnation," published in *In Search of God and Immortality* (Garvin Lectures 1949–1960). Boston: Beacon Press, 1961, pp. 142–44.
4. James M. Robinson, ed., *The Nag Hammadi Library in English*. New York: Harper & Row, 1977, p. 3.
5. Geddes MacGregor, *Reincarnation as a Christian Hope*. London: Macmillan, 1982, p. 36.
6. Loran Hurnscot, *A Prison, a Paradise*. New York: Viking, 1959, p. 263.
7. The procrastination question is discussed more fully in *Reincarnation, the Phoenix Fire Mystery* (cited in Preface), pp. 174–75, 307.
8. Geddes MacGregor, taped lecture "Reincarnation in Christianity," 1979, at The Theosophical Society in Wheaton, Illinois.
9. Krister Stendahl and Emilie T. Sander, "New Testament Canon, Texts, and Versions," *Encyclopedia Britannica, Macropedia*, II: 938, et seq.
10. Gospel statements quoted and discussed in *Death and Eternal Life* by John Hick (cited in chapter 3), p. 183.
11. Rudolf Frieling, *Christianity and Reincarnation*. Edinburgh: Floris Books, 1977, p. 44.
12. Geddes MacGregor, *Reincarnation in Christianity*, p. 60.
13. William Kingsland, *The Gnosis or Ancient Wisdom in the Christian Scriptures*. London: Allen & Unwin, 1937, p. 31.
14. Quoted in S. Radhakrishnan's *Eastern Religions and Western Thought*. Oxford: Oxford University Press, 1940, p. 343.
15. Geddes MacGregor, taped lecture "Reincarnation in Christianity."
16. Reverend Thomas Strong, *Mystical Christianity*. London: Regency Press, 1978, p. 37.
17. MacGregor, *Reincarnation as a Christian Hope*, p. 44.
18. Alexander Roberts and James Donaldson, eds., *Ante-Nicene Christian Library*. Edinburgh: Clark, 1867, XV: 496–97.
19. Geddes MacGregor, taped lecture "Reincarnation in Christianity."
20. Werner George Kümmel, *Introduction to the New Testament*. Nashville, Tennessee: Abingdon, 1975, p. 37.
21. MacGregor, *Reincarnation as a Christian Hope*, p. 62.
22. Elaine Pagels, *The Gnostic Gospels*. New York: Random House, 1979, p. xxiv.
23. Geddes MacGregor, *Gnosis, a Renaissance in Christian Thought*. Wheaton, Illinois: Quest Books, 1979, p. 6.
24. MacGregor, *Reincarnation as a Christian Hope*, p. 63.
25. MacGregor, *Reincarnation in Christianity*, p. 44.
26. MacGregor, *Reincarnation as a Christian Hope*, p. 64.
27. London: John Murray, 1883, article "Irenaeus," III, p. 269.
28. C. G. Jung, *Psychology and Alchemy*. New York: Pantheon, 1953, p. 35.
29. C. G. Jung, *Aion, Researches into the Phenomenology of the Self*. New York: Pantheon, 1959, pp. 190, 196, 222.
30. *Proceedings of the International Colloquium on Gnosticism*. Stockholm, August 20–25, 1973, p. 13.

31. Elaine Pagels, *The Gnostic Gospels*, pp. xxiv–xxvii.
32. *Reincarnation, the Phoenix Fire Mystery*, p. 156.
33. Elaine Pagels, *The Gnostic Gospels*, pp. xxiv, xxxv.
34. D. M. Scholer, *Nag Hammadi Bibliography*. Leiden: 1971, periodically updated.
35. MacGregor, *Reincarnation in Christianity*, pp. 43–44.
36. G.R.S. Mead, *Fragments of a Faith Forgotten*. New York: University Books, 1960, p. 142.
37. Ibid.
38. Jean Doresse, *The Secret Books of the Egyptians*. New York: Viking, 1960, pp. 112–13.
39. *The Pistis Sophia*, trans. G.R.S. Mead. London: John M. Watkins, revised edition, 1921, pp. 220, 262–63, 293–94, 313, 315, 320, 322–23.
40. Mircea Eliade, *The Myth of the Eternal Return*. New York: Pantheon, 1954, pp. 87–88.
41. *Reincarnation, the Phoenix Fire Mystery*, "Reincarnation in the Dark Ages," pp. 160–65.
42. MacGregor, *Reincarnation as a Christian Hope*, pp. 61–62, 64.
43. "An Interview with Geddes MacGregor," *American Theosophist*, August 1978, pp. 199–204.
44. MacGregor, taped lecture "Reincarnation in Christianity."

14 KRISHNA AND *THE BHAGAVAD-GITA*

1. S. Radhakrishnan, *The Principle Upanishads*. New York: Harper, 1953, pp. 18–19.
2. William Q. Judge, *Echoes from the Orient*. New York: Aryan Press, 1890, pp. 35–36. Currently reprinted, Theosophy Co. Los Angeles.
3. See index under *Bhagavad-Gita* in *Reincarnation, the Phoenix Fire Mystery* (cited in Preface).
4. Henry David Thoreau, *Walden and Other Writings*. New York: Modern Library, 1950, p. 266.
5. Arthur Christy, *The Orient in American Transcendentalism*. New York: Columbia University Press, 1932, p. 23.
6. *The Nation*, May 10, 1910, p. 481.
7. N. V. Guberti, *Materials for Russian Bibliography*. Moscow: 1978, II: 309–13.
8. Kathleen Raine, *Blake and Tradition*. Princeton University Press, 1968, pp. 350–53.
9. *Selected Writings of Ralph Waldo Emerson*, ed., Brooks Atkinson. New York: Modern Library, p. 660.
10. M. K. Gandhi, *Gandhi's Autobiography: The Story of My Experiments With Truth*. Washington, D.C.: Public Affairs Press, 1948, pp. 90–91, 321. Boston: Beacon Press, (paper).
11. James Hunt, *Gandhi in London*. New Delhi: Promilla & Co., 1978, p. 31. *Reincarnation, the Phoenix Fire Mystery*, pp. 487, 507–10.
12. Louis Fischer, *The Life of Mahatma Gandhi*. New York: Harper, 1950, pp. 131–32.
13. Eknath Easwaran, *Gandhi, the Man*. Petaluma, California: Nilgiri Press, 1978.
14. Elizabeth Seeger, *The Five Brothers*. New York: John Day, 1948, p. xii.
15. Walt Whitman, "As I Ponder'd in Silence," *Leaves of Grass*. New York: Modern Library, p. 4.
16. *The Bhagavad-Gita*, trans. William Q. Judge. Los Angeles: Theosophy Co.
17. William Q. Judge, *Notes on the Bhagavad Gita*. Los Angeles: Theosophy Co.
18. Ian Stevenson, *Twenty Cases Suggestive of Reincarnation* (cited in chapter 4), p. 15.
19. Quoted on front flap of M. K. Gandhi's *The Teaching of the Gita*, ed. Anand T. Hingorani. Bombay: Bharatiya Vidya Bhavan, 1971 (Pocket Gandhi Series No. 5).

20.   Geoffrey Ashe, *Gandhi*. New York: Stein & Day, 1968, p. xi.
21.   *Harijan*, March 1936.
22.   *The Bhagavad-Gita*, op. cit.
23.   Albert Schweitzer, *Indian Thought and Its Development*. Boston: Beacon Press, 1952, pp. 222–23.

15   THE LIFE AND TEACHINGS OF BUDDHA

1.   Sir Edwin Arnold, *The Light of Asia*. Los Angeles: Theosophy Co., 1977.
2.   Buddha, *The Dhammapada*. Los Angeles: Cunningham Press, 1955.
3.   Lafcadio Hearn, *Gleanings in Buddha-Fields*. Boston: Houghton Mifflin, 1900, pp. 208–10.
4.   *The Dhammapada*, p. vi.
5.   Nyanaponika Thera, *The Heart of Buddhist Meditation*. London: Rider, 1969, pp. 178–79.
6.   Edward Conze, trans. *Buddhist Scriptures*. Penguin Classics, 1959, pp. 19–20.
7.   *Reincarnation, the Phoenix Fire Mystery*, pp. 61–67, 92–93.
8.   George Grimm, *The Doctrine of the Buddha*. Berlin: Akademie-Verlag, 1958, p. 5 (in English).
9.   *The Dhammapada*. Verses 21, 46, 47, 160, 218, 326, 327, 334, 379, 411, 419, 423.
10.   Typewritten transcript of lecture by the Dalai Lama (available from Harvard University Center for World Religions), pp. 5, 7, 8.
11.   Taped lecture, "The Buddha Nature," by the Dalai Lama. Available at The Theosophical Society, Wheaton, Illinois.
12.   D. T. Suzuki, *The Field of Zen*. London: Buddhist Society, 1969, p. 58.
13.   D. T. Suzuki, "Self the Unattainable." *The Eastern Buddhist* (Kyoto) (New Series), October 1970, p. 3.
14.   Ibid., pp. 2, 57. See also D. T. Suzuki, "What Is the I?" *The Eastern Buddhist* (New Series), May 1971.
15.   Lynn White, *Frontiers of Knowledge in the Study of Man*. New York: Harper & Row, 1956, pp. 304–5.
16.   William Kingsland. *The Real H. P. Blavatsky*. London: John H. Watkins, 1928.
17.   *The Eastern Buddhist* (Old Series), ed. D. T. Suzuki, V: 377.
18.   Jamshed K. Fozdar, *The God of Buddha*. New York: Asia Publishing House, 1973, pp. 152–53.
19.   *The Middle Way* (London), volume 27, p. 76.
20.   "Edwin Arnold," *Dictionary of National Biography*, 2nd supplement. Oxford: Oxford University Press.
21.   Rick Fields, *How the Swans Came to the Lake: A Narrative History of Buddhism in America*. Boulder, Colorado: Shambhala, 1981, p. 68.
22.   *The International Review*, October 1879.
23.   *Gandhi's Autobiography* (cited in chapter 14), p. 92.
24.   "Claude Fayette Bragdon," *American Theosophist*, September 1983.
25.   Edward Conze, *Buddhism, Its Essence and Development*. New York: Harper Torchbook, 1959, appendix.
26.   William Peiris, *Edwin Arnold*. Kandy, Sri Lanka: Buddhist Publication Society, 1970, pp. 66–67.
27.   Brooks Wright, *Interpreter of Buddhism to the West: Sir Edwin Arnold*. New York: Bookman Associates, 1957, p. 39.
28.   Peiris, *Edwin Arnold*, p. 35.
29.   Wright, *Interpreter of Buddhism to the West: Sir Edwin Arnold*, p. 56.
30.   Conze, *Buddhism, Its Essence and Development*, pp. 24–25.

31. *Buddhism in England*, (London) vol. 7, no. 2.
32. Theosophy Co., Los Angeles.
33. *The Fo-Sho-Hing-Tsan-King: Life of Buddha*, trans. Samuel Beal. Oxford: Clarendon Press, 1883.
34. Edwin Burtt, *The Teachings of the Compassionate Buddha*. New York: New American Library, 1955, p. 134.
35. Judge, *Notes on The Bhagavad Gita*, p. 152.
36. Burtt, *The Teachings of the Compassionate Buddha*, p. 162.
37. *The Voice of the Silence*, trans. H. P. Blavatsky. Los Angeles: Theosophy Co., pp. 44–46, 78. Dr. D. T. Suzuki called this translation "the real Mahayana Buddhism" (*The Middle Way*, August 1965). The Dalai Lama autographed Christmas Humphrey's copy in India in 1956 (*The Middle Way*, November 1963).

16 WAR AND ITS TRANSCENDENCE

1. Leo Tolstoy, "Christianity and Patriotism," trans. Boris de Zirkoff, *Theosophia* (Los Angeles), vol. 7, no. 2, p. 13.
2. Dalai Lama, *My Land and My People*. New York: McGraw-Hill, 1962, pp. 50–51.
3. *Tibetan Messenger*, Winter 1973, p. 6. Published in English in Utrecht, The Netherlands.
4. Gandhi, *Gandhi's Autobiography* (cited in chapter 14), p. 92.
5. Ralph Waldo Emerson, "War," address before the American Peace Society, Winter— Spring 1838. *Complete Works of Ralph Waldo Emerson*. Boston: Houghton Mifflin, XI: 164.

17 MY RACE, MY RELIGION, MY COUNTRY, MY STATUS

1. Gina Cerminara, *The World Within*. New York: William Sloane, 1957, pp. 136–37.
2. C. J. Ducasse, *Nature, Mind, and Death*. LaSalle, Illinois: Open Court, 1951, chapter 21.
3. Ian Stevenson, "The Explanatory Value of the Idea of Reincarnation" (cited in chapter 4), pp. 316–17.
4. Ian Stevenson, *Cases of the Reincarnation Type* (cited in chapter 4), III: 7.
5. Samuel Butler, *The Note-Books of Samuel Butler*, ed. Henry Festing Jones. New York: Dutton, 1917, p. 397.
6. Ibid., p. 394.
7. H. P. Blavatsky, *Collected Writings*, ed. Boris de Zirkoff. Adyar, Madras and Wheaton, Illinois: Theosophical Publishing House, 1960, VIII: 405–6.

18 OUR PLUNDERED PLANET AND DISREGARD FOR ITS CREATURES

1. Jonathan Schell, *The Fate of the Earth*. New York: Knopf, 1982.
2. *Reincarnation, the Phoenix Fire Mystery* (cited in Preface), p. 595, note 74.
3. Lord Hugh Dowding, *Lychgate*. London: Rider, 1945, p. 94.
4. Lord Hugh Dowding, "Painful Experiments on Animals," address reprinted in pamphlet of the Antivivisection Society in London, n.d.
5. Lady Muriel Dowding, *Beauty Without Cruelty*. London: Neville Spearman, 1980; Wheaton, Illinois: Quest Books, 1982.
6. H. P. Blavatsky, *Collected Writings*. Wheaton, Illinois: Theosophical Publishing House, VII: 12–49. Also in booklet "Modern Ignorance of Life and Soul." Los Angeles: Theosophy Co. n.d.

19 REINCARNATION AND THE POPULATION EXPLOSION

1. Ian Stevenson, "Some Questions Related to Cases of the Reincarnation Type" (cited in chapter 4), October 1974, pp. 399–400.

NOTES

2. "New Fossil Discoveries Indicate That Advanced Man Had Evolved by 3.75 Million Years Ago," *The New York Times*, March 9, 1976.
3. *New York Post*, April 5, 1984 (Associated Press release).
4. N. Keyfitz, "How Many People Have Lived on the Earth?" *Demography*, 1966, III: 581–82. F. Wellemeyer, and others, "How Many People Have Ever Lived on Earth?" *Population Bulletin*, 1962, XVIII: 1–19.
5. Plato, *Phaedo* (81) and (107); *The Republic*, X (615). Vergil, *Aeneid*, VI (758). *The Bhagavad-Gita*, Chapter 6.
6. Ian Stevenson, "Some Questions Related to Cases of the Reincarnation Type," op. cit., pp. 400–401.

1. Marilyn Ferguson, *The Aquarian Conspiracy*. Los Angeles: J. P. Tarcher, 1980, p. 156.
3. Ibid., pp. 243–45.
4. Ibid., pp. 263–64.
5. Norman Mailer, *Marilyn*. New York: Grosset & Dunlap, 1973, pp. 22–23.
6. Walt Whitman, *Leaves of Grass*. New York: Modern Library, p. 364, n.d.
8. Larry Dossey, *Time, Space and Medicine*. Boulder, Colorado: Shambhala, 1982.
9. C. G. Jung, *Dreams, Memories, Reflections* (cited in chapter 3), p. 301.
10. Noel Langely, *Edgar Cayce on Reincarnation*. New York: Paperback Library, 1967, pp. 41–42.
11. Gina Cerminara, *Many Mansions*. New York: William Sloane, 1950, p. 23.
12. Ibid., pp. 26–27.
13. Thomas Sugrue, *There Is a River*. New York: Henry Holt, 1942, pp. 234–35.
14. Cerminara, *Many Mansions*, pp. 44–45.
15. Ibid., pp. 88–89.
17. Gina Cerminara, *The World Within*. New York: William Sloane, 1957, p. 53.
19. Geddes MacGregor, "Up and Down Jacob's Ladder." *American Theosophist*, Spring 1981.

1. Ian Stevenson, "The Explanatory Value of the Idea of Reincarnation" (cited in chapter 4), pp. 317–18.
2. Marilyn Ferguson, *The Aquarian Conspiracy* (cited in chapter 20), p. 226.
5. D. Alfred Bertholet, *Transmigration of Souls*. London and New York: Harper, 1909, p. 104.
8. Saul Bellow, *Herzog*. New York: Avon Books, 1961, pp. 216–17.
9. Maurice Maeterlinck, *The Treasure of the Humble*, trans. Alfred Sutro and A. B. Walkley. New York: Dodd, Mead, 1909; pp. 160, 162–64.

22 THE ACHING PROBLEM OF SUICIDE, AND A REMEDY THAT WORKS

1. Kenneth Ring, *Life at Death* (cited in chapter 8), p. 261.
2. Raymond Moody, *Life After Life* (cited in chapter 3), p. 143–44.
3. Raymond Moody, *Reflections on Life After Life* (cited in chapter 8), pp. 43–49.
4. George G. Ritchie, *Return From Tomorrow* (cited in chapter 8), pp. 58–59.
5. Ring, op. cit., p. 118.
6. "Life After Death: The Growing Evidence." *McCalls*, March 1981; also *Reader's Digest*, August 1981.
7. George Gallup, Jr., *Adventures in Immortality* (cited in chapter 1), p. 141.
8. *Richard Wagner Briefe an Hans von Bülow.* Jena: 1916, p. 107.
9. *Richard Wagner an Mathilde Wesendonck Lagebuchblätter und Briefe 1853–1871.* Leipzig: 1922, p. 285 (letter 106a).
10. Leo Tolstoy, *Diary of Leo Nickolaevich Tolstoy* (cited in chapter 3).
11. J. B. Priestley, *I Have Been Here Before.* London: William Heinemann, 1937, pp. 98–101.
12. Ritchie, *Return From Tomorrow*, pp. 114–16.

23 COLUMBIA UNIVERSITY LECTURES ON REINCARNATION

1. Morey Bernstein, *The Search for Bridey Murphey* (cited in chapter 3), pp. 93–95.
2. Op. cit. (see our chapter 12).
3. Elisabeth Kübler-Ross, *To Live Until We Say Goodbye.* Englewood Cliffs, New Jersey: Prentice-Hall, 1978.
4. New York: Warner Books, 1979.
5. Walt Whitman, *Leaves of Grass.* New York: Modern Library, pp. 29 and 72, n.d.
6. W. Macneile Dixon, *The Human Situation* (cited in chapter 1), pp. 422, 427.
7. H. Fielding Hall, *The Soul of a People.* London: Macmillan, 1905, pp. 93–100.
8. Edwin Arnold, *The Light of Asia,* Book the Eighth.
9. Quoted in *Lucifer* (London), April 1888, II: 147.
10. H. P. Blavatsky, *The Key to Theosophy.* Los Angeles: Theosophy Co., 1980, p. 248.

24 PLIGHT OF THE ELDERLY

1. Hermann Keyserling, *Travel Diary of a Philosopher,* trans. J. Holyroyd Reese. New York: Harcourt, Brace, 1925, I: 250–52.
2. *Standard Edition of the Complete Psychological Works of Sigmund Freud.* London: Hogarth Press, 1957, XIV: 289–95.
3. Lewis Thomas, *Lives of a Cell* (cited in chapter 8), p. 47.
4. Gandhi, *Gandhi's Letters to a Disciple,* pp. 31, 89.

25 CAREERS OF FAMOUS PEOPLE INFLUENCED BY REINCARNATION

1. *San Francisco Examiner,* April 27, 1938.
2. Ernest Thompson Seton, *The Gospel of the Redman* (cited in chapter 10), foreword.
3. Charles Lindbergh, *Autobiography of Values.* New York: Harcourt, Brace & Jovanovich, 1978, p. 304.
4. Charles Lindbergh, *The Spirit of St. Louis.* New York: Scribner's, 1956, pp. 352–53, 361–62, 375, 378, 387.
5. Charles Lindbergh, *Autobiography of Values,* pp. 304–5, 401–2.
6. Carl F. Glasenap, *The Life of Richard Wagner,* trans. William Ashton Ellis. London: Kegan Paul, 1900–1906, V: 254.

7. S. Radhakrishnan, *Eastern Religions and Western Thought*. New York: Oxford University Press, 1940, p. 248.
8. *The Aryan Path* (Bombay), September 1966, pp. 417–18.
9. Richard Wagner, *Collected Writings*, Kapp edition, VI: 278.
10. *The Aryan Path*, September 1966, pp. 417–18.
11. Georg Neidhart, *Werden Wir Wieden Geboren*. Munich, n.d., p. 59.
12. *Richard Wagner an Mathilde Wesendonck* (cited in chapter 22), p. 285.
13. Richard Wagner, *Richard Wagner's Letters to August Roeckel*, trans. Eleanor C. Sellar. London: 1897, pp. 137–38. *Richard Wagner an August Röckel*. Leipzig: 1912, p. 60.
14. Richard Specht, *Gustav Mahler*. Berlin: Schuster & Loeffler, 1913, p. 39.
15. Program notes on cover of Mahler's Third Symphony published by London Records. CSA 2223, Conductor Georg Solti.
16. Joseph Head and S. L. Cranston, *Reincarnation, an East-West Anthology*. New York: Julian Press, 1961, p. 195. Paperback Quest Books, Wheaton, Illinois, 1968.
17. *Irish Statesman*, November 21, 1925. *The New York Times*, February 7, 1928.
18. Stuart Gilbert, *James Joyce's Ulysses*. New York: Vintage, 1955, pp. 33–34, 36.
19. *Reincarnation, the Phoenix Fire Mystery* (cited in Preface), "Ireland's Literary Renaissance," pp. 358–63.
20. Stuart Gilbert, *James Joyce's Ulysses*, pp. vii–viii.
21. *We Moderns, 1920–1940*. Anniversary catalog of the famous Gotham Book Mart in New York City. In this catalog, well-known authors commented on fellow authors of the day.
22. James Atherton, *The Books of the Wake*. New York: Viking, 1960.
23. James Joyce, *A Portrait of the Artist as a Young Man*. New York: Viking, 1927.
24. *Newsweek*, April 9, 1956.
25. Richard Ellmann, *The Identity of Yeats*. New York: Oxford University Press, 1964, pp. 44–45, 256.
26. Shankar Mokashi-Punekar, *Later Phase in the Development of W. B. Yeats*. Dharwar, India: Karnatak University, 1966, p. 157.
27. William Butler Yeats, *The Collected Poems of W. B. Yeats*. New York: Macmillan, 1960, p. 341.
28. Frank Lester Pleadwell, trans. Privately printed, 1927. Original manuscript and translation in archives of St. Louis Art Museum, St. Louis, Missouri.
29. Joseph Head and S. L. Cranston, *Reincarnation in World Thought*. New York: Julian Press, 1967, pp. 353–54. Frank Elgar, *Mondrian*. New York: Praeger, 1968, pp. 88–89.
30. Sixten Ringbom, *The Sounding Cosmos, a Study in the Spiritualism of Kandinsky and the Genesis of Abstract Art*. Helsingsfors: Abo Akademi, 1970 (in English), chapter II, "The Colourful Worlds of Theosophy," pp. 57–108; see especially p. 80.
31. Michel Seuphor, *Piet Mondrian: Life and Work*. New York, n.d. (1960s), p. 58.
32. Edouard Schuré, *The Great Initiates*, trans. Gloria Rasberry. West Nyack, New York: St. George Books, 1961, p. 17.
33. Schuré, *The Great Initiates*, trans. Fred Rothwell. Philadelphia: David McKay, 1925, II: 109–10, 132–33.

26 HORIZONS FAR AND HORIZONS NEAR

1. H. P. Blavatsky, *Isis Unveiled* (cited in chapter 8), II: 264–65.
2. Feodor Dostoevsky, *The Brothers Karamazov*, trans. Constance Garnett. New York: Heritage, 1957, part 4, book XI, chapter 9.
3. Harlow Shapley, *The View from a Distant Star*. New York: Basic Books, 1963, pp. 63–65.

4. Ernest J. Opik, *The Oscillating Universe*. New York: Mentor, 1960, p. 114.
5. Ibid., pp. 136–37.
6. *The Bhagavad-Gita*, trans. Prabhavananda and Christopher Isherwood. New York: Harper, 1944, chapter 8.
7. Friedrich Von Schlegel, *Philosophie des Lebens*. Vienna Lectures, 1827, Lecture 6, p. 193.
8. Matthew Arnold, *Poetry and Prose*, ed. John Bryson. Cambridge, Mass.: Harvard University Press, 1967, "Empedocles on Etna," Act 2.
9. William Blake, *Complete Poetry of William Blake*. New York: Modern Library, 1941, p. 810.
10. S. Radhakrishnan and Charles Moore, eds., *A Source Book in Indian Philosophy*. Princeton University Press, 1957, pp. 610–11.
11. S. Radhakrishnan, *An Idealist View of Life*. London: Allen & Unwin, 1929, chapter 3.
12. W. Macneile Dixon, *The Human Situation* (cited in chapter 1). Selections from chapter 21, "The Verdict."

Acknowledgments

Grateful acknowledgment is hereby made to the following publishers, authors, and/or copyright holders for permission to quote from the following published works:

Allen & Unwin, Ltd., London. *An Idealist View of Life* by S. Radhakrishnan.

American Journal of Diseases of Children and Melvin Morse, M.D., "A Near-Death Experience in a 7-Year-Old Child," October 1983, volume 137, p. 959. Copyright 1983, American Medical Association.

George H. Baird, "The Inevitable Impact on Education of the Emerging Concepts Concerning Death and the Reincarnating Child." Presented to the Symposium on the Child and Death, Columbia University's College of Physicians and Surgeons, New York, January 1979.

Bantam Books, Inc., New York. *Out on a Limb* by Shirley MacLaine. Copyright © 1983 by Shirley MacLaine. All Rights Reserved.

Basic Books, New York. *The Thirteen Petalled Rose* by Rabbi Adin Steinsaltz. Copyright © 1980 by Basic Books, Inc.

Beacon Press, Boston. *Indian Thought and Its Development* by Albert Schweitzer.

Morey Bernstein. *The Search for Bridey Murphy*, published by Doubleday, New York.

Bobbs-Merrill Company, Inc., Indianapolis, Indiana. *Lifetimes: True Accounts of Reincarnation*, Copyright © 1979 by Frederick Lenz.

Cambridge University Press. *J. McT. E. McTaggart* by G. Lowes Dickinson; *The Realm of Ends* by James Ward.

Coward, McCann Publishers, New York. *Life at Death* by Dr. Kenneth Ring. Permission by The Putnam Publishing Group.

Daily News, New York. "Something's Happened to Your Mom," by Dave Hirshey, copyright © 1979 New York News, Inc.

Caren M. Elin, "Juvenile Crime and Beliefs in the Hereafter." Paper presented at Columbia University.

Family Circle Magazine, New York. "Have You Lived Before?" Interview with Ian Stevenson, M.D., by Eugene Kinkead. Reprinted from the June 14, 1978, issue of Family Circle Magazine. © 1978 The Family Circle.

Marilyn Ferguson, Inc., Los Angeles. Excerpts from *The Aquarian Conspiracy: Personal and Social Transformation in the 1980s*, © 1980 by Marilyn Ferguson, published by J. P. Tarcher, Inc. (9110 Sunset Blvd., Los Angeles, CA 90060) $15.00, $8.95 soft cover.

The Georgia Review, Athens, Georgia. "The Mystery of Blind Tom," by Ella May Thornton. *The Georgia Review*, vol. XV (1961), pp. 395–400, © 1961 by the University of Georgia.

Grosset & Dunlap, Inc., New York. *Marilyn* by Norman Mailer. Copyright © 1973 by Alfkog, Inc. and Norman Mailer.

Arthur Guirdham, M.D., selections from his articles, and from *The Cathars and Reincarnation*.

W. P. Halliday, London. *The Human Situation* by W. Macneile Dixon.

Harper & Row, Publishers, New York. *Gandhi's Letters to a Disciple*. Copyright 1950 by Harper & Brothers; *The Art of Loving* by Erich Fromm. Copyright © 1956 by Erich

Fromm; *The Religions of Man* by Huston Smith. Copyright © 1958 by Huston Smith; *The Unfinished Animal* by Theodore Roszak. Copyright © 1975 by Theodore Roszak; "Some New Directions" by Carl Rogers, from *Explorers of Humankind,* edited by Thomas Hanna. Copyright © 1979 by Thomas Hanna; *Recollections of Death* by Michael B. Sabom. Copyright © 1982 by Michael B. Sabom.

Hodder & Stoughton Limited, London. *A Religious Outlook for Modern Man* by Raynor C. Johnson.

Holt, Rinehart and Winston, New York. *There is a River* by Thomas Sugrue. Copyright 1942, 1945 by Holt, Rinehart and Winston. Copyright © 1970 by Mary Ganey Sugrue. Copyright © 1973 by Patricia Sugrue Channon.

Jeffrey Iverson, Cardiff, Wales. *More Lives Than One* by Jeffrey Iverson, pp. 8, 25, 27, and 130–45.

Jewish Publication Society of America, Philadelphia, Pennsylvania. *For the Sake of Heaven* by Martin Buber, translator Ludwig Lewisohn. Copyright © 1945, 1953, 1981.

Journal of Nervous and Mental Disease, published by Williams and Wilkins Company, Baltimore. Editorial of Eugene B. Brody, M.D., September 1977.

Myrra Lee, "Reincarnation in the Classroom: Problems and Suggestions." Presented to the Symposium on the Child and Death, Columbia University's College of Physicians and Surgeons, New York, January 1979.

Liveright Publishing Corporation, New York. *The Dybbuk,* a play by S. Ansky, translated by Henry G. Alsberg and Winifred Katzin. Copyright 1926 by Henry G. Alsberg, copyright renewed 1953 by Herman G. Alsberg and Winifred Katzen.

Geddes MacGregor. Selections from his books, lectures, and articles.

Macmillan & Co. Ltd., London. *The Soul of a People* by H. Fielding Hall.

Macmillan Publishing Co., Inc., New York. *Poems* by John Masefield. Copyright 1912 by Macmillan Publishing Co., Inc., renewed 1940 by John Masefield; *Collected Poems* by William Butler Yeats. Copyright 1940 by Georgie Yeats, renewed 1968 by Bertha Georgie Yeats, Michael Butler Yeates and Anne Yeates.

Mockingbird Books, Inc., St. Simons Island, Georgia. *Life After Life,* and *Reflections on Life After Life,* by Raymond Moody, Jr., M.D.

William Morrow & Company, New York. *Male and Female* by Margaret Mead. Copyright 1949, 1967 by Margaret Mead; *Many Mansions* by Gina Cerminara. Copyright 1950 by Gina Cerminara.

The New American Library, Inc., New York. *The Oscillating Universe* by Ernest J. Öpik, Copyright © 1960 by Ernest J. Öpik.

The New Humanity Journal, London. "Coping with Stress" by Ian Pearce, M.D.

New York Post. "Population 'Boom' Is Going Bust," by Ben Wattenberg, April 28, 1981.

The New York Times. Selections from six articles. Copyright © 1938, 1939, 1967, 1979 by The New York Times Company.

W. W. Norton & Co., Inc., New York. *Toward a Philosophy of History* by José Ortega y Gasset, translated by Helene Weyl. Copyright 1941, renewed 1968, by W. W. Norton & Co., Inc.

Open Court Publishing Company, La Salle, Illinois. *Nature, Mind, and Death* by C. J. Ducasse. Copyright by Open Court Publishing Company, 1951.

Penguin Books, Ltd., London. *Buddhist Scriptures,* translator Edward Conze, pp. 19–20. Copyright © Edward Conze, 1959.

A. D. Peters & Co. Ltd., London. *I Have Been Here Before* by J. B. Priestley, published by William Heinemann, Ltd.

M. C. Peto, Surrey, England. "The Case for Reincarnation," by Reverend Leslie Weatherhead.

Playboy Magazine, Chicago. Interview of Marcia Seligson with Elisabeth Kübler-Ross, May 1981, Copyright © 1981 by *Playboy*.

Prentice-Hall, Inc., Englewood, Cliffs, New Jersey. *To Live Until We Say Good-Bye* by Elisabeth Kübler-Ross. © 1978 by Ross Medical Associates, S.C., and Mal Warshaw.

Princeton University Press, Princeton, New Jersey; *Word and Image* by C. G. Jung, editor Aniela Jaffé. Copyright © 1979 by Princeton University Press.

Random House, Inc., New York. *The Gnostic Gospels* by Elaine Pagels. Copyright © 1979 by Elaine Pagels; *Dreams, Memories, Reflections* by C. G. Jung, published by Pantheon Books, New York. Copyright © 1962, 1963 by Random House, Inc.; *James Joyce's Ulysses* by Stuart Gilbert, published by Vintage Books. Copyright 1930, 1932 by Stuart Gilbert, copyright renewed 1958 by Arthur Stuart Gilbert.

George G. Ritchie, M.D., *Return from Tomorrow*, and his taped talk "To Live Again and Again." ,

Robinson & Watkins, London. *The Pistis Sophia*, translator G. R. S. Mead, published by John A. Watkins, 1921.

Routledge & Kegan Paul, London. *The Secret of the Golden Flower: A Chinese Book of Life*, translated by Richard Wilhelm with commentary by C. G. Jung. Copyright © by Routledge, Kegan Paul.

Russell & Russell, New York. Friedrich Nietzsche, *The Complete Works of Friedrich Nietzsche*, editor Oscar Levy, vol. XVI (1909–1911), published by Russell & Russell, 1964.

Schocken Books, Inc., New York. *Major Trends in Jewish Mysticism* by Gershom Scholem. Copyright © 1941 by Schocken Publishing House, Jerusalem, copyright 1946, © 1954 by Schocken Books, Inc. New York.

Gershom Scholem, "Seelenwanderung und Sympathie der Seelen in der Judischen Mystik," *Eranos* 24–1955, published by Eranos Foundation, Ascona, Switzerland.

Julia M. Seton, Santa Fe, New Mexico. *The Gospel of the Redman* by Ernest Thompson Seton and Julia M. Seton.

Shambhala Publications, Inc., Boulder, Colorado. *Space, Time, and Medicine*, by Larry Dossey, M.D. Copyright © 1982 by Larry Dossey.

Ian Stevenson, M.D., and University of Virginia Press. *Cases of The Reincarnation Type*, volume III.

St. Louis Art Museum, Missouri. *Modern Thought and Catholicism* by Paul Gauguin.

Star, New York. "Professor Recalls Life As Doctor in 1620."

Lyle Stuart, Inc., Secaucus, New Jersey. *Out-Of-The-Body Experiences* by Robert Crookall.

Time, New York. Excerpts from "The Metaphysics of War," by Lance Morrow. Copyright 1982 Time Inc. All rights reserved.

Time Books/The New York Times Book Co., Inc. *Kabbalah* by Gershom Scholem. Copyright © 1974 by Keter Publishing House Jerusalem Ltd.

University of Minnesota Press, Minneapolis. *Physics as Metaphor*, by Roger S. Jones.

Van Nostrand Reinhold, New York. "Reincarnation: Field Studies and Theoretical Issues" by Ian Stevenson, M.D., in *Handbook of Parapsychology*, editor Benjamin B. Wolman, published by Van Nostrand Reinhold © 1977.

Viking Penguin Inc., New York. *A Prison, a Paradise* by Loran Hurnscot. Copyright © by Victor Gollancz Ltd; *The Lives of a Cell* by Lewis Thomas. Copyright © 1972 by the

Massachusetts Medical Society. Originally published in the *New England Journal of Medicine; The Medusa and the Snail* by Lewis Thomas. Copyright © 1977, 1979 by Lewis Thomas. Originally published in the *New England Journal of Medicine*.
Robert Welsh. "Mondrian and Theosophy," in *Piet Mondrian Centennial Exhibition*, 1971, published by the Solomon R. Guggenheim Foundation.

Index